Reader's Digest

Quick, Thrifty Cooking

The Reader's Digest Association, Inc.

Pleasantville, New York / Montreal

Editor	Inge N. Dobelis
Art Director	Gerald Ferguson
Food Editor	Ben Etheridge
Associate Editor	Robert V. Huber
Art Production Associate	Lisa Drescher
Assistant Editor	Carol Davis
Editorial Assistant	Lydia Howard
Group Editor	Norman Mack
Group Art Director	David Trooper
Chief Consultant	Jean Anderson
Consultants	Ruth Cousineau, Sarah Belk Rian
Calorie Consultant	Elaine Hanna
Copy Editors	Sybil Pincus, Harriet Bachman
Permissions	Dorothy M. Harris, JoAnn T. Schmitt

Quick,
Thrifty
Cooking

The acknowledgments that appear on pages 246-247 are hereby made a part of this copyright page.

Copyright © 1985 The Reader's Digest Association, Inc.
Copyright © 1985 The Reader's Digest Association (Canada) Ltd.
Copyright © 1985 Reader's Digest Association Far East Ltd.
Philippine Copyright 1985 Reader's Digest Association Far East Ltd.

Library of Congress Cataloging in Publication Data
Main entry under title:

Quick, thrifty cooking.

At head of title: Reader's digest.
Includes index.
1. Low budget cookery.   I. Dobelis, Inge.   II. Reader's
Digest Association.   III. Reader's digest.
TX652.Q47   1985   641.5′5   84-3465
ISBN 0-89577-181-0

Printed in the United States of America

Contents

Introduction

This is a book designed for busy people who want to eat tasty, well-prepared food made from fresh, inexpensive ingredients. There are more than 450 recipes in QUICK, THRIFTY COOKING, all of which have been tested by professional cooks for quality and taste as well as ease and speed of preparation. Almost all the recipes take less than 50 minutes to prepare; the great majority—over 300 of them—can be made in 30 minutes or less. What is more, you need not be an experienced cook to get good results. The step-by-step directions, written in clear, everyday language (no culinary jargon is used), assure even the novice of success. Here, then, is a book that will show you how to work magic in the kitchen, using the commonest ingredients, for only a little money, with lots of style and no fuss.

How to Use This Book

Alongside most of the recipe titles you will find one or more of the following symbols:

tells you that the recipe is extra thrifty.

means that preparation and cooking are extra quick for that type of dish.

indicates that the recipe can be halved.

- Immediately below the title the preparation and cooking times for the recipe are listed, so that you can quickly tell whether you have the time to make it. Because some people work faster than others, use preparation times only as a guide. Generally, preparation involves procedures that do not require cooking, such as peeling, chopping, and slicing. But there are some exceptions, such as bringing water to a boil, and cooking onions or garlic in butter before mixing them with other ingredients. If you can prepare one part of a dish while the other part is cooking, only one of these times (the longer one) is counted.
- The number of average-size servings or the approximate amount a recipe will yield is given on the line with the preparation and cooking times.
- Last on the line is the number of calories per serving, to help you plan your menu whether you are dieting or just keeping an eye on your weight.
- Ingredients for each recipe are listed in a column on the left-hand side of the page; the instructions, on the right. Often there is a choice of an ingredient in a recipe: butter or margarine, half-and-half or milk, chutney or apple sauce. When there is a choice of ingredients, the calorie count is based on the first choice.
- To make the recipes easy to follow, the instructions are spelled out clearly and in detail. You will never have to guess what size skillet or saucepan to use, whether to set your burner high or low, or whether to cook a dish covered or uncovered. The first time an ingredient is mentioned in the instructions, it is printed in **boldface** type and in the order in which it appears in the list of ingredients. That way, as you follow the recipe, you can easily check to make sure you have not left out an ingredient.
- Many recipes are accompanied by tips that suggest ways you can vary the recipe by making a substitution for the main ingredient or by changing the seasoning. These tips also tell you which dishes can be made ahead, for how long, and how to reheat them, and which recipes are suitable for one-dish meals.

Before You Begin

When you decide to put a recipe on your menu, make a list of the ingredients required. Don't take anything for granted. Check your cupboard and refrigerator for items you will need, and make certain you have them. Read the instructions thoroughly, too, to be sure you have the proper utensils. Just before you start to cook, assemble all the ingredients and equipment and read the instructions again to familiarize yourself with what you will have to do and when. These precautions take just a few minutes, and they prevent major disappointments.

Now you are ready to begin. Turn to any recipe and discover for yourself how amazingly easy and fast it is to put wholesome, appetizing meals on the table for very little money.

> The cover of QUICK, THRIFTY COOKING converts into a stand for easy reading as you cook, while keeping the counter clear and the book free of stains. To set up the stand, open the cover so that the binding is flat, fold it backward across the bottom at the crease, and set the book upright.

TIME-SAVING, MONEY-SAVING TIPS

Although recipes are the heart of QUICK, THRIFTY COOKING, there are additional ways to economize without sacrificing quality—from your choice of cookware to the way you organize your menus and shopping and the use of time- and money-saving techniques in the kitchen.

COOK'S TOOLS

Walking through a housewares shop or the cookware section of a department store can be a breathtaking experience. Shelves from floor to ceiling are filled with nearly every kind of pot, pan, appliance, and gadget imaginable in a dazzling assortment of shapes, colors, materials, and prices. While it is exciting to have such an array of choices when you shop, it can also be disconcerting. How do you select cookware that will perform well in the kitchen without requiring a major investment?

First, realize that for every astronomically priced "gourmet" utensil there is almost always a moderately priced one that will do the job just as well. Second, buy equipment that you *know* you will use often. Third, remember that auxiliary items, ranging from inexpensive pastry blenders to food processors and microwave ovens, are worthwhile only if you use them. The guidelines below will help you in selecting basic, durable cookware that no cook should be without and in adding optional equipment as you like.

SAUCEPANS AND SKILLETS

Choose among a variety of good-quality materials discussed on page 6. Avoid such goods as flimsy decorative enamelware and thin aluminum pans, which are less expensive but do not last, distribute heat unevenly, and cause food to burn easily.

Recommended saucepans and skillets:
- *1-, 2-, and 3-quart saucepans with lids.*
- *2-quart double boiler with lid* for egg-thickened sauces and other mixtures that require gentle heat. A double boiler is also useful for reheating pasta, rice, and other dishes.
- *6- or 7-quart pot* for cooking pasta or preparing soups or stews for a crowd.
- *6-, 7-, or 8-inch skillet with lid.*
- *9- or 10-inch skillet with lid.*
- *12- or 14-inch skillet with lid.* Note that QUICK, THRIFTY COOKING often calls for this size skillet, which is just right for cooking 4 pork chops, a 2½- to 3-pound cut-up chicken, or a number of other skillet dishes that serve 4 to 6. Without a large skillet, you will often have to use 2 smaller ones.
- *9- or 10-inch nonstick skillet* for omelets, crêpes, and low-fat or fat-free cooking.

OVENWARE

Baking pans (made of stainless steel, aluminum, and other metals) and baking dishes (made of ovenproof glass or porcelain) are for roasting, baking casseroles, and reheating leftovers, as well as for baking cakes and breads, pies and cookies. Some recipes call for ovenware by volume, others by dimension. This information should be stamped into the bottom of the pan or dish. If it is not, check the volume by filling the pan with measuring cupsful of water to see how much the pan holds. Check dimensions with a ruler. Bakeware may be shallow or deep; a deep pan or dish will require a different cooking time and temperature than a shallow one. For best results, always use the specific pan called for in the recipe.

Recommended ovenware:
- *1-quart baking dish.*
- *1½-quart baking pan.*
- *13"x 9"x 2" baking-roasting pan with a rack.*
- *9"x 9"x 2" baking pan or dish.*
- *8"x 8"x 2" baking pan or dish.*
- *Two 8-inch or 9-inch round layer-cake pans.*
- *8- and 9-inch pie plate or pan.*
- *15½"x 10½"x 1" baking sheet.*
- *Two 9"x 5"x 3" loaf pans for breads, cakes, and meat loaves.*

Although appearance cannot be discounted, material counts most when selecting cookware. To choose wisely, you should know the characteristics of the basic materials from which cookware is made and the care that each requires.

Aluminum

An inexpensive metal that conducts heat quickly and evenly, aluminum is one of the best all-round cooking materials available: durable, lightweight, and rust-resistant. Choose heavy-gauge pots and pans for better heat distribution and longer wear. Hard water and alkaline foods such as eggs tend to discolor aluminum, but the stain is easily removed with a scouring pad. Aluminum also interacts with acid foods such as tomatoes and vinegar, so remove foods from the pot immediately after cooking. *Care:* Keep aluminum pots and pans clean by washing in hot, sudsy water; scrub with a soap-filled scouring pad. Do not expect it to retain its original sheen.

Stainless Steel

Sturdy and relatively inexpensive but a poor heat conductor, stainless steel is usually bonded with copper or aluminum in the making of saucepans and skillets. Stainless steel does not discolor as readily as aluminum and will retain its shininess. *Care:* Wash in hot, sudsy water, using a soft brush or nylon scouring pad.

Cast Iron

Because of its ability to absorb and hold heat, cast iron remains the favorite of many cooks for frying chicken, fish, potatoes, and many other foods. Properly seasoned and cared for, a cast iron interior acts almost like a nonstick finish, but unseasoned cast iron will rust. To season, rub the clean, dry utensil with cooking oil or melted shortening, and heat in a moderate oven for two hours. Cast iron utensils are inexpensive, but they are heavy and harder to handle than other metal cookware. *Care:* Avoid harsh abrasives, and wash gently in order to maintain the patina that builds up with use. Dry cast iron utensils thoroughly before putting away, and store uncovered to prevent trapped moisture from causing rust.

Copper

Beautiful and expensive, copper transmits heat quickly and evenly and is the first choice of many cooks despite its cost and the fact that it is difficult to clean. Because copper reacts easily with food, liquids, and air to form a poisonous green layer, saucepans and skillets should be lined with tin or stainless steel. *Care:* Avoid extremely high heat, and use only wooden implements when cooking with tin-lined copper. Soak before washing gently with nonabrasive cloths and cleansers. Never use scouring powder or steel wool pads. To retain the red-gold burnish, rub dry with a soft cloth, and clean occasionally with a lemon juice and salt mixture.

Stick-Resistant Aluminum

Made by a variety of manufacturers, stick-resistant aluminum utensils are recognizable by their dark gray color and shiny aluminum lids. Durable and easy to clean, stick-resistant aluminum is a good heat conductor and will not interact with foods as solid aluminum does. Do not confuse stick-resistant cookware with nonstick finishes. *Care:* Wash in hot, sudsy water.

Nonstick Finishes

Nonstick surfaces have improved greatly in recent years. The newest ones are less easily scratched or scraped, although the finishes still tend to chip over time. Nonstick skillets are especially useful for cooking eggs and fish fillets and for sautéing vegetables without adding any oil to the pan. *Care:* Wipe the pan with paper toweling before washing according to manufacturer's instructions. Store wrapped in plastic to prevent scratching.

Enameled Iron (Porcelain Enamelware)

Because it is heavy and holds and distributes heat evenly, enameled ironware (cast iron coated with porcelain enamel) is ideal for stews and other dishes that require long, slow cooking. Many enameled iron utensils have decorative finishes and can go from stove or oven directly to the table, but the finish is subject to chipping, cracking, scratching, and staining. *Care:* Soak if necessary to loosen food deposits, and wash gently in warm, sudsy water. Do not use abrasive pads or cleansers. Extreme temperature changes, as from refrigerator to hot oven, may cause the enamel to crack.

Flameproof Glass

Flameproof glass (both the sturdy, transparent variety and the more expensive, dazzling white glass) can be used over direct heat as well as in the oven. Flameproof glass is easy to clean and fairly strong, although it may break if subjected to sharp temperature changes. Note that not all glass utensils are flameproof, and check before buying. *Care:* Soak in hot water before washing in hot suds.

Substitutes for Common Ingredients

7⁵⁰
34

If the recipe calls for:	Amount	Use instead:
Baking powder	1 teaspoon	¼ teaspoon baking soda plus ½ teaspoon cream of tartar
Bread crumbs, fine dry	1 cup	¾ cup finely crumbled crackers
Broth, chicken or beef	1 cup	1 bouillon cube or 1 envelope instant broth dissolved in 1 cup boiling water
Buttermilk	1 cup	1 cup plain yogurt or 1 cup whole milk plus 1 tablespoon lemon juice or vinegar (let stand 5 minutes)
Cake flour	1 cup	1 cup sifted all-purpose flour less 2 tablespoons
Chocolate, unsweetened	1 square (1 ounce)	3 tablespoons cocoa plus 1 tablespoon butter
Cornstarch (for thickening)	1 tablespoon	2 tablespoons all-purpose flour
Corn syrup, light (not for baking)	1 cup	1¼ cups granulated sugar plus ⅓ cup water
Cracker crumbs, fine	1 cup	1¼ cups dry bread crumbs
Cream, heavy (not for whipping)	1 cup	¾ cup milk plus ⅓ cup melted butter
Cream, light	1 cup	¾ cup milk plus ¼ cup melted butter
Cream, sour	1 cup	⅞ cup plain yogurt or buttermilk plus 3 tablespoons melted butter
Garlic	1 small clove	⅛ teaspoon garlic powder
Half-and-half	1 cup	⅞ cup milk plus 1½ tablespoons melted butter
Herbs, fresh	1 tablespoon	1 teaspoon dried herbs or ⅔ teaspoon ground herbs
Honey	1 cup	1¼ cups granulated sugar plus ¼ cup water
Ketchup or chili sauce	½ cup	½ cup tomato sauce plus 2 tablespoons sugar, 1 tablespoon vinegar, and ⅛ teaspoon ground cloves
Lemon juice	1 teaspoon	½ teaspoon vinegar
Liquid hot red pepper seasoning	3 to 4 drops	⅛ teaspoon cayenne pepper
Milk, whole	1 cup	½ cup evaporated milk plus ½ cup water, or 1 cup water plus ⅓ cup instant nonfat dry milk powder and 2 teaspoons melted butter, or 1 cup skim milk plus 2 teaspoons melted butter
Mushrooms, fresh	8 ounces	1 6-ounce can mushrooms, drained
Mustard, prepared	1 tablespoon	1 teaspoon dried mustard
Onion	1 small	1 tablespoon instant minced onion
Oregano, dried	1 teaspoon	1 teaspoon dried marjoram
Pork, ground	½ pound	½ pound mild sausage
Sugar, brown	1 cup, firmly packed	1 cup granulated sugar
Sugar, granulated	1 cup	1 cup firmly packed brown sugar
Tartar sauce	½ cup	6 tablespoons mayonnaise plus 2 tablespoons sweet pickle relish
Tomato paste	1 tablespoon	1 tablespoon ketchup
Vinegar	1 teaspoon	2 teaspoons lemon juice
Yogurt, plain	1 cup	1 cup buttermilk

- *Muffin tins.* The standard size is 2 to 2½ inches in diameter and holds about ½ cup when full.
- *Six 6-ounce custard cups* for cooking or chilling individual servings of pudding, custard, or gelatin.

CUTLERY AND CUTTING SURFACES

Good-quality knives are essential for quick, efficient chopping, slicing, and dicing. They are expensive, but if well cared for, they will last a lifetime. Choose knives made of hard carbon steel or stainless steel. Carbon steel knives take a keener edge and maintain it longer, but they must be wiped clean immediately after use or they will discolor or rust. Choose knives with blades that extend inside the handle all the way to the end and that feel comfortable in your hand. If a knife feels uncomfortable, it may be too large or too small for you.

Don't wash knives in the dishwasher or let them soak in water. Always use knives on a surface such as wood or plastic that is softer than the blade itself. Use knives for cutting only, and store them in a knife rack or some other place where they will not get bent or nicked. Keep knives well honed with a sharpening stone or a butcher's steel the length of your longest knife. Avoid electric sharpeners, which tend to ruin the edge.

Recommended cutlery and cutting boards:
- *Chef's knife,* or French knife, for chopping. A chef's knife has a triangular-shaped blade 7 to 14 inches long. The shape prevents the knuckles from hitting the chopping surface.
- *Serrated knife* for slicing bread, tomatoes, citrus fruits, cakes, and other foods.
- *Utility knife* for slicing and chopping vegetables and fruit, disjointing poultry, filleting fish, and trimming the fat from meat. An all-purpose utility knife with a straight 5- to 8-inch blade can also do the work of a chef's knife.
- *Swivel-bladed vegetable peeler or paring knife* for paring, trimming, and coring fruits and vegetables. A swivel-bladed peeler removes only the peel, while a paring knife takes off a layer of pulp as well.
- *Chopping board.* Wooden boards should be at least 1 inch thick to prevent warping. Because excessive dampness causes a wooden board to crack, wipe after each use with a damp sponge and dry immediately. Scour the board occasionally with lemon juice or a baking soda solution; rinse and dry thoroughly. Polyethylene boards can go into the dishwasher or be soaked in hot, sudsy water.

MISCELLANEOUS BASIC COOKWARE

Besides pots, pans, ovenware, and cutlery, the number of kitchen utensils that you can buy is endless. Here are the basics.
- *Set of mixing bowls,* preferably stainless steel.
- *Set of metal measuring cups,* in 1-, ½-, ⅓-, and ¼-cup sizes, for measuring dry ingredients and fats.
- *Set of spouted glass measuring cups* in 1-, 2-, and 4-cup sizes, for measuring liquids.
- *2 or 3 wooden spoons* for mixing and stirring. Wooden spoons will not scratch enamel or nonstick saucepans or skillets and will never burn your hand.
- *Wooden fork,* for use with a wooden spoon to toss pasta and salads.
- *Tongs* of wood or metal for turning meat without piercing it, lifting and serving pasta, and removing vegetables from boiling water.
- *Flexible rubber or plastic scraper,* with a blade 1 to 3 inches wide, for scraping bowls, saucepans, and skillets clean.
- *Long-handled cooking fork,* preferably of stainless steel, for piercing and turning meats.
- *Long-handled cooking spoon,* preferably of stainless steel, for stirring, blending, and mixing, and for basting meats and poultry.
- *2 metal spatulas,* one short and wide for spreading butter and sandwich spreads, and one long and narrow for spreading cake frostings and fillings.
- *Pancake turner* for turning eggs, hamburgers, croquettes, and the like, as well as pancakes.
- *Long-handled slotted spoon* for retrieving vegetables or dumplings from boiling water or broth, or deep-fried food from fat.
- *Wire whisk* for beating egg whites, whipping cream, and beating sauces, batters, salad dressings, and other mixtures.
- *Rotary beater* for beating sauces, batters, salad dressings, and other mixtures. A rotary beater whips cream and egg whites faster than a whisk, but not to as great a volume.
- *Rolling pin* for rolling out dough, crushing nuts and peppercorns, and pounding meat to tenderize it.

- *4-sided grater* for shredding and grating cheese, nutmeg, lemon rind, etc.
- *Metal colander,* with legs, for draining pasta and vegetables.
- *2 sieves* (strainers), one fine- and one coarse-mesh, preferably of stainless steel, for sifting dry ingredients and straining foods.
- *2 funnels,* one small and one large, for transferring liquids from one container to another without spilling.
- *Hand citrus juicer.*
- *Wire rack* for cooling baked goods.
- *Oven thermometer* for double-checking oven heat and locating hot spots. A surprisingly large number of ovens register heat inaccurately, and there is a difference in temperature between the top and bottom shelves.
- *Meat thermometer* for accurately determining the doneness of meat.
- *Kitchen twine* for trussing poultry, tying roasts, and tying up herb bouquets.
- *Can opener.*
- *Corkscrew.* Choose a lever corkscrew.
- *Ladle.*
- *2 or more pot holders.*
- *Bulb baster.*
- *Automatic timer* to remind the cook when to turn off the stove or oven.

USEFUL BUT NOT ESSENTIAL EQUIPMENT

From the descriptions below, you can tell which of the items you want to put on your kitchenware shopping list.
- *A food mill* for mashing and grinding food and straining out skins, seeds, and fiber. It is useful if you do not have a blender or food processor.
- *Salad spinner* for drying salad greens better and more quickly than paper toweling does.
- *Dutch oven,* a heavy, flameproof pot with a lid, for braising large pieces of meat, such as pot roasts, and for cooking in quantity.
- *Pepper mill* to provide the flavor of freshly ground black peppercorns.
- *Pastry blender.* You can use a fork or 2 knives to work shortening or butter into flour, but a pastry blender is quicker.
- *Sifter* for sifting confectioners' sugar, flour, cocoa, and other dry ingredients.
- *Pastry brush* for spreading melted butter or beaten egg on pastry, for coating the inside of bakeware with melted butter or oil, and for basting poultry and meats.

- *Cheesecloth* for squeezing moisture from cooked greens, for tying up herb bouquets, and, when dipped in melted butter, for covering roasting poultry to keep it from drying out.
- *Garlic press,* an inexpensive gadget that juices and shreds garlic quickly.
- *Kitchen shears* for snipping kitchen twine, disjointing poultry, trimming fins and tails from fresh fish, and cutting pizza into wedges.
- *Blender.* A relatively inexpensive electric appliance, a blender has a host of uses: blending soups and purées, making bread crumbs, and making milk shakes, to name a few.
- *Food processor* for speeding many tedious jobs, such as chopping, slicing, shredding, and grating. A food processor will purée fruits and vegetables; grind meat; make mayonnaise, hollandaise, and other fragile sauces; blend batters; knead dough; and perform many other tasks. Choose a model with a compact design and a strong motor.
- *Toaster.* A toaster is quicker to use and cheaper to operate than an oven broiler for making toast. Choose a model with slots large enough to take thick slices of bread and rolls.
- *Toaster oven.* More energy efficient than a large oven, a toaster oven is perfect for baking potatoes and small casseroles or for quick broiling. It can be used in place of a conventional oven for preparing many foods.
- *Griddle* for cooking grilled cheese sandwiches, pancakes, hamburgers, and the like.
- *Electric skillet* for braising, stewing, roasting, steaming, and broiling as well as frying, and for use as an extra burner.
- *Crock pot.* Ingredients added to an electric crock pot in the morning cook slowly during the day and are ready to be served at night.
- *Hand-held electric mixer.* Portable and easy to clean, a hand mixer is faster and less tiring to use than a rotary beater or a wire whisk. Choose a model with at least 3 speeds and a heavy-duty motor.
- *Microwave oven.* A microwave oven uses high frequency energy to cook food. The energy penetrates the food, so that cooking takes place from the center outward. Speed is the primary advantage. However, the larger the amount of food in the oven, the longer it takes to cook. Microwave ovens are especially handy for cooking vegetables (frozen vegetables can be cooked in the package, and baked potatoes are hot and flaky in minutes), cook-

ing bacon, thawing frozen foods, and reheating leftovers. But they will not brown food unless they have a special browning element.

● *Convection oven.* A convection oven has a built-in fan that creates a continuous flow of hot air and maintains even heat throughout the oven. Foods therefore require less cooking time or a lower temperature or both than do those cooked in a conventional oven. Foods brown more evenly and shrink less.

SAVING TIME IN THE KITCHEN

The recipes in this book are themselves excellent time-savers, but there are many tricks and techniques that can save you even more time in the kitchen—from the way you organize your kitchen to shortcuts that minimize dreaded cleanup chores.

PLANNING AND WORKING AHEAD

One key to saving time in the kitchen is to have a place for everything. Arrange utensils for your convenience according to the type and amount of use they get. If your kitchen is not functionally designed, invest in a few inexpensive kitchen organizers—a pegboard, a spice rack, or drawers that can be attached to the bottom of a wall-hung kitchen cabinet. And be sure to keep your refrigerator as well organized as your cabinets and drawers. Designate spots for such items as mayonnaise, salad dressings, milk, and juice that you always have on hand. Maintaining an orderly refrigerator not only saves time but also cuts down on food waste.

Efficient tools are important, too. Always make sure that your knives are sharp and your small appliances in good repair. Cutting up a chicken can be a 10-minute job with a sharp knife and kitchen shears or a 20-minute hassle with dull tools. Keep knives well honed by running them over a sharpening stone once or twice every time you use them.

Efficient Freezer Storage

When you bring poultry, meats, and fish home from the supermarket, don't freeze them in large packages that will take a long time to thaw. Cut up chickens and wrap each piece individually in aluminum foil or moisture-proof, vapor-proof freezer paper. Then freeze. Similarly, wrap steaks and chops individually with foil or freezer paper before storing in the freezer. You will be able to remove any number of pieces you need with ease.

Don't freeze ground beef in one chunky piece. It takes too long to freeze and to thaw. Instead, shape the meat into a rectangle about ½ inch thick, wrap, and freeze. It will thaw quickly for use in meat loaves and casseroles. Or shape the meat into patties and wrap individually before freezing. There is no need to thaw them before frying or broiling.

Making Extras for Later Use

It is no secret that many dishes can be made in double portions, with the extra one frozen for later use, but some of the items listed below that you can make in extra quantities may surprise you.

● *Onions and garlic.* When you chop onions, prepare several cups more than you need, and freeze them in a plastic bag for future use. You can also mince several bulbs of garlic and store, refrigerated, in a jar of oil, ready for instant use.

● *Broth.* Freeze beef and chicken broth in ice cube trays, then store the cubes in plastic bags. When a recipe calls for a small amount of broth, you can remove just the amount that you need.

● *Hard-cooked eggs.* Keep a few unpeeled hard-cooked eggs on hand for quick sandwiches, salads, and appetizers. Mark the eggs with a pencil to distinguish them from uncooked eggs, and store for up to a week in the refrigerator. Peeled hard-cooked eggs will keep for two or three days. Place in a bowl or jar, covered with water, and refrigerate.

● *Rice.* Cook extra rice. It will keep in your refrigerator for as long as a week. Remove the rice as you need it, place in a sieve over a pot of simmering water, cover, and heat for 4 to 5 minutes until the rice is hot.

● *Sandwiches.* Make lunch box sandwiches in batches, wrap individually, and freeze for daily use. Some sandwich fillings that freeze well are peanut butter; ground or sliced cooked meat, poultry, tuna, and salmon; hard-cooked egg yolks; and cream cheese. Do not freeze sandwiches that contain mayonnaise, tomatoes, celery, lettuce, or cucumbers.

● *Bacon.* Have you ever thought of cooking bacon in advance? Arrange the slices side by side on a rack in a shallow baking pan, and bake, uncovered, in a preheated 400°F oven for 10 to 12 minutes, or until crisp. Drain on paper toweling and cool. Then stack the slices, wrap tightly in aluminum foil, and freeze. When you are ready to serve, warm the bacon in a skillet over low heat.

● *Sausages.* Link sausages can also be prepared ahead. Boil the links for 10 minutes, remove from the water, drain, dry, wrap, and store in the freezer. The links will need only browning when you want to use them.

SPEEDING UP PREPARATION AND COOKING

You don't need to have the experience of a French chef in order to save time preparing food—just follow the tips below.

Fruits and Vegetables

Don't peel fruits and vegetables unless the skins are tough or the recipe calls for peeling. You will save vitamins and minerals as well as time. Even the skins of beets, eggplant, acorn and butternut squash, and sweet potatoes are edible. When you use vegetables unpeeled, be sure to scrub them well.

When you do peel, work over sheets of newspaper spread on the counter. Then simply wrap up the peelings when you have finished, and toss them out.

● *Apples.* To core an apple quickly, cut it into quarters and use the point of the knife to remove the core and seeds. Or cut slices from the fruit, stopping at the core.

● *Onions.* The fastest way to peel an onion is to cut off both ends, slice the onion in half, and then peel each half. Small white onions to be cooked whole can be blanched for about 30 seconds in boiling water. Then cut off the ends, and the skins will slip right off.

● *Garlic.* To peel garlic quickly, put the clove on a chopping board, then place the flat side of a heavy knife on top of the clove. Hit the knife with your fist. You will be surprised how easily the peel comes off.

● *Tomatoes.* To peel tomatoes easily without removing any of the flesh, try one of these methods. Drop the tomatoes into boiling wa-

ter for 20 seconds. Using a slotted spoon, remove them immediately, run cold water over them, and peel them with a sharp knife. The skin will slip off like magic. Or spear each tomato through the stem with a long fork and hold over a gas flame until the skin splits and loosens. Peel. Note that these methods soften the flesh and should be used only for tomatoes that are going to be cooked.

The easiest way to chop canned tomatoes is with kitchen shears—right in the can itself.

● *Parsley.* Chop parsley by gathering as much as you need into a tight ball and slicing it as thin as possible with a sharp knife.

● *Salads.* The speediest salad of all is iceberg lettuce cut crosswise into slices 1 or 1½ inches thick. Spoon dressing over each slice, and serve.

To separate the leaves of iceberg lettuce, hit the core end sharply against the kitchen counter top. The core will twist out, and the leaves will separate without tearing.

There is no culinary law that says you must tear salad greens. Cutting them is much faster, and the salad will taste just the same.

If you are making a salad ahead of time, don't bother to dry the greens. Wash the greens, shake off the water, then place them in a bowl lined with paper towels. Cover the greens with another paper towel, and let the bowl stand in the refrigerator for at least an hour. The towels will absorb the excess moisture, and the greens will be dry and crisp.

● *Green beans.* To "snap" green beans in a jiffy, line them up in a row, their tips even with one another, and slice off the ends. Then line up the other ends and slice again.

● *Corn.* Remove the silk from fresh corn easily and quickly by rubbing the corn with a vegetable brush under cold water.

● *Potatoes.* To bake potatoes in about half the usual time, cover them with an iron skillet, or skewer them with aluminum potato nails. When preparing potatoes for mashing or for salads, peel and dice them, then cook in a small amount of water to retain vitamins. They will cook faster and more evenly. But if they are to be used whole, peel after boiling.

● *Dried beans.* Rinse dried beans in a sieve under cold running water.

Poultry, Meats, and Fish

● To bone chicken breasts, partially freeze (or defrost) them first. Beef, pork, or lamb

15-MINUTE RECIPES

When you are especially pressed for time or when you just want to get out of the kitchen extra fast, check this list for recipes that take no more than 15 (or, in a few cases, 16) minutes to prepare.

11

that has been cut into thin slices before cooking is much easier to handle if partially frozen.

- To form meatballs or hamburger patties quickly, shape the ground meat or meat mixture into a log, and slice. Roll the slices into balls or shape into patties.
- *Bacon.* To cook bacon quickly for drippings and crumbs, stack the slices needed and snip them crosswise with kitchen shears into ¼- to 1-inch pieces.
- Cook frozen fish without thawing, but be sure to allow extra broiling or baking time.

Dairy Products

- Egg whites will separate more easily if the eggs are cold, so don't remove them from the refrigerator until you are ready to use them.
- To peel hard-cooked eggs smoothly, plunge them into cold water immediately after they are cooked. Crack them as you submerge them, then peel them under cold running water.
- To soften butter quickly, cut it into small pieces, and knead it in a bowl with your fingers. Or simply grate the cold butter into a bowl.
- Heavy cream will whip faster if you chill the bowl and the beaters in the freezer. Also, avoid using the ultrapasteurized variety of heavy cream; it takes longer to whip.

Cleanup

Cleaning up as you go along saves time, reduces clutter, and makes the work easier.

- Make sure that everyone in your family is responsible for washing the utensils he or she uses. Keep a bottle of detergent at the sink as a reminder.
- Always heat the skillet before you add oil or butter. Foods will stick less.
- Keep fat from spattering when panfrying foods by covering the skillet with a colander. The holes allow the steam to escape so that the food will brown even though covered.
- When you heat milk, rinse the pan in cold water first to prevent sticking.
- Let your utensils wash themselves as you cook. The minute you finish with a bowl or saucepan, fill it with hot, sudsy water and let it soak. Later it should need little more than a rinse. The exception is utensils in which you have beaten or cooked eggs or egg-rich mixtures. Soak these in cool water; hot water will cook the egg right onto the bowl or pan.

ONE-STOP SHOPPING FOR THE WEEK

Every trip to the supermarket or corner grocery is a potential threat to your pocketbook. The way to avoid impulse buying and to save yourself the additional annoyance of hopping into the car countless times during the week is to do all your shopping at one time. One-stop shopping requires a special kind of planning, as you will see, but it will save you several hours weekly and who knows how much money.

The menus on the next two pages provide varied dinners that follow the principles of one-stop shopping. The first of these is planning menus around the perishability of food. Fish is cooked on Day 1, for example, because it should be cooked as soon as possible after purchase. Hamburger is the choice for Day 2 because ground meat is best served no later than the second day after purchase. All the other food will keep well in the refrigerator or freezer or on the shelf.

Another basic principle illustrated here is the importance of maintaining a stock of the staples listed in "Stocking Up," page 15. When the ingredients required by each recipe are divided between "Staples" and items for the "Shopping List," you will find that the shopping list is surprisingly short. In instances where the recipe calls for a larger than usual amount of a particular staple, the amount is noted in the Staples column.

Recipes are not specified for all dishes on the menu. For example, you can prepare the peas recommended in the menu for Day 2 as you like them; suggested flavorings for these dishes are listed in the Staples column. Only evening-meal menus are given because breakfasts are fairly routine in most households and lunches are often eaten away from home. Use the menus to plan and shop for a week's dinners. Then use the one-stop shopping and planning method to work out your own menus for other weeks. Return to a week's menus every 4 to 6 weeks.

Menus	Shopping List	Staples
Day 1		
Crumbed Oven-Fried Fish, page 156	1½ pounds flounder, sole, halibut, cod, or haddock fillets	Milk, salt, fine dry bread crumbs, paprika, butter or margarine, 1 lemon (optional)
Coleslaw, page 45	1 small firm head cabbage (about 1¼ pounds)	Mayonnaise, salt, pepper
	Sour cream or plain yogurt (for ½ cup)	
Carrots	8 medium-size carrots (1 pound)	Salt, butter or margarine
Italian Custard, page 241	Marsala wine	Eggs (6), sugar, salt
Day 2		
Hamburgers Diane, page 114	1 pound lean ground beef Parsley (for 2 tablespoons, chopped)	Salt, pepper, thyme, rosemary, butter or margarine, vegetable oil, Dijon or prepared spicy brown mustard, 1 lemon, Worcestershire sauce
Baked Sliced Potatoes, page 73	4 medium-size baking potatoes (about 1 pound)	Vegetable oil or butter; salt; pepper; thyme, oregano, sage, or basil (optional)
Peas	2 pounds fresh green peas or 1 package (10 ounces) frozen green peas	Salt, butter or margarine
Strawberries with Raspberry Sauce, page 238	1 package (10 ounces) quick-thaw frozen raspberries 1 pint strawberries	
Day 3		
Baked Eggs with Onions and Cheese, page 185		Butter or margarine, onions, flour, milk (1½ cups), salt, pepper, eggs (6), mild Cheddar cheese
Dry-Sautéed Broccoli, page 62	2 pounds broccoli	Peanut or vegetable oil, salt, pepper
Romaine Lettuce with Oil and Vinegar Dressing for Green Salads, page 51	1 large head romaine lettuce	Vegetable oil, red wine vinegar, salt, Dijon or prepared spicy brown mustard
Fresh fruit	A selection of fresh fruit	
Day 4		
Hot and Spicy Ham Steak, page 134	1 pound fully cooked ham steak, about ½ inch thick	Vegetable oil, ketchup (½ cup), sugar, cider vinegar, prepared spicy brown mustard, Worcestershire sauce, crushed dried red pepper (optional)
Spinach	2 packages (10 ounces each) fresh or frozen spinach	Salt, butter or margarine
Glorious Mashed Potatoes, page 74	3 large baking potatoes Sour cream (for ¼ cup) 1 package (3 ounces) cream cheese with chives Fresh or freeze-dried chives (for 1 tablespoon, optional)	Milk, butter or margarine, salt, pepper
Lemon Pudding Cake, page 240		Eggs, butter or margarine, sugar, 3 medium-size lemons (for grated rind of 1 lemon and ⅓ cup lemon juice), milk, flour

(continued on page 14)

Menus	Shopping List	Staples
Day 5		
Chicken with Sweet Peppers, page 90	Green onions 2 whole chicken breasts (4 halves) 2 medium-size green peppers	Soy sauce, ketchup, cider vinegar, ground ginger, cornstarch, salt, garlic, vegetable oil
Cucumber Salad with Soy and Sesame Dressing, page 46	2 medium-size cucumbers 2 teaspoons sesame oil (or creamy peanut butter)	Salt, sugar, soy sauce, cider vinegar, vegetable oil
Rice		Rice (1½ cups)
Blender Chocolate Mousse, page 242	1 package (6 ounces) semisweet chocolate bits	Eggs (4), vanilla extract or rum
Day 6		
Sausage Patties with Cream Gravy, page 141	1½ pounds mild or hot sausage meat 1 cup half-and-half (or milk)	Onion, flour, salt, pepper
Red Cabbage with Apples, page 65	1 small head red cabbage (about 1¼ pounds) 1 medium-size tart green apple	Onion, vegetable oil, cider vinegar, light or dark brown sugar or honey, salt, pepper
Green beans	1 pound green beans	Salt, butter or margarine
Fresh fruit	Assorted fresh fruit	
Day 7		
Beef with Curry Sauce, page 111	1½ pounds flank or skirt steak	Sugar, soy sauce, garlic, ground ginger, vegetable oil, onion, cornstarch, curry powder
Buttered Egg Noodles		Egg noodles (8 ounces), salt, butter or margarine
Pear, Celery, and Pecan Salad, page 57	Celery (for 3 stalks) 3 large firm, ripe pears Lettuce leaves for garnish	Mayonnaise or plain yogurt, vegetable oil, lemon (for 1 teaspoon juice), salt, pepper, pecan halves (½ cup)
Vanilla Ice Cream with Butterscotch Sauce, page 243	1 pint vanilla ice cream Half-and-half	Light brown sugar, butter or margarine, light corn syrup

SAVING MONEY IN THE KITCHEN

You don't want to take the time and energy to save money at the supermarket only to throw away much of the savings in the kitchen. To get the most out of every food dollar, learn how to avoid waste, use leftovers wisely, and cut energy costs.

PREVENTING SPOILAGE

Spoiled food is money lost. You can greatly reduce kitchen waste if you store foods properly so that they do not dry out or go bad. Make sure all refrigerated items are wrapped or covered and that containers are sealed to keep out air. Here are some tips for storing some hard-to-keep foods.

● To keep parsley fresh, wash gently in cool water, cut off the stem ends at an angle (as you would cut a bunch of flowers), then stand the parsley stalks in a glass of cold water. Slip a plastic bag over the glass of parsley and store in the refrigerator. The parsley should keep for 10 days. Or you can freeze parsley; chop and store it in a plastic container. Because parsley does not freeze solidly, you can spoon out just the amount you need.
● Green peppers can be chopped and frozen in a plastic bag for use as needed.
● To prevent pimientos from spoiling once the jar has been opened, cover with vinegar and refrigerate.

14

Keep these foods on hand. Be sure to replace them well before they run out, and you will avoid last-minute dashes to the store.

Bread and Grains

Bread, white or whole wheat
Bread crumbs, dry
Cereal, dry
Cornmeal
Cornstarch
Crackers
Flour, all-purpose
Quick-cooking oats
Rice
Spaghetti, egg noodles, and other pasta

Leavenings

Baking powder
Baking soda
Yeast, active dry

Fats and Oils

Olive oil
Vegetable oil
Vegetable shortening

Dairy Products

Butter or margarine
Cheese, sharp or extra sharp Cheddar
Cheese, Parmesan
Eggs
Milk, evaporated
Milk, whole

Sugars and Syrup

Brown sugar, light and dark
Confectioners' sugar
Corn syrup, light and dark
Granulated (white) sugar
Honey
Maple syrup

Chocolate and Cocoa

Chocolate, semisweet, unsweetened, and sweet
Cocoa

Herbs and Spices

Allspice, ground
Basil, dried
Bay leaves
Caraway seeds
Chili powder
Chives, freeze-dried
Cinnamon, ground
Cloves, ground
Cloves, whole
Cumin, ground
Curry powder
Dillweed
Ginger, ground
Marjoram, dried

Mint, dried
Mustard, dry
Nutmeg, ground
Oregano, dried
Paprika
Pepper, black
Pepper, cayenne
Pepper, crushed dried red
Rosemary, dried
Sage, dried
Tarragon, dried
Thyme, dried

Prepared Foods, Sauces, Condiments, and Seasonings

Anchovy fillets, flat
Beef and chicken broth, canned
Capers
Chilies, canned green
Chili sauce
Horseradish
Ketchup
Liquid hot red pepper seasoning
Mayonnaise
Mustard, Dijon or prepared spicy brown
Olives
Pickles, dill and sweet

Pickle relish
Pimientos, canned
Soy sauce
Steak sauce
Tomato paste
Tomato sauce
Tomatoes (1-pound cans)
Tuna, canned (6- or 7-ounce cans)
Vinegar, cider and red wine
Worcestershire sauce

Miscellaneous

Almond extract
Coffee
Garlic
Gelatin, unflavored
Lemons
Nuts, including almonds, pecans, and walnuts
Onions
Oranges
Peanut butter
Preserves, jellies, and marmalade
Raisins
Salt
Tea
Vanilla extract

● Leftover canned tomato paste spoils quickly, so buy tomato paste in tubes from which you can squeeze just the amount you need. Or freeze leftover canned tomato paste in one-tablespoon mounds in the dull side of aluminum foil. When hard, bundle in a plastic bag and store in the freezer.

● Mushrooms keep better if they are unwrapped and refrigerated in a loose brown paper bag. Those you cannot use right away can be chopped in a blender with a few tablespoons of water or chicken or beef broth, poured into ice cube trays, and frozen for use in sauces, stews, or soups.

● Strawberries will keep longer in the refrigerator if stored, uncovered, in a colander, which allows air to circulate around them.

● Don't throw away overripe bananas. Peel, slice, sprinkle with lemon juice, and freeze for use in milk shakes, puddings, or banana bread. Or freeze bananas in their skins.

● Don't slice a lemon when you need only a few drops of juice. Instead, puncture it with a toothpick, squeeze out what you need, and replace the toothpick. The lemon will keep longer whole than halved.

● Sliced bread stays fresher in the freezer than in the refrigerator. Just pop it frozen into the toaster.

● Fresh ginger keeps for months in the freezer. Wrap it tightly in aluminum foil, and chop off just as much as you need for a recipe.

RECYCLING

Much of what gets thrown away in the kitchen can be used. Here are some tips for putting

new life into items that usually get tossed out.
- Stale rolls will be perfectly good if you spray them lightly with cold water, place them in a paper bag or bundle them loosely in foil, and warm in a 375°F oven for about 7 minutes.
- Rejuvenate crystallized honey by placing the open jar in a warm (250°F) oven and heat until the honey liquefies.
- Soften hardened brown sugar by sprinkling it with water and placing it in a shallow pan, uncovered, in a 200°F oven. When the sugar becomes soft, crumble it with a fork or whirl it in the container of an electric blender or food processor.
- Turn pickle juice into salad dressing by mixing it with vegetable oil, or use it to marinate thinly sliced cucumbers or beets.
- Onions often come in plastic mesh bags that make handy pot and dish scrubbers. Cut the mesh to the desired size, fill with scraps of soap, and tie the ends.
- Save the nutritious water from cooked vegetables to use as a base for soup or as a substitute for chicken or beef broth in recipes.
- Collect and freeze leftover beef and chicken bones, then simmer to make a rich broth.
- Grate and freeze dried-out cheese for use in casseroles or omelets or as garnishes.

DO-IT-YOURSELF

Often the most expensive items on grocery bills are "convenience foods" (precooked, prepared, or packaged foods). Sometimes the saving in time is worth the price, but you can save money by making some of these foods at home. For example:
- Use leftover bread for making dry bread crumbs or croutons. Slice the bread into cubes or whirl it into crumbs in an electric blender. Then freeze or store in a dry glass jar.
- Instead of buying expensive meat extenders in the supermarket, use leftover bread crumbs in hamburgers and meat loaves. Or try uncooked bulgur (cracked wheat) or oatmeal, grated raw potato, or zucchini.
- Make your own seasoned stuffing by drying bread in a cooling, turned-off oven and then adding sage or poultry herbs. Crush the bread in an electric blender; or put it into a plastic bag, press out the air, and then crush with a rolling pin until the crumbs are very fine.
- It is cheaper to make your own whipped butter than to buy it. Just soften a stick of

butter to room temperature, beat with an electric beater until light and fluffy, and add ½ cup of vegetable oil one tablespoon at a time. Refrigerate in a covered container.
- Home-ground meat is cheaper and tastes better than store-bought.
- Learning to cut up a whole chicken can save as much as $1 per bird. All you need is a good sharp knife and a little practice.
- Save on boneless chicken breasts by doing the boning yourself with a sharp knife.
- Make your own desserts whenever possible—home-baked cookies, cakes, and other sweets or just fruit salad or fruit and cheese.

SUBSTITUTES

Recipes are not carved in stone. You will enjoy them just as much if on occasion you use less expensive ingredients. A little experimentation can produce some superb dishes that cost less than "the real thing."
- Try using pork or lamb instead of beef; they are often cheaper per serving. But if you do substitute pork for beef, be sure to cook it until it is well done.
- One type of seafood can often substitute for another. If crab is too expensive, try tuna. Choose the least expensive fish available for broiled or baked dishes.
- Make your own natural food snacks from dried fruits and nuts.
- Pork butt (porkette) is an inexpensive substitute for bacon. It does not taste the same, but it is very good. Just slice thin and fry a few minutes on each side. Unlike bacon, pork butt has very little shrinkage.

LEFTOVERS

Yesterday's leftovers can be today's main course, salad, or sandwich, or they can be frozen for use later as ingredients in soups and casseroles. These tips will help remind you of the many uses leftovers can be put to.

Vegetables

Leftover vegetables spoil more quickly than you might think, so either use or freeze them right away.
- Shape mashed potatoes into patties, roll in flour, dip in beaten egg and then in bread crumbs, and cook in butter or margarine for about 2 minutes on each side.
- Whip mashed potatoes with milk or half-

and-half, add grated onion, top with grated cheese, and bake, uncovered, in a preheated 350°F oven for 20 minutes.
● Freeze leftover vegetables for later use in soups or casseroles.
● Cold cooked vegetables make an excellent quick salad. Just toss with a dressing.
● Purée leftover vegetables with some half-and-half or cream and reheat with butter.
● Use minced vegetables in fillings for stuffed peppers or eggs.

Poultry, Meats, Fish

A number of the recipes in this book make imaginative use of leftover chicken and turkey, beef, pork, and lamb. Here are some additional ideas.
● Dice cooked chicken for use in soups, salads, sandwiches, casseroles, chicken pies, or curries.
● Chop leftover chicken, turkey, beef, or pork, and add to a white sauce or a spaghetti sauce. Season, heat, and serve over pasta.
● Add cubed beef, lamb, or pork to cooked rice, along with onions and other vegetables, to make a rice casserole.
● Grind cooked beef, pork, or lamb, and substitute for raw meat in meat patties or meat loaves.
● Mix cubed ham with coleslaw.
● Make omelets, salads, or scalloped potatoes heartier by adding chopped ham. Ham is also good with green beans, in casseroles, or ground up for ham loaf, patties, or croquettes.
● Create a sandwich spread from leftover ham by grinding it and mixing it with mayonnaise, horseradish or pickle relish, and onion.
● For richer flavor, fry eggs or potatoes, or brown meat, in bacon drippings. Use drippings for seasoning greens, limas, squash, and spinach and other leafy green vegetables.
● Turn leftover spaghetti sauce into chili by adding pinto beans, onions, and chili powder.
● Use chopped cooked lamb as a base for a curry or shepherd's pie or as a stuffing for zucchini or eggplant.
● Add leftover gravies and pan juices to soups, stews, and casseroles.
● Add cooked fish to salad greens for a main course salad. Or turn the fish into a sandwich filling or salad by mixing with capers, chopped celery, onion, sweet pickle relish, and mayonnaise.

Dairy Products

Don't shy away from recipes calling for egg yolks but not the whites, or vice versa, because you don't know what to do with the unused whites or yolks.
● Use uncooked egg yolks for making mayonnaise, hollandaise sauce, or custards (2 yolks equal 1 egg). Or add to mashed potatoes.
● Make a creamy salad dressing by mixing a raw egg yolk with ¼ cup of regular dressing.
● To save unused egg whites, freeze them in ice cube trays, one white per segment. They will thaw easily for later use in angel food cakes, meringues, macaroons, and soufflés.
● Egg yolks will keep if poached firm. Let them cool, then put them through a sieve and store refrigerated in a covered bowl. Use as a garnish on salads, appetizers, and soups.

SAVING ENERGY

You can pare your utility bills with efficient use of kitchen appliances. Over a period of time, the small savings will add up.
● Your oven can do double duty if you cook two items instead of one whenever possible. Roast two chickens at a time and save one for later use, or bake two pies and freeze one.
● Turn off the oven after most of the cooking is done. There will still be enough heat to finish things off.
● Don't peek inside the oven to check on a dish. You will waste energy.
● Don't bother preheating the oven when the cooking time is long, as for roasting meat.
● Don't worry about exact oven temperatures when you have more than one dish to cook. You can set the oven for 375°F when one recipe calls for 350°F and another for 400°F. You will save both energy and time.
● Whenever possible, cook stews, pot roasts, and the like on top of the stove instead of in the oven.
● If you have an electric stove, be sure the bottoms of your pots are smooth and lie flat on the burner.
● Match pots and pans to burner size. Using a large burner for a small pan wastes energy.
● Make sure that the lids on your pots and pans are tight-fitting.
● Put a lid on the saucepan when you are boiling water. The water will come to a boil faster.
● Whenever possible, use your toaster oven or electric skillet instead of the oven.

SMART SUPERMARKET SHOPPING

Because food is one of the largest single expenditures in the family budget, learning to shop efficiently is essential. You will get more for your food dollar and cut down on waste if you plan ahead, tailor your menus to your family's tastes, and learn to resist the impulse purchases. It is most efficient to restrict your shopping to one trip per week—the less time you spend in the market, the more money you will save.

HOME—THE PLACE TO START

Your shopping list should be precise and well organized. Begin by taking inventory of both your refrigerator and your cupboard. You will want to stock up on staples that are running low, purchase the ingredients for the next week's meals, and get the best buys on everything you need.

● Plan around your leftovers. Do you have what you need to turn the remains of last night's roast into tomorrow's casserole?

● Check newspaper ads for specials that you can plan a meal around. Not all items advertised as specials are good buys, so whenever possible, comparison-shop among the ads.

● Choose your supermarket carefully, and stick with it. Don't spend time and gasoline money running from store to store looking for the lowest price on every item on your list.

● Base your choice of supermarket not just on price but also on the quality and freshness of the meat and produce.

● Even after you have selected your market, keep an eye on the competition. Stores do change their pricing policies occasionally.

COUPONS AND SPECIALS

If you are watching the ads and clipping coupons, you know where savings are to be found each week. Learn how to use coupons and specials to your best advantage.

● Find out when your supermarket redeems coupons at "double value" and shop then, even if the store is busier than usual.

● Never, never buy anything just because you have a coupon.

● Don't buy a brand name for which you have a coupon without checking to see whether another brand is cheaper.

● Remember that many coupons are for heavily processed convenience foods that probably can be made cheaper from scratch.

● To avoid letting coupons expire before you have a chance to use them, redeem your oldest coupons first. Before you leave home, review your coupons and match them to items on your shopping list.

LEARNING SUPERMARKET STRATEGY

No one likes to think he or she is susceptible to impulse buying, but stores are designed to weaken resistance. The soft music and bright lights are there to lull customers into a trance, and the displays are aimed at tempting you to buy items you really do not need. Here are a few tips to help you resist those urges.

● Stick to your list. Any decision to buy made inside the store is considered impulse buying.

● If you need only a single item, don't take a cart. Get what you came in for, then head back to the checkout counter. (The milk and meat counters are often placed at the back of the store to entice you to pick up something else en route.)

● Never shop when you are hungry or tired.

● Be aware that the crackers and cookies at the ends of aisles and the candies, chewing gum, and magazines at checkout counters are there to tempt you with items that are probably not on your list.

● Shop alone as often as possible, or entrust the task to the family member who is least likely to stray from the list.

● Above all, try to leave the children at home. It is no accident that a lot of widely advertised junk food is placed on the shelves at the eye level of a three-year-old.

● Look around for less well known brands; they are generally less expensive. The nationally advertised brands are usually placed on the shelves at an adult's eye level, the cheaper brands above and below them.

● Look behind newly marked, higher-priced items at the front of a shelf. You may find a few still marked at the old price.

● Try to unload your cart completely before the checker starts totaling your bill. Watch the checkout process carefully for inadvertent errors. At home, review the register tape. If you find mistakes, save the tape and call the mistakes to the attention of the manager the next time you are in the store.

CHOOSING PRODUCTS WISELY

Even the most price-conscious shoppers can waste money by not thinking their needs through carefully, by failing to recognize quality, by neglecting to compute unit prices, or by resisting new brands.

● Always buy the form of the product that best fits your menu. For instance, less expensive crushed pineapple is more economical than chunk style if you are mixing it in gelatin. Tuna flakes are fine for tuna salad. The lower price is due to appearance, not quality.

● Make iced tea at home instead of buying the presweetened canned teas. It is far cheaper.

● If you need just a little ham for a recipe, ask for ham ends at the delicatessen counter.

● Never buy frozen food covered with frost—it has been defrosted. Similarly, it is best not to buy reduced-price dented cans—the contents may have spoiled.

● Check the dates on perishable foods carefully, and note that the fresher ones usually are toward the back of the case.

● Use reduced-price meat and produce right away before they spoil. Do not freeze.

● Check the unit price of all products you buy. This information should be neatly and legibly displayed and easy to compute. Also carry a pocket calculator with you to figure unit prices yourself. Be aware that the largest quantities are *not* always the best buys.

● Buy only as much as you know you can use. You are not getting a bargain when you choose a large size on the basis of unit price if you need only a small amount for your recipe and you do not know what you are going to do with the rest.

● Sample the less expensive generic and store brands. Don't judge on appearance alone; it may matter not at all when it comes to a final use. When you try out a new brand, buy the smallest size first to find out whether your family likes it.

● Don't throw away a spoiled product if you have just bought it. Return it to the store and ask for a refund.

● Request a rain check when your supermarket is out of an advertised special. Even if the store is not required by law to give it to you, the manager probably will do so if you ask.

Dairy Products

● Save on cheese for grating and for use in recipes by buying the low-priced ends at the delicatessen counter.

● Buy cheese spreads in jars, not the more expensive pressurized cans.

● Buy only plain cottage cheese, and add fruit or vegetables at home.

● Substitute nonfat dry milk for fluid milk. Not only is it cheaper, but it keeps for months when stored in a cool, dry place.

Vegetables and Fruits

● Use fresh vegetables in season. They require more preparation, it is true, but they are cheaper, better for you, and taste better.

● Buy frozen vegetables without added butter, almonds, or sauces. These extras inflate the price; add them yourself at home.

● Avoid prepackaged produce. Select fruits and vegetables from the bins to get the size, quality, and quantity you need.

Bread, Rice, and Cereals

● Buy bread by weight, not by size. The largest loaf is not always the best buy.

● Buy marked-down, day-old baked goods and freeze what you cannot use right away.

● Don't waste money on seasoned rice. Add your own herbs and spices.

● Avoid cereals with added sugar and fruit. They run up the price.

● Go for the large box of cereals instead of expensive individual serving-size packages.

SAVING TIME

Here are a few tips for streamlining your shopping so that you can whiz in and out of the store.

● If you have a large freezer, limit major shopping trips to every other week. In between, all you will need will be perishables like milk, fresh fruits, and fresh vegetables.

● Ask the checkout people when the store is least crowded, and shop at those times, usually early in the morning or at the dinner hour.

● Learn your supermarket layout so that you can breeze through without having to backtrack time and again.

● Whenever possible, cluster your errands. Choose a market in a shopping center that includes a dry cleaner, shoe repair shop, and photo development shop, for example.

APPETIZERS

Using these recipes, you can turn a piece of ordinary Cheddar cheese into a special Cocktail Cheese Spread in 8 minutes, or prepare an aromatic Herbed Cream Cheese in 5 minutes. If hot hors d'oeuvres are called for, you can make Crispy Chicken Tidbits or Sausage and Cheese Balls in 30 minutes or less. Even more convenient, 8 of these dishes can be made at least a day ahead. One of them, Black Olive Pâté, will keep in the refrigerator for a solid month. As you look through these recipes for ones that appeal to you, make a note to keep the ingredients on hand—for example, a can of sardines or a jar of artichoke hearts. This way, you'll be able to take care of unexpected guests at a moment's notice.

Artichoke Spread

Preparation: **8 minutes**   Cooking: **20 minutes**   Yield: **1½ cups**   Calories per tablespoon: **50**

The ingredients for this spread will have everyone guessing—some may even think it contains expensive crabmeat.

1 jar (6 ounces) artichoke hearts

½ cup grated Parmesan cheese

½ cup mayonnaise

1 large clove garlic, peeled and minced

1. Preheat the oven to 350°F. Drain the **artichoke hearts** (reserve the oil and use it in a salad dressing), and chop them coarsely.

2. In a mixing bowl, combine the artichokes, **cheese, mayonnaise,** and **garlic.** Using a rubber spatula, scrape the mixture into an ungreased ½-quart baking dish and bake, uncovered, for 20 minutes, or until bubbly and slightly browned. Serve hot, warm, or chilled as a spread for crackers or toast rounds.

Black Olive Pâté ⊚

Preparation: **10 minutes**   Cooking: **1 minute**   Yield: **⅔ cup**   Calories per tablespoon: **135**

Here is a pâté that you can store in the refrigerator for up to a month, so make it now and have it on hand for unexpected company.

⅔ cup (about 26) imported black Greek or Italian olives, drained

6 cloves garlic, peeled

½ cup (1 stick) butter (preferably unsalted), softened

Pinch cayenne pepper

¼ teaspoon salt (optional)

1. Pit the **olives,** chop them very fine, and set aside.

2. Bring 1 cup of water to a boil in a 1-quart saucepan, add the **garlic,** and cook for 1 minute. Drain the garlic, then mince.

3. Place the olives, garlic, **butter,** and **cayenne pepper** in a mixing bowl, and blend thoroughly. Taste, and add the **salt** if desired.

4. Pack the mixture into a 1-cup crock, custard cup, or small bowl. Chill for 10 to 15 minutes if you wish. Serve as a spread for thin slices of crusty French or Italian bread.

Middle Eastern Chick Pea Spread 🐷 ◎ ◍

Preparation: 15 minutes   Yield: **1½ cups**   Calories per tablespoon: **45**

1 can (10½ ounces) chick peas

1 or 2 cloves garlic, peeled and minced

4 teaspoons lemon juice

¼ cup creamy peanut butter

⅛ teaspoon ground cumin

Pinch cayenne pepper

¼ teaspoon salt

1 tablespoon olive oil

This variation on a classic Middle Eastern dish uses peanut butter instead of tahini (sesame paste), which may not be available everywhere and is quite expensive.

1. Drain the **chick peas** and reserve the liquid. Mash them with a potato masher, or purée in an electric blender or food processor.

2. Blend in the **garlic, lemon juice, peanut butter, cumin, cayenne pepper, salt,** and **oil.** Add enough of the reserved chick pea liquid to make a smooth, but not runny, paste. Serve at room temperature or chilled, with pita bread cut up into small triangles.

Tips: 1. This recipe can be halved. 2. You can make this spread ahead and refrigerate it for 3 to 5 days.

Cocktail Cheese Spread ◎

Preparation: 8 minutes   Yield: **1 cup**   Calories per tablespoon: **70**

1 cup shredded sharp Cheddar cheese (about 4 ounces)

1 package (3 ounces) cream cheese, softened

2 tablespoons butter or margarine, softened

¼ cup chopped walnuts or pecans

In a mixing bowl, blend the **Cheddar cheese, cream cheese, butter,** and **walnuts.** Pack the spread into a 1-cup crock, custard cup, or small bowl. Serve at room temperature or slightly chilled as a spread for crackers or toast rounds.

Herbed Cream Cheese 🐷 ◎ ◍

Preparation: 5 minutes   Yield: **1 cup**   Calories per tablespoon: **75**

This technique is traditionally used with goat cheese; if goat cheese is available where you live, try it.

1 package (8 ounces) cream cheese

3 tablespoons olive oil

½ teaspoon dried thyme, crumbled

½ teaspoon dried rosemary, crumbled

2 cloves garlic, peeled and minced

1. Shape the block of **cream cheese** into a disk about ½ inch thick, and place it in a shallow bowl. Prick the cheese all over with a toothpick.

2. Pour the **oil** over the cheese, and sprinkle with the **thyme, rosemary,** and **garlic.** Serve with slices of French or Italian bread.

Tips: 1. This recipe can be halved; use a 3-ounce package of cream cheese. 2. You can make this spread ahead and refrigerate it for up to 7 days.

Chicken Liver Pâté 🐷 ◑

Preparation: 10 minutes   Cooking: **16 minutes**   Yield: **1 cup**   Calories per tablespoon: **75**

If you don't have a hard-cooked egg on hand, boil one while you cook the onions and chicken livers.

5 tablespoons butter or margarine

2 medium-size yellow onions, peeled and coarsely chopped

³/₄ pound chicken livers, drained

3 tablespoons brandy

1 hard-cooked egg

³/₄ teaspoon salt

¹/₈ teaspoon black pepper

1 clove garlic, peeled and minced

> *Tips: 1. This recipe can be halved. 2. You can make this spread a day ahead. 3. You can use an electric blender or food processor for blending the mixture, but the consistency will be creamier.*

1. Melt 2 tablespoons of the **butter** in a heavy 9-inch skillet over moderately low heat. Add the **onions** and cook, uncovered, until soft and golden but not brown—about 10 minutes. Remove the onions to a mixing bowl and set aside.

2. Raise the heat to moderate. Add 1 tablespoon of the butter and the **chicken livers** to the skillet, and cook, stirring occasionally, for 5 minutes, or until the livers are pink all the way through. Add the livers to the onions.

3. Pour the **brandy** into the skillet and boil until only 1 tablespoon remains, scraping up any brown bits stuck to the skillet. Add to the onions and livers.

4. Mash the mixture with a fork until fairly smooth. Mix in the yolk of the **egg** along with the remaining 2 tablespoons of butter, and season with the **salt, pepper,** and **garlic.** Pack the pâté into a 1-cup crock, custard cup, or small bowl. Mince the egg white and sprinkle on top. Chill until serving, preferably at least 1 hour.

Caviar Pie ◑

Preparation: 30 minutes   Yield: **5 cups**   Calories per tablespoon: **30**

This sounds extravagant, but lumpfish caviar is relatively inexpensive. Moreover, the pie is always a hit. It must be made just before serving, or the caviar will discolor the sour cream, but you can save time by cooking and even chopping the eggs ahead.

6 hard-cooked eggs, finely chopped

2 tablespoons mayonnaise

1 medium-size yellow onion, peeled and finely chopped

1 jar (7 ounces) red or black lumpfish caviar

2 cups sour cream

¹/₄ cup finely chopped parsley

1. Combine the **eggs** and **mayonnaise,** and press the mixture into a buttered 9-inch pie plate.

2. Scatter the **onion** over the mixture, then spread the **caviar** evenly over the onion. Spoon the **sour cream** onto the center of the pie, and carefully spread it to the edges so that it completely covers the caviar.

3. Decorate the center and edge of the pie with the **parsley.** Serve as a spread with party-size dark pumpernickel bread or crackers.

> *Tips: 1. This recipe can be halved. 2. You can substitute 1 cup of plain yogurt for 1 of the cups of sour cream. If you do, you will reduce the number of calories per tablespoon to 25.*

22

Sardine Pâté 🐷

Preparation: **30 minutes**   Yield: **1 cup**   Calories per tablespoon: **45**

1 can (3¾ ounces) boneless sardines, drained

3 tablespoons butter or margarine, softened

2 tablespoons lemon juice

¾ cup finely chopped pimiento-stuffed olives

2 teaspoons prepared horseradish

1 clove garlic, peeled and minced

½ teaspoon Dijon or prepared spicy brown mustard

½ teaspoon paprika

⅛ teaspoon black pepper

½ teaspoon Worcestershire sauce

Pinch cayenne pepper

3 tablespoons finely chopped walnuts (optional)

Some sardines are packed without salt while others have a great deal, so be sure to taste this spread for seasoning after you have made it, and add salt only if necessary. Note that the preparation time includes 15 minutes of chilling in the refrigerator.

1. In a mixing bowl, mash the **sardines** with a fork, then blend in the **butter** to make a smooth paste. Add the **lemon juice, olives, horseradish, garlic, mustard, paprika, black pepper, Worcestershire sauce,** and **cayenne pepper,** and the **walnuts** if used. Blend well and taste the mixture for seasoning.

2. Chill for 15 minutes. Serve as a spread for crackers or toast, or use as a stuffing for celery.

Tips: 1. You can make this spread ahead and refrigerate it for 1 or 2 days. 2. Try this with a 3½-ounce can of tuna instead of the sardines.

Egg Chutney Madras 🐷 ◐

Preparation: **25 minutes**   Yield: **1 cup**   Calories per tablespoon: **55**

4 hard-cooked eggs, chopped

1 package (3 ounces) cream cheese, softened

1 tablespoon Worcestershire sauce

1 teaspoon curry powder

Pinch cayenne pepper

3 or 4 drops liquid hot red pepper seasoning

2 tablespoons mayonnaise

¼ cup chopped chutney or applesauce

¼ teaspoon salt

⅛ teaspoon black pepper

A mildly spicy, very spreadable egg salad, this recipe is quicker to prepare than it appears—15 minutes of the preparation time is for cooking the eggs.

Mash the **eggs** and **cream cheese** together with a fork. Add the **Worcestershire sauce, curry powder, cayenne pepper, red pepper seasoning, mayonnaise, chutney, salt,** and **black pepper,** and blend thoroughly. Chill until ready to serve. Serve as a spread for crackers, or for ½-inch slices of cucumber or raw zucchini.

Tips: 1. This recipe can be halved, or leftovers can be refrigerated for 1 or 2 days. 2. This is delicious as a sandwich filling.

Cheese Puffs 🐷 ⊘

Preparation: 5 minutes   Cooking: **2 minutes**   Yield: **16 pieces**   Calories per piece: **75**

1/2 **cup mayonnaise**

1/2 **cup grated Parmesan cheese**

2 **tablespoons grated yellow onion**

2 **teaspoons Dijon or prepared spicy brown mustard**

4 **slices rye bread**

1. Preheat the broiler. Combine the **mayonnaise, cheese, onion,** and **mustard.**

2. Place the **bread** in a shallow baking pan and toast one side lightly under the broiler. Spread the cheese mixture over the untoasted sides, then cut each slice into 4 triangles or squares.

3. Broil 6 inches from the heat for 2 minutes, or until the cheese spread is golden brown and slightly puffed. Serve immediately.

> *Tip: You can complete this recipe through Step 2 about 1 or 2 hours ahead of time, then broil the cheese-spread bread just before serving.*

Cheese Wafers 🐷

Preparation: 10 minutes   Cooking: **12 minutes**   Yield: **12 pieces**   Calories per piece: **85**

These rich and flavorful appetizers are sure to disappear fast. You may want to double or even triple the recipe.

4 **tablespoons (**1/2 **stick) butter or margarine, softened**

1 **cup shredded extra sharp Cheddar cheese (about 4 ounces)**

1/2 **cup unsifted all-purpose flour**

Pinch cayenne pepper

1. Preheat the oven to 350°F. In a mixing bowl, combine the **butter** and **cheese** with a fork, then blend in the **flour** and **cayenne pepper.**

2. Roll the mixture into 1-inch balls, place on a buttered 15½"x 10½"x 1" baking pan, and flatten with the heel of your hand until the balls are about 1/4 inch thick. Bake, uncovered, for 12 to 15 minutes, or until golden brown and crisp. Serve warm or at room temperature.

> *Tip: You can make these wafers 1 or 2 days ahead and store them in an airtight container.*

Pimiento Cheese Canapés 🐷 ⊘ ⎗

Preparation: 15 minutes   Yield: **40 pieces**   Calories per piece: **55**

2 **cups shredded extra sharp Cheddar cheese (about 8 ounces)**

1 **jar (4 ounces) pimientos, drained and finely chopped**

1/2 **cup mayonnaise or plain yogurt**

10 **slices white or whole wheat bread, with the crusts removed**

This all-time favorite not only is a tempting hors d'oeuvre but also can be used as a wholesome sandwich filling.

In a mixing bowl, combine the **cheese, pimientos,** and **mayonnaise.** Spread the mixture evenly over the slices of **bread,** then cut each slice into 4 squares or triangles.

> *Tips: 1. This recipe can be halved. 2. You can make this spread ahead and refrigerate it for up to 4 days.*

Pastrami Canapés ◑ ◖

Preparation: **12 minutes**   Cooking: **3 minutes**   Yield: **24 pieces**   Calories per piece: **90**

3 tablespoons sour cream

2 tablespoons Dijon or prepared spicy brown mustard

24 slices party rye or pumpernickel bread

1/4 pound pastrami, thinly sliced and trimmed of fat

1 can (8 ounces) sauerkraut, drained

1/2 pound Swiss cheese, sliced

1. Preheat the broiler. In a small bowl, combine the **sour cream** and **mustard**. Spread the mixture thinly on each slice of **bread**. Top with the **pastrami, sauerkraut,** and **cheese**.

2. Put the slices on a baking sheet and broil 4 inches from the heat for 3 minutes, or until the cheese is bubbly.

Tips: 1. This recipe can be halved. 2. Instead of party bread, use 6 regular-size slices of rye or pumpernickel, remove the crusts, and cut the slices into quarters.

Crispy Chicken Tidbits

Preparation: **15 minutes**   Cooking: **10 minutes**   Yield: **32 pieces**   Calories per piece: **50**

1/2 cup (1 stick) butter or margarine

4 teaspoons lemon juice

2 large whole chicken breasts (4 halves), about 1 1/2 pounds

1/2 cup fine dry bread crumbs

1 teaspoon salt

1 teaspoon dried rosemary, crumbled

3 cloves garlic, peeled and minced

1. Preheat the oven to 400°F. Melt the **butter** in a 1-quart saucepan, stir in the **lemon juice,** and set aside. Meanwhile, cut each half **chicken breast** into 8 pieces.

2. Combine the **bread crumbs, salt, rosemary,** and **garlic** on a plate or a sheet of wax paper. Dip the chicken into the lemon butter, then roll in the bread-crumb mixture.

3. Place the tidbits in one layer on a greased 15 1/2"x 10 1/2"x 1" baking pan, and bake for 10 to 15 minutes, or until the pieces are golden brown.

Sausage and Cheese Balls

Preparation: **15 minutes**   Cooking: **15 minutes**   Yield: **36 pieces**   Calories per piece: **65**

1 cup unsifted all-purpose flour

1/4 teaspoon baking powder

1/4 teaspoon salt

1/2 pound ground pork sausage

1 cup shredded sharp Cheddar cheese (about 4 ounces)

4 tablespoons (1/2 stick) butter or margarine, softened

1. Preheat the oven to 450°F. Combine the **flour, baking powder,** and **salt** in a large bowl, then add the **sausage, cheese,** and **butter**. Blend well with a wooden spoon or with your hands.

2. Roll the mixture into 1-inch balls; it should yield about 36 pieces. Place the balls about 1/2 inch apart on a greased 15 1/2"x 10 1/2"x 1" baking sheet and flatten them slightly with the heel of your hand. Bake for 15 to 20 minutes, or until the pieces are golden brown at the bottom. Serve hot or warm.

SOUPS

Soups often take hours to prepare, but all of these can be made in 45 minutes or less, and many can be served as main courses or one-dish meals. Light and hearty soups, hot and cold soups, soups with meat, fish, or vegetables—there's something here for everyone.

Spanish Black Bean Soup

Preparation: **10 minutes**   Cooking: **12 minutes**   Serves **4**   Calories per serving: **310**

2 tablespoons bacon drippings

1 medium-size yellow onion, peeled and chopped

1 clove garlic, peeled and minced

1/4 teaspoon dried thyme, crumbled

2 cans (15 to 16 ounces each) black beans, undrained

1 1/2 cups beef broth

3 tablespoons dry sherry

1 tablespoon chopped chives

This soup takes minutes to make, yet it is a meal in itself.

1. Heat the **bacon drippings** in a heavy 3-quart saucepan over moderate heat. Add the **onion** and **garlic,** and cook, uncovered, about 5 minutes, or until the onion is soft.

2. Add the **thyme, beans** and their liquid, and **beef broth.** Simmer, uncovered, stirring occasionally, for 10 minutes. Stir in the **sherry,** and simmer 1 or 2 minutes longer. Sprinkle each serving with some of the **chives.**

Tip: *This recipe can be halved, or leftovers can be refrigerated for up to 3 days.*

Plantation Peanut Soup

Preparation: **7 minutes**   Cooking: **10 minutes**   Serves **6**   Calories per serving: **355**

2 tablespoons butter or margarine

1 large yellow onion, peeled and chopped

1/2 cup tomato sauce

1/2 teaspoon dried thyme, crumbled

1/8 teaspoon black pepper

Pinch nutmeg

2 cups beef or chicken broth

1 cup creamy or chunky peanut butter

1 1/2 cups milk

2 tablespoons chopped chives

Don't hesitate to try this updated version of an old Southern classic dish.

1. Melt the **butter** in a 2-quart saucepan over moderate heat, add the **onion,** and cook, uncovered, for 5 minutes, or until soft.

2. Stir in the **tomato sauce, thyme, pepper, nutmeg, broth, peanut butter,** and **milk.** Simmer, stirring occasionally, for 10 minutes.

3. If you wish, purée the soup in an electric blender, then return the soup to the saucepan and reheat, uncovered, to serving temperature. Do not let the soup boil or it may curdle. Stir in the **chives.**

Tip: *This recipe can be halved, or leftovers can be refrigerated for up to 3 days or frozen.*

Lentil and Sausage Soup

Preparation: **10 minutes**   Cooking: **30 minutes**   Serves **6**   Calories per serving: **895**

3 tablespoons olive or vegetable oil

1 medium-size yellow onion, peeled and chopped

1 clove garlic, peeled and minced

3 medium-size carrots, peeled and cut into 1/2-inch slices

3 cups beef broth

1 can (8 ounces) tomato sauce

1 1/2 cups water

1/2 bay leaf

6 sprigs parsley, tied together

1 cup dry brown lentils, rinsed and sorted

1 cup uncooked rice

1 1/2 pounds chorizo or pepperoni, cut into 1/2-inch slices

This is a one-dish meal that is rich in vitamins, protein, and fiber—even if you omit the sausage.

1. Heat 2 tablespoons of the **oil** in a heavy 2-quart saucepan over moderate heat. Add the **onion, garlic,** and **carrots,** and cook, uncovered, for 5 minutes, or until the onion is soft.

2. Add the **beef broth, tomato sauce, water, bay leaf, parsley,** and **lentils.** Cover, bring to a boil, then reduce the heat and simmer for 10 minutes.

3. Add the **rice** to the soup, cover, and simmer for 20 to 30 minutes longer, or until the rice and lentils are tender. Meanwhile, place the remaining oil in an 8-inch skillet over moderate heat, add the **chorizo** slices, and cook, uncovered, for 10 minutes, or until browned. Drain on paper toweling.

4. Add the sausage slices to the soup when it is done, and heat them through. Serve with thick, crusty bread and a green salad.

Broccoli Chowder

Preparation: **12 minutes**   Cooking: **4 minutes**   Serves **4**   Calories per serving: **500**

For a complete meal, serve this nutritious soup with bread and a fresh-fruit dessert.

1 pound broccoli

1 1/2 cups chicken broth

3 cups milk

1 cup cubed cooked ham (about 1/2 pound)

1/4 teaspoon salt

1/8 teaspoon black pepper

1/2 cup half-and-half or milk

2 tablespoons butter or margarine

1 cup shredded Swiss or mild Cheddar cheese (about 4 ounces)

1. Trim the leaves and coarse stems from the **broccoli,** and cut the stems and florets into bite-size pieces. Meanwhile, bring the **chicken broth** to a boil in a 3-quart saucepan. Add the broccoli and cook, uncovered, for 5 minutes, or until the broccoli is crisp-tender. Using a slotted spoon, remove the broccoli from the saucepan, chop coarsely, and set aside.

2. Add the **milk, ham, salt,** and **pepper** to the broth, bring to a boil, then stir in the **half-and-half, butter,** and the broccoli. Heat until the soup returns to a simmer. Top each serving with 1/4 cup of the **cheese.**

Tips: 1. For a smooth soup, purée the cooked broccoli in an electric blender or food processor before returning it to the saucepan. 2. You can substitute cauliflower for the broccoli. 3. This recipe can be halved, or leftovers can be refrigerated for up to 3 days. 4. For a plain broccoli soup, omit the ham and cheese.

Carrot Soup 🐷 ◑

Preparation: **10 minutes**   Cooking: **20 minutes**   Serves **6**   Calories per serving: **55**

4 cups water

1½ teaspoons salt

4 medium-size carrots (about ½ pound), peeled and cut into ¼-inch slices

1 large all-purpose potato, peeled and diced

1 large yellow onion, peeled and chopped

⅛ teaspoon black pepper

¼ teaspoon dried basil, crumbled (optional)

1 tablespoon butter or margarine, softened

1 cup croutons (optional)

This light and refreshing soup is easy to prepare and thrifty in any season.

1. Place the **water** and **salt** in a 3-quart saucepan, and bring to a boil. Add the **carrots, potato,** and **onion,** cover, and simmer for 10 to 15 minutes, or until the vegetables are tender. Purée the vegetables with the cooking water in an electric blender or food processor.

2. Return the purée to the saucepan. Add the **pepper,** and the **basil** if used, and reheat, uncovered, to serving temperature. Stir in the **butter** just before serving. Garnish with the **croutons** if desired.

Tips: 1. This recipe can be halved. 2. As a variation, omit the basil and reheat with ½ cup of half-and-half and a pinch of ground nutmeg or curry powder. 3. You can make this dish ahead and refrigerate it for 1 or 2 days, but do not add the butter until just before serving.

Easy Cauliflower Soup ◑

Preparation: **10 minutes**   Cooking: **12 minutes**   Serves **4**   Calories per serving: **245**

3 tablespoons butter or margarine

1 medium-size yellow onion, peeled and chopped

1 small head cauliflower (¾ to 1 pound)

4 cups chicken broth

1 cup half-and-half

¼ teaspoon salt

⅛ teaspoon black pepper

2 tablespoons shredded Swiss or Jarlsberg cheese (optional)

1. Melt the **butter** in a 3-quart saucepan over moderate heat, add the **onion,** and cook, uncovered, for 5 minutes, or until soft. Meanwhile, separate the **cauliflower** into florets, then chop the florets into ½-inch pieces.

2. Add the cauliflower and **chicken broth** to the onion in the saucepan. Cover and simmer about 10 minutes, or until the cauliflower is tender.

3. Add the **half-and-half, salt,** and **pepper,** and heat until the soup returns to a simmer. Sprinkle each serving with some of the **cheese** if desired.

Tips: 1. This recipe can be halved, or leftovers can be refrigerated for 1 or 2 days. You need not reheat; the soup is excellent chilled. 2. For a smooth soup, purée it in an electric blender or food processor at the end of Step 2, then continue with the recipe. 3. To make a spicy variation, cook 1½ teaspoons of curry powder in the butter for 3 or 4 minutes before adding the onion.

SOUPS

Curried Celery Soup 🐷 ◑

Preparation: **14 minutes**   Cooking: **10 minutes**   Serves **6**   Calories per serving: **120**

3 tablespoons butter or margarine

4 stalks celery, finely chopped

3 tablespoons all-purpose flour

1½ teaspoons curry powder

¾ teaspoon salt

¼ teaspoon black pepper

2 cups milk

4 cups water or chicken broth

1. Melt the **butter** in a 3-quart saucepan over moderate heat. Add the **celery,** and cook, uncovered, for 5 minutes, or until crisp-tender, stirring occasionally.

2. Remove the pan from the heat, and blend in the **flour, curry powder, salt,** and **pepper** to make a paste. Gradually stir in the **milk** and **water.**

3. Return the mixture to the heat and stir constantly until it comes to a boil. Reduce the heat, cover, and simmer for 10 minutes.

Tips: **1.** *This recipe can be halved, or leftovers can be refrigerated for up to 3 days.* **2.** *For a garnish, top each serving with 1 tablespoon shredded, sweetened coconut, chopped pecans, or chopped raisins or with 1 teaspoon chopped chives.* **3.** *For a richer soup, use half-and-half instead of the milk.*

Corn Chowder ◑

Preparation: **10 minutes**   Cooking: **13 minutes**   Serves **4**   Calories per serving: **355**

4 slices bacon, cut into 1-inch strips

4 green onions, trimmed and chopped, or 1 medium-size yellow onion, peeled and chopped

1 medium-size sweet red or green pepper, cored, seeded, and chopped

1 cup water

2 cups fresh sweet corn (cut from 4 medium-size ears) or 1 package (10 ounces) frozen whole-kernel corn

2 cups half-and-half or milk

2 tablespoons minced parsley

¼ teaspoon salt

⅛ teaspoon black pepper

1. Cook the **bacon** in a 2-quart saucepan over moderately high heat until crisp—about 5 minutes. Using a slotted spoon, remove the bacon to paper toweling to drain. Set aside.

2. Pour all but 2 tablespoons of the bacon drippings from the saucepan, add the **green onions** and **red pepper,** and cook for 5 minutes over moderate heat, or until the vegetables are soft. Add the **water** and **corn,** and simmer, covered, for 10 minutes. If you are using frozen corn, break up the block with a fork and cook for 5 minutes.

3. Add the **half-and-half,** and reheat, uncovered, to serving temperature. Do not let the soup boil or it may curdle. Stir in the **parsley, salt,** and **black pepper.** Sprinkle each serving with some of the reserved bacon.

Tips: **1.** *This recipe can be halved.* **2.** *You can make this dish ahead and refrigerate it for 1 or 2 days.*

Cucumber Soup 🐷 ◑

Preparation: **12 minutes** Cooking: **22 minutes**   Serves **6** Calories per serving: **120**

2 tablespoons butter or margarine

2 tablespoons finely chopped yellow or green onion

2 large cucumbers, peeled, seeded, and diced

1 tablespoon white wine vinegar or cider vinegar

1 tablespoon all-purpose flour

4 cups chicken broth

1/4 teaspoon salt

1/2 teaspoon dried tarragon, crumbled, or 1/2 teaspoon dried dillweed (optional)

1/2 cup sour cream

3 tablespoons minced parsley (optional)

1. Melt the **butter** in a 2-quart saucepan over moderate heat, add the **onion,** and cook, uncovered, for 5 minutes, or until soft. Add the **cucumbers** and **vinegar.** Stir in the **flour** and cook, stirring constantly, for 1 or 2 minutes. Gradually stir in the **chicken broth,** then add the **salt** and the **tarragon** if used.

2. Cover and simmer for 20 minutes, or until the cucumbers are very soft, then purée the mixture in an electric blender or food processor. Return the mixture to the saucepan and reheat, uncovered, to serving temperature—about 2 minutes. If you plan to serve the soup cold, chill it in the refrigerator for 1 or 2 hours.

3. Top each serving with a heaping teaspoon of the **sour cream** and a sprinkling of the **parsley** if used.

> *Tips: 1. If serving the soup cold, you can substitute plain yogurt for the sour cream (yogurt would curdle in the hot soup). 2. This recipe can be halved. 3. You can make this dish ahead and refrigerate it for 1 or 2 days.*

Fresh Mushroom Soup ◑ ◑

Preparation: **10 minutes** Cooking: **5 minutes**   Serves **6** Calories per serving: **165**

4 tablespoons (1/2 stick) butter or margarine

1/2 pound mushrooms, thinly sliced

2 cups chicken broth

3 egg yolks

1 cup half-and-half

1/4 teaspoon salt

1/8 teaspoon black pepper

> *Tips: 1. This recipe can be halved; use 1 large or jumbo egg yolk. 2. For a smooth, more elegant soup, set aside 6 cooked mushroom slices, purée the soup in an electric blender or food processor, and top each serving with a mushroom slice.*

Serve this soup as a first course for dinner for 6, or with sandwiches and a salad for a lunch for 4.

1. Melt the **butter** in a 2-quart saucepan over moderate heat. Reduce the heat to low, add the **mushrooms,** and cook for 5 minutes, stirring frequently. Add the **chicken broth,** raise the heat to moderate, and bring to a boil.

2. Beat the **egg yolks** in a small bowl. Remove the mushroom mixture from the heat. Beat 1/2 cup of the hot broth into the yolks until the mixture is frothy. Gradually pour this mixture back into the saucepan, stirring constantly to prevent the eggs from curdling.

3. Return the saucepan to the stove over moderate heat, and add the **half-and-half, salt,** and **pepper.** Reheat, uncovered, stirring constantly, but do not let the soup boil.

French Onion Soup with Cheese Toast

Preparation: 17 minutes   Cooking: **13 minutes**   Serves **4**   Calories per serving: **320**

3 tablespoons butter or margarine

2 large yellow onions, peeled, halved lengthwise, and cut crosswise into very thin slices

1½ teaspoons all-purpose flour

4 cups beef broth

¼ teaspoon salt

⅛ teaspoon black pepper

4 slices French bread, about ¾ inch thick

4 thin slices Gruyère or Swiss cheese (about 4 ounces)

Tip: This recipe can be halved.

1. Melt 2 tablespoons of the **butter** in a 3-quart saucepan over moderate heat. Reduce the heat to moderately low, add the **onions,** and cook, uncovered, for 10 minutes, or until golden but not brown, stirring occasionally. Stir in the **flour** and cook for 1 minute.

2. Add the **beef broth, salt,** and **pepper,** and simmer, covered, for 10 minutes. Taste, and add additional salt and pepper if needed.

3. While the soup is simmering, spread the remaining tablespoon of butter over the slices of **bread,** and top each slice with a piece of the **cheese** to completely cover the bread. Preheat the broiler 5 minutes before the soup is done.

4. Just before serving, place the bread slices briefly under the broiler about 3 inches from the heat until the cheese melts. Put one slice into the bottom of each soup bowl and ladle the hot soup over it.

Old-Fashioned Potato Soup

Preparation: 24 minutes   Cooking: **5 minutes**   Serves **4**   Calories per serving: **320**

You may never want to buy canned potato soup again once you've made this thrifty, start-from-scratch recipe.

4 medium-size baking potatoes (about 2 pounds), peeled and cut into ½-inch slices

2 tablespoons butter or margarine

1 small yellow onion, peeled and chopped

3 cups milk

Pinch celery salt

¼ teaspoon salt

Pinch cayenne pepper

2 tablespoons minced parsley

1. Place the **potatoes** in a 2-quart saucepan with enough water to cover. Set the lid askew on the pan, and boil for 10 minutes, or until tender.

2. Meanwhile, melt the **butter** in a 7-inch skillet over moderate heat. Add the **onion,** and cook, uncovered, for 5 minutes, or until soft. Set aside.

3. When the potatoes are done, drain them in a colander, then mash them with a potato masher while they are still warm.

4. Return the potatoes to the saucepan, and add the onion and any butter remaining in the skillet. Stir in the **milk, celery salt, salt,** and **cayenne pepper.** Cook over moderate heat, stirring frequently, until smooth and steaming—about 5 minutes. Do not let the soup boil or it will curdle. Sprinkle each serving with some of the **parsley.**

Tips: 1. This recipe can be halved. 2. For a cold soup (vichyssoise), substitute heavy cream for the milk, chill the soup, and top each serving with 2 teaspoons of chopped chives.

Winter Squash Soup 🐷 ⏸

Preparation: 12 minutes   Cooking: 32 minutes   Serves **4**   Calories per serving: **245**

3½ cups water or chicken broth

½ teaspoon salt

1 large butternut squash (about 2 pounds), peeled, halved, seeded, and diced

8 to 10 cloves garlic, peeled and quartered

2 slices stale white bread, with the crusts removed, diced

¼ teaspoon black pepper

1 teaspoon dried basil, crumbled

¼ cup olive or vegetable oil

2 tablespoons minced parsley

This soup is rich and satisfying, yet it is delicately flavored because the garlic becomes very subtle when boiled.

1. Bring the **water** and **salt** to a boil in a 3-quart saucepan. Add the **squash** and **garlic,** and simmer for 25 minutes, covered, or until the squash is very tender, stirring occasionally.

2. Add the **bread, pepper,** and **basil,** reduce the heat, and simmer, uncovered, for 2 or 3 minutes longer. Purée the soup in an electric blender or food processor, then return it to the saucepan and reheat, uncovered, to serving temperature. Stir in the **oil,** and sprinkle each serving with some of the **parsley.**

> **Tips: 1.** *This recipe can be halved.* **2.** *You can make this dish ahead and refrigerate it for 1 or 2 days.* **3.** *If you like, substitute pumpkin for the butternut squash. You can also use zucchini in place of the butternut squash, but cook it only 10 to 15 minutes.*

Buttermilk Gazpacho 🐷 ⏸

Preparation: 23 minutes   Serves **4**   Calories per serving: **105**

2 hard-cooked eggs, halved

1 can (12 ounces) tomato or mixed vegetable juice

1½ cups buttermilk

½ cup chopped Spanish or Bermuda onion

1 stalk celery, diced

1 medium-size sweet green or red pepper, cored, seeded, and chopped

⅛ teaspoon black pepper

1 tablespoon snipped fresh dill or ¼ teaspoon dried dillweed (optional)

1 lime, thinly sliced (optional)

Wonderfully quick and cooling, this soup is low in calories and high in vitamin C. You can reduce the preparation time to 8 minutes if you cook the eggs in advance. Use very cold ingredients for serving immediately, or prepare in advance and chill.

1. Press the yolks of the **eggs** through a sieve into a mixing bowl. Add the **tomato juice, buttermilk, onion, celery, green pepper,** and **black pepper,** and the **dill** if used. Stir to mix.

2. Mince the egg whites, and divide among 4 mugs or soup bowls. Pour the soup over the whites. Garnish each serving with a slice of **lime** if desired.

> **Tip:** *This recipe can be halved.*

French Cream of Tomato Soup 🐷 ◑

Preparation: **10 minutes** Cooking: **20 minutes** Serves **6** Calories per serving: **205**

4 tablespoons (1/2 stick) butter or margarine

1 tablespoon olive or vegetable oil

1 large yellow onion, peeled and chopped

3 medium-size fresh tomatoes, peeled and chopped, or 1 can (1 pound) tomatoes, chopped, with their juice

3 tablespoons tomato paste

4 tablespoons all-purpose flour

2 1/2 cups chicken broth

1/2 teaspoon sugar

1/4 teaspoon salt

1/8 teaspoon black pepper

1 cup half-and-half

Save a few minutes' preparation time by peeling and chopping the tomatoes while the onion is cooking.

1. Heat 2 tablespoons of the **butter** with the **oil** in a 3-quart saucepan over moderate heat. Add the **onion** and cook, uncovered, for 5 minutes.

2. Stir in the **tomatoes** and **tomato paste,** and cook for 2 or 3 minutes. Blend in the **flour,** then add the **chicken broth, sugar, salt,** and **pepper.** Cover and simmer for 15 minutes.

3. Purée the mixture in an electric blender or food processor, then return the purée to the saucepan and add the **half-and-half.** Bring the soup to a simmer, and simmer, uncovered, for 2 or 3 minutes. Stir in the remaining 2 tablespoons of butter.

Tips: **1.** *For a richer soup, use heavy cream instead of the half-and-half.* **2.** *Top each serving with 2 tablespoons of shredded Swiss or sharp Cheddar cheese, or a few croutons.* **3.** *This recipe can be halved.* **4.** *You can make this dish ahead and refrigerate it for 1 or 2 days. When reheating, do not let the soup boil or it may curdle.*

Creamy Watercress Soup ◑

Preparation: **11 minutes** Cooking: **18 minutes** Serves **4** Calories per serving: **265**

5 tablespoons butter or margarine

1 medium-size yellow onion, peeled and chopped

1 medium-size all-purpose potato, peeled and diced

1 cup water

1 bunch watercress

A few grains ground nutmeg

2 cups chicken broth

1 cup half-and-half

1/2 teaspoon salt

Tip: This recipe can be halved.

1. Melt 3 tablespoons of the **butter** in a 3-quart saucepan over moderate heat. Add the **onion** and **potato,** and cook, uncovered, for 5 minutes, or until the onion is soft. Add the **water,** cover, and simmer for 10 to 15 minutes, or until the potato is tender.

2. Meanwhile, cut the stems from the **watercress** and discard them. Wash, drain, and chop the leaves. Purée the watercress along with the onion-potato mixture in an electric blender or food processor.

3. Pour the purée into the saucepan and stir in the **nutmeg, chicken broth,** and **half-and-half.** Heat, uncovered, over low heat, to serving temperature, but do not let the soup boil. Season with the **salt,** and stir in the remaining 2 tablespoons of butter. Serve hot or cold.

Speedy Cream of Chicken Soup ▷ ⬯

Preparation: **4 minutes**   Cooking: **3 minutes**   Serves **4**   Calories per serving: **340**

4 cups chicken broth

1½ cups cubed cooked chicken

4 tablespoons (½ stick) butter or margarine

1 teaspoon Worcestershire sauce

1 clove garlic, peeled and minced

3 to 4 drops liquid hot red pepper seasoning

1 cup half-and-half

¼ teaspoon salt (optional)

⅛ teaspoon black pepper (optional)

In a 2-quart saucepan, mix the **chicken broth, chicken, butter, Worcestershire sauce, garlic, red pepper seasoning,** and **half-and-half.** Cook over moderate heat, stirring, for 3 minutes, or until the soup reaches serving temperature. Taste for seasoning, and add the **salt** and **pepper** if desired.

Tips: 1. This recipe can be halved, or leftovers can be refrigerated for 1 or 2 days or frozen. 2. You can substitute cooked turkey for the chicken. 3. If you like, add leftover vegetables such as corn, peas, green beans, lima beans, or diced carrots; or add 2 tablespoons of uncooked rice and increase the cooking time by 15 minutes.

Beef and Cabbage Soup ⬯

Preparation: **15 minutes**   Cooking: **8 minutes**   Serves **6**   Calories per serving: **260**

1 small yellow onion, peeled and chopped

2 large carrots, peeled and chopped

2 stalks celery, chopped

1 small head cabbage (about ¾ pound), cored and thinly sliced

1 bay leaf

6 whole black peppercorns

5 cups beef broth

¼ teaspoon salt

¼ teaspoon black pepper

2 cups cubed cooked beef

6 tablespoons sour cream (optional)

Use leftover beef to make this quick, thrifty, and full-flavored soup. Serve it with thick slices of dark, crusty bread for a light lunch or supper.

1. Place the **onion, carrots, celery, cabbage, bay leaf, peppercorns,** and **beef broth** in a 3-quart saucepan. Cover and bring to a boil. Reduce the heat and simmer for 8 to 10 minutes, or until the cabbage is crisp-tender. (Cook about 2 minutes longer if you like very tender cabbage.) Add the **salt** and **pepper.**

2. Divide the **beef** equally among 6 soup bowls and ladle the soup over it. Top each serving with 1 tablespoon of the **sour cream** if desired, or serve the sour cream on the side.

Tips: 1. You can use chicken broth instead of the beef broth and leftover chicken or turkey instead of the beef. 2. This recipe can be halved, or leftovers can be refrigerated for 1 or 2 days or frozen.

Ground Beef and Vegetable Chowder ⊕

Preparation: **15 minutes**   Cooking: **30 minutes**   Serves **6**   Calories per serving: **375**

1/4 **pound salt pork or slab bacon, cut into** 1/4**-inch cubes, or 6 slices bacon, cut into 1-inch strips**

1 pound lean ground beef

1 medium-size yellow onion, peeled and chopped

2 medium-size carrots, peeled and chopped

1 stalk celery, chopped

3 medium-size fresh tomatoes, peeled and chopped, or 1 can (1 pound) tomatoes, chopped, with their juice

1/4 **cup uncooked rice**

2 medium-size all-purpose potatoes, scrubbed (but not peeled) and diced

1/2 **teaspoon dried basil or rosemary, crumbled**

6 cups water or beef broth

1 teaspoon salt

1/4 **teaspoon black pepper**

Serve this chowder as a main course with garlic bread and a tossed salad, which you can make while the soup is cooking. To speed preparation of the soup, peel and chop the onion and get ready as many of the remaining vegetables as you can while the salt pork is browning; finish the chopping while the beef and onion cook.

1. Cook the **salt pork,** uncovered, in a 3-quart saucepan over moderate heat until golden brown and crisp—about 5 minutes. Using a slotted spoon, remove the pork to paper toweling to drain. Set aside.

2. Add the **beef** to the drippings in the saucepan, and cook, stirring, for 5 minutes. Add the **onion** and cook 5 minutes longer.

3. Add the **carrots, celery, tomatoes, rice, potatoes, basil, water, salt, pepper,** and the salt pork. Cover and bring to a boil. Reduce the heat and simmer for 25 minutes, or until the rice and potatoes are tender.

Tips: **1.** *This recipe can be halved.* **2.** *You can cook this soup ahead and refrigerate it for 1 or 2 days or freeze it.* **3.** *Lean ground pork can be substituted for the beef.* **4.** *You can stretch this recipe to serve 8 by adding 1 package (10 ounces) frozen peas or whole-kernel corn during the last 10 minutes of cooking.*

Meatball Soup ⊕

Preparation: **10 minutes**   Cooking: **19 minutes**   Serves **6**   Calories per serving: **435**

6 cups beef broth

3/4 **pound lean ground beef**

3/4 **pound lean ground pork**

1 egg, lightly beaten

1 1/2 **teaspoons salt**

1/8 **teaspoon black pepper**

3 medium-size fresh tomatoes, peeled and chopped, or 1 can (1 pound) stewed tomatoes, with their juice

1 can (15 to 16 ounces) kidney beans, drained

1/4 **cup chopped parsley**

1. Bring the **beef broth** to a boil in a 4-quart saucepan. Meanwhile, in a mixing bowl, combine the **beef, pork, egg, salt,** and **pepper.** Shape the mixture into 3/4-inch balls.

2. Reduce the heat, and add the meatballs and **tomatoes** to the broth. Cover and simmer for 15 minutes. Add the **beans** and **parsley,** and simmer until heated through—about 2 minutes.

Tips: **1.** *You can use all ground beef instead of the beef and pork, and chick peas instead of the kidney beans.* **2.** *This recipe can be halved.* **3.** *You can make this dish ahead and refrigerate it for 1 or 2 days or freeze it.*

Italian Sausage Soup ⊕

Preparation: **15 minutes**   Cooking: **10 minutes**   Serves **4**   Calories per serving: **425**

½ pound mild pork sausage or sweet Italian sausage, with the casings removed

1 medium-size yellow onion, peeled and chopped

3 medium-size fresh tomatoes, peeled and chopped, or 1 can (1 pound) tomatoes, chopped, with their juice

3 cups chicken broth

1 teaspoon dried basil, crumbled

1 cup uncooked elbow macaroni

¼ teaspoon salt

This main-course soup needs only a salad and Italian bread to make a meal.

1. Cook the **sausage,** uncovered, in a 2-quart saucepan over moderate heat, using a spoon to break up the meat into small pieces. Cook for 5 minutes, or until no pink remains.

2. Add the **onion** and continue cooking, uncovered, for 5 minutes, or until the onion is soft. Add the **tomatoes, chicken broth,** and **basil,** and bring to a boil. Stir in the **macaroni** and simmer, covered, for 10 minutes, or until the macaroni is tender. Add the **salt** and serve.

> *Tips: **1.** For added richness, top each serving with 2 tablespoons of grated Parmesan cheese. **2.** This recipe can be halved, or leftovers can be refrigerated for 1 or 2 days or frozen.*

Clam Chowder ⊕

Preparation: **16 minutes**   Cooking: **22 minutes**   Serves **4**   Calories per serving: **340**

2 slices bacon, cut into 1-inch strips

1 medium-size yellow onion, peeled and chopped

3 medium-size all-purpose potatoes, scrubbed (but not peeled) and diced

1½ cups water

2 cans (10½ ounces each) minced clams, with their juice

1 bottle (8 ounces) clam juice

1 cup half-and-half

2 tablespoons all-purpose flour

¾ teaspoon salt

¼ teaspoon black pepper

2 tablespoons minced parsley

> *Tip: This recipe can be halved.*

1. Cook the **bacon** in a 3-quart saucepan over moderately high heat until crisp—about 5 minutes. Using a slotted spoon, remove the bacon to paper toweling to drain. Set aside.

2. Reduce the heat to moderate, add the **onion** to the bacon drippings in the saucepan, and cook, uncovered, for 5 minutes, or until soft.

3. Add the **potatoes** and **water.** Cover and simmer for 15 minutes, or until the potatoes are tender. Meanwhile, drain the liquid from the **clams** into a mixing bowl; reserve the clams. Add the bottled **clam juice** and **half-and-half.**

4. When the potatoes are done, remove the pan from the heat. Using a wire whisk, blend in the **flour** until smooth, then stir the clam-juice mixture into the saucepan. Cook, stirring, over moderate heat until thick and bubbly—about 1 minute.

5. Add the clams, **salt,** and **pepper,** and simmer, uncovered, for 5 minutes. Do not let the soup boil or it may curdle. Sprinkle each serving with some of the **parsley** and the reserved bacon.

Haddock Chowder ⊕

Preparation: **22 minutes** Cooking: **15 minutes**   Serves **6** Calories per serving: **345**

Serve this chowder as a main course with a lettuce and tomato salad.

2 medium-size yellow onions, peeled and coarsely chopped

2 large all-purpose potatoes, peeled and diced

2 cups water

2 ounces salt pork, cut into 1/4-inch cubes, or 3 slices bacon, cut into 1-inch strips

1 1/2 pounds fresh or frozen haddock or cod fillets

2 cups milk

1 cup half-and-half

2 tablespoons butter or margarine

1 1/2 teaspoons salt

1/8 teaspoon black pepper

1. Bring the **onions, potatoes,** and **water** to a boil in a 2-quart saucepan. Cover and cook over moderate heat for 15 minutes.

2. Meanwhile, cook the **salt pork,** uncovered, in a 3-quart saucepan over moderate heat until golden brown and crisp—about 5 minutes.

3. When the onions and potatoes are done, add them and their cooking water to the salt pork and the drippings. Add the **haddock,** cover, and simmer for 10 to 15 minutes, stirring once or twice, until the haddock is tender (the haddock will break apart as it cooks).

4. Add the **milk, half-and-half, butter, salt,** and **pepper.** Reheat, uncovered, over low heat to serving temperature—about 5 minutes. Do not let the soup boil or it may curdle.

Tip: This recipe can be halved.

Canadian Cheddar Cheese Soup ⊕

Preparation: **14 minutes** Cooking: **25 minutes**   Serves **4** Calories per serving: **370**

4 tablespoons (1/2 stick) butter or margarine

1/3 cup minced yellow onion

1/3 cup grated carrot

2 tablespoons all-purpose flour

2 cups chicken broth

1/2 teaspoon dry mustard

1/2 teaspoon paprika

1 cup half-and-half

1 cup shredded sharp Cheddar cheese (about 4 ounces)

1 cup beer

This nippy cheese soup from Ontario is an example of classic Canadian cooking. Because of the saltiness of the broth and cheese, you will not need to add any salt.

1. Melt the **butter** in a 3-quart saucepan over moderate heat. Reduce the heat to low, add the **onion** and **carrot,** and cook, covered, for 5 minutes, or until the onion is soft. Stir in the **flour,** and cook 3 or 4 more minutes. Gradually add the **chicken broth,** stirring constantly. Stir in the **mustard** and **paprika.**

2. Simmer, uncovered, for 20 to 25 minutes. Add the **half-and-half, cheese,** and **beer.** Stirring constantly, continue to simmer until the soup is heated through and the cheese has melted. Do not let the soup boil or the cheese will be stringy.

Tips: 1. This recipe can be halved. 2. As a variation, substitute 3 cups of strong beef broth for the chicken broth and beer, and use Swiss cheese instead of the Cheddar cheese.

SALADS AND SALAD DRESSINGS

The ancient Romans ate green leafy vegetables seasoned only with salt, and it is from their word for salt that we get the word "salad." Today salads can be anything from a side dish of lettuce tossed with oil and vinegar to a main course of meat or fish or a dessert of fresh fruits. This section contains a representative selection from virtually the whole range of salads. Here you will find not only instructions on how to make and dress crisp green salads but the recipe for the classic Caesar Salad. You will find old-fashioned Macaroni Salad as well as Chinese Noodle Salad. There are three recipes for perking up everyday tuna, and a Curried Chicken Salad sumptuous enough for guests. You will also discover new ways to use carrots, green peppers, tomatoes, even turnips in tasty, thrifty salads.

Ham and Cheese Salad with Walnut Dressing ①

Preparation: 18 minutes **Cooking: 2 minutes** **Serves 6** **Calories per serving: 540**

1 package (9 ounces) frozen artichoke hearts

2 cups cubed cooked ham

2 cups cubed Swiss or sharp Cheddar cheese (about 10 ounces)

¼ pound mushrooms, sliced

¼ cup minced parsley

½ cup walnut meats

½ cup water

3 tablespoons white or red wine vinegar

1 clove garlic, peeled

½ teaspoon salt

Pinch cayenne pepper

5 tablespoons olive or vegetable oil

Lettuce leaves and whole radishes for garnish

1. Bring about ¼ cup of lightly salted water to a boil in a 1- or 2-quart saucepan. Thaw the **artichoke hearts** under hot running water, then place them in the saucepan and cook, covered, for 2 minutes. Drain the artichoke hearts, rinse with cold water, drain again, and pat them dry with paper toweling. Cut each heart in half and put the pieces into a large serving bowl. Add the **ham, cheese, mushrooms,** and **parsley.**

2. Put the **walnuts** into an electric blender jar or a food processor fitted with the metal chopping blade. Add the **water, vinegar, garlic, salt, cayenne pepper,** and **oil,** and blend until the nuts are pulverized—5 to 10 seconds nonstop. If you are not using a blender or food processor, mince the nuts and the garlic, and shake them with the other ingredients in a tightly capped jar.

3. Toss the salad with the dressing. The salad tastes best if left to stand at room temperature for an hour. If you refrigerate it, bring it back to room temperature before serving. Serve on the **lettuce leaves** and garnish with the **radishes.**

Tips: 1. This recipe can be halved. 2. You can omit the artichoke hearts and cheese, and substitute 1 cup of cooked green beans.

Summer Meat and Cabbage Salad ⊘ ⬙

Preparation: **10 minutes**   Serves **4**   Calories per serving: **510**

1/3 cup vegetable oil

3 tablespoons red wine vinegar

1/2 teaspoon Dijon or prepared spicy brown mustard

1/8 teaspoon salt

1/8 teaspoon black pepper

1-pound piece of bologna

1 small yellow onion, peeled and thinly sliced

1/2 small head cabbage, trimmed and finely shredded

1 medium-size tart apple, cored and diced (optional)

Lettuce leaves for garnish

On a hot summer day, this salad can be a meal in itself.

1. In a serving bowl, combine the **oil, vinegar, mustard, salt,** and **pepper.**

2. Cut the **bologna** into 1/4-inch slices, then stack the slices and cut them into 1/4-inch strips.

3. Put the strips into the serving bowl along with the **onion** and **cabbage,** and the **apple** if used. Toss thoroughly to mix. If you have time, chill the salad for 45 minutes to 1 hour—it will taste better. Spoon the salad over the **lettuce leaves.** Serve with pumpernickel bread and butter.

> *Tips: 1. This recipe can be halved; use 1 small apple instead of half a medium-size one. 2. You can use ham instead of the bologna.*

Spicy Beef Salad ⊘

Preparation: **15 minutes**   Serves **4**   Calories per serving: **445**

1 tablespoon red wine vinegar

1 teaspoon Dijon or prepared spicy brown mustard

1/4 teaspoon salt

Pinch black pepper

1/4 cup olive or vegetable oil

1 tablespoon minced parsley

1 teaspoon ground cumin

1 clove garlic, peeled and minced

2 cups cubed cooked beef

2 stalks celery, chopped

1/4 cup finely chopped yellow onion

2 medium-size sweet green or red peppers, cored, seeded, and chopped

Lettuce leaves for garnish

Here is a way to turn leftover beef into another main course. Serve with corn on the cob or corn bread and with a fruit salad.

1. In a small serving bowl, combine the **vinegar, mustard, salt, pepper, oil, parsley, cumin,** and **garlic.**

2. Add the **beef, celery, onion,** and **sweet peppers.** Toss well. Serve on the **lettuce leaves.**

> *Tips: 1. You can substitute cooked pork, ham, turkey, or chicken for the beef. 2. For a more elaborate salad, add one or more of the following: 1/2 cup cubed Cheddar or Swiss cheese, 1 cup cooked corn kernels, 1 chopped ripe tomato.*

Curried Chicken Salad with Green Grapes

Preparation: **20 minutes**   Cooking: **4 minutes**   Serves **6**   Calories per serving: **390**

Serve this as a main course, with a cucumber salad, or as part of a cold buffet. If you make this salad with yogurt instead of mayonnaise, you will reduce the calories per serving to 265.

1/4 **cup vegetable oil**

2 **tablespoons grated yellow onion**

3/4 **teaspoon curry powder**

1/2 **teaspoon salt**

1/2 **cup mayonnaise or plain yogurt**

2 **teaspoons lemon juice**

1/2 **teaspoon Dijon or prepared spicy brown mustard**

3 **cups cubed cooked chicken**

2 **stalks celery, chopped**

1 **cup green seedless grapes**

1. In a small saucepan, heat 2 tablespoons of the **oil,** add the **onion,** and cook over low heat for 3 minutes. Stir in the **curry powder** and **salt,** and cook another 30 seconds. Remove the mixture from the heat and let it cool. Stir in the **mayonnaise, lemon juice,** and **mustard.**

2. Put the **chicken** into a serving bowl and add the curry-mayonnaise mixture, the remaining 2 tablespoons of oil, and the **celery.** Toss to mix. Add the **grapes** and toss again, gently. Chill the salad before serving if there is time. If time is short, start with very cold chicken and grapes.

> *Tips: 1. Leftovers will keep well in the refrigerator for a day and, in fact, will taste even better after 24 hours. 2. You can use cubed cooked ham, turkey, or lamb instead of the chicken. 3. In place of the grapes, use 1 chopped apple, 1/2 cup raisins, or 1 cup drained, canned pineapple chunks. 4. Garnish with 1/2 cup chopped walnuts, pecans, or peanuts.*

Mediterranean Tuna Salad

Preparation: **10 minutes**   Serves **4**   Calories per serving: **370**

2 **cans (6**1/2 **or 7 ounces each) tuna, drained and flaked**

3 **tablespoons finely chopped yellow onion**

3 **stalks celery, finely chopped**

1/2 **cup olive oil or** 1/4 **cup each olive oil and vegetable oil**

2 **tablespoons red wine vinegar**

3 **tablespoons chopped fresh basil or 1**1/2 **teaspoons dried basil, crumbled**

1 **teaspoon Dijon or prepared spicy brown mustard**

1/4 **teaspoon salt**

1. Place the **tuna** in a large serving bowl. Mix in the **onion** and **celery,** and set aside.

2. In a small bowl, combine the **oil, vinegar, basil, mustard,** and **salt.**

3. Pour the dressing over the tuna. Toss to blend, and serve on lettuce leaves or use as a sandwich filling.

> *Tips: 1. This recipe can be halved. 2. For another version of this salad, add 1/2 sweet green or red pepper, chopped; 3 tablespoons chopped pitted black olives; 2 chopped anchovy fillets; and 2 chopped medium-size ripe tomatoes.*

Curried Tuna Salad ⊘

Preparation: **10 minutes**   Serves **4**   Calories per serving: **455**

2 cans (6½ or 7 ounces each) tuna, drained and flaked

3 tablespoons finely chopped yellow onion

3 stalks celery, finely chopped

¾ cup mayonnaise or plain yogurt

2 teaspoons lemon juice

Pinch salt

1 tablespoon curry powder

1 medium-size apple, cored and diced (optional)

¼ cup raisins (optional)

If you use plain yogurt instead of mayonnaise, you will reduce the number of calories per serving to 185.

1. Place the **tuna, onion,** and **celery** in a serving bowl. Add the **mayonnaise, lemon juice, salt,** and **curry powder,** and the **apple** and **raisins** if used. Toss to mix well.

2. Taste the salad for seasoning and add more curry powder if desired. Serve on lettuce leaves or in pita bread.

> **Tip:** *As a variation, substitute ½ to 1 teaspoon dried dillweed for the curry powder, and use ½ cup walnuts instead of the apples and raisins.*

Tuna and Chick Pea Salad 🐷 ⊘

Preparation: **10 minutes**   Serves **4**   Calories per serving: **400**

1 can (15 to 16 ounces) chick peas, drained

⅓ cup finely chopped yellow onion

1 stalk celery, finely chopped

1 clove garlic, peeled and minced

1 teaspoon dried dillweed

2 tablespoons finely chopped parsley (optional)

2 tablespoons red wine vinegar

⅓ cup olive or vegetable oil

⅛ teaspoon salt

Pinch black pepper

1 can (6½ or 7 ounces) tuna, drained

2 small tomatoes, chopped (optional)

Lettuce leaves for garnish

Served with French or Italian bread, this salad is a satisfying main course. You can also omit the tuna and serve the salad as a side dish.

1. In a large serving bowl, combine the **chick peas, onion, celery, garlic,** and **dillweed,** and the **parsley** if used. Add the **vinegar, oil, salt,** and **pepper,** and toss to blend.

2. Break the **tuna** into chunks and add it to the salad along with the **tomatoes** if used. Toss gently to blend. Serve on the **lettuce leaves** at room temperature or slightly chilled.

> **Tip:** *As a variation, substitute a 7-ounce can of salmon for the tuna. Be sure to pick over the salmon and remove the dark skin and bones before adding it. You can also substitute cooked or canned Italian white beans (cannellini) for the chick peas.*

Macaroni Salad

| Preparation: **10 minutes** | Cooking: **9 minutes** | Serves **6** | Calories per serving: **350** |

Why not make a macaroni salad occasionally instead of the old standby—potato salad. It's much easier and keeps well in the refrigerator. You save on preparation time by chopping the vegetables while the macaroni cooks.

1/2 **pound elbow macaroni, bow ties, or similar pasta**

2 **stalks celery, chopped**

1/2 **medium-size sweet green or red pepper, cored, seeded, and chopped**

1 **small yellow onion, peeled and finely chopped**

3/4 **cup mayonnaise**

4 **teaspoons white vinegar or lemon juice**

1 1/2 **teaspoons Dijon or prepared spicy brown mustard**

1/2 **teaspoon salt**

1/8 **teaspoon black pepper**

Lettuce leaves for garnish

1. Cook the **macaroni** according to package directions, drain in a colander, and rinse under cold running water. Drain again thoroughly.

2. While the macaroni is cooking, combine the **celery, sweet pepper, onion, mayonnaise, vinegar, mustard, salt,** and **black pepper** in a serving bowl. Add the macaroni to the bowl and toss well to mix. Serve on the **lettuce leaves.**

Tips: **1.** *This recipe can be halved.* **2.** *Macaroni salad should not be kept at room temperature for long periods of time, because the mayonnaise will spoil. (For a picnic, make the salad without mayonnaise, substituting 1/2 cup olive oil, increasing the amount of mustard to 2 teaspoons, and adding 2 cloves of garlic, peeled and minced.)* **3.** *For variety, add 1/2 cup chopped black olives, 1 large, coarsely chopped tomato, or 2 or 3 chopped anchovy fillets.*

Chinese Noodle Salad

| Preparation: **5 minutes** | Cooking: **4 minutes** | Serves **4** | Calories per serving: **545** |

3/4 **pound very thin egg noodles or thin spaghetti**

5 **tablespoons creamy peanut butter**

5 **tablespoons warm water**

6 **tablespoons vegetable oil**

5 **tablespoons soy sauce**

1/8 **teaspoon salt**

1 **tablespoon sugar**

1/4 **cup red or white wine vinegar**

2 **cloves garlic, peeled and minced**

1/4 **cup chopped green onions**

1. Cook the **noodles** according to package directions, drain in a colander, and rinse under cold running water. Drain again thoroughly.

2. While the noodles are cooking, mix the **peanut butter** and **warm water** in a serving bowl to make a smooth paste. Stir in the **oil, soy sauce, salt, sugar, vinegar, garlic,** and **green onions.** Add the noodles and toss thoroughly. Serve the salad at room temperature.

Tip: *You can store leftovers in the refrigerator for 1 or 2 days, but be sure to let them return to room temperature before serving.*

Green Noodle and Pimiento Salad 🐷 ⊙

Preparation: **7 minutes**   Cooking: **7 minutes**   Serves **4**   Calories per serving: **435**

1/2 **pound spinach noodles**

1/3 **cup chopped green onions**

3 **radishes, thinly sliced**

2 **stalks celery, chopped**

1 **jar (4 ounces) pimientos, drained and chopped**

2 **tablespoons lemon juice**

1/3 **cup olive oil**

1/4 **cup sour cream**

1 **teaspoon dried basil, crumbled**

1 **teaspoon salt**

1/4 **teaspoon black pepper**

Use the time while the noodles are cooking to chop the onions, celery, and pimiento and to slice the radishes.

1. Cook the **noodles** according to package directions, drain in a colander, and rinse under cold running water. Drain again thoroughly.

2. Transfer the noodles to a large serving bowl, add the **green onions, radishes, celery,** and **pimientos.** Toss. Add the **lemon juice, oil, sour cream, basil, salt,** and **pepper.** Toss again and serve at room temperature.

Tip: You can vary this salad in a number of ways, including the following: 1. Use fusilli (corkscrew pasta) or ziti instead of green noodles. 2. Omit the salt and add 2 chopped anchovy fillets to the salad. 3. Add 2 tablespoons of drained capers and 1 tablespoon of finely chopped parsley, and decrease the amount of salt to 1/2 teaspoon. 4. Add 1 can (6 1/2 or 7 ounces) of tuna, drained and broken into small chunks.

Rice, Green Pea, and Red Pepper Salad ◑

Preparation: **5 minutes**   Cooking: **20 minutes**   Serves **4**   Calories per serving: **380**

2 **cups water**

1 **teaspoon salt**

1 **cup uncooked rice**

2 **stalks celery, finely chopped**

1 **medium-size sweet red pepper, cored, seeded, and chopped**

2 **green onions, trimmed and finely chopped**

1/4 **cup finely chopped parsley**

1 **package (10 ounces) frozen green peas**

1/4 **cup olive or vegetable oil**

2 **tablespoons red or white wine vinegar**

1/2 **teaspoon Dijon or prepared spicy brown mustard**

1/8 **teaspoon black pepper**

Rice salad is ideal for entertaining, because it can easily be prepared in large amounts and well in advance. Note: Prepare the celery, sweet pepper, green onions, and parsley while the rice is cooking.

1. Pour the **water** into a heavy 2- or 3-quart saucepan, add the **salt,** and bring to a boil over high heat. Stir in the **rice,** reduce the heat to moderate, and simmer, covered, for 20 minutes.

2. Put the **celery, sweet pepper, green onions,** and **parsley** into a serving bowl. When the rice is done, break the block of frozen **peas** into chunks, and add them to the bowl along with the rice. The hot rice will thaw the peas and the peas will help cool the rice.

3. Let the mixture stand for 4 or 5 minutes while you prepare the dressing. In a small bowl, thoroughly combine the **oil, vinegar, mustard,** and **black pepper.** Pour the dressing over the salad and toss gently to mix.

Tips: 1. This recipe can be halved or doubled. 2. You can turn this salad into a main course by adding either a cup of cubed Cheddar or Swiss cheese, or a cup of drained, cooked chick peas, navy beans, or pea beans.

Middle Eastern Cracked Wheat Salad 🐷 ◑

Preparation: **18 minutes**   Serves **6**   Calories per serving: **240**

2 cups water

1 cup uncooked bulgur
(cracked wheat)

1 teaspoon salt

¼ cup lemon juice

1 large clove garlic, peeled
and minced

4 green onions, trimmed and
thinly sliced

¼ cup chopped mint

¼ cup olive oil or
2 tablespoons each olive oil
and vegetable oil

Pinch black pepper

2 medium-size tomatoes, cut
into bite-size pieces

⅔ cup minced parsley

1 small cucumber, peeled
and cut into bite-size pieces

Because there is no meat or mayonnaise to spoil, this is an excellent salad for picnics or camping trips. Serve it with fruit and cheese for a complete meal. A good time to mince the garlic and parsley, slice the onions, cut up the tomatoes and cucumber, and chop the mint is while the bulgur is soaking.

1. Bring the **water** to a boil in a 1- or 2-quart saucepan. Add the **bulgur** and **salt**. Cover the pan, remove it from the heat, and let the bulgur soak about 15 minutes, or until it is chewable.

2. When the bulgur is tender, turn it out into a serving bowl. Add the **lemon juice, garlic, green onions, mint, oil,** and **pepper.** Toss to mix. Cover the salad and set it aside until you are ready to serve. Just before serving, add the **tomatoes, parsley,** and **cucumber,** and toss again.

> **Tips: 1.** *The taste will improve if you prepare the salad 45 minutes to 2 hours ahead to let the flavors blend, but this is not essential.* **2.** *This recipe can be halved and the leftovers can be refrigerated.*

Beet and Apple Salad with Yogurt Dressing

Preparation: **17 minutes**   Serves **4**   Calories per serving: **130**

Raw beets are used in this nutritious salad from Czechoslovakia. It tastes even better when chilled.

4 or 5 small young beets
(about 10 ounces)

¾ cup plain yogurt

¼ teaspoon salt

¼ teaspoon sugar

2 teaspoons lemon juice

2 tablespoons mayonnaise

2 medium-size apples, cored
and diced

½ small yellow onion, peeled
and chopped

1. Peel the uncooked **beets** and halve them. Cut each half into ⅛-inch slices.

2. In a serving bowl, combine the **yogurt, salt, sugar, lemon juice,** and **mayonnaise.** Add the beets and **apples,** and toss until they are nicely coated with the yogurt mixture. Top with the **onion** and serve.

> **Tips: 1.** *Sour cream can be substituted for the yogurt, but it increases the number of calories per serving from 130 to 195.* **2.** *You can use 2 teaspoons of prepared horseradish instead of the chopped onion.*

Bean Sprout and Bacon Salad ⬭

Preparation: **15 minutes**   Cooking: **5 minutes**   Serves **4**   Calories per serving: **165**

4 slices bacon, cut into 1-inch strips

3 tablespoons red wine vinegar

1 clove garlic, peeled and minced

1/4 teaspoon Worcestershire sauce

1/8 teaspoon dry or Dijon mustard

1/4 teaspoon salt

1/8 teaspoon black pepper

1 pound fresh or canned mung bean sprouts, drained

6 green onions, trimmed and thinly sliced

1/2 medium-size sweet green or red pepper, cored, seeded, and chopped

Lettuce leaves for garnish

A quick way to cut bacon is to stack the slices and then snip them crosswise with kitchen shears.

1. Cook the **bacon** in a 9- or 10-inch skillet over moderately high heat until crisp—about 5 minutes. Remove the bacon, drain on paper toweling, and reserve. Pour off all but 3 tablespoons of the drippings.

2. Let the drippings cool to room temperature, then add the **vinegar, garlic, Worcestershire sauce, mustard, salt,** and **black pepper.** Set aside.

3. Put the **bean sprouts** into a colander and run hot water over them for 2 to 3 minutes to wash and wilt them. Drain well, place in a serving bowl, and toss with the **green onions** and **sweet pepper.** Crumble the reserved bacon and add.

4. Reheat the dressing and pour it while still hot over the salad. Toss and serve on **lettuce leaves.**

Tip: This recipe can be halved.

Coleslaw ▷ ⬭

Preparation: **8 minutes**   Serves **4**   Calories per serving: **290**

This basic coleslaw recipe lends itself to many variations, including the ones listed in the Tip below. You can also easily reduce the amounts of the ingredients to serve 1 or 2. Making this coleslaw with plain yogurt instead of sour cream reduces the calories per serving to 110.

1 small firm head cabbage (about 1 1/4 pounds)

1/2 cup mayonnaise

1/2 cup sour cream or plain yogurt

1/2 teaspoon salt

1/8 teaspoon black pepper

1. Cut the stalk end from the **cabbage,** and remove any discolored or limp outer leaves. Quarter the cabbage lengthwise, and trim off and discard the core at the point of each quarter.

2. Cut the sections of cabbage into very thin slices. Place the slices in a bowl and toss with the **mayonnaise, sour cream, salt,** and **pepper.**

Tip: You can add any of the following ingredients or combinations of ingredients to vary the slaw:
1. 1 tablespoon prepared horseradish; 2. 1/2 sweet green or red pepper, cored, seeded, and chopped; 3. 2 tablespoons snipped fresh dill or 1 teaspoon dillweed; 4. 1 teaspoon caraway or celery seeds; 5. 1 or 2 grated carrots; 6. 1 cup leftover cooked vegetables, diced; 7. 1 or 2 chopped pimientos; 8. 1 apple, cored and chopped, but not peeled, with 1/2 cup chopped nuts; 9. 1/2 cup raisins or seedless grapes, or 1/2 cup diced peaches, pears, pineapple, or orange.

Shredded Carrots with Herbs and Lemon 🐷 ◑

Preparation: 20 minutes   Cooking: 6 minutes   Serves 6   Calories per serving: 135

12 medium-size carrots (about 1½ pounds)

¼ cup olive or vegetable oil

1 large red onion, peeled and finely chopped

1 or 2 cloves garlic, peeled and minced

½ teaspoon dried marjoram or oregano, crumbled

¼ teaspoon dried thyme, crumbled

¼ cup lemon juice

¼ teaspoon salt

⅛ teaspoon black pepper

1. Peel the **carrots**, then shred them using the second coarsest side of a four-sided grater.

2. Heat the **oil** in a 12-inch skillet, and add the shredded carrots, **onion**, and **garlic**. Cook over moderately high heat, stirring constantly, for 5 minutes.

3. Sprinkle in the **marjoram** and **thyme**, and continue cooking and stirring another 1 or 2 minutes. Add the **lemon juice** and toss lightly, then season with the **salt** and **pepper**. Toss well again and chill until ready to serve.

> *Tips: 1. This recipe can be halved; use 1 medium-size onion instead of half a large one. 2. You can also serve this dish hot.*

Cucumber Salad with Soy and Sesame Dressing ◉

Preparation: 5 minutes   Serves 4   Calories per serving: 45

2 medium-size cucumbers

½ teaspoon salt

1 teaspoon sugar

1 tablespoon soy sauce

1 tablespoon cider vinegar

2 teaspoons sesame oil or 2 teaspoons creamy peanut butter blended with 2 teaspoons vegetable oil

Try this Chinese cucumber salad whenever you tire of cucumbers with the traditional oil and vinegar dressing.

1. Peel the **cucumbers** and cut them in half lengthwise. Scoop out the seeds with a spoon. Cut each half crosswise into ¼-inch slices.

2. Combine the **salt, sugar, soy sauce, vinegar,** and **oil.** Pour the dressing over the cucumbers and toss to mix. Serve chilled.

Cucumber Salad with Walnuts ◉

Preparation: 7 minutes   Serves 4   Calories per serving: 110

2 medium-size cucumbers

1 cup plain yogurt

¼ cup chopped walnuts

1 small yellow onion, peeled and finely chopped

¼ teaspoon salt

¼ teaspoon black pepper

1 tablespoon snipped dill

1. Peel the **cucumbers** and cut them in half lengthwise. Scoop out the seeds with a spoon. Cut each half crosswise into ¼-inch slices.

2. Combine the **yogurt, walnuts, onion, salt, pepper,** and **dill.** Pour the dressing over the cucumbers and toss to mix. Serve chilled.

Roasted Pepper Salad

Preparation: **5 minutes**   Cooking: **20 minutes**   Serves **4**   Calories per serving: **135**

Serve these sweet and mellow roasted peppers as a salad or an appetizer.

8 medium-size sweet red or green peppers

1/8 teaspoon salt

Pinch black pepper

1 clove garlic, peeled and minced

2 tablespoons minced parsley

5 teaspoons red wine vinegar

1/4 cup olive oil or 2 tablespoons each olive oil and vegetable oil, mixed

4 lemon wedges

1. Preheat the broiler. Place the **sweet peppers** on their sides on the broiler pan and broil 2 inches from the heat, turning frequently, until the skins are blackened—about 20 minutes.

2. Cool the peppers under cold running water, then peel, core, and seed them. Cut the peppers into strips about 1 inch wide and 2 inches long.

3. Arrange the strips of pepper on a dish, and sprinkle with the **salt, black pepper, garlic, parsley, vinegar,** and **oil.** Serve at room temperature, garnished with the **lemon wedges.**

Tips: 1. The peppers will peel more easily if you close them up tight in a paper bag until slightly cooled.
2. As a variation, omit the salt and add 1 cup of sliced mushrooms and 2 tablespoons drained capers.
3. If you omit the olive oil, you will reduce the number of calories per serving to 40.

Basic Potato Salad with Variations

Preparation: **10 minutes**   Cooking: **5 minutes**   Serves **4**   Calories per serving: **240**

The basic recipe for this salad can be varied in many ways, three of which are given at the end of the recipe. Use the time while the potatoes are cooking to chop the parsley, onion, and celery.

4 medium-size all-purpose potatoes (about 1 pound), peeled and diced

1 tablespoon minced parsley

1 tablespoon finely chopped yellow onion

1 stalk celery, chopped

1 tablespoon vegetable oil

1 tablespoon cider vinegar

1/2 teaspoon salt

1/3 cup mayonnaise

1 teaspoon Dijon or prepared spicy brown mustard

Salad greens for garnish

1. Bring about 1 inch of lightly salted water to a boil in a 2-quart saucepan. Add the **potatoes,** set the lid askew on the pan, and cook about 5 minutes, or until just tender.

2. While the potatoes are cooking, mix the **parsley, onion, celery, oil, vinegar, salt, mayonnaise,** and **mustard** in a serving bowl.

3. Drain the cooked potatoes and let them cool slightly. Add them to the bowl and toss gently to mix all the ingredients. Cover and refrigerate until chilled. Serve on the **salad greens.**

Tip: Start with the basic recipe and add or substitute ingredients as shown to make the following variations:
Caesar Potato Salad. *Eliminate the onion and salt, and add 2 chopped anchovy fillets, 1 clove garlic (peeled and minced), 2 teaspoons Worcestershire sauce, and 1/4 cup grated Parmesan cheese.*
German Potato Salad. *Use half a medium-size onion (peeled and sliced), in place of the smaller amount of onion, double the vinegar, eliminate the celery, and add 4 slices of bacon, fried crisp and crumbled.*
Potato Salad with Egg. *Add 1 sliced hard-cooked egg, 2 tablespoons sweet pickle relish or finely chopped sweet green pepper, and 2 tablespoons snipped fresh dill or 1/2 teaspoon dried dillweed.*

47

Spanish Potato Salad ⊘

Preparation: **10 minutes**   Cooking: **5 minutes**   Serves **4**   Calories per serving: **235**

4 medium-size all-purpose potatoes (about 1 pound), peeled and diced

1 tablespoon finely chopped yellow onion

1 stalk celery, chopped

1 clove garlic, peeled and minced

1/4 cup chopped sweet green or red pepper

1/4 cup sliced pimiento-stuffed olives

1/4 teaspoon dried thyme, crumbled

5 tablespoons olive or vegetable oil

2 tablespoons lemon juice

1/2 teaspoon salt

1/4 teaspoon black pepper

Put the potato cooking time to good use by chopping the onion, celery, and pepper, mincing the garlic, and slicing the olives.

1. Bring about 1 inch of lightly salted water to a boil in a 2-quart saucepan. Add the **potatoes,** set the lid askew on the pan, and cook about 5 minutes, or until just tender.

2. While the potatoes are cooking, mix the **onion, celery, garlic, sweet pepper, olives, thyme, oil, lemon juice, salt,** and **black pepper** in a serving bowl.

3. Drain the cooked potatoes and let them cool slightly. Add them to the bowl and toss gently to mix all the ingredients. Cover and refrigerate until chilled.

> **Tip:** *To vary the recipe, add 1/4 cup of finely chopped parsley and half a can of boneless sardines, drained and chopped.*

Spinach-Bacon Salad with Warm Dressing ⊕

Preparation: **10 minutes**   Cooking: **6 minutes**   Serves **4**   Calories per serving: **260**

Compare the cost of making spinach salad at home with the cost of eating it in a restaurant. Compare the taste, too!

1 package (10 ounces) fresh spinach

1/4 pound mushrooms, thinly sliced

1 small red onion, peeled and thinly sliced

8 slices bacon, cut into 1-inch strips

2 teaspoons Dijon or prepared spicy brown mustard

2 teaspoons sugar

2 teaspoons red wine vinegar

1 teaspoon Worcestershire sauce

3 tablespoons lemon juice

1. Trim the **spinach** of coarse stems and blemished leaves, and wash it. Pat the spinach dry with paper toweling, tear into bite-size pieces, and put into a large serving bowl along with the **mushrooms** and **onion.** Set aside.

2. Meanwhile, cook the **bacon** in a 12-inch skillet over moderately high heat until crisp—about 5 minutes. Drain on paper toweling and reserve. Pour off all but 5 tablespoons of the drippings.

3. Reduce the heat to low. Add the **mustard, sugar, vinegar, Worcestershire sauce,** and **lemon juice** to the drippings. Stir to mix well.

4. Pour the dressing over the salad, crumble the bacon over it, and toss thoroughly. Serve immediately on room-temperature plates.

> **Tips: 1.** *This recipe can be halved.* **2.** *To make ahead, prepare the salad and dressing, but do not combine. Cover the salad with plastic food wrap and refrigerate. Before serving, heat the dressing and toss with the salad.*

Tomato and Red Pepper Salad ⧗ ⧗

Preparation: **15 minutes**   Serves **4**   Calories per serving: **175**

1/3 cup olive or vegetable oil

2 tablespoons cider vinegar

1 clove garlic, peeled and minced

1/2 teaspoon salt

1/8 teaspoon black pepper

1 teaspoon paprika

6 to 8 drops liquid hot red pepper seasoning

2 tablespoons finely chopped parsley

4 medium-size ripe tomatoes, cut into 1/4-inch slices

2 medium-size sweet red peppers, cored, seeded, and cut into 1/4-inch strips

1 medium-size red onion, peeled and thinly sliced

Lettuce leaves for garnish

The nippy dressing on this recipe is good with other raw vegetables as well as cold, cooked ones.

1. In a small bowl, combine the **oil, vinegar, garlic, salt, black pepper, paprika, red pepper seasoning,** and **parsley.** Set aside.

2. Put the **tomatoes, sweet peppers,** and **onion** into a serving bowl. Pour the dressing over the vegetables and toss gently to coat. Serve on the **lettuce leaves.** The salad should be served cool, but not cold.

> **Tip:** *This recipe can be halved: use a small clove of garlic, a pinch of pepper, and a small onion, and half the amounts of the other ingredients.*

Farmer's Turnip and Pear Salad

Preparation: **18 minutes**   Serves **4**   Calories per serving: **225**

The ingredients of this salad may be surprising, but the result is pleasing.

1/3 cup vegetable oil

2 tablespoons cider vinegar

4 teaspoons sugar

1/2 teaspoon salt

1/4 teaspoon dry or Dijon mustard

Pinch ground nutmeg

1/8 teaspoon paprika

1 teaspoon lemon juice

2 large, firm, ripe pears

4 or 5 medium-size turnips (about 3/4 pound)

1 large head romaine lettuce

1. In a serving bowl, combine the **oil, vinegar, sugar, salt, mustard, nutmeg, paprika,** and **lemon juice.** Quarter, core, and cube the **pears,** and add them to the dressing.

2. Peel the **turnips** and coarsely shred them, using the second coarsest side of a four-sided grater. (You should have about 2 cups.) Add the turnips to the pears and dressing.

3. Wash the **lettuce,** pat it dry with paper toweling, then tear it into bite-size pieces. Add it to the salad and toss well until nicely dressed.

> **Tips: 1.** *You can substitute 3/4 pound of rutabaga (yellow turnip) for the white turnips.* **2.** *Instead of tearing the lettuce into bite-size pieces and tossing it with the salad, toss the other ingredients without the lettuce and serve on whole lettuce leaves. Serve with cottage cheese on the side to round out a lunch.*

Creating a Green Salad

The simple green salad, made from one or more types of raw green leafy vegetables and tossed with a dressing, is the most basic of side dishes. It should not, however, be dull or routine, and it need not be so if you follow the guidelines below for choosing, combining, and preparing greens, and serving them with a suitable dressing.

Choosing Salad Greens

To improve appearance, texture, and flavor, use more than one variety of greens in a single salad: dark green with light green and mild with tangy. Here is a descriptive list of the most common types of reasonably priced and readily available greens.

Boston (butterhead) lettuce: Fragile, mild-flavored medium-green leaves with a buttery texture. Boston tastes best with a mild Oil and Vinegar Dressing for Green Salads, page 51.

Chicory (curly endive): Frilly, slightly bitter bright-green leaves. Combine it with milder lettuces, and toss with a robust dressing, such as Creamy Blue Cheese Dressing, page 51.

Escarole: Broad, slightly bitter green leaves, not as crisp or tender as iceberg or romaine. Combine it with romaine, and serve with Russian Dressing, page 51.

Iceberg (crisphead) lettuce: Crisp pale-green leaves in a compact head. Because iceberg has less flavor than other greens, combine it with other lettuces, and toss with Oil and Vinegar Dressing for Green Salads, page 51.

Leaf (garden) lettuce: Ruffled, mild-tasting pale-green leaves. Leaf lettuce wilts quickly and should be used soon after purchase or harvesting. Combine it with stronger-tasting greens such as chicory or escarole, and serve with Oil and Vinegar Dressing for Green Salads, page 51.

Romaine (cos) lettuce: Broad, very crisp medium-dark to dark leaves in a long, tapering head. This delicate-tasting lettuce gives a wonderful crunch to salads and is good in combination with any of the other lettuces. Try it with Low-Calorie Yogurt Dressing, page 52. It is the required lettuce for Caesar Salad, page 53.

Spinach: Bland dark-green leaves, which should be young and tender for a salad. Use spinach alone (see Spinach-Bacon Salad with Warm Dressing, page 48), or add it to pale-green salads for color.

Watercress: Small deep-green leaves with a peppery taste. It mixes well with greens such as leaf lettuce and romaine.

How To Prepare Salad Greens

Separate the leaves of the salad greens and wash them in cold water. Be sure to get rid of any grit that clings to them. Dry the leaves with paper toweling, roll them gently in soft absorbent cloth towels, or dry them in a salad spinner, which will do the job in seconds. Be sure the leaves are thoroughly dry, or the dressing will not cling to them.

Tear, do not cut, the greens into bite-size pieces. The exception to this rule is iceberg lettuce, which can be sliced or shredded.

Dressing and Serving Green Salads

Use only fresh, good-quality oil for making salad dressings. Mix and serve the salad in a glass, ceramic, or stainless steel salad bowl. It is best not to use wooden bowls, because the wood soaks up oils and seasonings, which eventually impart a rancid taste to the greens. When adding the dressing to the salad, be stingy. Use just enough to coat the leaves lightly, then serve the salad at once.

Green Salad Extras

Here are a few combinations of vegetables and other extras to add to your salad greens for contrast in taste, color, and texture.

- Avocado, tomato, and crumbled bacon.
- Bean sprouts, carrot, green onions, and bamboo shoots.
- Cheese, ham, hard-cooked egg, tomato, and onion.
- Onion, orange sections, and rosemary.
- Radishes, green onions, cucumber, tomato, and mushrooms.
- Tomato, crumbled bacon, and hard-cooked egg.
- Zucchini, radishes, green onions, and blue cheese.
- Cooked green beans, cooked potato, tuna, tomato, and black olives.
- Cooked cauliflower, capers, anchovies, and hard-cooked egg.
- Cooked peas, hard-cooked egg, Cheddar cheese, and sweet pickle relish.

Oil and Vinegar Dressing for Green Salads

Preparation: 2 minutes   Yield: **1¼ cups**   Calories per tablespoon: **100**

1 cup vegetable oil or ½ cup each vegetable oil and olive oil

¼ cup red wine vinegar

1 teaspoon salt

½ teaspoon Dijon or prepared spicy brown mustard

Put all the ingredients into a jar, cap the jar securely, and shake vigorously. Store in the refrigerator. Shake again just before serving.

> **Tip:** *You can add any one or more of the following to the above basic dressing: 1 large clove garlic, peeled and minced; ½ teaspoon curry powder or dried herbs, such as oregano, thyme, basil, or dillweed; 2 tablespoons grated Parmesan cheese; 2 tablespoons crumbled Roquefort or blue cheese; 2 tablespoons drained capers; 2 tablespoons chili sauce or ½ teaspoon chili powder; 2 tablespoons sour cream; 2 minced anchovy fillets.*

Creamy Blue Cheese Dressing

Preparation: 5 minutes   Yield: **1¾ cups**   Calories per tablespoon: **75**

½ cup crumbled blue cheese (about 4 ounces)

3 tablespoons half-and-half

½ cup mayonnaise or sour cream

6 tablespoons olive or vegetable oil

¼ cup white vinegar

1 teaspoon prepared yellow mustard (optional)

⅛ teaspoon salt

⅛ teaspoon black pepper

If you like a salad dressing with bite, this one is for you.

1. In a small bowl, mash the **cheese** together with the **half-and-half** until creamy.

2. Add the **mayonnaise, oil,** and **vinegar,** and the **mustard** if used, then the **salt** and **pepper.** Using a rotary beater or wire whisk, beat the ingredients together until well mixed. Cover and store in the refrigerator. Serve over greens with a strong flavor, such as escarole, chicory, or watercress.

> **Tip:** *If you reduce the amount of half-and-half to 2 tablespoons, you can use the dressing for stuffing celery.*

Russian Dressing

Preparation: 5 minutes   Yield: **1 cup**   Calories per tablespoon: **55**

½ cup mayonnaise

2 tablespoons chili sauce or ketchup

2 tablespoons finely chopped yellow onion

2 tablespoons finely chopped sweet green pepper

2 tablespoons lemon juice

¼ teaspoon salt

This creamy dressing can be used in many ways: on wedges of iceberg lettuce or on cold seafood; as a dip for raw vegetables; as a spread for chicken or turkey sandwiches; or even spooned over hard-cooked eggs, boiled potatoes, carrots, or beets.

Put all the ingredients into a small bowl and stir well to mix. Cover and store in the refrigerator.

Avocado Dressing

Preparation: **8 minutes**   Yield: **1¼ cups**   Calories per tablespoon: **60**

1 medium-size ripe avocado

½ cup vegetable oil

2 tablespoons lemon juice

1 tablespoon grated yellow onion

¼ teaspoon salt

¼ teaspoon liquid hot red pepper seasoning

Do not prepare this dressing more than 1 or 2 hours in advance because it will darken.

Cut the **avocado** in half and scoop out the flesh into an electric blender jar. Add the **oil, lemon juice, onion, salt,** and **red pepper seasoning,** and blend until smooth. Chill. Serve over wedges of lettuce, tomato slices, or cold, cooked seafood.

Low-Calorie Yogurt Dressing

Preparation: **4 minutes**   Yield: **½ cup**   Calories per tablespoon: **25**

2 teaspoons lemon juice

1 tablespoon vegetable oil

½ cup plain yogurt

½ teaspoon paprika

Dash liquid hot red pepper seasoning

½ teaspoon salt

¼ teaspoon minced garlic

Put all the ingredients into a jar, cap the jar securely, and shake vigorously. Store in the refrigerator. Shake again just before serving. Use to dress sliced cucumbers or tomatoes, cooked vegetables, or cold poached fish.

> *Tip: To vary the dressing, add 1 teaspoon curry powder, or substitute 1 finely chopped trimmed green onion for the garlic and add 1 tablespoon minced fresh mint or snipped dill, or 1 teaspoon dried mint or dillweed.*

Low-Calorie Tomato Dressing

Preparation: **3 minutes**   Yield: **1¼ cups**   Calories per tablespoon: **4**

1 cup tomato juice

¼ cup red wine vinegar

2 tablespoons finely chopped yellow onion

⅛ teaspoon black pepper

¼ teaspoon salt

1 teaspoon minced garlic (optional)

1 teaspoon Worcestershire sauce

Put all the ingredients into a jar, cap the jar securely, and shake vigorously. Store in the refrigerator. Shake again just before serving.

> *Tips: 1. For extra flavor, add one of the following to the dressing: 1 tablespoon snipped dill (or 1 teaspoon dried dillweed); 1 teaspoon dried tarragon, crumbled; 1 teaspoon crushed fennel seeds and ½ teaspoon dried thyme, crumbled; or ½ teaspoon each dried basil and oregano, crumbled. 2. You can heat this dressing until thick and use it as barbecue sauce.*

Caesar Salad

Preparation: **12 minutes**   Cooking: **5 minutes**   Serves **4**   Calories per serving: **300**

Here is one of the best of all salads. Enjoy it as a first course or as a light lunch.

1/2 cup olive oil

2 slices firm-textured white bread

1 egg

1/8 teaspoon salt

1/8 teaspoon black pepper

1 clove garlic, peeled and minced

2 tablespoons lemon juice

3 tablespoons grated Parmesan cheese

3 or 4 anchovy fillets, rinsed and chopped (optional)

1 large head romaine lettuce

1. Heat 3 tablespoons of the **oil** in a 10-inch skillet over moderate heat. Cut the **bread** into 1/2-inch cubes (you need not remove the crusts) and cook in the oil, uncovered, over low heat for 5 minutes, or until golden brown. Drain on paper toweling and reserve.

2. While the bread cubes are browning, break the **egg** into a large serving bowl and beat it together with the **salt, pepper, garlic,** and **lemon juice** until all the ingredients are well combined. Beat in the remaining oil, the **cheese,** and the **anchovies** if used.

3. Wash the **lettuce,** pat it dry with paper toweling, tear it into bite-size pieces, and add to the bowl. Toss well and top with the bread cubes.

> *Tip: You can use 1 cup of packaged croutons in place of the bread cubes, and omit Step 1.*

Romaine Salad with Blue Cheese and Walnuts ⊙

Preparation: **10 minutes**   Serves **4**   Calories per serving: **275**

1 large head romaine lettuce

1/4 cup olive or vegetable oil

1 tablespoon red wine vinegar

1/4 cup crumbled blue cheese (about 2 ounces)

1/2 cup coarsely chopped walnuts

8 cherry tomatoes or 1 medium-size tomato cut into 8 wedges

1. Wash the **lettuce** and pat it dry with paper toweling. Tear the lettuce into bite-size pieces.

2. Put the **oil, vinegar,** and half the **cheese** into a large serving bowl. Mash the cheese with a fork, then blend it thoroughly with the oil and vinegar.

3. Add the lettuce, the remaining cheese, and the **walnuts** and **tomatoes,** and toss thoroughly. Serve immediately.

> *Tip: You can substitute pecans for the walnuts.*

Tossed Watercress Salad with Radishes and Pear

Preparation: **17 minutes**   Serves **4**   Calories per serving: **170**

1 bunch watercress

1 small yellow onion, peeled and thinly sliced

12 radishes, thinly sliced

1 medium-size firm, ripe pear, peeled, cored, and thinly sliced

3 tablespoons vegetable oil

1 tablespoon lemon juice

¼ teaspoon salt

½ teaspoon Dijon or prepared spicy brown mustard

Spicy, peppery watercress is the basis of this tossed salad. Try it for a change in flavor and you will also get a bonus in nutrition—watercress is far richer than lettuce in protein, calcium, and vitamin C.

1. Wash the **watercress** and dry it with paper toweling. Cut off and discard the stem ends, tear the watercress into bite-size pieces, and place in a serving bowl. Add the **onion, radishes,** and **pear** slices.

2. In a small bowl, mix the **oil, lemon juice, salt,** and **mustard.** Pour this dressing over the salad, toss, and serve.

Greek Salad ▷ ◖▶

Preparation: **10 minutes**   Serves **4**   Calories per serving: **385**

½ cup olive oil or ¼ cup each olive oil and vegetable oil

¼ teaspoon salt

1 tablespoon red wine vinegar

1 teaspoon Dijon mustard

⅛ teaspoon black pepper

1 tablespoon capers, drained

½ cup pitted black olives

4 to 6 anchovy fillets, rinsed and chopped

1 medium-size head romaine lettuce

1 medium-size yellow onion, peeled and thinly sliced

2 medium-size tomatoes, each cut into 8 wedges

1 medium-size cucumber, peeled and thinly sliced

1 cup feta cheese (about 4 ounces), cut into ½-inch cubes, or 1 cup large-curd cottage cheese

Here is a perfect salad for a soup-and-salad meal. To savor the true flavor of this salad, make an effort to find feta cheese for it. Probably the best known of Greek cheeses, pure white feta is made from sheep's milk and preserved in brine.

1. In a large serving bowl, place the **oil, salt, vinegar, mustard, pepper, capers, olives,** and **anchovies,** and stir with a fork to mix well.

2. Wash the **lettuce,** pat it dry with paper toweling, and tear it into bite-size pieces. Add it to the bowl along with the **onion, tomatoes,** and **cucumber.** Toss to coat with the dressing.

3. Add the **cheese** and toss gently to prevent the cheese from crumbling.

> **Tip:** *To make this salad a main course for 4, double the ingredients and serve with warmed pita bread or with crusty French bread. To make it a main dish for 1 or a side dish for 2, halve the amounts of all the ingredients.*

SALADS AND DRESSINGS

Creating a Fruit Salad

What is more refreshing than a salad made of fresh fruit served plain or with a simple dressing? Fruit salad can be served as an appetizer, side dish, or dessert. And a good fruit salad is quick and simple to make. Create your own salad of fresh fruits by following the suggestions given below, or use one of the recipes that follow.

Choosing Fruits

Your choice of fruits will be limited by what is in season, but try to select those that complement one another. Consider color, contrast, and texture when combining fruits. For example, the crispness of a tart apple is a good foil for sweet ripe bananas. You can add nuts, sour cream, or cottage cheese, or even a raw vegetable. Here are a few combinations.

- Sliced avocado with orange and grapefruit sections.
- Honeydew melon or cantaloupe balls with blueberries and cubed watermelon.
- Cantaloupe balls with grapes and whole or sliced strawberries.
- Sliced apples and bananas with orange sections.
- Orange sections, pitted prunes, and nuts with ricotta or cottage cheese.
- Sliced peaches and toasted almonds with cottage cheese.
- Sliced peaches, plums, and bananas with whole or sliced strawberries.
- Pineapple chunks, orange sections, raisins, and nuts with ricotta or cottage cheese.
- Sliced apples and shredded cabbage with sour cream.

To brighten your fruit salad still further, add a bit of shredded coconut, chopped fresh mint, crystallized or preserved ginger.

Preparing Fruits

Prepare the fruits by removing any inedible parts, including tough skins, seeds, or cores. If you are using oranges or other citrus fruits, divide the peeled fruit into sections and remove all the white membrane from each section. Slice, dice, or cube large fruits so that they are in bite-size pieces. Count on about 1 cup of prepared fruit per person.

Apples, avocados, bananas, peaches, and pears darken when exposed to air. When using these fruits, dip them into a bowl of lemon water (3 tablespoons of lemon juice mixed with 1 cup of water) as you cut the fruits to keep them bright and colorful.

Dressing and Serving Fruit Salads

Fruit salads can be served chilled or at room temperature, with or without a dressing. If you prefer to use a dressing, try one of the recipes below. Use a tangy dressing for appetizer salads and toss dessert salads with a sweet dressing or top with whipped cream.

Fruit salads are good side dishes for pork and poultry. If you want a change from cranberry sauce, try serving turkey with ambrosia, a classic fruit salad made of orange sections, pineapple chunks, and shredded coconut, moistened with a little orange juice, sprinkled with sifted confectioners' sugar, tossed, and chilled.

Oil and Vinegar Dressing for Fruit Salads

Preparation: **3 minutes**   Yield: **3/4 cup**   Calories per tablespoon: **90**

1/2 cup vegetable oil

1/4 cup red wine vinegar

1 tablespoon honey

**Grated rind and juice of
1 small lemon**

1/2 teaspoon salt

Put all the ingredients into a jar, cap the jar securely, and shake vigorously. Store in the refrigerator. Shake again just before serving.

> *Tip: Instead of the honey and lemon juice and rind, you can use any of the following: 2 tablespoons cut-up chutney; 1 tablespoon lemon or lime juice and 1/4 cup each currant jelly and chopped walnuts; or 2 teaspoons sugar and 2 tablespoons minced fresh mint.*

Yogurt and Honey Dressing

Preparation: 5 minutes　　　　　Yield: **²/₃ cup**　Calories per tablespoon: **30**

1 teaspoon grated lemon rind

2 tablespoons lemon juice

1 tablespoon vegetable oil

¹/₂ cup plain yogurt

2 tablespoons honey

¹/₄ teaspoon paprika

Dash liquid hot red pepper seasoning

¹/₄ teaspoon salt

Put all the ingredients into a jar, cap the jar securely, and shake vigorously. Store in the refrigerator. Shake again just before serving on a fruit salad.

> *Tip: As a variation, you can omit the paprika and red pepper seasoning and add 1 or 2 teaspoons of minced fresh mint.*

Sour Cream, Orange, and Honey Dressing

Preparation: 2 minutes　　　　　Yield: **1¹/₄ cups**　Calories per tablespoon: **30**

1 cup sour cream

2 tablespoons honey

2 tablespoons orange or lemon juice

¹/₈ teaspoon ground ginger (optional)

Put all the ingredients into a small bowl and stir well to mix. Cover and store in the refrigerator. Serve with berries, peaches, nectarines, bananas, or other fruit.

Low-Calorie Fruit Dressing

Preparation: 2 minutes　　　　　Yield: **1¹/₃ cups**　Calories per tablespoon: **10**

1 cup pineapple, orange, or tangerine juice

5 tablespoons lemon juice

1 tablespoon honey or light corn syrup

1 clove garlic, peeled and minced

¹/₂ teaspoon salt

¹/₄ teaspoon paprika

Put all the ingredients into a jar, cap the jar securely, and shake vigorously. Store in the refrigerator. Shake again just before serving.

> *Tips: 1. For variety, add 1 tablespoon of chopped fresh mint, dill, or basil. 2. This is a good dressing for apples, pears, and bananas because the citrus juice keeps them from turning brown. 3. You can use this dressing for a green salad too.*

Poppy Seed Dressing

Preparation: **8 minutes**   Yield: **1¹⁄₃ cups**   Calories per tablespoon: **80**

¹⁄₄ **cup sugar**

³⁄₄ **teaspoon dry mustard**

³⁄₄ **teaspoon salt**

3 tablespoons cider vinegar

1 tablespoon grated or minced yellow onion

³⁄₄ **cup vegetable oil**

1 tablespoon poppy seeds

1. In a small saucepan, combine the **sugar, mustard, salt, vinegar,** and **onion.** Stir over moderate heat for 3 minutes, or until the sugar dissolves. Remove from the heat.

2. Using a wire whisk or a rotary beater, gradually beat the **oil** into the mixture and continue beating until the mixture thickens. Stir in the **poppy seeds.** Store in the refrigerator and beat again just before serving.

Apple Salad with Sour Cream Dressing ⊘ ⊘

Preparation: **10 minutes**   Serves **4**   Calories per serving: **280**

¹⁄₂ **cup sour cream or plain yogurt**

1 tablespoon lemon juice

¹⁄₈ **teaspoon ground cinnamon**

4 medium-size tart apples

¹⁄₂ **cup raisins**

¹⁄₂ **cup chopped pecans or walnuts**

Lettuce leaves for garnish

1. In a serving bowl, combine the **sour cream** and **lemon juice.** Stir in the **cinnamon.**

2. Cut the **apples** into quarters lengthwise and cut out the cores. Dice the apple quarters, one by one, and stir the pieces into the sour cream mixture as you dice, to keep the apples from turning brown.

3. Mix in the **raisins** and **pecans.** Serve on the **lettuce leaves.** The salad tastes best slightly chilled.

Tip: This recipe can be reduced to serve 1 or 2.

Pear, Celery, and Pecan Salad 🐷 ⊘

Preparation: **14 minutes**   Serves **4**   Calories per serving: **335**

¹⁄₃ **cup mayonnaise or plain yogurt**

1 tablespoon vegetable oil

1 teaspoon lemon juice

¹⁄₄ **teaspoon salt**

¹⁄₈ **teaspoon black pepper**

3 stalks celery, diced

3 large firm, ripe pears

Lettuce leaves for garnish

¹⁄₂ **cup pecan halves**

1. In a serving bowl, combine the **mayonnaise, oil, lemon juice, salt,** and **pepper.** Add the diced **celery.**

2. Stem and peel the **pears,** quarter them lengthwise, and cut out the cores. Dice each quarter into 1-inch pieces. Add the pears to the bowl and toss. Mound on the **lettuce leaves** and top with the **pecans.** The salad tastes best slightly chilled.

Tip: For variety, add ¹⁄₄ cup cubed ham or Cheddar or blue cheese. You can also use apples instead of the pears, and walnuts instead of the pecans.

VEGETABLES

Vegetables not only provide nutrition but add a variety of flavors and colors to a meal. Most vegetables can be cooked simply by steaming, boiling, or sautéeing; and few people need to be reminded that the fresher the vegetable and the less it is cooked, the more wholesome and flavorful it is. Indeed, fresh vegetables are so good that you will often want to eat them raw or slightly cooked and tossed with butter. But even natural goodness can be tedious if it is never varied. The recipes that follow show you new ways of cooking everyday carrots, cabbage, and green beans; ingenious ways to shorten the cooking time of slow-cooking beets and winter squash; and quick, simple ways to turn staple potatoes into delectable dishes. The vegetables presented here are inexpensive either year-round—for example, cabbage and carrots—or seasonally—for example, asparagus, corn, and zucchini.

Skillet Asparagus ◎ ◑

Preparation: **4 minutes**   Cooking: **8 minutes**   Serves **4**   Calories per serving: **110**

Put asparagus on your menu in the spring, when it is in season.

1¹⁄₂ pounds asparagus

3 tablespoons butter or margarine

2 tablespoons grated Parmesan cheese

> **Tip:** *This recipe is suitable for 1 or 2, since the ingredients can be halved and the leftovers reheated.*

1. Break off the tough stem ends of the **asparagus** as far down as the stalks snap easily. Wash the asparagus thoroughly.

2. Bring about 1 inch of lightly salted water to a boil in a 10- or 12-inch skillet. Add the asparagus and cook, covered, for 5 minutes, or until the asparagus is crisp-tender. Drain well.

3. Reduce the heat to moderate, add the **butter** to the asparagus, and warm for 2 or 3 minutes.

4. Sprinkle with the **cheese** and, leaving the broiler door open, place the skillet (but not the handle) under the broiler until the cheese melts.

Asparagus Chinese Style ◎

Preparation: **7 minutes**   Cooking: **5 minutes**   Serves **4**   Calories per serving: **110**

1¹⁄₂ pounds asparagus

2 tablespoons vegetable or peanut oil

1 clove garlic, peeled and minced

¹⁄₄ teaspoon salt

³⁄₄ cup chicken broth

1 tablespoon each cornstarch and cold water mixed with 2 tablespoons soy sauce

¹⁄₈ teaspoon black pepper

1. Break off the tough stem ends of the **asparagus** as far down as the stalks snap easily. Wash the asparagus thoroughly and cut the stalks at an angle into ¹⁄₂-inch slices.

2. Heat the **oil** in a 10- or 12-inch skillet, add the **garlic, salt,** and asparagus, and sauté over moderate heat for 2 minutes.

3. Pour in the **chicken broth** and bring to a boil.

4. Add the **cornstarch, water,** and **soy sauce** mixture, stir, and bring to a boil again. Stir for 1 minute, add the **pepper,** and serve at once.

Green Beans with Garlic and Cheese ◁ ◁D

Preparation: **6 minutes**   Cooking: **10 minutes**   Serves **4**   Calories per serving: **250**

1 pound green beans

1 medium-size lemon

6 tablespoons olive
or vegetable oil

3 cloves garlic, peeled
and minced

1/2 teaspoon black pepper

1/4 cup grated
Parmesan cheese

Tip: This recipe can be halved.

1. Wash the **beans** and cut off the ends. Bring about 1 inch of lightly salted water to a boil in a 2-quart saucepan. Add the beans, cover, and cook for 8 minutes, or until crisp-tender.

2. Meanwhile, remove the peel from the **lemon** in strips with a swivel-bladed vegetable peeler. Cut the peel into very narrow strips about 1½ inches long. Squeeze the juice from the lemon. Set both aside.

3. When the beans are done, drain them in a colander. Put the **oil** into the same saucepan and sauté the **garlic** for 1 minute. Add the beans and toss to coat them with the oil and garlic.

4. Add the strips of lemon peel, lemon juice, and **pepper**, and toss again. Spoon the beans into a heated serving dish and sprinkle with the **cheese**. Serve at once.

Green Beans Italian Style

Preparation: **5 minutes**   Cooking: **25 minutes**   Serves **4**   Calories per serving: **180**

Serve this dish hot or make it ahead and serve it cold. And if you prefer, use wax beans instead of green beans.

1 pound green beans

1/4 cup vegetable or olive oil

1 clove garlic, peeled
and minced

2 tablespoons chopped
parsley

1 teaspoon sugar

3/4 teaspoon salt

1/8 teaspoon black pepper

3/4 cup beef broth

1 medium-size tomato, peeled
and thinly sliced

1. Wash the **beans** and cut off the ends. Put the beans into a 10-inch skillet with the **oil, garlic, parsley, sugar, salt,** and **pepper**, and cook, covered, over low heat for 15 minutes.

2. Add the **broth**. Cook, uncovered, for 5 more minutes, or until the beans are almost tender. Raise the heat to moderate, add the **tomato**, and cook, uncovered, for another 5 minutes.

Tip: To serve the leftovers warm, sprinkle grated Parmesan cheese and a little oil over the top, and bake in a 400°F oven until the cheese melts.

Warm Green Beans Vinaigrette 🐷 ⊙

Preparation: **5 minutes**   Cooking: **8 minutes**   Serves **4**   Calories per serving: **155**

1 pound green beans

2 tablespoons cider vinegar

1/2 teaspoon salt

1/4 teaspoon black pepper

1 teaspoon Dijon or prepared spicy brown mustard

5 tablespoons vegetable oil

1 small red or yellow onion, peeled and finely chopped

1. Wash the **beans** and cut off the ends. Bring about 1 inch of lightly salted water to a boil in a 2-quart saucepan and add the beans. Cook, covered, for 8 minutes, or until crisp-tender.

2. Meanwhile, make the dressing by mixing together the **vinegar, salt, pepper, mustard, oil,** and **onion.** Drain the beans when done and toss immediately with the dressing.

Tip: Serve leftovers cold or toss them with hot pasta.

Green Beans in Egg Sauce 🐷 ⊙

Preparation: **5 minutes**   Cooking: **10 minutes**   Serves **4**   Calories per serving: **80**

1 pound green beans

2 eggs

2 tablespoons cider vinegar

1/2 small yellow onion, peeled and finely chopped

1 clove garlic, peeled and minced

1/4 teaspoon salt

1/8 teaspoon black pepper

Tip: Use the egg sauce with broccoli, carrots, or asparagus.

1. Wash the **beans** and cut off the ends. Bring about 1 inch of lightly salted water to a boil in a 2-quart saucepan and add the beans. Cook, covered, for 8 minutes, or until crisp-tender. Drain, reserving 2 tablespoons of the cooking water. Return the beans to the pan and set over lowest heat.

2. Mix the **eggs** and **vinegar** in a bowl, add the reserved water, and beat the ingredients together with a fork. Pour the mixture over the beans.

3. Add the **onion, garlic, salt,** and **pepper,** and stir until the beans are coated with the sauce.

Lima Beans in Sour Cream

Preparation: **36 minutes**   Cooking: **22 minutes**   Serves **4**   Calories per serving: **340**

You can make this dish in less than 15 minutes if you use frozen Fordhook limas.

3 pounds fresh baby lima beans, shelled (about 3 cups), or 2 packages (10 ounces each) frozen limas

2 tablespoons butter or margarine

2 tablespoons grated yellow onion

1 cup sour cream or plain yogurt at room temperature

2 teaspoons paprika

1. Bring about 1 inch of lightly salted water to a boil in a 2-quart saucepan. Add the **lima beans** and cook, covered, for 20 to 25 minutes. If you are using frozen beans, cook according to package directions. Drain in a colander.

2. In the same saucepan, melt the **butter** and cook the **onion** over low heat for 1 minute.

3. Return the beans to the saucepan, add the **sour cream** and **paprika,** and stir all the ingredients together. Heat the mixture, but do not let it boil or the cream will curdle.

Baby Lima Beans with Herbs

Preparation: **25 minutes**   Cooking: **33 minutes**   Serves **4**   Calories per serving: **180**

This hearty dish tastes even better reheated the next day after the flavors have blended. Using frozen limas greatly reduces the preparation time.

2 slices bacon, cut into 1-inch strips

1 medium-size yellow onion, peeled and sliced

2 medium-size carrots, peeled and thinly sliced

1/8 teaspoon ground nutmeg

1/4 teaspoon dried thyme, crumbled

1/8 teaspoon fennel or anise seeds (optional)

1 1/2 pounds fresh baby lima beans, shelled (about 1 1/2 cups), or 1 package (10 ounces) frozen lima beans

1 teaspoon salt

1/4 teaspoon black pepper

2 tablespoons minced parsley

1 1/4 cups water

1. Cook the **bacon** in a heavy 2-quart saucepan over moderately high heat until crisp—about 5 minutes. Remove the bacon, drain on paper toweling, and reserve.

2. Place the **onion, carrots, nutmeg,** and **thyme,** and the **fennel seeds** if used, in the saucepan with the bacon drippings. Cook, uncovered, over moderate heat until the onion starts to color—about 8 to 10 minutes.

3. Add the **lima beans** (breaking up the block if you are using frozen limas), the **salt** and **pepper,** 1 tablespoon of the **parsley,** and the **water.**

4. Bring to a simmer, cover, turn the heat to low, and cook for 15 minutes. Uncover and cook another 5 minutes. Before serving, sprinkle with the remaining tablespoon of parsley and crumble the reserved bacon over the top.

> *Tip: For a main course, omit the bacon and substitute 2 tablespoons of butter or vegetable oil for the drippings. Brown 1 pound of mild Italian or link sausage, cut it into chunks, and simmer it with the beans.*

Grated Beets Russian Style

Preparation: **10 minutes**   Cooking: **20 minutes**   Serves **4**   Calories per serving: **85**

Although this recipe is considered typically Russian, it is of Polish origin.

2 tablespoons butter or margarine

4 cups coarsely shredded beets (about 2 large beets)

2 tablespoons lemon juice

1 1/2 teaspoons salt

1/8 teaspoon black pepper

1/2 cup water

1 tablespoon all-purpose flour

1. Heat the **butter** in an 8-inch skillet. Add the **beets, lemon juice, salt, pepper,** and **water.** Cover and cook over moderately low heat for 15 minutes, stirring from time to time.

2. Sprinkle the **flour** over the beets but do not stir in. Cover and cook another 5 minutes.

> *Tips: 1. If you halve this recipe, do not reduce the amount of butter called for. 2. For variety, garnish with 1 teaspoon of prepared horseradish mixed with 1/2 cup of sour cream or plain yogurt.*

Sweet and Sour Broccoli ⬭

Preparation: **6 minutes**   Cooking: **8 minutes**   Serves **4**   Calories per serving: **275**

This richly flavored broccoli adds zest to a main course of pasta and cheese or roast chicken.

2 pounds broccoli

8 slices bacon, cut into 1-inch strips

¼ cup minced green onions

1 tablespoon dark or light brown sugar

2 tablespoons cider vinegar

⅛ teaspoon dry mustard

¼ teaspoon salt

⅛ teaspoon black pepper

> **Tips: 1.** *This recipe can be halved.* **2.** *This dish is best eaten right away, since the bacon drippings congeal as they cool.* **3.** *You can substitute cauliflower for the broccoli.* **4.** *If you want to omit the bacon, cook the green onions in vegetable oil, add the sugar, vinegar, mustard, salt, and pepper, and heat the mixture. Toss it with the broccoli and about ¼ cup of chopped pecans or walnuts.*

1. Trim the leaves and coarse stem ends from the **broccoli,** and cut the stems and the florets into bite-size pieces.

2. Bring about 1 inch of lightly salted water to a boil in a 3-quart saucepan. Add the broccoli and cook, covered, for 5 minutes, or until crisp-tender.

3. Meanwhile, place the **bacon** into a 6-inch skillet and cook over moderately high heat for 5 minutes, or just until crisp and brown. Remove from the skillet and drain on paper toweling.

4. Pour out all but ¼ cup of the bacon drippings. Add the **green onions** to the skillet and cook, uncovered, over low heat for 1 to 2 minutes, or until they are golden. Add the **sugar, vinegar, mustard, salt,** and **pepper** to the green onions, and heat the mixture for 1 to 2 minutes.

5. Just before serving, crumble the bacon over the broccoli. Add the dressing and toss.

Dry-Sautéed Broccoli 🐷 ▷

Preparation: **8 minutes**   Cooking: **5 minutes**   Serves **4**   Calories per serving: **150**

2 pounds broccoli

3 tablespoons peanut or vegetable oil

1 teaspoon salt

⅛ teaspoon black pepper

> **Tips: 1.** *This recipe works well with tender young green beans.* **2.** *To use leftovers, add a tablespoon of oil before reheating.* **3.** *Turn this into an Italian dish by substituting olive oil and adding 4 large slivered cloves of garlic. Heat the oil for 1 minute, remove the garlic, and stir-fry the broccoli as directed above. Before serving, squeeze the juice of a small lemon over the broccoli, add salt and pepper, and toss.*

Here is a simple way to cook broccoli that turns it a dazzling emerald green while retaining its nutritive value.

1. Trim the leaves and coarse stem ends from the **broccoli.** Wash the broccoli and pat it dry with paper toweling. Cut the florets from the stems, then divide them into smaller florets, roughly 1 to 1½ inches long. Halve any unusually chunky stems vertically. Slice the stems, slightly on the diagonal, about ¼ inch thick.

2. Heat the **oil** in a 9- or 10-inch skillet until small ripples appear. Add the broccoli, lower the heat to moderately high, and cook, stirring constantly, for 4 to 5 minutes, or until the broccoli is crisp-tender.

3. Add the **salt** and **pepper,** and toss well.

Broccoli with Sweet Red Peppers ⬙ ⬙

Preparation: **10 minutes**   Cooking: **5 minutes**   Serves **4**   Calories per serving: **125**

2 pounds broccoli

2 tablespoons butter
or margarine

4 green onions, trimmed and
chopped

1/2 sweet red pepper, cored,
seeded, and chopped

Grated rind and juice
of 1 medium-size lemon

1 teaspoon salt

1/4 teaspoon black pepper

*Tips: 1. This recipe can be halved.
2. For a variation that is almost a
total change, substitute
cauliflower for the broccoli.*

1. Trim the leaves and coarse stem ends from the **broccoli.** Cut the stems into 3/4-inch pieces and the florets into 1-inch pieces.

2. Bring about 1 inch of lightly salted water to a boil in a 3-quart saucepan. Add the broccoli and cook, covered, for about 5 minutes, or until it is crisp-tender.

3. Meanwhile, melt the **butter** in a 6-inch skillet. Add the **green onions** and the **sweet red pepper** and cook, uncovered, over moderately low heat about 5 minutes, or until soft.

4. Remove the skillet from the heat. Add the **lemon rind, lemon juice, salt,** and **pepper.** Drain the broccoli in a colander, put it into a serving dish, and toss it with the green-onion–red-pepper mixture.

Brussels Sprouts with Walnuts ⬙ ⬙

Preparation: **5 minutes**   Cooking: **10 minutes**   Serves **4**   Calories per serving: **245**

*Brussels sprouts with walnuts are
festive enough to serve at Thanksgiving
or Christmas.*

1 pound Brussels sprouts

1/4 cup (1/2 stick) butter
or margarine

1/2 cup walnut
or pecan halves

1/4 teaspoon salt

1/8 teaspoon black pepper

*Tips: 1. This recipe can be halved.
2. Omit the walnuts and add 1 or
2 chopped anchovies and 1 clove
garlic, peeled and chopped, to
the butter.*

1. Remove the loose and faded leaves and trim the stalk ends from the **Brussels sprouts.**

2. Bring about 1 inch of lightly salted water to a boil in a 2-quart saucepan. Add the Brussels sprouts, and cook, covered, for 8 to 10 minutes, or until they are tender but still bright green. Drain them in a colander and rinse them quickly with cold water to preserve their color and to stop the cooking.

3. Melt the **butter** in an 8-inch skillet, add the **walnuts,** and cook, uncovered, over low heat for 3 minutes, or until the nuts brown lightly. Add the Brussels sprouts and the **salt** and **pepper,** and continue cooking about 2 minutes—or just long enough to heat through.

Skillet Cabbage

Preparation: **8 minutes**   Cooking: **10 minutes**   Serves **4**   Calories per serving: **230**

Cabbage and bacon are a robust combination. To speed preparation of this dish, get the carrots, onion, and celery ready while the bacon is cooking, and while they are cooking, peel and chop the tomatoes.

1 small head cabbage (about 1¼ pounds)

4 slices bacon, cut into 1-inch strips

2 medium-size carrots, peeled and coarsely shredded

1 medium-size yellow onion, peeled and thinly sliced

2 stalks celery, thinly sliced (optional)

2 medium-size tomatoes, peeled and chopped

1 tablespoon sugar

½ teaspoon salt

⅛ teaspoon black pepper

1. Quarter the **cabbage,** trim off and discard the core at the point of each quarter, then cut the quarters into ⅛-inch-thick slices. Set aside.

2. Cook the **bacon** in a 12- or 14-inch skillet over moderately high heat for 5 minutes, or until crisp. Remove from the skillet and drain on paper toweling.

3. To the bacon drippings in the skillet add the cabbage, **carrots,** and **onion,** and the **celery** if used. Cook, uncovered, stirring occasionally, over moderate heat for 5 to 7 minutes, or until the vegetables are crisp-tender.

4. Mix in the **tomatoes,** remove the skillet from the heat, and season with the **sugar, salt,** and **pepper.** Crumble the reserved bacon over the top and serve.

> *Tips: 1. If you prefer to omit the bacon, cook the vegetables in 3 tablespoons of butter or vegetable oil. For an even quicker dish, use only the cabbage, bacon, and onions. 2. Leftovers can be refrigerated and reheated. When reheating, if the cabbage seems dry, add 1 tablespoon of butter, vegetable oil, or bacon drippings.*

Shredded Cabbage with Garlic

Preparation: **5 minutes**   Cooking: **16 minutes**   Serves **4**   Calories per serving: **135**

Serve this full-flavored cabbage as a side dish. Or cook 8 ounces of egg noodles, butter them, and mix them with the cabbage for a light meal.

1 small head cabbage (about 1¼ pounds)

4 tablespoons (½ stick) butter or margarine

2 cloves garlic, peeled and minced

½ teaspoon salt

¼ teaspoon black pepper

1. Quarter the **cabbage,** trim off and discard the core at the point of each quarter, then cut the quarters into ⅛-inch-thick slices.

2. Melt the **butter** in a 12- or 14-inch skillet, over moderately high heat. Add the cabbage and **garlic,** and stir to coat the cabbage with the butter. Sauté about 1 minute.

3. Cover the skillet and cook the cabbage over low heat about 15 minutes, or until it is tender but still crisp, stirring occasionally. Season with the **salt** and **pepper.**

> *Tips: 1. This recipe can be halved. 2. As a variation, sauté a diced sweet green pepper with the cabbage and season with 2 to 3 tablespoons of white wine vinegar.*

VEGETABLES

Cabbage with Lemon Sauce 🐷 ▱ ◖

Preparation: 5 minutes   Cooking: **10 minutes**   Serves **4**   Calories per serving: **115**

Serve this dish with roast pork, baked ham, or sausages.

1 small head cabbage (about 1¼ pounds)

2 tablespoons butter or margarine

4 teaspoons all-purpose flour

¾ to 1 cup chicken broth

5 teaspoons lemon juice

¼ teaspoon salt

⅛ teaspoon black pepper

3 tablespoons grated Parmesan cheese

Tip: This recipe can be halved.

1. Quarter the **cabbage,** trim off and discard the core at the point of each quarter, then cut the quarters into ¼-inch-thick slices.

2. Bring 1 inch of lightly salted water to a boil in a 4-quart pot, and add the cabbage. Cover and cook for 5 minutes, or until crisp-tender. Drain, and return the cabbage to the pot.

3. Melt the **butter** in a 1-quart saucepan. Mix in the **flour** and cook, uncovered, over low heat for 2 minutes, stirring constantly.

4. Gradually stir in the **chicken broth.** Cook, uncovered, over moderate heat, stirring constantly, for 3 minutes, or until the liquid becomes thickened and smooth.

5. Stir in the **lemon juice, salt,** and **pepper.** Pour the sauce over the cabbage and toss to mix. Top with the **cheese** and serve immediately.

Red Cabbage with Apples 🐷

Preparation: 10 minutes   Cooking: **13 minutes**   Serves **4**   Calories per serving: **155**

1 small head red cabbage (about 1¼ pounds)

1 medium-size yellow onion, peeled and coarsely chopped

2 tablespoons vegetable oil

¼ cup cider vinegar

2 tablespoons light brown sugar or honey

¼ teaspoon salt

⅛ teaspoon black pepper

1 medium-size tart green apple, cored and thinly sliced

1. Quarter the **cabbage,** trim off the core at the point of each quarter, then cut each quarter into ⅛-inch-thick slices, and set aside.

2. In a 12- or 14-inch skillet over moderate heat, sauté the **onion** in the **oil** until it is soft— about 5 minutes. Stir in the **vinegar, sugar, salt,** and **pepper.** Add the **apple** and cabbage.

3. Raise the heat to high and bring the liquid to a boil, then reduce the heat to moderate. Cover the skillet and cook the cabbage just until it wilts, about 8 to 10 minutes, stirring occasionally.

Orange-Ginger Carrots 🐷 ◑

Preparation: 8 minutes   Cooking: 13 minutes   **Serves 4   Calories per serving: 85**

8 medium-size carrots (about 1 pound)

1 tablespoon sugar

1 teaspoon cornstarch

1/4 teaspoon salt

1/4 teaspoon ground ginger

1/4 cup orange juice

1 tablespoon butter or margarine

Tips: 1. This recipe can be halved. 2. You can make this dish ahead of time and refrigerate it for 1 or 2 days; add a little more orange juice if necessary.

1. Peel the **carrots,** then slice, cutting them at a slight angle, about 1 inch thick.

2. Bring about 1 inch of lightly salted water to a boil in a 2-quart saucepan. Add the carrots and cook, covered, for 10 to 15 minutes, or until the carrots are crisp-tender. Drain.

3. Meanwhile, in a small bowl combine the **sugar, cornstarch, salt, ginger,** and **orange juice.** Pour the mixture over the carrots, and cook over low heat, stirring, for 3 minutes. Remove from the heat and add the **butter.** Toss gently to mix.

Creamed Diced Carrots with Green Pepper 🐷

Preparation: 10 minutes   Cooking: 18 minutes   **Serves 4   Calories per serving: 230**

These creamed carrots are particularly good with turkey, chicken, or pork.

3 tablespoons butter or margarine

8 medium-size carrots (about 1 pound), peeled and diced

1 small yellow onion, peeled and chopped

1/3 cup coarsely chopped sweet green pepper

3 tablespoons all-purpose flour

1/2 cup chicken broth or water

1 cup half-and-half or milk

1 pinch each dried rosemary, crumbled, and ground nutmeg or 1 teaspoon curry powder

1/4 teaspoon salt

1/8 teaspoon black pepper

1. Melt the **butter** in a 2-quart saucepan over moderate heat. Add the **carrots** and **onion,** and stir. Cover, lower the heat, and cook for 10 minutes. Add the **green pepper,** cover, and cook another 2 minutes.

2. Sprinkle in the **flour,** stir, then add the **broth, half-and-half,** and **seasonings.** Stir well.

3. Bring the mixture to a simmer, stirring constantly, then cover and cook over low heat for 4 or 5 minutes, or until the carrots are done—they should be slightly crunchy.

Tips: 1. If you want to prepare this dish ahead, slightly undercook the carrots and reheat slowly. 2. For extra taste and richness, add 1/2 cup grated Swiss cheese to the carrots at the end of the cooking. 3. An additional 4 to 5 cups of broth will transform this dish into a soup.

Carrots Amana Style 🐷

Preparation: **10 minutes** Cooking: **25 minutes** Serves **4** Calories per serving: **175**

1 medium-size yellow onion, peeled and chopped

2 tablespoons bacon drippings, butter, or margarine

8 medium-size carrots (about 1 pound), peeled and cut into 1/2-inch slices

3 small all-purpose potatoes, peeled and quartered

1 1/4 cups water

1 tablespoon sugar

1/2 teaspoon salt

1/8 teaspoon black pepper

3 tablespoons minced parsley

Tip: For a different taste, substitute turnips for the potatoes.

In the 19th century, members of a small religious society arrived in the United States from Germany and ultimately settled in Iowa. Known today as the Amana Colonies, they are made up of farm people who believe in good hearty food. This is how they prepare carrots.

1. In a 2-quart saucepan over moderately high heat, cook the **onion**, uncovered, in the **bacon drippings** or other fat until soft and golden—about 3 or 4 minutes. Add the **carrots, potatoes,** and **water,** and bring to a boil. Cover, reduce the heat to moderate, and simmer for 20 to 25 minutes, or until the vegetables are tender.

2. Remove the carrots and potatoes with a slotted spoon, and mash them well. Return the vegetables to the saucepan, add the **sugar, salt,** and **pepper,** and stir. Cook, uncovered, about 5 minutes longer, or until the mixture thickens slightly. Serve sprinkled with the **parsley.**

Cauliflower Fritters

Preparation: **10 minutes** Cooking: **15 minutes** Serves **4** Calories per serving: **160**

Transform cauliflower into fritters by using this recipe from Peru.

1 small head cauliflower (about 1 1/4 pounds)

3 tablespoons all-purpose flour

1/2 teaspoon salt

1/8 teaspoon black pepper

2 tablespoons water

1 egg, lightly beaten

1 medium-size yellow onion, peeled and chopped

1/4 cup vegetable oil

Tip: You can make these fritters with broccoli instead of cauliflower.

1. Separate the **cauliflower** into small florets. Bring about 1 inch of lightly salted water to a boil in a 2-quart saucepan. Add the cauliflower, bring to a boil again, cover, and cook for 5 minutes. Drain in a colander. Coarsely chop the cauliflower and set aside.

2. While the cauliflower is cooking, mix the **flour, salt, pepper, water,** and **egg** in a bowl, then stir in the **onion** and chopped cauliflower.

3. In a 12-inch skillet, heat the **oil** over moderate heat until hot but not smoking. Drop the cauliflower mixture by tablespoonsful into the hot oil and sauté about 3 minutes on each side until brown. Drain the fritters on paper toweling and set them in a keep-warm (250°F) oven until ready to serve. Cook the remaining mixture the same way.

Cauliflower with Tomatoes

Preparation: **10 minutes**　Cooking: **11 minutes**　　Serves **4**　Calories per serving: **230**

Originating in sunny Italy, this dish is ideal for warm weather and picnics, but it is good anytime.

1 medium-size head cauliflower (about 2 pounds)

¼ cup vegetable oil

2 tablespoons olive oil

1 large yellow onion, peeled and chopped

3 tablespoons cider vinegar

1 large tomato, peeled and chopped

½ teaspoon dried oregano, crumbled

½ teaspoon dried basil, crumbled

½ teaspoon salt

⅛ teaspoon black pepper

1. Separate the **cauliflower** into small florets. Bring about 1 inch of lightly salted water to a boil in a 2-quart saucepan. Add the cauliflower. When the water returns to a boil, remove the cauliflower and drain.

2. Put the **vegetable oil, olive oil,** and cauliflower into a 12-inch skillet and cook, uncovered, over moderate heat until the edges of the cauliflower begin to brown—3 to 4 minutes.

3. Add the **onion** and continue cooking about 3 minutes. Add the **vinegar** and cover the skillet. Lower the heat and cook for another 3 or 4 minutes.

4. Add the **tomato, oregano, basil, salt,** and **pepper.** Cover and simmer until the cauliflower is tender—about 2 minutes. Do not overcook.

> **Tip:** *Serve leftovers slightly chilled as a salad.*

Confetti Corn

Preparation: **15 minutes**　Cooking: **11 minutes**　　Serves **4**　Calories per serving: **225**

6 medium-size ears fresh sweet corn or 2 packages (10 ounces each) frozen whole-kernel corn

4 tablespoons (½ stick) butter or margarine

1 large sweet green pepper, cored, seeded, and finely chopped

1 jar (4 ounces) pimientos, drained and finely chopped

1 medium-size yellow onion, peeled and finely chopped

½ teaspoon salt

⅛ teaspoon black pepper

1. Remove the husks and silk from the **corn** and, with a knife, scrape the kernels and the milk from the cobs into a bowl. If you are using frozen corn, cook according to package directions, then drain thoroughly.

2. Melt the **butter** in a 1-quart saucepan over moderate heat, and add the **green pepper, pimientos,** and **onion.** Cook, stirring constantly, for 8 to 10 minutes, or until the onion is golden.

3. Add the corn, **salt,** and **pepper,** cover the pan, and simmer for 3 to 4 minutes, or just long enough to heat the corn through.

> **Tip:** *You can halve this recipe. If you do, cover any unused pimientos with vinegar and refrigerate them— they will keep for days—or freeze them for another use.*

Corn in Parsley Cream ▷ ⬨

Preparation: **10 minutes**   Cooking: **7 minutes**   Serves **4**   Calories per serving: **195**

6 medium-size ears fresh
sweet corn or 2 packages
(10 ounces each) frozen
whole-kernel corn

2 tablespoons butter
or margarine

1/2 teaspoon salt

1/4 teaspoon black pepper

2 teaspoons minced parsley

1 teaspoon paprika

1/2 cup half-and-half

1. Remove the husks and silk from the **corn** and,
with a knife, scrape the kernels and the milk
from the cobs into a bowl. If you are using frozen
corn, cook according to package directions, then
drain thoroughly.

2. Melt the **butter** in a 10- or 12-inch skillet over
moderately low heat. Add the corn and cook,
uncovered, for 4 to 5 minutes, stirring constantly
to prevent sticking.

3. Season with the **salt, pepper, parsley,** and
paprika. Stir in the **half-and-half,** and bring just
to serving temperature, but do not boil.

> *Tip: This recipe can be halved or the leftovers can be
> refrigerated and reheated.*

Skillet Corn with Chilies ⬨

Preparation: **15 minutes**   Cooking: **11 minutes**   Serves **4**   Calories per serving: **410**

*This Mexican-flavored dish is
substantial enough for a light lunch.*

4 tablespoons (1/2 stick)
butter or margarine

1 large yellow onion, peeled
and finely chopped

6 medium-size ears fresh
sweet corn or 2 packages
(10 ounces each) frozen
whole-kernel corn

2 canned green chilies (each
about 2 inches long), minced

3 medium-size fresh tomatoes,
peeled and chopped, or
1 can (1 pound) tomatoes,
chopped, with their juice

1 1/2 teaspoons dried oregano,
crumbled

1 teaspoon salt

1 1/2 cups shredded sharp
Cheddar cheese (about
6 ounces)

1. Melt the **butter** in a 12-inch skillet, add the
onion, and cook, covered, over moderate heat
for 5 minutes.

2. Meanwhile, remove the husks and silk from
the **corn** and, with a knife, scrape the kernels
and the milk from the cobs into a bowl. (If
you are using frozen corn, leave it frozen.)

3. To the onion and butter add the **chilies,
tomatoes, oregano, salt,** and corn. (If you are
using frozen corn, break up the block with a
fork.) Cover and cook over moderate heat,
stirring once or twice, for 10 minutes, or until the
corn is tender.

4. Top with the **cheese,** reduce the heat to low,
and cook, uncovered, for 1 minute, or until the
cheese melts.

> *Tips: 1. This recipe can be halved. 2. To make a milder
> version of this dish, use 1 medium-size sweet green
> pepper, finely chopped, in place of the chilies.*

Broiled Eggplant ⊡ ⬭

Preparation: **5 minutes** Cooking: **10 minutes** Serves **4** Calories per serving: **240**

- **2 medium-size eggplants (about 1 pound each), peeled**
- **2 medium-size tomatoes, peeled and coarsely chopped**
- **1 large yellow onion, peeled and chopped**
- **3 cloves garlic, peeled and minced**
- **1 teaspoon salt**
- **1/8 teaspoon black pepper**
- **1 teaspoon dried basil, crumbled**
- **5 tablespoons olive or vegetable oil**
- **2 tablespoons grated Parmesan cheese**

1. Preheat the broiler. Slice the **eggplant** into 1-inch rounds and put them into an oiled 13"x 9"x 2" baking pan. Scatter the chopped **tomatoes** and **onion** over the eggplant.

2. In a small bowl, combine the **garlic, salt, pepper, basil**, and **oil**. Drizzle the mixture over the eggplant.

3. Broil 4 inches from the heat for 10 to 15 minutes, or until the eggplant is soft and begins to brown at the edges. Sprinkle with the **cheese** and serve.

> *Tips: 1. This recipe can be halved; use a medium-size onion instead of half a large one. 2. For variety, garnish the eggplant with 4 tablespoons of chopped ripe olives.*

Scalloped Eggplant 🐷

Preparation: **12 minutes** Cooking: **30 minutes** Serves **4** Calories per serving: **220**

Rich and hearty, yet low in fat, this is a good main-course vegetable dish.

- **2 medium-size eggplants (about 2 pounds)**
- **1 tablespoon olive oil, butter, or margarine**
- **1 medium-size yellow onion, peeled and chopped**
- **2 cloves garlic, peeled and minced**
- **1 teaspoon dried rosemary, crumbled**
- **1 teaspoon dried oregano, crumbled**
- **1/2 teaspoon salt**
- **3 medium-size fresh tomatoes, peeled and chopped, or 1 can (1 pound) tomatoes, coarsely chopped, with their juice**
- **1 cup shredded Swiss cheese (about 4 ounces)**

1. Preheat the oven to 375°F. Peel the **eggplant** and cut it into 1-inch cubes. Bring about 1 inch of lightly salted water to a boil in a 2-quart saucepan, and add the eggplant. Boil for 1 minute—do not overcook. Drain the eggplant and set aside.

2. Heat the **oil** in the saucepan, add the **onion** and **garlic,** and cook, uncovered, over low heat for 5 minutes.

3. Place the eggplant in a buttered 2-quart baking dish and top it with the onion, garlic, **rosemary, oregano,** and **salt**. Distribute the **tomatoes** with 1/2 cup of their juice evenly over the top.

4. Bake, uncovered, for 25 minutes. Sprinkle with the **cheese** and bake an additional 5 minutes, or until the cheese melts.

> *Tips: 1. For a richer dish, omit the oregano, rosemary, and tomatoes, and substitute 1 egg beaten with 1/2 cup half-and-half; pour the mixture over the eggplant just before baking. 2. This dish can easily be made ahead—just refrigerate and reheat.*

Onions and Apples 🐷 ▷

Preparation: **5 minutes**   Cooking: **15 minutes**   Serves **4**   Calories per serving: **210**

4 slices bacon, cut into 1-inch strips

2 medium-size tart apples, cored and cut into ½-inch slices

1 tablespoon light or dark brown sugar

1 large yellow onion, peeled and thinly sliced

¼ cup water

1. Cook the **bacon** in a 12-inch skillet over moderately high heat until crisp—about 5 minutes. Drain on paper toweling. Reserve the drippings.

2. Put the **apple** slices into the skillet with the bacon drippings, sprinkle the slices with the **sugar,** and scatter the **onion** on top. Cook, uncovered, over moderate heat for 5 minutes.

3. Add the **water,** then cover and simmer for 10 to 15 minutes, or until the onions are soft. If necessary, add more water during cooking. Crumble the reserved bacon over the top.

Sturbridge-Style Creamed Hashed Onions 🐷

Preparation: **5 minutes**   Cooking: **20 minutes**   Serves **4**   Calories per serving: **80**

2 large sweet onions, peeled and cut in half crosswise

¼ cup milk

1 tablespoon butter or margarine

¼ teaspoon salt

Pinch black pepper

Pinch ground nutmeg

¼ cup half-and-half

This recipe comes from Old Sturbridge Village in Massachusetts, where the dish was served long ago.

1. Place the **onions** in a heavy 2-quart saucepan. Add the **milk** and enough water to cover the onions. Simmer for 10 to 12 minutes.

2. Drain the onions in a colander, let them cool slightly, then chop them coarsely. Return the onions to the pan. Add the **butter, salt, pepper, nutmeg,** and **half-and-half.** Simmer, uncovered, stirring occasionally, for 10 minutes.

Peas with Orange and Mint ◐

Preparation: **34 minutes**   Cooking: **12 minutes**   Serves **4**   Calories per serving: **200**

2 oranges

4 tablespoons (½ stick) butter or margarine

2 pounds fresh green peas, shelled (about 2 cups), or 1 package (10 ounces) frozen green peas

1 bunch green onions, sliced

2 tablespoons minced fresh or 2 teaspoons dried mint

¼ teaspoon salt

⅛ teaspoon black pepper

Preparation time for fresh peas runs long, so if you are in a rush, use frozen peas.

1. Grate the rind from both **oranges** and squeeze the juice of one.

2. Melt the **butter** in a 2-quart saucepan, add the orange juice and **peas,** and cook, covered, over moderate heat for 5 minutes.

3. Add the orange rind, **green onions,** and **mint,** and continue cooking until the peas are tender—7 to 10 more minutes. Season with the **salt** and **pepper,** and serve.

> *Tip: This recipe can be halved and also reheated.*

French Green Peas ⓓ

Preparation: 29 minutes   Cooking: 11 minutes   **Serves 4   Calories per serving: 150**

½ medium-size head
iceberg lettuce

3 tablespoons butter
or margarine

¼ cup water

1 teaspoon sugar

¼ teaspoon salt

1 small yellow onion, peeled
and chopped

2 pounds fresh green peas,
shelled (about 2 cups), or
1 package (10 ounces) frozen
green peas

1 tablespoon chopped fresh
or 1 teaspoon dried parsley

The addition of lettuce to green peas reduces the amount of water needed to cook the peas and adds a touch of elegance. Using frozen peas reduces the preparation time to 5 minutes.

1. Remove the core and outer leaves of the **lettuce.** Slice the head into thin shreds.

2. Place the **butter, water, sugar,** and **salt** into a 2-quart saucepan. Top with the lettuce, then the **onion,** then the **peas.** Sprinkle with the **parsley** and cover.

3. Bring to a boil, then lower the heat and simmer about 10 minutes, or until the peas are tender. Spoon the peas along with any juices into individual dishes.

Tips: 1. If you use frozen peas, there is no need to thaw them. Simply add the frozen block and break it up with a fork. 2. This recipe can be halved.

Sautéed Green Peppers ▷

Preparation: 3 minutes   Cooking: 15 minutes   **Serves 4   Calories per serving: 85**

4 medium-size sweet
green peppers

2 tablespoons olive or
vegetable oil

3 cloves garlic, peeled and
cut in half lengthwise

½ teaspoon red wine vinegar

⅛ teaspoon sugar

2 tablespoons capers, drained

1 tablespoon chopped pitted
ripe olives

¼ teaspoon dried oregano,
crumbled

¼ teaspoon dried rosemary,
crumbled

⅛ teaspoon salt

¼ teaspoon black pepper

In summer, when peppers are plentiful, cook them northern Italian style and serve hot or cold as a vegetable or as an appetizer.

1. Core and seed the **green peppers,** and slice lengthwise into ¼-inch-wide strips. Heat the **oil** in a 12-inch skillet, add the sliced peppers and the **garlic,** and cook over moderate heat, uncovered, for 10 minutes, or until the peppers are slightly limp.

2. Add the **vinegar, sugar, capers, olives, oregano,** and **rosemary,** and cook, uncovered, 5 minutes longer. Remove the garlic and season with the **salt** and **black pepper.**

Tips: 1. If you have time, add 5 to 15 minutes to the final cooking for an even more flavorful dish. 2. To add color to this dish, use a combination of sweet red and green peppers.

New Potatoes with Green Onions 🐷

| Preparation: **3 minutes** | Cooking: **18 minutes** | Serves **4** | Calories per serving: **160** |

1½ pounds small new potatoes, scrubbed (but not peeled)

1 teaspoon salt

2 tablespoons butter or margarine

Grated rind of 1 lemon

Juice of ½ lemon

¼ cup thinly sliced green onions (green part only)

1. Place the **potatoes** in a 2-quart saucepan with water to cover. Add the **salt** and bring to a boil—about 3 minutes. Set the lid on the pan askew and cook the potatoes for 15 to 20 minutes, depending on their size, until fork tender. Drain.

2. Add the **butter, lemon rind,** and **lemon juice,** and stir well until the potatoes are glazed. Sprinkle with the **green onions** and serve.

Tip: The cooked potatoes can be refrigerated and reheated as long as two days later with good results.

Curried New Potatoes 🐷 ◫

| Preparation: **3 minutes** | Cooking: **25 minutes** | Serves **4** | Calories per serving: **210** |

4 tablespoons (½ stick) butter or margarine

1½ pounds small new potatoes, scrubbed (but not peeled) and quartered

1 teaspoon curry powder

1 teaspoon dry mustard

¼ cup chopped green onions

½ teaspoon salt

⅛ teaspoon black pepper

Tip: This recipe can be halved.

1. Melt the **butter** in a 12-inch skillet, preferably nonstick. Add the **potatoes** and cook them, uncovered, over moderate heat about 10 minutes, stirring occasionally.

2. Sprinkle the **curry powder** and **mustard** over the potatoes, and stir well. Reduce the heat to low, cover the skillet, and cook the potatoes another 10 minutes, or until they are tender.

3. Stir in the **green onions, salt,** and **pepper.** Increase the heat to moderately high and cook, uncovered, until the potatoes are crisp and lightly browned—about 5 minutes.

Baked Sliced Potatoes 🐷 ◫

| Preparation: **10 minutes** | Cooking: **20 minutes** | Serves **4** | Calories per serving: **195** |

Some of these potatoes are crisp, some are chewy—but all are good to eat.

4 medium-size baking potatoes (about 1 pound)

¼ cup vegetable oil or melted butter or margarine

1 teaspoon salt

½ teaspoon black pepper

½ teaspoon dried thyme, oregano, sage, or basil, crumbled (optional)

1. Preheat the oven to 450°F. Peel the **potatoes** and cut them into slices about ⅛ inch thick. Place the slices in a bowl with the **oil, salt,** and **pepper,** and the **thyme** or other herbs, if desired. Toss to mix well. Place the slices in a greased 15½"x 10½"x 1" baking pan, spreading out the slices so that they overlap slightly.

2. Bake the potatoes, uncovered, for about 20 minutes—or longer if you prefer them crisper.

Tip: This recipe can be halved.

Glorious Mashed Potatoes ⊕

Preparation: **9 minutes**   Cooking: **15 minutes**   Serves **4**   Calories per serving: **240**

These potatoes always draw raves, yet present a dilemma—should you tell how easy they are to prepare?

3 large baking potatoes (about 1½ pounds)

¼ cup milk

2 tablespoons butter or margarine, softened

¼ cup sour cream

1 package (3 ounces) cream cheese with chives at room temperature

½ teaspoon salt

⅛ teaspoon black pepper

1 teaspoon minced fresh or freeze-dried chives (optional)

1. Peel the **potatoes** and cut them into ¼-inch slices. Place the slices in a 2-quart saucepan, add water to cover, set the lid on the pan askew, and boil for 15 minutes, or until tender.

2. Drain the potatoes and mash them with a potato masher or fork, adding the **milk** to moisten them. Mix in the **butter, sour cream,** and **cream cheese** until well blended. Season with the **salt** and **pepper,** and sprinkle with the **chives** if used.

Tips: 1. To reduce this recipe to serve 2, use 2 medium-size potatoes instead of 3 large ones and halve the amounts of all the other ingredients. 2. If you have any leftover potatoes, shape them into patties and fry them in vegetable oil 5 minutes per side. 3. To keep the potatoes warm for up to half an hour, cover with aluminum foil and set in a 250°F oven.

Potato Pancakes 🐷

Preparation: **10 minutes**   Cooking: **20 minutes**   Serves **4**   Calories per serving: **275**

Try these with roast beef or pork, or as a main course with applesauce for a light meal. The recipe will give you about 16 pancakes, each about 2 inches in diameter and ½ inch thick.

3 large baking potatoes (about 1½ pounds), peeled and coarsely grated

1 small yellow onion, peeled and finely chopped

1 egg

2 tablespoons all-purpose flour

¼ teaspoon salt

6 tablespoons vegetable oil

1. Combine the **potatoes** with the **onion** and set aside. Beat together the **egg, flour,** and **salt.** Heat 3 tablespoons of the **oil** in a 12-inch skillet.

2. Quickly mix the potatoes and onion with the egg mixture to form a batter. Drop the batter by rounded tablespoonsful into the skillet, spacing the pancakes about 1 inch apart. (You will be able to cook only 8 at a time.) Flatten each pancake slightly with a pancake turner.

3. Cook the pancakes, uncovered, for 5 minutes, then flip them over with the turner and cook an additional 5 minutes. Drain the pancakes on paper toweling, put them on a platter, and set them, uncovered, in a keep-warm (250°F) oven while you make the remaining pancakes.

4. Add the remaining 3 tablespoons of oil to the skillet and cook the remaining pancakes precisely as you did the first batch. Serve hot.

Spanish Sweet Potatoes ⬡

Preparation: **10 minutes**   Cooking: **15 minutes**   Serves **4**   Calories per serving: **265**

Instead of candying sweet potatoes, try this recipe for a change of pace.

4 medium-size sweet potatoes (about 1½ pounds)

3 tablespoons olive or vegetable oil

1 medium-size sweet red or green pepper, cored, seeded, and chopped

1 medium-size yellow onion, peeled and chopped

½ teaspoon salt

½ teaspoon paprika

1 tablespoon minced parsley (optional)

1. Peel the **sweet potatoes** and cut them into ½-inch cubes. Bring about 1 inch of lightly salted water to a boil in a 2-quart saucepan. Add the potatoes and cook, covered, for 5 to 6 minutes, or until they are tender but not too soft. Drain.

2. Heat the **oil** in a 12-inch skillet, and add the potatoes, **sweet pepper, onion, salt,** and **paprika,** and the **parsley** if used. Sauté over moderate heat for about 10 minutes, or until the potatoes begin to brown. Drain and serve.

> **Tip:** *This recipe can be halved.*

Sweet Potato Pancakes 🐖 ⬡

Preparation: **7 minutes**   Cooking: **10 minutes**   Serves **4**   Calories per serving: **165**

This unusual way to use sweet potatoes is a wonderful variation on the traditional potato pancake recipe.

2 cups grated peeled raw sweet potatoes (about ½ pound potatoes)

2 eggs, lightly beaten

1 teaspoon salt

1 tablespoon all-purpose flour

Pinch baking powder

1 tablespoon light or dark brown sugar

2 tablespoons vegetable oil

1. Mix the grated **sweet potatoes** with the **eggs, salt, flour, baking powder,** and **brown sugar.** Heat the **oil** in a 12-inch skillet over moderately high heat.

2. Drop the batter into the hot oil by rounded tablespoonsful, flattening them slightly with a pancake turner. You will get about 8 pancakes.

3. Fry the pancakes about 5 minutes, or until they are golden brown on the bottom. Flip the pancakes over with the turner and cook for 4 or 5 more minutes. Drain briefly on paper toweling, and serve hot.

> **Tip:** *To vary the flavor, omit the brown sugar from the batter and substitute 1 small yellow onion, minced, and a pinch each of dried thyme and dried rosemary.*

Spinach Dressed with Oil and Vinegar ⊙ ⊕

Preparation: **5 minutes**   Cooking: **5 minutes**   Serves **4**   Calories per serving: **155**

Dress up spinach the Italian way.

2 packages (10 ounces each) fresh spinach

¼ cup olive oil

2 cloves garlic, peeled and minced

3 tablespoons red wine vinegar

½ teaspoon salt

Pinch black pepper

1. Trim the **spinach** of coarse stems and blemished leaves, and wash it.

2. Heat the **olive oil** and **garlic** in a large (6- or 7-quart) pot over moderate heat, and cook until the garlic releases its fragrance—about 1 minute. Add the spinach by handfuls, stirring occasionally with a wooden spoon.

3. When all the spinach has been added, stir in the **vinegar, salt,** and **pepper.** Serve hot, at room temperature, or slightly chilled.

> *Tip: This recipe can be halved.*

Spinach with Two Cheeses

Preparation: **15 minutes**   Cooking: **10 minutes**   Serves **4**   Calories per serving: **315**

Even if spinach is not your favorite vegetable, you should like this.

2 packages (10 ounces each) fresh spinach or 2 packages (10 ounces each) frozen chopped spinach

5 tablespoons butter or margarine

1 cup ricotta cheese or small-curd cottage cheese

1 egg

3 tablespoons all-purpose flour

¼ teaspoon salt

⅛ teaspoon black pepper

⅛ teaspoon ground nutmeg

3 tablespoons grated Parmesan cheese

1. Preheat the oven to 425°F. Trim the fresh **spinach** of coarse stems and blemished leaves, and wash it.

2. Place the spinach in a large (6- or 7-quart) pot with just the water that clings to the leaves and cook, covered, for 5 minutes, or until it is just limp. If you are using frozen spinach, cook according to package directions. Drain the cooked spinach in a sieve or colander, pressing out most of the liquid from the spinach with the back of a large spoon. Chop the spinach fine.

3. Melt 3 tablespoons of the **butter** in the same pot. Remove from the heat. Add the chopped spinach, **ricotta cheese, egg, flour, salt, pepper,** and **nutmeg.** Beat with a spoon until thoroughly mixed.

4. Place the mixture in a buttered 8"x 8"x 2" baking dish. Dot with the remaining 2 tablespoons of butter, and sprinkle the top with the **Parmesan cheese.** Bake, uncovered, for 10 minutes, or until the cheese melts.

> *Tip: This dish reheats well. Place the spinach in the top of a double boiler over simmering water. Cover and heat.*

VEGETABLES

Sweet and Sour Spinach

Preparation: **5 minutes** Cooking: **7 minutes**   Serves **4** Calories per serving: **115**

2 packages (10 ounces each)
fresh spinach or 2 packages
(10 ounces each) frozen
chopped spinach

4 slices bacon, cut into
1-inch strips

1 tablespoon all-purpose
flour

1/2 cup water

3 tablespoons cider vinegar

1 1/2 teaspoons sugar

1/4 teaspoon salt

1/8 teaspoon black pepper

Tip: This recipe can be halved.

1. Trim the fresh **spinach** of coarse stems and blemished leaves, and wash it.

2. Place the spinach into a large (6- or 7-quart) pot with just the water that clings to the leaves, and cook, covered, for 5 minutes, or until it is just limp. If you are using frozen spinach, cook according to package directions. Drain the cooked spinach well and press out as much liquid as you can. Put the spinach into a serving bowl and set in a keep-warm (250°F) oven.

3. While the spinach is cooking, cook the **bacon** in a 10-inch skillet over moderately high heat until crisp—about 5 minutes. Drain on paper toweling, set aside, and pour out all but 1 tablespoon of the bacon drippings. Blend the **flour** into the remaining drippings.

4. Mix together the **water, vinegar, sugar, salt,** and **pepper.** Add the mixture slowly to the bacon drippings and flour, blending until smooth and thick. Pour the sauce over the spinach. Serve with the bacon crumbled on top.

Sautéed Summer Squash

Preparation: **3 minutes** Cooking: **7 minutes**   Serves **4** Calories per serving: **85**

1 tablespoon butter
or margarine

1 tablespoon olive oil

1 clove garlic, peeled and
minced (optional)

3/4 pound summer squash,
sliced into 1/4-inch rounds

1/2 teaspoon dried basil,
crumbled

2 medium-size tomatoes,
peeled and chopped

1/2 teaspoon salt

1/4 teaspoon black pepper

1. In a 10-inch skillet, heat the **butter** and **oil,** add the **garlic** if used, and cook, uncovered, over moderate heat for 30 seconds.

2. Add the **squash,** tossing to coat it with butter and oil. Sprinkle the **basil** over the top. Cook, tossing occasionally, for 5 or 6 minutes, or until the squash is just tender.

3. Add the **tomatoes, salt,** and **pepper.** Heat through, toss, and serve. (Note: It is important to add the salt at the end. If used early in the cooking, it releases moisture from the squash and makes it too soft.)

Tip: Try the following variation: Omit the olive oil and basil, increase the butter to 2 tablespoons, and add 1/4 cup snipped fresh dill.

Yellow Squash Casserole ◁▷

Preparation: **10 minutes**   Cooking: **12 minutes**   Serves **4**   Calories per serving: **295**

This squash and cheese casserole with its bread-crumb topping is a perfect vegetable dish for dinner parties or potluck suppers.

4 tablespoons (¹/₂ stick) butter or margarine

1 large yellow onion, peeled and finely chopped

1 pound yellow squash or zucchini

1 egg, lightly beaten

1 cup shredded sharp Cheddar cheese (about 4 ounces)

¹/₈ teaspoon ground nutmeg

Pinch salt

¹/₈ teaspoon black pepper

¹/₂ teaspoon dried marjoram, crumbled (optional)

Pinch dried thyme, crumbled (optional)

¹/₃ cup fine dry bread crumbs

1. Preheat the oven to 425°F. Melt 3 tablespoons of the **butter** in a 12-inch skillet over moderate heat. Add the **onion** and cook, covered, for 5 minutes, or until soft.

2. Meanwhile, cut the **squash** into ¹/₄-inch slices. If they are large, quarter them. Add the squash to the onion, cover, and cook for 3 minutes, or until crisp-tender.

3. In a bowl, blend the **egg, cheese, nutmeg, salt,** and **pepper,** and the **marjoram** and **thyme** if used. Remove the squash from the heat, and blend in the egg and cheese mixture.

4. Pour into a buttered 9"x 9"x 2" baking dish, top with the **bread crumbs,** and dot with the remaining butter. Bake, uncovered, for 10 minutes, or until bubbly, then broil for 2 minutes, or until golden brown.

Tips: 1. This recipe can be halved. 2. Because of the sharpness of the cheese, you will need very little salt. 3. This dish may be prepared—but not baked—a few hours ahead, covered, and refrigerated.

Zucchini Patties 🐷

Preparation: **8 minutes**   Cooking: **16 minutes**   Serves **4**   Calories per serving: **225**

In summer, when you're desperate for a new way to cook the zucchini from your garden, try these patties.

2 tablespoons butter or margarine

3 tablespoons vegetable oil

3¹/₂ cups coarsely grated zucchini (3 or 4 medium-size zucchini)

¹/₄ cup all-purpose flour

2 eggs, lightly beaten

¹/₂ teaspoon salt

¹/₈ teaspoon black pepper

1. Heat the **butter** and **oil** together in a 12-inch skillet over moderate heat. Meanwhile, quickly mix the **zucchini** with the **flour, eggs, salt,** and **pepper** to form a batter.

2. Drop tablespoonsful of batter into the hot butter and oil to form 6 patties 2 to 2¹/₂ inches in diameter. Flatten each patty slightly with the back of a spoon. Reserve the remaining batter.

3. Cook the patties for about 4 minutes on each side, or until they are golden brown and crusty. Remove them to a platter covered with paper toweling and set in a keep-warm (250°F) oven. Using the remaining batter, cook 6 more patties in the same manner, adding 1 more tablespoon of oil to the skillet, if needed.

VEGETABLES

78

Stuffed Zucchini

Preparation: **15 minutes**   Cooking: **15 minutes**   Serves **4**   Calories per serving: **125**

2 narrow 6- to 7-inch-long zucchini or yellow squash (about 1 pound)

1 cup fresh sweet corn kernels (cut from 2 medium-size ears of corn) or 1 cup frozen whole-kernel corn

1/2 cup small-curd cottage cheese

1/8 teaspoon salt

1/8 teaspoon black pepper

2 tablespoons chopped green onions (optional)

1/4 cup grated Parmesan cheese

Serve as a vegetable main course. While the squash is baking, you'll have more than enough time to make a tomato salad to serve with it.

1. Preheat the oven to 400°F. Cut the **squash** in half lengthwise and scoop the seeds out of each half with a teaspoon.

2. Mix together the **corn, cottage cheese, salt, pepper,** and **green onions.** Spoon the mixture into the squash halves, mounding it slightly. Top with the **Parmesan cheese.**

3. Place the squash in a buttered 8"x 8"x 2" baking dish and bake, uncovered, for 15 minutes, or until the squash is tender and the cheese topping has melted.

Baked Zucchini with Tomatoes ⏺

Preparation: **10 minutes**   Cooking: **25 minutes**   Serves **4**   Calories per serving: **170**

This colorful dish has a distinctly Mediterranean flair. Serve it with something simple—roast chicken, for example, or pasta and cheese.

3 medium-size zucchini (about 1 pound)

2 medium-size tomatoes

1 medium-size sweet green pepper, cored, seeded, and chopped

1 medium-size yellow onion, peeled and finely chopped

1/2 teaspoon salt

1/8 teaspoon black pepper

1/4 cup olive or vegetable oil

1. Preheat the oven to 400°F. Trim the ends off the **zucchini** and remove the stem ends from the **tomatoes.** Cut both vegetables into 1/2-inch slices and arrange them in a buttered 1- or 1½-quart baking dish with their edges overlapping slightly, alternating the tomato with the zucchini.

2. Scatter the **green pepper, onion, salt,** and **black pepper** over the slices. Drizzle the **oil** evenly over the vegetables.

3. Place the dish in the oven and bake, uncovered, about 25 minutes, or until the squash is crisp-tender.

> **Tips: 1.** *You can substitute yellow squash for the zucchini.* **2.** *This dish may be prepared ahead and baked just before serving, or it may be cooked and reheated.* **3.** *This recipe can be halved.*

VEGETABLES

Sautéed Butternut Squash Slices 🐷

Preparation: 12 minutes   Cooking: 20 minutes   **Serves 4   Calories per serving: 155**

1 medium-size butternut squash (about 1¼ pounds)

4 tablespoons (½ stick) butter or margarine

½ teaspoon salt

¼ teaspoon black pepper

¼ teaspoon ground nutmeg

2 tablespoons finely chopped parsley

Who would ever believe that a winter squash can take so little time to cook!

1. Cut the **squash** into ¼-inch slices, peel the slices, and discard the seeds and stringy pith.

2. Melt the **butter** in a 12-inch skillet over moderate heat. Add the squash and **salt.** Cover.

3. Cook about 20 minutes, or until the squash is tender, turning the slices frequently. Season with the **pepper, nutmeg,** and **parsley,** and serve.

Baked Winter Squash 🐷

Preparation: 5 minutes   Cooking: 30 minutes   **Serves 4   Calories per serving: 185**

4 tablespoons (½ stick) butter or margarine

1 large butternut or acorn squash (about 2 pounds)

Tip: To vary the dish, about 5 minutes before the squash is done, sprinkle with 1 tablespoon brown sugar, a pinch of ground nutmeg, and a pinch of ground allspice.

If you like winter squash but don't have time to bake it in halves or quarters, this recipe is perfect for you.

1. Preheat the oven to 400°F. Melt the **butter** in the oven in a 9"x 9"x 2" baking dish. Meanwhile, trim the **squash,** cut it in half lengthwise, and scoop out the seeds. Cut the squash into 1½-inch chunks.

2. Add the squash to the baking dish and toss to coat with the melted butter. Bake, uncovered, for 15 minutes, toss again, and bake another 15 minutes. Serve with a little of the butter spooned over each portion.

Cherry Tomatoes in Brown-Butter Sauce ⊘

Preparation: 4 minutes   Cooking: 5 minutes   **Serves 4   Calories per serving: 130**

4 tablespoons (½ stick) butter or margarine

1 tablespoon lemon juice

¼ cup finely chopped parsley

1 teaspoon dried tarragon, crumbled (optional)

1 pint (2 cups) cherry tomatoes, washed and stemmed

Redolent of herbs and rich with butter, this savory way of cooking cherry tomatoes comes from France.

1. Melt the **butter** in a heavy 10-inch skillet and stir over low heat until the butter turns a deep golden brown. Stir in the **lemon juice** and **parsley,** and the **tarragon** if used.

2. Add the **tomatoes,** raise the heat to moderate, and cook, swirling the skillet constantly, until the tomato skins begin to burst—about 3 minutes. Serve with French bread for soaking up the herb butter.

Broiled Tomatoes ⊘

Preparation: **15 minutes** Cooking: **3 minutes** Serves **4** Calories per serving: **340**

4 large, firm, ripe tomatoes

1/2 teaspoon salt

1/8 teaspoon black pepper

1 1/2 cups shredded Swiss cheese (about 6 ounces)

3 tablespoons grated Parmesan cheese

4 teaspoons Dijon mustard

1/2 teaspoon dried marjoram or oregano, crumbled

1/2 teaspoon dried basil, crumbled

1/4 cup half-and-half

2 tablespoons butter or margarine, melted

3/4 cup fine dry bread crumbs

Although this is an ideal recipe for good summer tomatoes, it is also a way to add flavor to dull winter ones. It's a fine dish for lunch.

1. Preheat the broiler. Remove the stem ends from the **tomatoes,** and cut the tomatoes into 1/2-inch slices. Place the slices on an ungreased 15 1/2"x 10 1/2"x 1" baking sheet and sprinkle them with the **salt** and **pepper.**

2. In a bowl, combine the **cheeses, mustard, marjoram, basil,** and **half-and-half.** Spread this mixture evenly over the sliced tomatoes.

3. In another bowl, combine the **butter** and **bread crumbs.** Spoon over the tomatoes and broil 5 inches from the heat for 3 minutes, or until bubbly and touched with brown.

> **Tip:** *You can substitute Cheddar cheese for the Swiss cheese, if you wish.*

Baked Stuffed Tomatoes ⊘

Preparation: **10 minutes** Cooking: **10 minutes** Serves **4** Calories per serving: **135**

2 large, firm, ripe tomatoes, each about 2 1/2 inches across

1/4 teaspoon salt

1/4 teaspoon black pepper

1 small clove garlic, peeled and minced

2 teaspoons grated yellow onion

1/4 teaspoon dried basil, crumbled

1/4 teaspoon dried thyme, crumbled

1/3 cup fine dry bread crumbs

1/4 cup finely chopped parsley

2 tablespoons olive or vegetable oil

1/4 cup grated Parmesan cheese

Fill tomato halves with spicy bread crumb stuffing and bake them in the oven for a special treat.

1. Adjust the oven rack to the upper third of the oven and preheat the oven to 400°F.

2. Remove the stem ends from the **tomatoes** and cut the tomatoes in half crosswise. Remove the seeds from the tomatoes with your fingertip.

3. In a small bowl, mix together the **salt, pepper, garlic, onion, basil, thyme, bread crumbs, parsley, oil,** and **cheese.** Spoon the mixture into the tomato halves.

4. Place the tomatoes in an ungreased 8"x 8"x 2" baking pan and bake, uncovered, for 10 to 12 minutes. The tomatoes should be tender but still hold their shape. If baked longer than 12 minutes, they will be too soft. Serve hot or cold.

> **Tip:** *You can use sweet green peppers instead of the tomatoes if you double the filling recipe. Cut off the tops of 4 medium-size peppers and remove the seeds. Cook the peppers in boiling water for 10 minutes. Then stuff and bake them as you would the tomatoes.*

Fried Tomatoes ⊘

Preparation: **10 minutes** Cooking: **6 minutes**   Serves **4** Calories per serving: **185**

For best results use only firm tomatoes, not soft ones.

3 medium-size ripe or green tomatoes

1 egg

½ cup fine dry bread crumbs

½ teaspoon salt

½ teaspoon black pepper

½ teaspoon dried oregano or thyme, crumbled (optional)

¼ cup bacon drippings or vegetable oil

1. Wash and dry the **tomatoes,** but do not peel them. Cut a thin slice off the top and bottom of each tomato and discard. Cut the tomatoes into slices about ½ inch thick.

2. In one pie plate or shallow bowl, beat the **egg** lightly; in another, combine the **bread crumbs, salt,** and **pepper,** and the **oregano** if used. Dip the tomato slices on both sides into the beaten egg, then press the slices on both sides into the bread-crumb mixture.

3. Heat the **bacon drippings** in a 10- or 12-inch skillet over moderately high heat. Slip half the slices into the skillet using a pancake turner and fry, uncovered, until golden brown, then flip them with the turner, and fry on the other side—about 1½ to 2 minutes on each side. Transfer the tomatoes to paper toweling to drain. Cook the remaining slices in the same manner.

Glazed Turnips

Preparation: **8 minutes** Cooking: **17 minutes**   Serves **4** Calories per serving: **130**

Use either white or yellow turnips (rutabagas)—whichever you prefer. The brown sugar and orange bring out the natural sweetness of the turnips.

1 pound white or yellow turnips

1 tablespoon butter or margarine

⅓ cup firmly packed light brown sugar

Grated rind and juice of ½ orange

¼ teaspoon salt

¼ teaspoon black pepper

1. Peel the **turnips** and cut them into ½-inch cubes. Bring about 1 inch of lightly salted water to a boil in a 2-quart saucepan. Add the turnips, cover, and cook for 15 to 20 minutes. Drain.

2. Meanwhile, melt the **butter** in a 1-quart saucepan, and add the **sugar, orange rind**, and **orange juice.** Simmer the mixture, uncovered, for 2 or 3 minutes, or until it is slightly thickened. Keep warm until the turnips are done.

3. Add the drained turnips to the orange mixture and toss briefly over moderate heat until they are just glazed. Season with the **salt** and **pepper.**

Tips: 1. These turnips can be reheated. 2. Try turnips creamed, also. After boiling, drain the turnips. Melt 2 tablespoons of butter in the saucepan, add the turnips, ½ cup heavy cream, and ½ teaspoon grated lemon rind. Bring to a boil and serve.

POULTRY

Hardly any meat or fish is as inexpensive as poultry—especially chicken and turkey. But poultry has other attributes besides price. It is high in protein, low in cholesterol, and most people like it.

Chicken, in particular, is exceptionally versatile because of its mild flavor. It goes well with all types of vegetables, herbs, and spices, and even fruits. Here you'll find many new and interesting delicacies, including golden nuggets of chicken with herbs and cheese, chicken breasts with an elegant mustard cream sauce, and intriguingly spiced dishes from around the world. In some cases, chicken or turkey has been made to substitute for more costly beef and veal, as in Chicken Stroganoff, Sautéed Chicken Scallops with Marsala, and Chicken Scaloppine.

Although roast chicken and roast turkey breast take longer to cook than most foods in this book, they deserve a special place here. You will find that many quick, good dishes can be made from the leftovers, such as Chicken Hash and Chicken with Apples and Onions. Turkey can be substituted for chicken in these dishes, too, making them doubly useful.

Basic Broiled Chicken

Preparation: **3 minutes**   Cooking: **20 minutes**   Serves **4**   Calories per serving: **290-350**

Broiled chicken is one of the simplest and thriftiest of all meat dishes. It is also remarkably versatile. Whether you cook the basic broiled chicken described in the main recipe or one of the variations given in the Tip below, you will have a tasty, satisfying main course. Serve the chicken with Corn in Parsley Cream, page 69, or buttered noodles and a green vegetable or salad.

1 chicken (2½ to 3 pounds), split lengthwise or quartered

½ teaspoon salt

¼ teaspoon black pepper

4 tablespoons (½ stick) butter or margarine, melted, or ¼ cup vegetable oil

1. Preheat the broiler. Sprinkle the **chicken** with the **salt** and **pepper,** and brush with the **butter.**

2. Place the chicken, skin side down, on the rack of the broiler pan, and broil 6 to 9 inches from the heat for 10 to 15 minutes, basting occasionally with the melted butter.

3. Turn the chicken, brush with the butter, and broil 10 to 15 minutes longer, basting occasionally with the butter. Pierce the thickest part of the thigh with a small knife; if the meat is no longer pink, the chicken is done. If the chicken browns too quickly, reduce the heat or move the chicken farther away from the heat.

> *Tip: You can vary plain broiled chicken by adding a simple marinade. To make the marinade, melt ¼ cup butter or margarine in a small saucepan and heat for 3 to 5 minutes with the ingredient or ingredients for any of the variations suggested below. Brush the chicken with the mixture and broil immediately, basting occasionally. To give the chicken even more flavor, let it stand for 15 minutes or longer after you brush it with the marinade.*
> *Garlic-Broiled Chicken. Add to the butter 3 tablespoons lemon juice, 1 teaspoon crumbled dried oregano or rosemary, and 2 to 4 cloves garlic, minced.*
> *Orange-Broiled Chicken. Add 3 tablespoons orange marmalade to the butter.*
> *Curry-Broiled Chicken. Add to the butter 2 teaspoons curry powder, 1 tablespoon minced chutney, and ½ clove garlic, minced.*

Low-Calorie Celery-Broiled Chicken 🐷 ▷

Preparation: **3 minutes** Cooking: **20 minutes**   Serves **4**   Calories per serving: **240-300**

Broiled chicken is an ideal diet dish if it is not drowned in butter, but you may find dry-broiled chicken dull and monotonous. If so, brighten up your diet with this variation. The chicken is rubbed with lemon instead of butter and further flavored with celery. The only calories in this dish are the ones in the chicken itself. If you do not eat the skin, the calories per serving are reduced to 160 - 200, depending on the size of the chicken.

1 chicken (2½ to 3 pounds), split lengthwise or quartered

3 tablespoons lemon juice

½ teaspoon salt

½ to 1 teaspoon black pepper

4 stalks celery, cut in half

1. Preheat the broiler. Rub the **chicken** all over with the **lemon juice,** and sprinkle with the **salt** and **pepper.** Place the chicken, skin side down, on the rack of the broiler pan. Put 2 pieces of the **celery** into the cavity of each chicken half or 1 piece into each quarter.

2. Place the broiler pan 6 to 9 inches from the heat, and broil the chicken for 10 to 12 minutes. Turn the chicken skin side up, and place the remaining pieces of celery over the chicken. Broil until golden brown and tender—about 10 minutes. Pierce the thickest part of the thigh with a small knife; if the meat is no longer pink, the chicken is done. Discard the celery. Serve with Baked Stuffed Tomatoes, page 81.

Chicken Florentine

Preparation: **5 minutes** Cooking: **25 minutes**   Serves **4**   Calories per serving: **375**

2½ pounds chicken thighs or drumsticks

1 package (10 ounces) fresh spinach

6 tablespoons butter or margarine

3 cloves garlic, peeled and minced

¼ cup fine dry bread crumbs

¼ cup grated Parmesan cheese

> *Tips: 1. Save and freeze the water the chicken cooked in and use it as a broth at another time. 2. The chicken may be cooked ahead and refrigerated for a day or two. Reheat, uncovered, in a 350°F oven for 20 to 30 minutes.*

1. Skin the **chicken** while you bring 1 quart of lightly salted water to a boil in a 12- or 14-inch skillet. Add the chicken and simmer, covered, for 20 minutes.

2. Preheat the broiler. Trim the **spinach** of coarse stems and blemished leaves, and wash it. Melt 3 tablespoons of the **butter** in a 4-quart saucepan, add the **garlic,** and cook, uncovered, over moderately low heat for 1 or 2 minutes, or until golden but not brown. Add the spinach and cook, stirring, until it is just limp—4 to 5 minutes. Transfer the spinach to a buttered 9"x 9"x 2" flameproof baking dish.

3. Remove the chicken from the water, pat it dry with paper toweling, and place it on top of the spinach. Melt the remaining 3 tablespoons of butter, combine with the **bread crumbs** and **cheese,** and sprinkle the mixture over the chicken. Broil 4 inches from the heat until the chicken is golden brown—about 3 or 4 minutes.

Roast Chicken

Preparation: 5 minutes Cooking: **1¼ hours** Serves **4–8** Calories per 4-ounce serving: **285**

Not only is roast chicken an excellent main course, but the leftovers form the basis for a variety of imaginative dishes, as a number of recipes in this section prove. To serve 4 persons, roast a 2½-pound chicken. To obtain leftovers for recipes calling for cooked chicken, either roast a larger bird, which will take longer to cook, or 2 smaller ones, which cook as quickly as 1.

1 chicken (2½ to 8 pounds)

1 teaspoon salt

1 or 2 cloves garlic, peeled and minced

1 teaspoon dried thyme, oregano, rosemary, or sage, crumbled (optional)

2 tablespoons butter or margarine, softened, or 2 tablespoons vegetable oil

Tip: Freeze the gizzard, heart, and neck that come with the chicken. When you have collected 4 or more packages of giblets, make a chicken broth by simmering them, uncovered, in 1 quart of water with 1 sliced carrot, 1 sliced onion, and a pinch of thyme. Strain. Freeze the livers separately for another use.

1. Preheat the oven to 375°F. Remove the package of giblets from the cavity of the **chicken**. Pull out the loose fat from the inside of the chicken. Wash the chicken and pat it dry with paper toweling.

2. Rub the chicken inside and out with the **salt** and **garlic,** and the **thyme** or other herb if used. Fasten the neck skin to the back of the chicken with a skewer and fold the wings across the back of the chicken. Tie the ends of the drumsticks to the tail.

3. Rub the outside of the chicken with the **butter.** Place the chicken, breast side up, on a rack in a 13"x 9"x 2" roasting pan. Do not add water and do not cover.

4. Roast the chicken for 1¼ hours or more, depending on its size. A 2½- to 3-pound chicken should take 1¼ to 1¾ hours, a 3- to 4-pound chicken 1¾ to 2¼ hours. A 5- to 8-pound chicken should be roasted in a 325°F oven and takes 2½ to 3½ hours. The chicken is done when you can easily move the drumstick. To check further, pierce the thickest part of the drumstick with a small knife; if the juices run clear, the chicken is done. Let the chicken rest for 10 minutes to distribute the juices and settle the meat before carving.

Watercress Stuffing

Preparation: 17 minutes Cooking: **15 minutes** Serves **4** Calories per serving: **190**

5 tablespoons butter or margarine

1 medium-size yellow onion, peeled and minced

2 stalks celery, minced

1 bunch watercress, minced

2 cups diced dry bread

½ teaspoon salt

Assemble this while the chicken is roasting and bake it on a shelf above the bird.

1. Preheat the oven to 375°F. Melt the **butter** in a 12-inch skillet over moderate heat. Add the **onion** and **celery,** and cook, uncovered, for 10 minutes, or until the vegetables are soft.

2. Stir in the **watercress** and cook, stirring, for 3 minutes. Add the **bread** and **salt,** and toss to mix. Spoon the mixture into a buttered 8"x 8"x 2" baking dish and bake, uncovered, for 15 minutes.

Chicken Hash 🐷

Preparation: **15 minutes**   Cooking: **15 minutes**   Serves **6**   Calories per serving: **315**

3 medium-size all-purpose
potatoes, peeled and diced

6 slices bacon, cut into
1-inch strips

1 small yellow onion, peeled
and finely chopped

1/2 cup chopped green onions

3/4 cup diced celery

2 cups cubed cooked chicken

1 cup half-and-half

1/2 teaspoon salt

1/4 teaspoon black pepper

*Tips: 1. If you like, you can
substitute turkey for the chicken.
You can also omit the bacon and
use 3 tablespoons vegetable
oil instead of the bacon drippings.
2. This recipe can be made ahead,
refrigerated, and reheated.
When reheating, add a little oil to
the skillet.*

*To prepare this dish quickly, cut up the onions, celery,
and chicken while the potatoes and bacon are cooking.*

1. Bring 1 inch of lightly salted water to a boil in a
1-quart saucepan. Add the **potatoes,** set the lid
askew on the pan, and cook for 5 minutes.

2. Meanwhile, cook the **bacon** in a heavy 9- or
10- inch skillet over moderately high heat until
crisp—about 5 minutes. Drain the bacon on
paper toweling and reserve. Pour off half
the bacon drippings. Drain the potatoes.

3. Raise the heat to high and add the potatoes,
yellow onion, green onions, celery, and
chicken to the skillet. Cook, stirring, to brown all
the ingredients slightly—about 3 minutes.

4. Lower the heat to moderately high. Add half
the **half-and-half,** pressing down on the mixture.
Let the liquid cook off completely, then scrape
up any crust that forms, and mix into the hash.
Repeat with the rest of the half-and-half. This
should take about 12 minutes altogether.

5. Add the **salt** and **pepper,** and crumble the
bacon over the top. Serve with peas or broccoli.

Chicken and Dumplings 🐷

Preparation: **12 minutes**   Cooking: **15 minutes**   Serves **4**   Calories per serving: **580**

6 cups chicken broth

2 cups cubed cooked chicken

4 tablespoons (1/2 stick)
butter or margarine

1 clove garlic, peeled
and minced

1/4 teaspoon black pepper

1 cup cooked peas or carrots
(optional)

1 1/2 cups unsifted all-purpose
flour

3 teaspoons baking powder

1/2 teaspoon salt

1/4 cup vegetable shortening

1/2 to 2/3 cup ice water

1. In a 3-quart saucepan, combine the **chicken
broth, chicken, butter, garlic,** and **pepper,** and
the **peas** if used. Bring the mixture to a boil,
lower the heat, and simmer for 1 minute.

2. In a mixing bowl, combine the **flour, baking
powder,** and **salt.** Blend in the **vegetable
shortening** until the mixture is coarse and
mealy. Stir in just enough **ice water** to make a
light dough.

3. Bring the chicken mixture back to a boil, lower
the heat, and simmer for 1 minute. Drop the
dumpling dough by rounded tablespoonsful into
the gently bubbling broth, spacing them as
evenly as possible.

4. Cover and simmer for 15 minutes without
lifting the cover. Ladle into soup plates. Serve
with a green salad.

Chicken with Apples and Onions 🐷

Preparation: 10 minutes Cooking: **20 minutes** | Serves **4** Calories per serving: **400**

6 tablespoons butter or margarine

1 medium-size tart apple, peeled and diced

1 medium-size yellow onion, peeled and chopped

2 stalks celery, chopped

1/2 cup apple juice

1/2 teaspoon salt

1/4 teaspoon black pepper

Pinch ground nutmeg

2 tablespoons all-purpose flour

1 cup half-and-half

2 cups cubed cooked chicken

1. Melt 4 tablespoons of the **butter** in a 2-quart saucepan over moderate heat. Add the **apple, onion,** and **celery,** and cook, uncovered, for 5 minutes.

2. Add the **apple juice, salt, pepper,** and **nutmeg,** and simmer, covered, for 5 minutes, or until the vegetables are soft. Uncover and cook 5 minutes longer, or until most of the liquid has evaporated.

3. Meanwhile, melt the remaining 2 tablespoons of butter in a small saucepan over low heat. Blend in the **flour** and cook, stirring, for 1 minute. Gradually add the **half-and-half,** stirring constantly, to make a thick sauce.

4. Add the sauce and the **chicken** to the vegetables. Cover and heat through.

Spicy Curried Chicken with Tomatoes 🥘

Preparation: 18 minutes Cooking: **10 minutes** | Serves **4** Calories per serving: **355**

1/4 cup vegetable oil

1 medium-size yellow onion, peeled and coarsely chopped

2 medium-size sweet green peppers, cored, seeded, and chopped

1 clove garlic, peeled and minced

1/2 teaspoon ground cumin

1/8 teaspoon cayenne pepper

1/4 teaspoon paprika

1 1/2 teaspoons curry powder

1/4 teaspoon ground ginger

1/2 teaspoon salt

2 cups cubed cooked chicken

5 medium-size fresh tomatoes, peeled and sliced, or 1 can (28 ounces) tomatoes, sliced, with their juice

1 1/2 teaspoons lemon juice

This variation on a Burmese recipe has been adapted for the Western palate. Save time by cutting up the cooked chicken while the spices are cooking.

1. Heat the **oil** in a heavy 12-inch skillet over moderate heat. Add the **onion** and **green peppers,** and cook, covered, for 5 minutes, or until the onion is soft.

2. Add the **garlic, cumin, cayenne pepper, paprika, curry powder, ginger,** and **salt.** Reduce the heat to low and cook, covered, 8 minutes longer, stirring occasionally.

3. Put the **chicken** and the **tomatoes** with their juice into the skillet. Simmer, uncovered, for 10 minutes, or until the chicken is heated through and the liquid has thickened slightly.

4. Stir in the **lemon juice.** Serve with rice, noodles, or potatoes and with Baked Winter Squash, page 80.

Tips: 1. This recipe can be halved. 2. You can make this dish ahead and refrigerate it for 1 or 2 days. 3. Substitute beef or lamb for the chicken if you like.

Blue Ribbon Chicken Curry ◖D

Preparation: 20 minutes   **Cooking: 10 minutes**   **Serves 4**   **Calories per serving: 425**

4 tablespoons (½ stick) butter or margarine

¼ cup minced yellow onion

1 small apple, peeled, cored, and finely chopped

3 tablespoons all-purpose flour

1½ cups chicken broth

½ cup half-and-half

½ teaspoon salt

4 teaspoons curry powder

⅛ teaspoon cayenne pepper

¼ teaspoon ground ginger

3 cups cubed cooked chicken

1. Melt the **butter** in a heavy 9- or 10-inch skillet over moderately high heat. Add the **onion** and **apple,** and cook for 10 minutes, or until tender.

2. Blend in the **flour,** add the **chicken broth** and **half-and-half,** and cook, stirring constantly, until the sauce has thickened—about 5 minutes.

3. Stir in the **salt, curry powder, cayenne pepper,** and **ginger.** Add the **chicken,** and cook, covered, over very low heat for 10 minutes. Serve with rice and Shredded Cabbage with Garlic, page 64.

Tips: 1. This recipe can be halved. 2. You can substitute turkey for the chicken. 3. A condiment of plain yogurt mixed with chopped cucumbers, green onions, and radishes is good with curry.

Spicy Chicken Croquettes 🐷

Preparation: 30 minutes   **Cooking: 6 minutes**   **Serves 4**   **Calories per serving: 345**

5 tablespoons butter or margarine

1 small yellow onion, peeled and finely chopped

½ teaspoon dried thyme, crumbled

½ teaspoon dried marjoram, crumbled

2 cups finely chopped cooked chicken

2 tablespoons all-purpose flour

2 tablespoons minced parsley

1 tablespoon Dijon or prepared spicy brown mustard

1 teaspoon salt

⅛ teaspoon black pepper

2 tablespoons milk

1 egg, lightly beaten

¼ cup grated Parmesan or Romano cheese

Here is a thrifty company dish that uses leftover chicken. Serve it with Peas with Orange and Mint, page 71.

1. Melt 2 tablespoons of the **butter** in a heavy 12-inch skillet. Add the **onion,** and cook over moderate heat until soft—about 5 minutes. Blend in the **thyme** and **marjoram,** and cook 1 minute more. Stir in the **chicken, flour, parsley, mustard, salt, pepper,** and **milk,** and cook for 3 minutes. Remove the skillet from the heat, and stir in the **egg** and **cheese.**

2. Pour the mixture into a buttered 8"x 8"x 2" pan, spreading it evenly. Chill in the freezer for 15 minutes, or until stiff enough to shape.

3. Take the pan from the freezer and shape the mixture into 4 oval patties.

4. Melt the remaining 3 tablespoons of butter in the skillet over moderately high heat and brown the croquettes for 3 to 4 minutes on each side.

Tips: 1. You can substitute leftover turkey for the chicken if you wish. 2. These croquettes reheat well—a good make-ahead dish.

Chicken Breasts Geneva ⊘

Preparation: **17 minutes**   Cooking: **8 minutes**   Serves **4**   Calories per serving: **500**

4 tablespoons (½ stick) butter or margarine

¼ cup vegetable oil

1 stalk celery, cut into thin, 2-inch-long strips

2 small carrots, peeled and cut into thin, 2-inch-long strips

1 medium-size yellow onion, peeled and finely chopped

4 slices boiled ham, cut into thin strips

½ teaspoon salt

¼ teaspoon black pepper

¼ cup all-purpose flour

2 whole chicken breasts (4 halves), skinned and boned

4 thin slices Swiss cheese

1. Preheat the broiler. Melt 2 tablespoons of the **butter** with 2 tablespoons of the **oil** in a heavy 9- or 10-inch skillet over moderate heat. Add the **celery, carrots, onion,** and **ham.** Lower the heat, cover, and cook for 10 minutes, stirring occasionally. (The vegetables should not brown.) Meanwhile, blend the **salt, pepper,** and **flour** in a small bowl.

2. Remove the contents of the skillet to a plate, set aside, and in the same skillet, heat the remaining butter and oil over moderately high heat. Coat the **chicken breasts** with the flour mixture and shake off any excess. Place the breasts in the skillet and brown for 3 minutes on each side, lowering the heat to moderate, if necessary, to prevent burning.

3. Arrange the chicken pieces on an aluminum-foil–lined 15½"x 10½"x 1" baking pan. Top each piece with some of the vegetable-ham mixture, then with a slice of **cheese.** Broil just until the cheese melts. Watch carefully to prevent the cheese from burning.

Chicken Breasts with Tarragon ⊘ ◐

Preparation: **1 minute**   Cooking: **16 minutes**   Serves **4**   Calories per serving: **235**

2 tablespoons butter or margarine

2 whole chicken breasts (4 halves), skinned and boned

2 teaspoons all-purpose flour

½ teaspoon salt

½ teaspoon dried tarragon, crumbled

1 teaspoon Dijon or prepared spicy brown mustard

½ cup dry white wine or chicken broth

½ cup half-and-half

Tip: This recipe can be halved.

1. Melt the **butter** in a heavy 9- or 10-inch skillet over moderately high heat. Add the **chicken breasts** and brown about 3 minutes on each side. Do not overcook. Remove the breasts to a warm platter.

2. Add the **flour, salt, tarragon,** and **mustard.** Gradually stir in the **wine.** Cook, stirring and scraping up any brown bits stuck to the skillet. Continue to cook until the liquid has boiled down by half. Add the **half-and-half** and cook until the mixture thickens slightly. Return the breasts and any accumulated juices to the skillet to reheat. Spoon the sauce over the breasts. Serve with Skillet Asparagus, page 58, or buttered new potatoes.

Sautéed Chicken Scallops with Marsala ⊡ ⊕

Preparation: **7 minutes** Cooking: **6 minutes**   Serves **4** Calories per serving: **325**

Here is an ideal company dish. It has the flavor and delicacy of the finest cuisine, yet is fast and easy to prepare.

2 whole chicken breasts (4 halves), skinned and boned

3 tablespoons vegetable oil

1/2 cup all-purpose flour

1/2 teaspoon salt

1/8 teaspoon black pepper

1/3 cup Marsala or sweet vermouth

3 tablespoons butter or margarine

> *Tips: 1. This recipe can be halved. 2. You can use turkey cutlets instead of the chicken breasts.*

1. Lay each half **chicken breast** on the work surface, place your hand flat over it, and, cutting parallel to your hand, slice the breast in two.

2. Heat the **oil** in a heavy 9- or 10-inch skillet over moderately high heat. Place the **flour** in a shallow dish. Press the breasts into the flour, coating the pieces on both sides. Shake off any excess flour. Place half the pieces in the skillet and brown them for 1 minute on each side. Remove to a warm platter, and season with the **salt** and **pepper**. Cook the remaining pieces.

3. Tip the skillet and skim off most of the fat. Add the **Marsala,** and boil briskly for 1 minute, scraping up any brown bits stuck to the skillet. Add the **butter** and any juices that have accumulated from the chicken on the platter. When the sauce thickens, reduce the heat to low, add the breasts, and coat them with the sauce.

Chicken with Sweet Peppers ⊡

Preparation: **20 minutes** Cooking: **5 minutes**   Serves **4** Calories per serving: **235**

You can prepare this light, savory dish in almost the time that it takes to cook rice, which goes perfectly with it.

2 tablespoons soy sauce

2 tablespoons ketchup

1 teaspoon cider vinegar

1/4 teaspoon ground ginger

1 teaspoon cornstarch

1/4 teaspoon salt

1/3 cup water

1 clove garlic, peeled and minced

2 green onions, trimmed and thinly sliced

2 whole chicken breasts (4 halves), skinned and boned

2 medium-size sweet green or red peppers or 1 green and 1 red pepper

3 tablespoons vegetable oil

1. In a bowl, make a sauce by mixing the **soy sauce, ketchup, vinegar, ginger, cornstarch, salt, water, garlic,** and **green onions**. Set aside.

2. Cut the **chicken breasts** crosswise (against the grain) into 1/4-inch strips. Core and seed the **peppers,** and cut them into 1/4-inch strips.

3. Heat the **oil** in a heavy 9- or 10-inch skillet over moderately high heat. Add the peppers, raise the heat to high, and cook, stirring with a large spoon, for 2 minutes. The peppers should be crisp-tender. Remove them to a platter.

4. Add the chicken to the skillet. Cook, stirring, over high heat for 2 minutes, or until the chicken is no longer pink. Do not overcook.

5. Return the peppers to the skillet. Stir the sauce and add it to the skillet. Cook, stirring, over high heat until the sauce thickens—about 20 seconds.

> *Tips: 1. You can use flank steak instead of the chicken breasts. 2. This dish can be reheated; you may have to add a few teaspoons of water to thin the sauce.*

Chicken with Mustard Cream ⊘ ⬭

Preparation: 12 minutes   Cooking: **10 minutes**   Serves **4**   Calories per serving: **435**

This tasty dish—one of the specialties of a popular Swiss restaurant in New York City—is excellent for parties.

2 whole chicken breasts (4 halves), skinned and boned

1/2 teaspoon salt

1/4 teaspoon black pepper

3 tablespoons Dijon or prepared spicy brown mustard

1/2 cup all-purpose flour

3 tablespoons butter or margarine

1 cup heavy cream or half-and-half

Tip: 1. This recipe can be halved, or leftovers can be refrigerated for 1 or 2 days. When reheating, use low heat; high heat may curdle the sauce and dry out the meat.

1. Pound the **chicken breasts** between 2 sheets of wax paper to a thickness of about 1/4 inch. Season with the **salt** and **pepper.**

2. Spread both sides of the breasts with 2 tablespoons of the **mustard.** Put the **flour** in a shallow dish or on a sheet of wax paper, and press the breasts into the flour, coating them on both sides. Shake off any excess flour.

3. Melt the **butter** in a heavy 9- or 10-inch skillet over moderately high heat. Brown the breasts in the butter about 3 minutes on each side. (If the breasts have not started to brown after the first 2 minutes, turn up the heat.) Remove the breasts to a warm platter.

4. Pour the **cream** into the skillet and boil rapidly about 2 minutes, scraping up any brown bits stuck to the skillet. Remove the skillet from the heat and stir in the remaining tablespoon of mustard. Taste, and add more salt or mustard to the sauce, if you like.

5. Return the chicken to the skillet and reheat briefly, basting with the sauce. Serve with buttered green peas.

Orange Chicken ⊘ ⬭

Preparation: 5 minutes   Cooking: **15 minutes**   Serves **4**   Calories per serving: **195**

2 whole chicken breasts (4 halves), skinned and boned

2 tablespoons butter or margarine, melted

1/2 teaspoon paprika

1/4 cup finely chopped yellow onion

1 teaspoon salt

1/4 teaspoon dried rosemary, crumbled

Pinch black pepper

1 cup orange juice

Grated rind of 1 orange

1. Preheat the oven to 350°F. Arrange the **chicken breasts** in a 13"x 9"x 2" baking dish. Drizzle the **butter** evenly over the breasts and sprinkle them with the **paprika.**

2. In a small bowl, combine the **onion, salt, rosemary, pepper, orange juice,** and **orange rind.** Pour over the breasts. Bake, uncovered, for 15 minutes or until fork tender, basting the breasts occasionally with the pan juices. Serve with egg noodles or rice, and Green Beans Italian Style, page 59.

Tip: This recipe can be halved.

Golden Chicken Nuggets ⊘

Preparation: **10 minutes**   Cooking: **8 minutes**   Serves **4**   Calories per serving: **355**

Serve these tasty nuggets as a main course (about 8 pieces per serving) or as an hors d'oeuvre.

2 whole chicken breasts (4 halves), skinned and boned

¹⁄₂ cup fine dry bread crumbs

¹⁄₄ cup grated Parmesan cheese

1 teaspoon salt

1 teaspoon dried thyme, crumbled

1 teaspoon dried basil, crumbled

¹⁄₂ cup (1 stick) butter or margarine, melted

Lemon wedges

1. Preheat the oven to 400°F. Cut each half **chicken breast** into 1½-inch cubes.

2. Combine the **bread crumbs, cheese, salt, thyme,** and **basil,** and spread the mixture on a plate. Dip the chicken cubes into the melted **butter,** then coat with the crumb mixture.

3. Arrange the cubes in a single layer on an aluminum-foil–lined 15½"x 10½"x 1" baking pan. Bake for 8 minutes. Serve with **lemon wedges.**

> *Tip: You can prepare these nuggets ahead of time through Step 2. Cover and refrigerate, and bake just before serving.*

POULTRY

Chicken Scaloppine ⊘

Preparation: **10 minutes**   Cooking: **7 minutes**   Serves **4**   Calories per serving: **320**

Scaloppine should be made at the last minute—so make sure your vegetables are ready to serve when you begin the chicken. And because this recipe moves quickly from step to step, you should also have all the ingredients ready before you begin.

2 whole chicken breasts (4 halves), skinned and boned

3 tablespoons vegetable oil

¹⁄₂ cup all-purpose flour

¹⁄₂ teaspoon salt

¹⁄₈ teaspoon black pepper

3 tablespoons butter or margarine

Grated rind of 1 lemon

2 cloves garlic, peeled and minced

¹⁄₃ cup minced parsley

¹⁄₂ cup chicken broth

1. Lay each half **chicken breast** on the work surface, place your hand flat over it, and, cutting parallel to your hand, slice the breast in two.

2. Heat the **oil** in a heavy 9- or 10-inch skillet over moderately high heat. In a shallow dish, combine the **flour, salt,** and **pepper.** Press the chicken into the flour mixture, coating the pieces on both sides. Shake off any excess flour. Place half the pieces in the skillet and brown them for 1 minute on each side. Remove the breasts to a warm platter. Cook the remaining breasts the same way.

3. Add the **butter** to the skillet, along with the **lemon rind, garlic,** and **parsley.** Add the **chicken broth,** scraping up any brown bits stuck to the skillet. Bring the liquid to a boil and let it cook until it thickens slightly.

4. Return the breasts to the pan, along with any accumulated juices, and coat with the sauce. Serve with green beans and potatoes or rice.

> *Tip: You can use turkey cutlets instead of chicken breasts.*

Chicken Stroganoff ⊘ ⊕

Preparation: **8 minutes**   Cooking: **8 minutes**   Serves **4**   Calories per serving: **385**

Here is a lightning-fast main course, good for company. Be sure you have the onion chopped and the mushrooms sliced before you begin the cooking. If you're counting calories, note that using yogurt instead of sour cream reduces the number of calories per serving to 300.

2 whole chicken breasts (4 halves), skinned and boned

4 tablespoons (1/2 stick) butter or margarine

1 teaspoon salt

1 medium-size yellow onion, peeled and finely chopped

1/3 pound mushrooms, sliced

1 1/2 teaspoons paprika

1/4 cup water

2 tablespoons all-purpose flour

3 tablespoons dry sherry or water

1 cup sour cream or plain yogurt

1. Cut each half **chicken breast** crosswise (against the grain) into 10 or 12 strips. Melt the **butter** in a heavy 12-inch skillet over moderately high heat. Add the chicken and sprinkle with the **salt.** Cook for 2 minutes, stirring constantly. Add the **onion, mushrooms,** and **paprika,** and cook 2 minutes longer, continuing to stir. Add the **water.** Reduce the heat to moderate, cover, and cook an additional 2 minutes.

2. Meanwhile, combine the **flour** and **sherry** in a small bowl. Add the mixture to the skillet and cook, stirring rapidly, until the mixture thickens—about 1 minute.

3. Add the **sour cream** and stir until heated through. Do not let the mixture come to a boil. Serve over rice.

> *Tips: 1. This recipe can be halved or doubled.*
> *2. You can garnish the chicken with either 1 tablespoon snipped fresh dill or 1 teaspoon caraway seeds.*

Chicken with Sherry and Raisins

Preparation: **15 minutes**   Cooking: **18 minutes**   Serves **4**   Calories per serving: **460**

2 tablespoons butter or margarine

2 tablespoons vegetable oil

2 1/2 pounds chicken thighs

1 medium-size yellow onion, peeled and chopped

2/3 cup dry sherry

1 cup chicken broth

1/2 teaspoon salt

1/4 teaspoon black pepper

1/3 cup raisins

1/4 cup apricot or peach preserves

1. Heat the **butter** and **oil** in a heavy 12- or 14-inch skillet over moderately high heat. Add the **chicken thighs** and cook, uncovered, for 15 minutes, turning them frequently.

2. Add the **onion, sherry, chicken broth, salt,** and **pepper.** Cover, reduce the heat, and simmer for 15 minutes.

3. Remove the thighs to a platter and set them in a keep-warm (250°F) oven. Tilt the skillet and skim the fat from the pan juices. Add the **raisins** and **preserves** to the skillet. Boil, stirring, until the sauce has thickened—about 3 to 5 minutes. Pour the sauce over the thighs, and serve with sweet potatoes or Sturbridge-Style Creamed Hashed Onions, page 71.

Company Chicken with Orange and Almonds

Preparation: **15 minutes**   Cooking: **20 minutes**   Serves **4**   Calories per serving: **440**

2 tablespoons vegetable oil

3 tablespoons butter or margarine

2½ pounds chicken thighs

1 lemon

2 small navel oranges

½ cup water

¼ teaspoon ground ginger

¾ teaspoon salt

¼ teaspoon black pepper

¼ cup slivered blanched almonds

1. Heat the **oil** and 2 tablespoons of the **butter** in a heavy 12- or 14-inch skillet over moderately high heat. Add the **chicken thighs** and cook, uncovered, for 15 minutes, turning them occasionally. Meanwhile, grate the rind from the **lemon** and from 1 **orange,** then juice them.

2. Pour all but 2 tablespoons of the fat from the skillet. Add the lemon and orange rind and juice, the **water, ginger, salt,** and **pepper.** Cover, reduce the heat, and simmer for 15 minutes.

3. Meanwhile, peel the remaining orange, cut it into 8 sections, remove any seeds, and set the orange sections aside. Put the **almonds** and the remaining tablespoon of butter into a small skillet over moderately low heat, and cook until golden brown—3 to 5 minutes. Set aside.

4. When the chicken has cooked, remove the cover, tilt the skillet, and skim the fat from the pan juices. Add the reserved orange sections, and simmer, uncovered, 5 to 10 minutes longer, or until the sauce has thickened slightly. Sprinkle the almonds over the chicken and serve.

POULTRY

Savory Chicken ⊕

Preparation: **15 minutes**   Cooking: **20 minutes**   Serves **4**   Calories per serving: **445**

⅓ cup olive or vegetable oil

2½ pounds chicken thighs

1 medium-size yellow onion, peeled and chopped

2 cloves garlic, peeled and minced

3 or 4 anchovy fillets, rinsed and finely chopped

½ cup dry red or white wine

¼ cup red wine vinegar

1 tablespoon tomato paste

2 tablespoons capers, drained

½ teaspoon salt

¼ teaspoon black pepper

1. Heat the **oil** in a heavy 12- or 14-inch skillet over moderately high heat. Add the **chicken thighs** and cook, uncovered, for 15 minutes, turning them occasionally. Pour all but 2 tablespoons of the fat from the skillet.

2. Add the **onion, garlic, anchovies, wine, vinegar, tomato paste, capers, salt,** and **pepper.** Cover, reduce the heat, and simmer for 20 minutes, turning the chicken once or twice. Tilt the skillet and skim the fat from the sauce. Serve the chicken with buttered pasta or rice.

Tip: This recipe can be halved, or leftovers can be refrigerated for 1 or 2 days or frozen.

Chicken and Sausage Fricassee with Sage

Preparation: **17 minutes**   Cooking: **25 minutes**   Serves **4**   Calories per serving: **425-485**

1/2 **pound sweet or hot Italian sausage**

1 **tablespoon butter or margarine**

1 **tablespoon olive or vegetable oil**

1 **chicken (2 1/2 to 3 pounds), cut into serving pieces**

1/2 **teaspoon salt**

1/4 **teaspoon black pepper**

1 **cup dry white wine or chicken broth**

1 **teaspoon dried sage, crumbled**

1. Remove the **sausage** from the casing. In a heavy 12- or 14-inch skillet, brown the sausage over high heat—about 5 minutes. Remove with a slotted spoon and set aside. Discard the fat.

2. Reduce the heat to moderately high. In the same skillet, melt the **butter,** then add the **oil** and **chicken.** Sprinkle the chicken with the **salt** and **pepper,** and cook, uncovered, turning the pieces once or twice, until well browned—about 10 minutes.

3. Pour the **wine** over the chicken, and add the sausage and **sage.** Reduce the heat to low, cover, and cook until the chicken is done—about 25 minutes. Tilt the skillet, skim the fat from the pan juices, and serve the chicken immediately with the natural gravy.

Chicken with Red Wine ⓓ

Preparation: **8 minutes**   Cooking: **35 minutes**   Serves **4**   Calories per serving: **460-520**

1/4 **cup all-purpose flour**

1 **chicken (2 1/2 to 3 pounds), cut into serving pieces**

2 **tablespoons butter or margarine**

2 **tablespoons vegetable oil**

3/4 **cup dry red wine**

1/4 **cup water**

1 **small yellow onion, peeled and finely chopped**

2 **cloves garlic, peeled and minced**

1/2 **teaspoon dried thyme, crumbled**

1/2 **bay leaf**

1/2 **teaspoon salt**

1/8 **teaspoon black pepper**

1 **medium-size tomato, peeled and chopped**

1/4 **pound mushrooms, sliced**

Here is a quick version of coq au vin. *Speed up the total cooking time by preparing the onion and garlic while the chicken browns, the tomatoes and mushrooms while the chicken simmers for the first 15 minutes.*

1. Put the **flour** on a plate or piece of wax paper, and coat the **chicken** with it. Shake off any excess flour and set the chicken aside. Heat the **butter** and **oil** in a heavy 12- or 14-inch skillet over moderately high heat. Add the chicken and cook, uncovered, turning the pieces once or twice, until browned—about 5 minutes.

2. Add the **wine, water, onion, garlic, thyme, bay leaf, salt,** and **pepper.** Cover, reduce the heat, and simmer for 15 minutes.

3. Add the **tomato** and **mushrooms.** Cover and simmer 15 minutes longer.

4. Remove the cover, tilt the skillet, and skim the fat from the pan juices. Cook, uncovered, an additional 5 minutes, or until the sauce thickens slightly. Serve with buttered noodles.

Tips: 1. This recipe can be halved. 2. You can make this dish ahead and refrigerate it for 1 or 2 days.

Chicken Paprika ⊕

Preparation: 13 minutes **Cooking: 22 minutes** **Serves 4** **Calories per serving: 465-525**

1/3 cup vegetable oil

1/4 cup all-purpose flour

1 teaspoon salt

1/2 teaspoon black pepper

1 chicken (2 1/2 to 3 pounds), cut into serving pieces

1/2 medium-size yellow onion, peeled and finely chopped

3 tablespoons water

1 tablespoon paprika

1/2 cup sour cream at room temperature

> *Tips: 1. This recipe can be halved.*
> *2. You can substitute plain yogurt for the sour cream and reduce the number of calories per serving by 40.*

1. Heat the **oil** in a heavy 12- or 14-inch skillet over moderately high heat. In a shallow bowl, combine the **flour, salt,** and **pepper,** and coat the **chicken** with it. Shake off any excess flour.

2. Place the chicken in the skillet and cook, uncovered, turning the pieces once or twice, until well browned—about 10 minutes.

3. Add the **onion, water,** and **paprika,** cover, reduce the heat, and simmer for 20 minutes.

4. Place the chicken on a warm serving platter, and remove the skillet from the heat. Tilt the skillet and skim the fat from the pan juices. Stir in the **sour cream.** Pour the sauce over the chicken. Serve with Farmer's Turnip and Pear Salad, page 49.

Chicken with Vinegar Cream Sauce ⊕

Preparation: 23 minutes **Cooking: 15 minutes** **Serves 4** **Calories per serving: 460-520**

1 tablespoon butter or margarine

1 tablespoon vegetable oil

1 chicken (2 1/2 to 3 pounds), cut into serving pieces

4 cloves garlic, peeled and minced

4 large carrots, peeled and cut into 1/2-inch slices

1 large yellow onion, peeled and coarsely chopped

1/2 cup red wine vinegar

1 1/4 cups chicken broth

1/4 teaspoon salt

1/8 teaspoon black pepper

1/2 teaspoon dried thyme, crumbled

1 bay leaf

1 cup sour cream

1. Heat the **butter** and **oil** in a heavy 12- or 14-inch skillet over moderately high heat. Add the **chicken** and cook, uncovered, turning the pieces once or twice, until browned—about 10 minutes.

2. Add the **garlic, carrots,** and **onion,** and reduce the heat to moderate. Cover and cook for 10 minutes, or until the onion is soft.

3. Pour off and discard the fat from the skillet. Add the **vinegar,** raise the heat to moderately high, and cook, uncovered, until almost all of the vinegar has evaporated—3 to 5 minutes.

4. Add the **chicken broth, salt, pepper, thyme,** and **bay leaf.** Cook, uncovered, over moderate heat for 15 more minutes, stirring occasionally. Nearly all of the liquid will evaporate.

5. Remove the skillet from the heat, stir in the **sour cream,** and serve.

> *Tips: 1. This recipe can be halved. 2. This dish should not be reheated because the sauce will curdle. 3. To freeze, complete the recipe through Step 4 and add the sour cream just before serving.*

Mexican Chicken ◍

Preparation: **15 minutes**   Cooking: **30 minutes**   Serves **4**   Calories per serving: **510-570**

1/4 cup vegetable oil

1 chicken (2 1/2 to 3 pounds), cut into serving pieces

1 large yellow onion, peeled and finely chopped

2 cloves garlic, peeled and minced

1 tablespoon chili powder

1/2 cup uncooked rice

1 1/2 cups chicken broth

1/2 teaspoon salt

1/8 teaspoon black pepper

3 medium-size fresh tomatoes, peeled and chopped, or 1 can (1 pound) tomatoes, chopped, with their juice

2 tablespoons sliced pimiento-stuffed green olives

Add 2 cups of leftover corn or a package of frozen whole-kernel corn during the last 5 minutes of cooking, and you will have a complete meal. To streamline the preparation time, get the onion and garlic ready while the chicken is browning and prepare the tomatoes and olives while the chicken and rice are cooking.

1. Heat the **oil** in a heavy 12- or 14-inch skillet over moderately high heat. Add the **chicken** and cook, uncovered, turning the pieces once or twice, until well browned—about 10 minutes.

2. Add the **onion, garlic,** and **chili powder,** and stir to mix. Reduce the heat to moderate and cook, uncovered, for 5 minutes.

3. Add the **rice, chicken broth, salt,** and **pepper,** and cook, covered, for 25 minutes.

4. Add the **tomatoes** and **olives,** and stir. Cover and cook 5 minutes longer. Tilt the skillet, skim the fat from the pan juices, and serve.

> **Tip:** *This recipe can be halved.*

POULTRY

Braised Chinese Chicken

Preparation: **10 minutes**   Cooking: **22 minutes**   Serves **4**   Calories per serving: **390-450**

2 tablespoons vegetable oil

1 chicken (2 1/2 to 3 pounds), cut into serving pieces

1/4 cup soy sauce

1/4 teaspoon ground ginger

2 teaspoons creamy peanut butter

2 teaspoons sugar

3/4 cup chicken broth

1 medium-size yellow onion, peeled and chopped

2 cloves garlic, peeled and minced

2 teaspoons cornstarch

2 tablespoons cold water

2 teaspoons cider vinegar

1. Heat the **oil** in a heavy 12- or 14-inch skillet over moderately high heat. Add the **chicken** and cook, uncovered, turning the pieces once or twice, until well browned—about 10 minutes.

2. Meanwhile, in a small bowl, mix the **soy sauce, ginger, peanut butter,** and **sugar** until well blended. Stir in the **chicken broth** and pour the mixture over the chicken. Scatter the **onion** and **garlic** over the chicken.

3. Cover the skillet, reduce the heat, and simmer for 20 minutes. Remove the chicken to a deep platter. Tilt the skillet and skim the fat from the pan juices.

4. Combine the **cornstarch, water,** and **vinegar,** and add to the liquid in the skillet. Bring to a boil and cook, stirring constantly, for 2 minutes. Pour the sauce over the chicken. Serve with rice.

> **Tip:** *You can make this dish 1 or 2 days ahead, refrigerate it, and reheat it in a covered skillet.*

Chicken Creole ⓓ

Preparation: **12 minutes**   Cooking: **30 minutes**   Serves **4**   Calories per serving: **340-400**

POULTRY

2 tablespoons butter or margarine

1 chicken (2½ to 3 pounds), cut into serving pieces

1 medium-size yellow onion, peeled and thinly sliced

1 medium-size sweet green pepper, cored, seeded, and cut into ½-inch strips

2 stalks celery, chopped

3 medium-size fresh tomatoes, peeled and chopped, or 1 can (1 pound) tomatoes, chopped, with their juice

2 cloves garlic, peeled and minced

½ teaspoon paprika

½ teaspoon dried thyme, crumbled

½ bay leaf

½ teaspoon salt

⅛ teaspoon black pepper

¼ pound mushrooms, sliced

1. Melt the **butter** in a heavy 12- or 14-inch skillet over moderately high heat. Add the **chicken** and cook, uncovered, turning the pieces once or twice, until well browned—about 10 minutes.

2. Add the **onion, green pepper, celery, tomatoes, garlic, paprika, thyme, bay leaf, salt,** and **black pepper.** Cover, reduce the heat, and simmer for 25 minutes, turning the chicken once or twice.

3. Remove the cover, tilt the skillet, and skim the fat from the pan juices. Add the **mushrooms** and simmer, covered, 5 minutes longer. Serve with rice and a salad.

> *Tips: 1. This recipe can be halved. 2. You can make this dish ahead and refrigerate or freeze it.*

Chicken with Rosemary and Lime

Preparation: **10 minutes**   Cooking: **25 minutes**   Serves **4**   Calories per serving: **420-480**

⅓ cup vegetable oil

1 chicken (2½ to 3 pounds), cut into serving pieces

½ cup chicken broth

Grated rind and juice of 1 large lime

2 cloves garlic, peeled and minced

¼ teaspoon ground ginger

½ teaspoon dried rosemary, crumbled

1 teaspoon salt

½ teaspoon black pepper

1. Heat the **oil** in a heavy 12- or 14-inch skillet over moderately high heat. Add the **chicken** and cook, uncovered, turning the pieces once or twice, until well browned—about 10 minutes.

2. Add the **chicken broth, lime rind** and **juice, garlic, ginger, rosemary, salt,** and **pepper.** Cover, reduce the heat to moderately low, and simmer for 25 minutes. Skim the fat from the pan juices and serve the chicken with the natural gravy. Serve with Carrots Amana Style, page 67.

> *Tips: 1. You can cook this dish ahead, refrigerate it, and serve it the next day. 2. For variety, substitute 4 1-inch-thick pork chops, well trimmed, for the chicken.*

Oven-Barbecued Chicken 🐷 🍳

Preparation: 7 minutes   Cooking: **45 minutes**   Serves **4**   Calories per serving: **305-365**

This is an extremely easy main dish because the preparation time is so short. While the chicken is cooking, you can complete the rest of the meal.

1 chicken (2¹/₂ to 3 pounds), cut into serving pieces

¹/₂ teaspoon salt

¹/₄ teaspoon black pepper

¹/₃ cup water

¹/₂ cup ketchup

2 tablespoons light brown or white sugar

¹/₄ cup cider vinegar

1 tablespoon Dijon or prepared spicy brown mustard

1 tablespoon Worcestershire sauce

¹/₄ teaspoon crushed dried red pepper (optional)

1. Preheat the oven to 400°F. Arrange the **chicken** in a single layer in a 13"x 9"x 2" baking dish. Season with the **salt** and **black pepper.**

2. In a small bowl, mix the **water, ketchup, sugar, vinegar, mustard,** and **Worcestershire sauce,** and the **dried red pepper** if used. Pour the mixture over the chicken.

3. Bake, uncovered, for 45 minutes. Tip the baking dish and skim the fat from the sauce. Serve with Glorious Mashed Potatoes, page 74, or buttered noodles, and a green vegetable, such as Dry-Sautéed Broccoli, page 62.

> *Tips: 1. This recipe can be halved. 2. You can make this dish ahead and refrigerate or freeze it. 3. As a variation, substitute 4 ¹/₂-inch-thick pork chops for the chicken. Trim most of the fat from the chops before cooking them. Serve with Coleslaw, page 45.*

Oven-Fried Chicken Parmesan 🍳

Preparation: 10 minutes   Cooking: **35 minutes**   Serves **4**   Calories per serving: **520-580**

1 cup soft fresh bread crumbs

¹/₃ cup grated Parmesan cheese

2 tablespoons minced parsley

¹/₂ clove garlic, peeled and minced

1 teaspoon salt

¹/₄ teaspoon black pepper

¹/₂ cup (1 stick) butter or margarine, melted

1 chicken (2¹/₂ to 3 pounds), cut into serving pieces

1. Preheat the oven to 400°F. Butter a 13"x 9"x 2" baking dish. In a shallow bowl, combine the **bread crumbs, cheese, parsley, garlic, salt,** and **pepper.** Place the melted **butter** in another shallow bowl. Dip the **chicken** into the butter, then roll the pieces in the crumb mixture and put them into the baking dish.

2. Pour the remaining butter evenly over the chicken and bake, uncovered, for 35 to 40 minutes, basting occasionally with the pan juices. Serve with broccoli.

> *Tips: 1. One slice of bread torn into very small pieces or whirled in a blender at high speed makes ¹/₂ cup of crumbs. 2. This recipe can be halved.*

Indian Chicken 🐷

Preparation: **5 minutes**   Cooking: **44 minutes**   Serves **4**   Calories per serving: **265-325**

This intriguingly flavored chicken tastes even better when served warm rather than oven-hot.

1¼ teaspoons salt

2 cloves garlic, peeled and minced

½ teaspoon ground cardamom or cinnamon

2 teaspoons chili powder

½ teaspoon ground ginger

2 teaspoons all-purpose flour

1 chicken (2½ to 3 pounds), cut into serving pieces

½ cup plain yogurt

¼ cup water

1. Preheat the oven to 400°F. In a small bowl, combine the **salt, garlic, cardamom, chili powder, ginger,** and **flour.** Rub the mixture onto the **chicken.**

2. Arrange the chicken, skin side up, in a single layer in a buttered 13"x 9"x 2" baking dish. Bake, uncovered, for 40 minutes.

3. Remove the chicken to a warm serving platter. Pour all but 1 tablespoon of the fat from the baking dish. Let the dish cool about 2 minutes.

4. Meanwhile, in a small bowl, beat the **yogurt** and **water** with a fork until smooth, then mix thoroughly with the fat remaining in the baking dish, scraping up any brown bits stuck to the dish. Pour the yogurt mixture over and around the chicken, and serve with rice.

Lemon Chicken 🐷

Preparation: **5 minutes**   Cooking: **40 minutes**   Serves **4**   Calories per serving: **375-435**

½ cup all-purpose flour

1 teaspoon dried tarragon, crumbled

1¼ teaspoons salt

1 chicken (2½ to 3 pounds), cut into serving pieces

4 tablespoons (½ stick) butter or margarine

⅓ cup lemon juice

1 tablespoon grated yellow onion

1 clove garlic, peeled and minced

⅛ teaspoon black pepper

1. Preheat the oven to 400°F. Combine the **flour, tarragon,** and 1 teaspoon of the **salt** in a bag. Add the **chicken** a few pieces at a time. Shake the bag to coat the chicken with the flour mixture. Remove the pieces from the bag and shake off any excess flour mixture.

2. Melt the **butter** in the oven in a 13"x 9"x 2" baking dish. Coat the chicken on all sides with the butter, then turn the chicken skin side up.

3. In a small bowl, mix the **lemon juice, onion, garlic, pepper,** and the remaining ¼ teaspoon of salt. Drizzle this mixture evenly over the chicken, and bake, uncovered, for 40 minutes. Serve with Green Beans Italian Style, page 59, or French Green Peas, page 72.

> *Tip: You can substitute 4 to 6 shoulder lamb chops for the chicken; trim the fat from the chops and baste frequently as they bake.*

Chicken Vermont

Preparation: **10 minutes**   Cooking: **30 minutes**   Serves **4**   Calories per serving: **570-630**

6 tablespoons butter or margarine

1/2 cup maple syrup

1 teaspoon salt

1/8 teaspoon ground cloves

1/4 teaspoon dry mustard

1 teaspoon black pepper

1 chicken (2 1/2 to 3 pounds), cut into serving pieces

3/4 cup white or yellow cornmeal

1/2 cup apple juice

1. Preheat the oven to 400°F. Put the **butter, maple syrup, salt, cloves, mustard,** and **pepper** into a 13"x 9"x 2" baking dish. Place the dish in the oven and heat until the butter melts.

2. Remove the dish from the oven, stir the mixture in the dish, then coat the **chicken** with the mixture. Put the **cornmeal** on a plate or a piece of wax paper, and roll the chicken in the meal to coat the pieces thoroughly. Shake off any excess cornmeal.

3. Arrange the chicken, skin side up, in the baking dish. Pour the **apple juice** around the chicken, but not over it. Bake, uncovered, for 30 minutes, basting occasionally with the pan juices. Add more apple juice if the liquid evaporates. Serve with Confetti Corn, page 68.

Roast Turkey Breast with Herbs

Preparation: **10 minutes**   Cooking: **1 1/4 hours**   Serves **10**   Calories per 4-ounce serving: **255**

Cooking turkey does take time, but most of the cooking is unattended—and you will probably have leftovers for making Turkey Croquettes, page 102, or any of your own favorite recipes. Note that you can substitute turkey for chicken in any recipe calling for cooked chicken.

1 turkey breast (5 pounds), thawed if frozen

1 teaspoon dried thyme, crumbled

1 teaspoon dried sage, crumbled

2 tablespoons minced parsley

1/4 teaspoon salt

1/8 teaspoon black pepper

1/2 cup (1 stick) butter or margarine, melted

1. Preheat the oven to 475°F. Rinse the **turkey breast** and pat it dry with paper toweling. Sprinkle the **thyme, sage, parsley, salt,** and **pepper** over the breast. Brush the top all over with the **butter.**

2. Place the breast, skin side up, on a rack in a 13"x 9"x 2" roasting pan. Insert a meat thermometer, if you have one, into the thickest part of the breast and roast, uncovered, for 30 minutes, basting occasionally with the pan juices.

3. Reduce the heat to 425°F, and continue to roast, uncovered, for 30 more minutes. Check to see if the breast is browning too much. If it is, cover it loosely with aluminum foil. Roast 15 minutes longer, or until the thermometer registers 180°F to 185°F.

4. Remove from the oven and let stand at room temperature for 10 minutes before carving.

> *Tip: The cooking time given above is for a 5-pound turkey breast. If you use a larger one, you will have to increase the roasting time, allowing about 15 minutes per pound. The 255-calorie serving includes the skin.*

Turkey–Sweet Potato Bake 🐷

Preparation: **10 minutes** Cooking: **25 minutes**   Serves **6**   Calories per serving: **315**

This recipe performs wizardry with your Thanksgiving leftovers—turkey, stuffing, and sweet potatoes are all used up in one rich, hearty dish.

2 cups cubed cooked turkey

2 cups cooked turkey stuffing

1 egg

3/4 cup milk

1/4 teaspoon salt

Pinch black pepper

1 cup cooked sweet potatoes

3 tablespoons butter or margarine, softened

Pinch ground nutmeg

1. Preheat the oven to 375°F. In a mixing bowl, combine the **turkey** and **stuffing,** and spread the mixture into a buttered 9"x 9"x 2" baking dish. Beat together the **egg, milk, salt,** and **pepper.** Pour evenly over the turkey mixture.

2. Mash the **sweet potatoes,** blend in 2 tablespoons of the **butter,** and season with the **nutmeg.** Spread evenly over the turkey mixture. Dot with the remaining tablespoon of butter.

3. Bake, uncovered, for 25 minutes, or until heated through. Serve with steamed green beans or broccoli, which you can cook while the dish is in the oven.

Turkey Croquettes 🐷

Preparation: **30 minutes** Cooking: **12 minutes**   Serves **4**   Calories per serving: **410**

4 tablespoons (1/2 stick) butter or margarine

1/3 cup unsifted all-purpose flour

1 teaspoon salt

1/2 cup milk

2 cups finely chopped cooked turkey

1 tablespoon grated yellow onion

1 tablespoon lemon juice

1 teaspoon dried tarragon or parsley, crumbled

1 egg

1/3 cup fine dry bread crumbs

1/3 cup vegetable oil

Tips: 1. You can use chicken instead of the turkey. 2. The croquettes can be made 1 or 2 days ahead and reheated, uncovered, in a 350°F oven.

1. Melt the **butter** in a 2-quart saucepan over moderate heat, and blend in the **flour** and **salt,** stirring constantly.

2. Gradually stir in the **milk** and cook, continuing to stir, until the mixture thickens— about 3 minutes. Remove the saucepan from the heat, and stir in the **turkey, onion, lemon juice,** and **tarragon.**

3. Pour the mixture into a buttered 8"x 8"x 2" pan, spreading it evenly. Chill in the freezer for 15 minutes, or until stiff enough to shape.

4. Take the pan from the freezer and shape the mixture into 4 oval patties.

5. Put the **egg** and **bread crumbs** into separate small bowls. Beat the egg lightly. Heat the **oil** in a heavy 12-inch skillet over moderately high heat. Take each croquette and dip it first into the egg and next into the bread crumbs, then place it in the skillet. Fry the croquettes until they are nicely browned—about 6 minutes on each side.

Turkey Jambalaya

Preparation: **15 minutes** Cooking: **30 minutes**   Serves **6**   Calories per serving: **250**

4 tablespoons (¹⁄₂ stick) butter or margarine

³⁄₄ cup uncooked rice

1 stalk celery, finely chopped

¹⁄₂ medium-size sweet green pepper, cored, seeded, and chopped

1 small yellow onion, peeled and finely chopped

2 cups cubed cooked turkey

3 medium-size fresh tomatoes, peeled and chopped, or 1 can (1 pound) tomatoes, chopped, with their juice

1¹⁄₄ cups chicken broth or turkey broth and gravy combined

Dash cayenne pepper

¹⁄₄ teaspoon dried thyme or sage, crumbled

This dish is so fresh-tasting, you would never know it was made with leftover turkey. Served with a salad or green vegetable, this is a complete meal.

1. Melt the **butter** in a heavy 9- or 10-inch skillet over moderate heat. Add the **rice, celery, green pepper,** and **onion.** Cook, uncovered, stirring occasionally, until the vegetables are just tender—about 10 minutes.

2. Stir in the **turkey, tomatoes, chicken broth, cayenne pepper,** and **thyme.** Cover the skillet and simmer, stirring occasionally, for 30 to 35 minutes, or until the rice is tender.

Roast Cornish Game Hen with Curry

Preparation: **10 minutes** Cooking: **40 minutes**   Serves **4**   Calories per serving: **490**

Produced by crossing Cornish and White Rock chickens, the Rock Cornish Game Hen is the smallest of all chickens, yet is meaty, with a plump breast. These hens are easy to deal with, as you can allow one bird per person and there is no mess of carving.

4 Cornish game hens (about 1 pound each)

4 teaspoons curry powder

1 teaspoon salt

6 tablespoons butter or margarine, softened

2 large carrots, peeled and chopped

1 large yellow onion, peeled and finely chopped

1. Preheat the oven to 400°F. Wash the **hens** and pat them dry with paper toweling. Split each hen down the back, leaving the breast intact. Press down on the breasts to flatten slightly.

2. In a small bowl, combine the **curry powder, salt,** and 4 tablespoons of the **butter.** Rub this mixture onto both sides of the hens.

3. Grease a 13"x 9"x 2" roasting pan with the remaining 2 tablespoons of butter. Spread the **carrots** and **onion** evenly over the bottom of the pan, and place the hens on top of the vegetables.

4. Roast, uncovered, for 40 minutes. After 15 minutes of cooking, add 1 cup of water to the pan and baste the hens occasionally with the pan juices. When the hens are done, skim the fat from the pan juices. Serve with the vegetables, the natural gravy, and rice or Lima Beans in Sour Cream, page 60.

BEEF

Beef is one of our favorite foods—on the average, each of us consumes well over 100 pounds of it every year. Some people think that beef is expensive, others that it is slow too cook. In this section, however, you'll find delicious, low-cost, imaginative recipes for inexpensive steaks, hamburgers, stews, meat loaves, and one-dish beef meals. And as for speed—more than half the recipes require less than 30 minutes from start to finish.

Roast Beef

Preparation: 10 minutes   Cooking: 50 minutes   Serves 6   Calories per serving: 365

Cooking roast beef this way is both fast and efficient. Serve one piece immediately; 2½ pounds will give you 6 ample servings. Cube or slice the rest, freeze it, and use it to make recipes calling for cooked beef.

**1 boneless sirloin tip
(5 pounds)**

2 tablespoons soy sauce

2 tablespoons vegetable oil

½ teaspoon black pepper

1. Preheat the oven to 450°F. Cut the **sirloin tip** in half horizontally, and tie each half across the meat in two places and once lengthwise with cotton kitchen twine. Rub with the **soy sauce** and **oil,** and sprinkle with the **pepper.**

2. Place the pieces side by side on a rack in a 13"x 9" x 2" roasting pan, and insert a meat thermometer in the thickest part of one piece. Roast 50 to 60 minutes for rare (125°F); 1 hour to 1 hour 10 minutes for medium (150°F); and 1 hour 15 minutes to 1 hour 30 minutes for well done (160°F). Let the pieces stand for 10 to 15 minutes on a warm platter before slicing.

Beef with Scrambled Eggs ⊘

Preparation: 7 minutes   Cooking: 9 minutes   Serves 4   Calories per serving: 460

2 tablespoons vegetable oil

**2 cups finely chopped
cooked beef**

**⅓ cup finely chopped yellow
onion**

**2 medium-size tomatoes,
peeled and chopped**

**3 canned green chilies,
seeded and finely chopped**

1 teaspoon salt

¼ teaspoon ground cumin

**¼ teaspoon dried oregano,
crumbled**

6 eggs

1. Heat the **oil** in a heavy 12-inch skillet over moderate heat for about 1 minute. Add the **beef** and **onion,** and cook, uncovered, for 5 minutes.

2. Add the **tomatoes, green chilies, salt, cumin,** and **oregano** to the skillet, and cook, uncovered, for 5 more minutes, or until the mixture has thickened.

3. Beat the **eggs** lightly, add them to the mixture in the skillet, and scramble until the eggs are just set—about 4 minutes. Serve with tortillas.

Tip: You can substitute cooked pork for the beef.

French-Style Beef and Onions ⬭

Preparation: 20 minutes   Cooking: 15 minutes   Serves 4   Calories per serving: 1040

8 slices cooked roast beef, about ⅛ inch thick

¼ teaspoon salt

¼ teaspoon black pepper

3 tablespoons butter or margarine

2 large yellow onions, peeled and thinly sliced

1 tablespoon all-purpose flour

1½ cups leftover roast beef gravy mixed with beef broth, or 1½ cups beef broth

1 tablespoon cider vinegar

1½ cups shredded Swiss or sharp Cheddar cheese (about 6 ounces)

Here is a way to use leftover roast beef that will make the second meal as good as the first.

1. Preheat the oven to 425°F. Arrange the **beef** slices in a 13″ x 9″ x 2″ ungreased baking dish, overlapping the slices. Sprinkle with the **salt** and **pepper** and set aside.

2. Melt the **butter** in a 12-inch skillet over moderate heat. Add the **onions** and cook, covered, for 10 minutes. Stir in the **flour** and cook, uncovered, for 1 minute, stirring.

3. Gradually stir the **gravy** into the skillet, and cook until slightly thickened—3 to 5 minutes. Stir in the **vinegar** and pour the mixture over the beef. Sprinkle with the **cheese** and bake, uncovered, for 15 minutes.

> *Tips: 1. This recipe can be halved. 2. This dish can be prepared (but not baked) a day ahead.*

Deviled Beef Slices ▷ ⬭

Preparation: 10 minutes   Cooking: 9 minutes   Serves 4   Calories per serving: 585

8 drops liquid hot red pepper seasoning

4 tablespoons prepared spicy brown mustard

1 teaspoon salt

12 slices cooked roast beef, about 2 inches wide and ¼ inch thick

1 cup fine dry bread crumbs

3 tablespoons vegetable oil

3 tablespoons butter or margarine

1 clove garlic, peeled and minced

½ cup beef broth and ½ cup dry white wine, or 1 cup beef broth

1 teaspoon dried tarragon, crumbled

1. In a small bowl, combine the **red pepper seasoning,** 3 tablespoons of the **mustard,** and ½ teaspoon of the **salt.** Spread the mixture on both sides of the **beef** slices. Put the **bread crumbs** on a plate, and press the slices into them.

2. Heat the **oil** in a heavy 9- or 10-inch skillet over high heat for about 1 minute. Add half the beef slices and cook for 1 minute on each side. Remove the cooked slices to a platter and keep warm. Cook the remaining beef the same way.

3. To make the sauce, melt 1 tablespoon of the **butter** in the skillet over low heat. Add the **garlic** and brown lightly—about 1 minute. Add the **broth** and **wine, tarragon,** and the remaining mustard and salt. Bring the liquid to a boil, and boil for 2 minutes. Remove from the heat, stir in the remaining butter, and pour the sauce over the beef slices. Serve with mashed potatoes and Baked Zucchini with Tomatoes, page 79.

> *Tip: This recipe can be halved.*

BEEF

Roast Beef Hash ◐ ◑

Preparation: **7 minutes**   Cooking: **14 minutes**   Serves **4**   Calories per serving: **510**

1/4 cup vegetable oil

1 medium-size yellow onion, peeled and finely chopped

2 cups diced cooked potatoes

2 cups diced cooked roast beef

3/4 teaspoon salt

1/4 teaspoon black pepper

3/4 teaspoon dried thyme, crumbled

1/2 cup half-and-half

1. Heat the **oil** in a heavy 12-inch skillet over moderate heat. Add the **onion** and cook, uncovered, until soft—about 5 minutes. Add the **potatoes, beef, salt, pepper,** and **thyme,** and cook, uncovered, until the potatoes begin to brown—about 6 minutes.

2. Add the **half-and-half,** pressing down on the mixture with a pancake turner. Cook, uncovered, for 3 to 4 minutes, or until the half-and-half has almost evaporated. Serve with poached or fried eggs and a tossed green salad with Low-Calorie Tomato Dressing, page 52.

Tip: This recipe can be halved.

Beef Croquettes ◑

Preparation: **29 minutes**   Cooking: **6 minutes**   Serves **4**   Calories per serving: **630**

1/2 cup vegetable oil

1 medium-size yellow onion, peeled and finely chopped

3 tablespoons all-purpose flour

1 cup beef broth

2 cups very finely chopped cooked beef

1/2 teaspoon salt

1/4 teaspoon black pepper

1/2 teaspoon dried thyme, crumbled

1 tablespoon Worcestershire sauce

1 egg, lightly beaten

3/4 cup fine dry bread crumbs

1. Heat 1/4 cup of the **oil** in a heavy 10-inch skillet over moderate heat. Add the **onion** and cook, covered, until soft—about 5 minutes. Stir in the **flour,** cook for 1 minute, then gradually stir in the **beef broth.** Cook, stirring, for 1 minute, or until smooth and thickened.

2. Mix in the **beef, salt, pepper, thyme,** and **Worcestershire sauce.** Spread the mixture evenly in a buttered 8"x 8"x 2" baking dish.

3. Chill in the freezer for 15 minutes, or until stiff enough to shape. Form the mixture into 4 oval patties about 3/4 inch thick. Dip them into the **egg,** then coat them with the **bread crumbs.**

4. Rinse and dry the skillet. Heat the remaining oil in it over moderately high heat for 1 minute. Add the croquettes, and cook until brown—about 3 minutes on each side. Drain on paper toweling.

*Tips: **1.** This recipe can be halved. **2.** You can substitute lamb, pork, or ham for the beef. **3.** Add any of the following to the croquette mixture: 1 tablespoon prepared mustard or horseradish; 1/4 cup minced ripe olives; 1/2 cup chopped, sautéed mushrooms; 2 tablespoons chili sauce; 2 tablespoons minced capers, dill pickle, or sweet green pepper; 1 crushed clove garlic. **4.** You can make these croquettes ahead and refrigerate or freeze them. Reheat on a baking sheet in a 350°F oven.*

BEEF

Minute Steaks Monaco ⊘

Preparation: **5 minutes**   Cooking: **13 minutes**   Serves **4**   Calories per serving: **515**

1 teaspoon salt

4 cube steaks (about
6 ounces each)

1/4 cup vegetable oil

1 small eggplant (about
1/2 pound), peeled and cut
into 1/2-inch slices

1/4 pound mushrooms,
quartered

1 1/4 cups chicken broth

1 can (8 ounces) tomato
sauce

1/2 teaspoon dried oregano,
crumbled

1 tablespoon all-purpose
flour

2 tablespoons water

1. Heat a heavy 12-inch skillet over moderately high heat until very hot. Sprinkle the bottom of the skillet with the **salt,** add the **steaks,** and cook for 1 minute on each side for rare; cook an additional minute per side for well done. Remove the steaks to a platter and set in a keep-warm (250°F) oven.

2. Reduce the heat to moderate. Add the **oil** to the skillet, and brown the **eggplant** slices on both sides along with the **mushrooms**—about 5 minutes. Stir in the **chicken broth, tomato sauce,** and **oregano,** and simmer, covered, for 5 minutes, or until the eggplant is tender.

3. In a small bowl, blend the **flour** and **water** into a smooth paste. Stir into the liquid in the skillet. Cook, stirring constantly, until the mixture thickens and boils—about 1 minute.

4. Arrange the eggplant slices under the steaks on the serving platter, and top with the sauce and mushrooms. Serve with buttered noodles and a green salad.

Cube Steaks with Black Pepper and Cream ⊘ ⊕

Preparation: **2 minutes**   Cooking: **10 minutes**   Serves **6**   Calories per serving: **430**

6 cube steaks (about
6 ounces each)

2 tablespoons peppercorns,
crushed

2 tablespoons vegetable oil

3/4 cup beef broth

3 tablespoons half-and-half

3 tablespoons butter or
margarine

Here is a thrifty version of the classic French dish steak au poivre.

1. Dry the **steaks** with paper toweling. Press the **crushed peppercorns** evenly onto both sides of the steaks. Heat the **oil** in a heavy 12-inch skillet over moderately high heat for about 1 minute. Add the steaks and cook for 1 minute on each side for medium; cook an additional minute per side for well done. Remove the steaks to a platter and set in a keep-warm (250°F) oven.

2. Pour off and discard the oil from the skillet. Add the **beef broth** and boil, uncovered, over high heat until only 1/4 cup of the broth remains—about 5 minutes. Add the **half-and-half,** and heat briefly.

3. Remove the skillet from the heat. Stir in the **butter** until it melts, together with any accumulated juices from the platter. Pour the sauce over the steaks and serve.

Tips: 1. This recipe can be halved. 2. To crush peppercorns, place them in a 6-inch skillet. Select a saucepan that will fit inside the skillet, set the pan on top of the peppercorns, and press hard, with a rocking motion, until the peppercorns are coarsely crushed. You can also buy crushed peppercorns.

BEEF

Skirt Steak with Mushrooms ▷

Preparation: **6 minutes**   Cooking: **13 minutes**   Serves **4**   Calories per serving: **420**

The cooking time given is for rare steak. If you prefer beef more well done, cook the steak a bit longer.

1½ pounds skirt or flank steak, trimmed of fat

½ teaspoon salt

¼ teaspoon black pepper

1 tablespoon vegetable oil

3 tablespoons butter or margarine

1 clove garlic, peeled and minced

¼ pound mushrooms, thickly sliced

⅓ cup beef broth or water

1 tablespoon minced parsley

1. Cut the **steak** into 4 pieces, pat the pieces dry with paper toweling, and sprinkle them with the **salt** and **pepper.**

2. Heat the **oil** in a heavy 12-inch skillet over high heat for about 1 minute. Add the steak and cook, uncovered, for 3 minutes on each side. Remove the steak to a platter.

3. Melt the **butter** in the skillet, then add the **garlic,** and cook, stirring, for 1 minute. Add the **mushrooms,** toss, and cook, uncovered, for 4 minutes, tossing occasionally.

4. Add the **beef broth** and stir, scraping up any brown bits stuck to the skillet. Return the steak and any accumulated juices to the skillet, and heat through. Sprinkle with the **parsley,** and serve with boiled potatoes and green beans or Baked Stuffed Tomatoes, page 81.

Indian Steak ▷ ◑

Preparation: **15 minutes**   Cooking: **6 minutes**   Serves **4**   Calories per serving: **425**

Inspired by the cooking of India, this steak is mildly flavored with curried onion. The cooking time given is for rare steak. If you prefer beef more well done, cook the steak a bit longer.

2 tablespoons butter or margarine

2 tablespoons vegetable oil

1 large yellow onion, peeled and thinly sliced

1 teaspoon curry powder

1½ pounds flank or skirt steak

½ teaspoon salt

¼ teaspoon black pepper

1. Heat the **butter** and the **oil** in a heavy 8- or 9-inch skillet over moderate heat. Add the **onion** and **curry powder,** and cook, uncovered, until the onion is dark brown and crisp—about 12 minutes. (Be careful not to let the onion burn; turn down the heat if it is browning too quickly.) Remove the onion to a warm plate, cover with aluminum foil, and set aside.

2. Meanwhile, trim the **steak** of fat and cut it into 4 pieces. Pat the pieces dry with paper toweling, and sprinkle them with the **salt** and **pepper.** Put the steak into the skillet and cook, uncovered, over moderate heat for 3 minutes on each side.

3. Remove the steak to a warm serving platter. Scatter the onion over the steak, and serve with rice and Green Beans with Garlic and Cheese, page 59, or Orange-Ginger Carrots, page 66.

Tips: 1. This recipe can be halved. 2. As a variation, add 1 tablespoon of dried currants or raisins to the onion during the last 3 minutes of cooking and sprinkle with 1 tablespoon of chopped toasted almonds.

Oriental Steak Broil

Preparation: **35 minutes**   Cooking: **6 minutes**   Serves **4**   Calories per serving: **340**

3 tablespoons lemon juice

1 tablespoon vegetable oil

2 cloves garlic, peeled and minced

1 tablespoon soy sauce

1½ teaspoons salt

¼ teaspoon black pepper

¼ teaspoon aniseed, crushed, or ground allspice

1½ pounds flank steak

> *Tip: Use leftover steak, thinly sliced, for sandwiches.*

1. Preheat the broiler. In a 1-quart saucepan, combine the **lemon juice, oil, garlic, soy sauce, salt, pepper,** and **aniseed.** Bring to a boil over high heat and stir about 30 seconds, or until the salt dissolves.

2. Put the **steak** into a 9"x 9"x 2" nonaluminum baking dish and pierce all over with a fork. Pour the hot marinade over the steak, turn the steak over in the marinade to coat it well, and marinate at room temperature for 30 minutes (or longer, if you have the time), turning once.

3. Place the steak on the rack of the broiler pan about 2 or 3 inches from the heat. Broil for 3 minutes on each side for rare; broil an additional 2 minutes per side for medium. Cut the steak on the diagonal into ½-inch slices. Serve with baked potatoes.

Chuck Steaks with Herb Butter ▷ ◫

Preparation: **15 minutes**   Cooking: **4 minutes**   Serves **4**   Calories per serving: **615**

These steaks, with their accompanying herb butter, are quick to prepare and good for unexpected company. The cooking time given is for rare steak. If you prefer beef more well done, cook the steaks a bit longer.

1½ pounds lean boneless chuck blade or arm, 1½ to 2 inches thick

½ teaspoon salt

¼ teaspoon black pepper

4 tablespoons (½ stick) butter or margarine, softened

1 clove garlic, peeled and minced

1 tablespoon minced parsley

½ teaspoon dried basil, crumbled

¼ teaspoon dried thyme, crumbled

1 tablespoon vegetable oil

1. Put the **chuck** on the counter, place your hand flat over it, and, cutting parallel to your hand, cut the meat horizontally into 4 slices.

2. Pound the slices with a wooden mallet until they are ¼ inch thick. Trim off any excess fat.

3. Notch the edges of the steaks all around to prevent curling. Pat the steaks dry with paper toweling, and sprinkle them with the **salt** and ⅛ teaspoon of the **pepper.** Set aside.

4. In a small bowl, combine the **butter, garlic, parsley, basil,** and **thyme,** and the remaining ⅛ teaspoon of pepper. Set aside.

5. Heat the **oil** in a 12-inch skillet over moderately high heat for about 1 minute. Add the steaks and cook, uncovered, for 2 minutes on each side. Serve with a dollop of herb butter on top of each steak.

> *Tips: **1.** This recipe can be halved, but use the same amount of oil. **2.** Leftovers can be refrigerated or frozen, and used on sandwiches or stir-fried with vegetables.*

BEEF

Chinese Pepper Steak ⏺

Preparation: **20 minutes** Cooking: **12 minutes** Serves **4** Calories per serving: **560**

⅓ cup cornstarch

1 pound boneless top round steak, trimmed of fat and cut crosswise into strips ¼ inch thick and 2 inches long

½ cup vegetable oil

3 medium-size sweet green or red peppers, cored, seeded, and cut into ½-inch strips

3 medium-size yellow onions, peeled and sliced

3 cloves garlic, peeled and minced

½ cup soy sauce

1 cup water

Tip: This recipe can be halved.

1. Put the **cornstarch** into a large bowl and toss the **steak** slices in it to coat. Set aside.

2. Heat ¼ cup of the **oil** in a heavy 12-inch skillet over moderately high heat for about 1 minute. Add half the steak slices and cook, stirring once or twice, until no pink remains—about 1 or 2 minutes. Using a slotted spoon, remove the cooked slices to a platter. Cook the remaining steak the same way and add to the platter.

3. Reduce the heat to moderate, and add the remaining ¼ cup of oil. Add the **peppers, onions,** and **garlic,** and cook, uncovered, for 5 minutes, or until the onions are soft. Return the steak and any accumulated juices to the skillet.

4. Stir in the **soy sauce** and **water.** Continue cooking and stirring until the sauce has thickened—about 4 minutes. Serve with rice.

Beef Stroganoff ⏵ ⏺

Preparation: **15 minutes** Cooking: **10 minutes** Serves **4** Calories per serving: **540**

¼ cup all-purpose flour

1 teaspoon salt

¼ teaspoon black pepper

1½ pounds flank or skirt steak, trimmed of fat and cut crosswise into ¼-inch slices

4 tablespoons butter or margarine

1 medium-size yellow onion, peeled and chopped

2 cloves garlic, peeled and minced

½ pound mushrooms, sliced

1¼ cups beef broth

2 tablespoons tomato paste

¾ cup sour cream

Tips: 1. This recipe can be halved. 2. You can substitute plain yogurt for the sour cream.

1. In a large bowl, combine the **flour, salt,** and **pepper.** Toss the **steak** slices in the mixture until they are coated. Shake off any excess flour. Set the slices aside.

2. Heat the **butter** in a heavy 12-inch skillet over moderately high heat until bubbly. Add half the steak slices and cook, stirring once or twice, for 1 or 2 minutes, or until no pink remains. Using a slotted spoon, remove the cooked steak to a platter. Cook the remaining steak the same way and add to the platter.

3. Reduce the heat to moderately low. Add the **onion** and **garlic,** and cook, uncovered, for 5 minutes, or until the onion is soft. Add the **mushrooms, beef broth,** and **tomato paste,** raise the heat to high, and cook for 2 minutes, scraping up any brown bits stuck to the skillet.

4. Return the steak and any accumulated juices to the skillet, and heat through—about 1 minute. Remove the skillet from the heat and stir in the **sour cream.** Serve over buttered noodles and with a lettuce and tomato salad.

Beef with Curry Sauce ⊕

Preparation: 35 minutes   Cooking: 7 minutes   Serves 4   Calories per serving: 500

You can omit the 25-minute marinating time if you wish, but the dish will have a better flavor if it has a chance to absorb the seasonings.

1½ teaspoons sugar

3 tablespoons soy sauce

2 cloves garlic, peeled and minced

¾ teaspoon ground ginger

5 tablespoons vegetable oil

1½ pounds flank or skirt steak, trimmed of fat and cut crosswise into strips ¼ inch wide and 2 inches long

1 large yellow onion, peeled and thinly sliced

4½ teaspoons cornstarch

2 tablespoons curry powder

¾ cup cold water

1. In a large bowl, combine the **sugar, soy sauce, garlic, ginger,** and 2 tablespoons of the **oil.** Add the **steak** slices, toss to coat them with the mixture, and marinate for 25 minutes at room temperature.

2. Heat the remaining 3 tablespoons of oil in a heavy 12-inch skillet over moderately high heat for about 1 minute. Using a slotted spoon, transfer the steak from the marinade to the skillet. Cook for 1 minute, turning once. Remove the slices to a platter. Add the **onion** to the skillet, reduce the heat to moderate, and cook for 2 minutes.

3. Meanwhile, add the **cornstarch, curry powder,** and **water** to the marinade. When the onion has cooked, stir the marinade, pour it into the skillet, and cook, stirring, for 1 minute, or until the sauce has thickened. Return the steak and any accumulated juices to the skillet. Simmer, uncovered, until heated through—about 3 minutes. Serve with rice.

> **Tip:** *This recipe can be halved.*

Spicy Oriental Beef ◎ ⊕

Preparation: 16 minutes   Cooking: 10 minutes   Serves 6   Calories per serving: 460

2 pounds flank or skirt steak, trimmed of fat and cut crosswise into ¼-inch slices

6 tablespoons soy sauce

½ cup vegetable oil

2 large carrots, peeled and cut into ¼-inch slices

4 large stalks celery, cut into ¼-inch slices

1 teaspoon ground ginger

¼ to ½ teaspoon crushed dried red pepper

1 teaspoon salt

1. In a large bowl, combine the **steak** slices and **soy sauce.** Heat ¼ cup of the **oil** in a heavy 12-inch skillet over moderately high heat for about 1 minute. Add the steak and cook, stirring, for 5 minutes, or until no pink remains.

2. Return the steak and pan juices to the bowl, and set aside. Heat the remaining ¼ cup of oil in the same skillet and add the **carrots.** Cook for 1 minute, then add the **celery, ginger, dried red pepper,** and **salt.** Cook, stirring, 2 minutes longer, or until the vegetables are crisp-tender. Do not overcook.

3. Reduce the heat to moderate, and return the steak and any accumulated juices to the skillet. Simmer, uncovered, until heated through—about 2 minutes. Serve over rice or noodles and with Cucumber Salad with Soy and Sesame Dressing, page 46.

> **Tip:** *This recipe can be halved.*

Paprika Beef ⬭ ⬭

Preparation: **10 minutes**   Cooking: **19 minutes**   Serves **4**   Calories per serving: **560**

4 tablespoons (¹/₂ stick) butter or margarine

1¹/₂ pounds flank or skirt steak, trimmed of fat and cut crosswise into strips ¹/₄ inch thick and 2 inches long

2 cups half-and-half

1¹/₄ teaspoons paprika

³/₄ teaspoon salt

Tips: 1. This recipe can be halved. 2. You can make this dish ahead and refrigerate it for up to 3 days or freeze it. 3. If you like a richer sauce, use heavy cream instead of the half-and-half.

1. Heat 2 tablespoons of the **butter** in a heavy 12-inch skillet over moderately high heat until bubbly. Add half the **steak** slices and cook for 3 to 4 minutes on each side until brown. Using a slotted spoon, remove the slices to a platter. Cook the remaining steak the same way and add to the platter.

2. Raise the heat to high. Add the **half-and-half, paprika,** and **salt** to the skillet, and boil, stirring, for 4 to 6 minutes, or until the sauce has thickened slightly. Stir in the remaining 2 tablespoons of butter. Return the steak and any accumulated juices to the skillet. Reduce the heat, and simmer, uncovered, until heated through—about 3 minutes. Serve over buttered noodles or rice.

Sukiyaki ⬭ ⬭

Preparation: **8 minutes**   Cooking: **10 minutes**   Serves **4**   Calories per serving: **420**

3 tablespoons butter or margarine

1 medium-size yellow onion, peeled and thinly sliced

1 pound flank or skirt steak, trimmed of fat and cut crosswise into ¹/₄-inch slices

¹/₄ teaspoon salt

¹/₂ pound mushrooms, sliced

1 large stalk celery, thinly sliced

2 medium-size carrots, peeled and thinly sliced

1 pound fresh or canned mung bean sprouts, drained

1 can (5 ounces) water chestnuts, drained and thinly sliced

2 tablespoons soy sauce

1 cup beef broth

¹/₂ cup chopped green onions (optional)

The estimated preparation time above assumes that you first trim and slice the steak—about 3 minutes. Use the 5 minutes while the onion is cooking to slice the mushrooms and celery and the 5 minutes while the steak browns to peel and slice the carrots, slice the water chestnuts, and chop the green onions.

1. Melt the **butter** in a heavy 12-inch skillet over moderate heat. Add the **onion** and cook, uncovered, stirring occasionally, for 5 minutes. Remove the onion to a plate and set aside.

2. Raise the heat to moderately high. Add the **steak** slices and cook, uncovered, turning once or twice, until browned—about 5 minutes. Return the onion to the skillet. Add the **salt, mushrooms, celery, carrots, bean sprouts, water chestnuts, soy sauce,** and **beef broth.**

3. Reduce the heat and simmer, uncovered, for 5 minutes, or until the celery and carrots are crisp-tender. Do not overcook. Serve over rice and sprinkle with the **green onions** if used. Serve with additional soy sauce, if you like.

Tip: This recipe can be halved.

112

Greek Beef Kebabs

Preparation: **30 minutes** Cooking: **6 minutes** Serves **4** Calories per serving: **265**

2 tablespoons olive oil

2 tablespoons lemon juice

1/2 teaspoon dried oregano, crumbled

1/4 teaspoon salt

1/8 teaspoon black pepper

1 clove garlic, peeled and minced

1 1/2 pounds flank or skirt steak, cut into 1-inch cubes

1. In a large bowl, combine the **oil, lemon juice, oregano, salt, pepper,** and **garlic.** Add the **steak** cubes to the mixture and marinate for 20 to 25 minutes at room temperature. About 5 minutes before you are ready to cook the kebabs, preheat the broiler.

2. Remove the steak from the marinade and thread it onto 4 skewers. Broil 4 inches from the heat for 3 minutes on each side, basting occasionally with the marinade.

> *Tip: To make a more elaborate dish, skewer cherry tomatoes, sweet green pepper chunks, onion wedges, and mushrooms between the meat cubes.*

Just Plain Good Hamburgers ⊙

Preparation: **5 minutes** Cooking: **6 minutes** Serves **4** Calories per serving: **230**

Here are directions for making not only plain hamburgers but 8 variations and 7 toppings. The calorie count above is for a plain hamburger; calories may increase depending on the variation and topping used.

1 pound lean ground beef

1 small yellow onion, peeled and grated

1 teaspoon salt

1/4 teaspoon black pepper

1. In a large bowl, combine the **beef, onion, salt,** and **pepper.** Shape the mixture into 4 patties, each about 1 inch thick.

2. *To panbroil:* Heat a lightly oiled heavy 12-inch skillet over moderate heat until hot. Cook the patties, uncovered, 3 minutes on each side for rare, 4 for medium, 6 for well done. Do not press on the patties or you will force out the juices. *To broil:* Place the patties 3 inches from the heat, and cook 2 minutes on each side for rare, 3 to 4 for medium, 5 to 6 for well done. Serve sandwich style on toasted hamburger buns.

> **Variations:** *Add any of the following to the beef before shaping it into patties:* **1.** *1/2 cup bottled barbecue sauce;* **2.** *1 can (2 1/4 to 3 ounces) deviled ham, 1 tablespoon sweet pickle relish, and 1 teaspoon prepared spicy brown mustard;* **3.** *1/2 cup shredded sharp Cheddar cheese;* **4.** *1/3 cup chopped walnuts;* **5.** *1/4 cup sour cream, 1 tablespoon minced parsley, and 1/8 teaspoon each dried thyme and oregano, crumbled;* **6.** *1/2 cup chopped mushrooms;* **7.** *1/4 cup chopped stuffed green olives;* **8.** *1/4 cup grated Parmesan cheese, 1/4 cup tomato sauce, and 1/4 teaspoon dried oregano, crumbled.*

> **Toppings:** **1.** *1/4 cup chili sauce and 1/4 teaspoon chili powder heated until just bubbly with 1 tablespoon butter or margarine;* **2.** *1 package (3 ounces) cream cheese with chives blended with 1/4 cup sour cream;* **3.** *1 tablespoon melted butter or margarine and 1 tablespoon garlic-flavored oil and vinegar dressing mixed with 1 teaspoon minced parsley and 1/2 teaspoon chopped fresh or freeze-dried chives;* **4.** *1 tablespoon all-purpose flour blended with 1 tablespoon butter or margarine, 1/4 teaspoon curry powder, 1/4 teaspoon salt, 2 or 3 sliced fresh mushrooms, and 1/2 cup water cooked until the sauce thickens—about 1 minute;* **5.** *2 tablespoons butter or margarine heated with 1/4 cup ketchup and 1 tablespoon bottled steak sauce;* **6.** *2 cups shredded cabbage mixed with mayonnaise, 4 sliced stuffed olives, and 2 slices cooked bacon, crumbled;* **7.** *1 can (1 pound) barbecue beans or baked beans heated with 1/2 cup shredded sharp Cheddar cheese.*

BEEF

Barbecued Hamburgers 🐷 ▷ ⬭

Preparation: **7 minutes**   Cooking: **9 minutes**   Serves **6**   Calories per serving: **315**

½ **cup fine dry bread crumbs**

½ **cup milk**

½ **teaspoon salt**

¼ **teaspoon black pepper**

1½ **pounds lean ground beef**

2 **small yellow onions, peeled and finely chopped**

1 **tablespoon vegetable oil**

½ **cup cider vinegar**

1½ **teaspoons chili powder**

⅛ **teaspoon dried oregano, crumbled**

4 **teaspoons Worcestershire sauce**

3 **medium-size tomatoes, peeled and chopped, or 1 can (1 pound) tomatoes, chopped, with their juice**

1. In a large bowl, combine the **bread crumbs, milk, salt,** and **pepper.** Add the **beef** and half the chopped **onions.** Mix well and shape the mixture into 6 patties, each about 1 inch thick.

2. Heat the **oil** in a heavy 12-inch skillet over moderate heat for about 1 minute. Add the patties and cook, uncovered, for 2 minutes on each side. Meanwhile, in a small bowl, combine the remaining onions, the **vinegar, chili powder, oregano, Worcestershire sauce,** and **tomatoes.** Pour the mixture over the patties and cook, uncovered, for 5 to 8 minutes, or until the sauce has thickened. Serve.

> *Tips: 1. This recipe can be halved; make 4 patties instead of 3, if you like. 2. You can make this dish ahead and refrigerate it for up to 3 days. 3. Try the sauce on other kinds of hamburgers as well.*

Hamburgers Diane 🐷 ▷ ⬭

Preparation: **6 minutes**   Cooking: **7 minutes**   Serves **4**   Calories per serving: **310**

1 **pound lean ground beef**

½ **teaspoon salt**

¼ **teaspoon black pepper**

½ **teaspoon dried thyme, crumbled**

¼ **teaspoon dried rosemary, crumbled**

2 **tablespoons butter or margarine**

1 **tablespoon vegetable oil**

1 **tablespoon Dijon or prepared spicy brown mustard**

1 **tablespoon lemon juice**

1½ **teaspoons Worcestershire sauce**

2 **tablespoons chopped parsley**

Flavored with herbs and served with a tart butter sauce, this is a quick version of a famous dish—Steak Diane—using thrifty ground beef.

1. In a large bowl, combine the **beef, salt, pepper, thyme,** and **rosemary.** Shape the mixture into 4 patties, each about 1 inch thick.

2. Heat 1 tablespoon of the **butter** with the **oil** and **mustard** in a heavy 12-inch skillet over moderate heat for about 1 minute. Add the patties and cook, uncovered, 3 minutes on each side for rare, 4 minutes for medium, and 6 for well done. Remove the patties to a warm platter.

3. Add the **lemon juice** and **Worcestershire sauce** to the skillet, and stir for 30 seconds. Remove the skillet from the heat, and stir in the **parsley** and the remaining butter. Pour the sauce over the patties.

> *Tip: This recipe can be halved.*

Onion Burgers in Wine Sauce ⊚ ⊕

Preparation: **9 minutes**   Cooking: **12 minutes**   Serves **4**   Calories per serving: **395**

This dish is good enough for an informal dinner party.

1 small yellow onion, peeled and finely chopped

1 pound ground round

3/4 teaspoon salt

1/4 teaspoon black pepper

5 tablespoons all-purpose flour

3 tablespoons butter or margarine

1 1/4 cups dry red wine

*Tips: 1. This recipe can be halved.
2. You can substitute ground lamb for the beef.*

1. In a large bowl, combine the **onion, beef, salt,** and **pepper.** Shape the mixture into 4 patties, each about 1 inch thick.

2. Put 3 tablespoons of the **flour** on a plate or a sheet of wax paper, and press both sides of the patties into it. Brush off any excess flour.

3. Heat 1 tablespoon of the **butter** in a heavy 12-inch skillet over moderate heat until bubbly. Cook the patties, uncovered, 3 minutes on each side for rare, 4 minutes for medium, and 6 minutes for well done. Remove to a warm platter.

4. Discard the fat from the skillet. Add the **wine,** and boil until only about 1/2 cup wine remains— about 4 minutes. Meanwhile, blend the remaining 2 tablespoons each of flour and butter.

5. Reduce the heat to low. Stir in the flour-butter mixture and cook, stirring constantly, for about 1 minute, or until the sauce thickens. Pour the sauce over the patties.

Italian Cutlets with Tomato Sauce ⊚

Preparation: **17 minutes**   Cooking: **9 minutes**   Serves **4**   Calories per serving: **475**

1 pound lean ground beef

1/2 teaspoon salt

3 tablespoons all-purpose flour

1 egg, lightly beaten

1/2 cup fine dry bread crumbs

1/4 cup olive or vegetable oil

2 slices (1 ounce each) mozzarella cheese, cut in half

1 can (8 ounces) tomato sauce

1/4 cup water

1/2 teaspoon dried basil, crumbled

1/2 teaspoon dried oregano, crumbled

1. In a mixing bowl, combine the **beef** and **salt,** and shape the mixture into 4 oval-shaped cutlets, each about 1 inch thick.

2. Put the **flour, egg,** and **bread crumbs** into separate shallow bowls. Press the cutlets into the flour, dip them into the beaten egg, then coat them with the bread crumbs.

3. Heat the **oil** in a heavy 12-inch skillet over moderately high heat for about 1 minute, and cook the cutlets for 4 minutes on each side. Reduce the heat to moderate, place a piece of **cheese** on each cutlet, and pour the **tomato sauce** and **water** around the cutlets. Sprinkle with the **basil** and **oregano.**

4. Cook, uncovered, for 5 minutes. Cover, reduce the heat to low, and simmer 4 minutes longer, or until the cheese melts.

Tip: Use fewer dishes by putting the flour and bread crumbs on separate pieces of wax paper.

BEEF

Hamburger Pancakes 🐷 ⊙

Preparation: **6 minutes**   Cooking: **10 minutes**   Serves **4**   Calories per serving: **200**

1/2 **pound lean ground beef**

1 **tablespoon grated yellow onion**

1/2 **teaspoon salt**

1/4 **teaspoon black pepper**

1/4 **teaspoon baking powder**

3 **eggs, separated**

1 **tablespoon vegetable oil**

An ingenious cook from Saskatchewan, Canada, shows how to make 1/2 pound of ground beef go a long way. The recipe was undoubtedly born of necessity, perhaps during the Depression, but it still serves when you want to stretch a small amount of meat—or your food budget.

1. In a large bowl, combine the **beef, onion, salt, pepper, baking powder,** and **egg yolks.** In a separate bowl, beat the **egg whites** until just stiff, then fold them into the beef mixture.

2. Heat the **oil** in a heavy 9- or 10-inch skillet over moderate heat for about 1 minute. Using a large spoon, drop the beef mixture into the skillet, making 4 pancakes. Cook for 5 minutes, turn the pancakes with a pancake turner, and cook 5 minutes longer.

Salisbury Steak with Onion Sauce ⊙

Preparation: **10 minutes**   Cooking: **15 minutes**   Serves **6**   Calories per serving: **315**

Getting this dish on the table in 25 minutes takes some organization: prepare the ingredients for and shape the patties while the onion is cooking. Then, while the patties are on the stove, finish the sauce.

4 **tablespoons (1/2 stick) butter or margarine**

1 **tablespoon water**

1 **large yellow onion, peeled and finely chopped**

1 1/2 **pounds lean ground beef**

2 **cloves garlic, peeled and minced**

1 **tablespoon chopped fresh chives or freeze-dried chives**

1 **tablespoon finely chopped parsley**

1/4 **teaspoon dried thyme, crumbled**

1 **teaspoon salt**

1/4 **teaspoon black pepper**

2 **tablespoons all-purpose flour**

1 **cup beef broth**

1. Place 2 tablespoons of the **butter,** the **water,** and all but 2 tablespoons of the **onion** in a heavy 10-inch skillet over moderately low heat. Cover and cook for 10 minutes, stirring occasionally to prevent browning.

2. Meanwhile, in a large bowl, combine the **beef, garlic, chives, parsley, thyme, salt, pepper,** and the reserved 2 tablespoons of onion. Shape the mixture into 6 patties about 1 inch thick.

3. Heat the remaining 2 tablespoons of butter in a heavy 12-inch skillet over moderate heat until bubbly. Add the patties and cook about 4 minutes on each side for medium. Remove the patties to a warm platter and set aside.

4. To make the sauce, stir the **flour** into the cooked onion in the 10-inch skillet and cook for 1 minute over moderately high heat. Add the **beef broth** and boil for 4 minutes, stirring, until the sauce has thickened. Place the patties in the skillet to reheat briefly, and spoon the sauce over them. Serve with Glorious Mashed Potatoes, page 74.

Tips: 1. For a smoother sauce, purée it in a blender, reheat if necessary, and pour over the patties. 2. This dish can be made ahead and refrigerated for 1 or 2 days.

BEEF

116

Sweet and Sour Beef and Cabbage ⊕

Preparation: **21 minutes**   Cooking: **20 minutes**   Serves **6**   Calories per serving: **270**

1 pound lean ground beef

3 tablespoons uncooked rice

2 tablespoons grated onion

1 egg, lightly beaten

2 tablespoons water

1/2 teaspoon dried dillweed

1 teaspoon salt

1/2 teaspoon black pepper

2 tablespoons vegetable oil

1 medium-size yellow onion, peeled and chopped

3 medium-size fresh tomatoes, peeled and chopped, or 1 can (1 pound) tomatoes, chopped, with their juice

2 tablespoons lemon juice

1 tablespoon honey

1 small cabbage (about 1 pound), cut into 6 wedges

2 carrots, peeled and sliced

Here's a one-dish meal with all the flavor of stuffed cabbage but with only half the work. To save time, prepare the chopped onion, tomatoes, carrots, and cabbage while the beef patties are browning.

1. In a large bowl, combine the **beef, rice, grated onion, egg, water, dillweed,** 1/2 teaspoon of the **salt,** and 1/4 teaspoon of the **pepper.** Shape the mixture into 6 oval patties.

2. Heat the **oil** in a heavy 12-inch skillet over moderately high heat for about 1 minute. Add the patties and cook, uncovered, for 4 minutes on each side, or until browned. Remove the patties to a platter.

3. Pour all but 2 tablespoons of the drippings from the skillet. Add the **chopped onion, tomatoes, lemon juice, honey,** the remaining 1/2 teaspoon of salt and 1/4 teaspoon of pepper, and bring to a boil. Reduce the heat and add the **cabbage** wedges. Top with the patties and **carrots,** cover, and simmer for 20 minutes.

Tips: 1. This recipe can be halved. 2. You can substitute lamb for the beef.

Swedish Meatballs

Preparation: **13 minutes**   Cooking: **27 minutes**   Serves **4**   Calories per serving: **625**

3/4 cup fine dry bread crumbs

2 tablespoons finely chopped yellow onion

1 teaspoon salt

1/8 teaspoon ground nutmeg

1/2 cup milk

1/2 pound lean ground beef

1/2 pound ground pork

1/2 pound ground veal

3 tablespoons butter

4 teaspoons all-purpose flour

1 cup beef broth

3/4 cup half-and-half

1. In a large bowl, combine the **bread crumbs, onion, salt, nutmeg,** and **milk.** Add the ground **beef, pork,** and **veal,** and mix thoroughly. Shape the mixture into 1 1/2-inch balls.

2. Heat the **butter** in a heavy 12-inch skillet over moderate heat until bubbly. Cook the meatballs, uncovered, turning frequently, for 20 minutes. Remove them to a platter with a slotted spoon.

3. Add the **flour** to the drippings in the skillet, stir until bubbly, then blend in the **beef broth** and **half-and-half.** Boil, uncovered, for 4 to 5 minutes, stirring, until the sauce thickens.

4. Return the meatballs and any accumulated juices to the skillet. Spoon the sauce over the meatballs and heat through—about 2 minutes.

Tip: You can make this recipe using all ground beef.

Rice and Beef Porcupines

Preparation: **13 minutes**   Cooking: **30 minutes**   Serves **4**   Calories per serving: **405**

1 pound lean ground beef

1 teaspoon salt

3 tablespoons finely chopped yellow onion

1/2 teaspoon dried oregano, crumbled

1/4 teaspoon dried rosemary, crumbled

1/2 cup uncooked rice

2 tablespoons vegetable oil

2 cans (8 ounces each) tomato sauce

1 cup water

1. In a large bowl, combine the **beef, salt, onion, oregano, rosemary,** and **rice.** Shape the mixture into 1½-inch balls.

2. Heat the **oil** in a heavy 12-inch skillet over moderately low heat for about 1 minute. Cook the meatballs, uncovered, turning frequently, until browned on all sides—about 5 minutes.

3. Add the **tomato sauce** and **water,** cover and simmer for 30 minutes. Serve with a green salad and crusty Italian bread.

> *Tip: You can substitute 1 jar (15 or 16 ounces) meatless spaghetti sauce for the tomato sauce.*

Mediterranean Meatballs ⊕

Preparation: **20 minutes**   Cooking: **20 minutes**   Serves **4**   Calories per serving: **560**

1 pound lean ground beef

1/2 cup soft fresh bread crumbs (1 slice bread)

1 small yellow onion, peeled and finely chopped

1 clove garlic, peeled and minced

1 egg, lightly beaten

3/4 teaspoon salt

1/2 teaspoon black pepper

2 tablespoons flour

2 tablespoons vegetable oil

1/2 cup beef broth

3 medium-size fresh tomatoes, peeled and chopped, or 1 can (1 pound) tomatoes, chopped, with their juice

1 teaspoon dried tarragon, crumbled

3 medium-size zucchini (about 1 pound), sliced

1 can (20 ounces) chick peas, drained (about 2 cups)

Here is an easy skillet dinner that can be made ahead. What more could a cook-in-a-hurry ask for?

1. In a large bowl, combine the **beef, bread crumbs, onion, garlic, egg,** 1/2 teaspoon of the **salt,** and 1/4 teaspoon of the **pepper.** Shape the mixture into 1½-inch balls. Dust the meatballs lightly with the **flour.**

2. Heat the **oil** in a heavy 12-inch skillet over moderate heat for about 1 minute. Cook the meatballs, uncovered, turning frequently, until browned on all sides—about 5 minutes.

3. Pour off and discard the fat from the skillet. Add the **beef broth** to the meatballs, bring to a boil, and cook for 30 seconds, scraping up any brown bits stuck to the skillet. Add the **tomatoes,** the remaining 1/4 teaspoon each of salt and pepper, and the **tarragon.** Cover, reduce the heat, and simmer for 15 minutes.

4. Add the **zucchini** and **chick peas,** and cook, covered, for 4 to 5 minutes, or until the zucchini is crisp-tender.

> *Tip: This recipe can be halved; use 1/2 a beaten egg and refrigerate the other half and add to the next morning's scrambled eggs.*

Miniature Meat Loaves

Preparation: **13 minutes**   Cooking: **35 minutes**   Serves **6**   Calories per serving: **365**

Individual meat loaves cook in approximately half the time it takes to bake one large loaf.

2 tablespoons butter or margarine

1 medium-size yellow onion, peeled and finely chopped

1½ pounds ground beef, preferably ground chuck

½ cup fine dry bread crumbs

1 jar (4 ounces) pimientos, drained and chopped

1 egg, lightly beaten

¼ cup milk

½ teaspoon dried thyme, crumbled

1¼ teaspoon salt

¼ teaspoon black pepper

3 slices bacon, cut in half

1. Preheat the oven to 400°F. Melt the **butter** in a 6-inch skillet over moderate heat. Add the **onion** and cook, uncovered, for 5 minutes, or until soft.

2. In a large bowl, combine the cooked onion, the **beef, bread crumbs, pimientos, egg, milk, thyme, salt,** and **pepper.** Shape the mixture into 6 loaves, each about 4"x 1½"x 1½". Put the loaves into an unbuttered 9"x 9"x 2" baking dish. Place a piece of the **bacon** on top of each loaf.

3. Bake, uncovered, for 35 minutes. Serve with a tomato sauce, if desired, and mashed or boiled potatoes.

Tips: 1. You can substitute 1 tablespoon of finely chopped parsley for the pimientos. 2. This recipe can be made ahead, cooked, and refrigerated for up to 3 days or frozen.

Sweet and Sour Meat Loaf

Preparation: **8 minutes**   Cooking: **30 minutes**   Serves **4**   Calories per serving: **280**

1 pound lean ground beef

1 medium-size yellow onion, peeled and finely chopped

1 stalk celery, finely chopped

1 clove garlic, peeled and minced

1 teaspoon salt

1 teaspoon dry mustard

1 egg, lightly beaten

½ small sweet green pepper, cored, seeded, and minced

½ cup tomato sauce

1 tablespoon firmly packed light or dark brown sugar

1 tablespoon cider vinegar

1. Preheat the oven to 450°F. In a large bowl, combine the **beef, onion, celery, garlic, salt, mustard, egg,** and **pepper.** Pat the mixture into a 9-inch pie plate, leaving ½ inch of space around the edge to catch the drippings. Separate the pie into 4 equal wedges by cutting through the meat to the bottom of the pie plate.

2. In a small bowl, combine the **tomato sauce, brown sugar,** and **vinegar,** and pour over the meat mixture. Bake, uncovered, for 30 minutes, basting occasionally with the juices. Tip the pie plate and pour off the drippings. Serve the meat loaf with buttered new potatoes and Broccoli with Sweet Red Peppers, page 63.

Tips: 1. You can substitute ground lamb for the beef. 2. For extra flavor, add half an 8¼-ounce can of crushed pineapple, drained, to the meat mixture. 3. Leftovers can be refrigerated for 1 or 2 days or frozen. Reheat, uncovered, in a 350°F oven.

Beef and Sweet Potato Stew ◁ ⬭

Preparation: **13 minutes**   Cooking: **15 minutes**   Serves **4**   Calories per serving: **285**

2 cups beef broth

3/4 pound lean ground beef

2 medium-size sweet potatoes (about 3/4 pound), peeled and cut into 1/2-inch cubes

1 small yellow onion, peeled and finely chopped

1 clove garlic, peeled and minced

Pinch cayenne pepper

1/4 teaspoon dried thyme, crumbled

1/4 teaspoon dried marjoram, crumbled

2 tablespoons tomato paste

1. Bring the **beef broth** to a boil in a 2-quart saucepan. Add the **beef,** cover, and boil for 3 minutes, or until the meat is no longer pink, stirring frequently to break up any large clumps.

2. Add the **sweet potatoes, onion, garlic, cayenne pepper, thyme, marjoram,** and **tomato paste.** Reduce the heat, cover, and simmer for 15 minutes, or until the potatoes are tender. Serve with Farmer's Turnip and Pear Salad, page 49.

> *Tips: 1. This recipe can be halved, or leftovers can be refrigerated for 1 or 2 days. 2. You can substitute white potatoes for the sweet potatoes.*

Beef and Tomato Stew ◁ ⬭

Preparation: **12 minutes**   Cooking: **15 minutes**   Serves **4**   Calories per serving: **385**

2 tablespoons vegetable oil

1 pound lean ground beef

1 medium-size yellow onion, peeled and finely chopped

1 canned green chili, seeded and minced

2 cups fresh sweet corn (cut from 3 large ears) or 1 package (10 ounces) frozen whole-kernel corn

2 small zucchini or yellow squash (about 3/4 pound), cut into 1/2-inch slices

4 medium-size ripe or green tomatoes, peeled and cut into 1-inch pieces

1/2 teaspoon ground cumin

1/2 teaspoon dried oregano, crumbled

1 teaspoon salt

Here's how to streamline the preparation time of this dish. If you're using fresh corn, shuck it and cut the kernels from the cob before you start the recipe; peel and chop the onion and mince the chili pepper while the beef browns; prepare the tomatoes and squash while the onion and chili cook.

1. Heat the **oil** in a heavy 12-inch skillet over moderately high heat for about 1 minute. Cook the **beef,** uncovered, stirring frequently, for 5 minutes, or until browned. Add the **onion** and **chili,** and cook, uncovered, for 5 more minutes, or until the onion is soft.

2. Add the **corn** to the skillet (if you use frozen corn, put the frozen block into the skillet and break it up with a fork), then the **zucchini, tomatoes, cumin, oregano,** and **salt.** Simmer, uncovered, for 15 minutes, stirring occasionally. Serve in soup bowls.

> *Tips: 1. This recipe can be halved. 2. You can make this dish ahead and refrigerate it for up to 3 days, or freeze it. 3. If you like an extra spicy stew, substitute 1 or 2 minced serrano chilies for the milder canned chili pepper.*

BEEF

Spicy Texas Beef Stew ◐

Preparation: **11 minutes**   Cooking: **20 minutes**   Serves **4**   Calories per serving: **435**

1/4 cup vegetable oil

1 pound lean ground beef

1 medium-size yellow onion, peeled and finely chopped

1 clove garlic, peeled and minced

3 medium-size fresh tomatoes, peeled and chopped, or 1 can (1 pound) tomatoes, chopped, with their juice

1 teaspoon sugar

1 teaspoon ground cinnamon

1/8 teaspoon ground cloves

1/4 teaspoon ground cumin

1 teaspoon salt

1/2 cup raisins

A favorite from Texas, this stew has an unusual flavor, both sweet and spicy. Save time by peeling and chopping the tomatoes while the beef is browning.

1. Heat the **oil** in a heavy 2-quart saucepan over moderate heat for about 1 minute. Add the **beef, onion,** and **garlic,** and cook, uncovered, stirring frequently, about 7 minutes, or until the onion is soft and the beef has browned.

2. Add the **tomatoes, sugar, cinnamon, cloves, cumin, salt,** and **raisins.** Cover, reduce the heat, and simmer for 20 minutes, stirring occasionally. Add 2 or 3 tablespoons of water if the mixture gets too thick. Serve with rice, a green vegetable, buttered tortillas, and a fruit salad.

Tip: This recipe can be halved, or leftovers can be refrigerated for 1 or 2 days or frozen.

Chili Frittata 🐷

Preparation: **11 minutes**   Cooking: **22 minutes**   Serves **4**   Calories per serving: **375**

1/4 cup vegetable oil

1 medium-size yellow onion, peeled and chopped

1 medium-size sweet green pepper, cored, seeded, and chopped

1/2 pound lean ground beef

1/2 teaspoon dried oregano, crumbled

1/4 teaspoon dried basil, crumbled

2 teaspoons chili powder

1 teaspoon salt

1 medium-size tomato, peeled and chopped

4 eggs

1/4 cup milk

1/3 cup grated Parmesan cheese

1. Heat 2 tablespoons of the **oil** in a heavy 10-inch skillet over moderate heat for about 1 minute. Add the **onion** and **green pepper.** Cook, uncovered, for 3 minutes. Add the **beef** and cook, stirring, until browned—about 4 minutes.

2. Add the **oregano, basil, chili powder,** 1/2 teaspoon of the **salt,** and the **tomato.** Reduce the heat to low, cover, and cook for 15 minutes. Transfer the mixture to a bowl.

3. Preheat the broiler. In the same skillet, heat the remaining 2 tablespoons of oil. Beat the **eggs, milk,** and remaining salt together in a bowl, and pour into the skillet. Cook over moderate heat, without stirring, until the eggs begin to set around the edges—2 to 3 minutes.

4. Spoon the beef mixture evenly over the eggs and cook for 3 to 4 more minutes. Sprinkle the **cheese** over the mixture, place the skillet (but not the handle) under the broiler about 5 inches from the heat, and broil for 2 minutes. Cut the frittata into wedges and serve.

Quick Chili Con Carne

Preparation: **13 minutes**   Cooking: **25 minutes**   Serves **6**   Calories per serving: **295**

2 tablespoons vegetable oil

1 medium-size yellow onion, peeled and chopped

1 medium-size sweet green pepper, cored, seeded, and chopped

1 pound lean ground beef

2 cloves garlic, peeled and minced

2 cans (8 ounces each) tomato sauce

1/4 teaspoon ground cumin

1/4 teaspoon cayenne pepper

2 teaspoons chili powder

1/2 teaspoon dried oregano, crumbled

1 teaspoon salt

2 cans (15 ounces each) pinto or kidney beans, drained

1. Heat the **oil** in a heavy 3-quart saucepan over moderate heat for about 1 minute. Add the **onion, green pepper, beef,** and **garlic,** and cook, uncovered, stirring frequently, for 7 or 8 minutes, or until the onion is soft and the beef has browned.

2. Add the **tomato sauce, cumin, cayenne pepper, chili powder, oregano,** and **salt.** Cover, reduce the heat, and simmer for 20 minutes, stirring occasionally. Add 2 or 3 tablespoons of water if the mixture becomes too thick.

3. Stir in the **beans,** cover, and simmer for 5 more minutes, or until the beans are heated through. Serve with a green salad.

> *Tips:* **1.** *This recipe can be halved, or leftovers can be refrigerated for up to 3 days, or frozen.* **2.** *For an extra treat, serve the chili in bowls or taco shells and top with sour cream, chopped onions, and diced cucumber.*

Skillet Macaroni and Beef

Preparation: **10 minutes**   Cooking: **13 minutes**   Serves **4**   Calories per serving: **435**

3/4 pound ground beef

1 small zucchini (about 1/4 pound), coarsely chopped

1 small yellow onion, peeled and finely chopped

8 ounces uncooked elbow macaroni

2 cans (8 ounces each) tomato sauce

1 teaspoon salt

2 teaspoons Worcestershire sauce

3/4 teaspoon dried basil, crumbled

3/4 teaspoon dried oregano, crumbled

1 to 1 1/2 cups water

This satisfying one-dish meal gives you more dinner for the dollar than you are likely to find anywhere! To save time, chop the onion and zucchini while the beef browns.

1. In a heavy 12-inch skillet over moderately high heat, cook the **beef,** uncovered, stirring occasionally, for 5 minutes, or until browned. Using a slotted spoon, remove the beef to a bowl and set aside. Add the **zucchini, onion,** and **macaroni** to the skillet, and cook, uncovered, for 3 minutes.

2. Return the beef to the skillet, and add the **tomato sauce, salt, Worcestershire sauce, basil, oregano,** and enough **water** to cover the macaroni and beef. Cover the skillet, reduce the heat, and simmer for 13 to 15 minutes, or until the macaroni is tender. Stir occasionally.

> *Tips:* **1.** *You can substitute 1 medium-size chopped sweet green pepper for the zucchini.* **2.** *This recipe can be halved, or leftovers can be refrigerated for 1 or 2 days.*

Indian Spiced Beef and Chick Peas 🐷

Preparation: **16 minutes**   Cooking: **25 minutes**   Serves **4**   Calories per serving: **810**

2 tablespoons vegetable oil

1 medium-size yellow onion, peeled and chopped

2 cloves garlic, peeled and minced

1 pound lean ground beef

3/4 teaspoon ground cumin

1/4 teaspoon ground cinnamon

1/8 teaspoon ground cloves

1/8 teaspoon cayenne pepper

1 cup sour cream

3/4 teaspoon salt

1 1/2 cups uncooked rice

1 can (10 ounces) chick peas, drained

Spicy but not hot, this dish is good enough for company, and you can make it ahead—it's even better the next day.

1. Heat the **oil** in a heavy 12-inch skillet over moderate heat. Add the **onion** and cook, uncovered, for 5 minutes, or until soft. Add the **garlic** and cook 1 minute longer.

2. Add the **beef** and cook, uncovered, stirring frequently, for 5 minutes, or until browned. Skim off all but 1 tablespoon of the drippings.

3. Stir in the **cumin, cinnamon, cloves, cayenne pepper, sour cream,** and **salt.** Cover and simmer for 20 minutes, stirring once or twice. Meanwhile, cook the **rice** according to package directions.

4. Stir the **chick peas** into the beef mixture and simmer, uncovered, for 5 to 10 minutes, or until the sauce has thickened. Serve over the rice.

Tex-Mex Tortilla Bake

Preparation: **20 minutes**   Cooking: **20 minutes**   Serves **4**   Calories per serving: **695**

1 pound lean ground beef

1 medium-size yellow onion, peeled and finely chopped

2 stalks celery, finely chopped

2 cloves garlic, peeled and minced

6 medium-size fresh tomatoes, peeled and chopped, or 1 can (2 pounds 3 ounces) tomatoes, chopped, with their juice

3/4 teaspoon dried oregano, crumbled

1/2 teaspoon ground cumin

1 teaspoon salt

1 to 3 canned green chilies, rinsed, seeded, and minced

16 tortillas

1 1/2 cups shredded sharp Cheddar cheese (6 ounces)

When you know you've got a busy day ahead, make this dish the night before. To save time, while the beef is browning, prepare the onion, celery, and garlic, and while they are cooking, prepare the tomatoes and chilies.

1. Preheat the oven to 325°F. In a heavy 12-inch skillet over moderately high heat, cook the **beef,** uncovered, stirring frequently, for 5 minutes. Using a slotted spoon, remove the beef to a bowl.

2. Add the **onion, celery,** and **garlic** to the beef drippings in the skillet, and cook, uncovered, over moderately low heat for 5 minutes, or until the onion is soft.

3. Add the **tomatoes** and their juice, the **oregano, cumin, salt,** and **chilies.** Simmer, uncovered, for 10 minutes, or until thick. Stir in the beef and any accumulated juices.

4. Cut the **tortillas** into 1-inch strips and line the bottom of a buttered 13"x 9"x 2" baking dish with half of them. Cover with half the beef mixture. Repeat. Sprinkle with the **cheese,** and bake, uncovered, for 20 minutes.

Easy Taco Supper ⊘ ⍟

Preparation: **14 minutes**   Cooking: **10 minutes**   Serves **4**   Calories per serving: **925**

2 tablespoons vegetable oil

1 medium-size yellow onion, peeled and chopped

1 large sweet green pepper, cored, seeded, and chopped

1 pound lean ground beef

3/4 teaspoon ground cumin

1 teaspoon dried oregano

1 teaspoon chili powder

3/4 teaspoon salt

2 to 4 canned green chilies, rinsed, seeded, and chopped

1 can (15 to 16 ounces) pinto or kidney beans, drained

1 medium-size tomato, diced

12 taco shells

2 cups shredded sharp Cheddar cheese (8 ounces)

3/4 cup sour cream

1 medium-size cucumber, peeled and diced

2 cups shredded lettuce

1. Heat the **oil** in a heavy 12-inch skillet over moderate heat. Add the **onion** and **green pepper,** and cook, uncovered, for 5 minutes, or until the onion is soft.

2. Add the **beef** and cook, uncovered, stirring frequently, for 5 minutes, or until browned. Tilt the skillet and skim off all but 2 tablespoons of the fat.

3. Stir in the **cumin, oregano, chili powder, salt, chilies, beans,** and **tomato.** Cover and simmer for 10 minutes, stirring once or twice.

4. Meanwhile, heat the **taco shells** according to package directions. When the taco filling is cooked, transfer to a serving bowl. Serve with small bowls of the **cheese, sour cream, cucumber,** and **lettuce.** Let everyone stuff his own taco shells, allowing about 1/3 cup of beef filling per taco, and garnish as desired.

Tip: This recipe can be halved.

Creamed Dried Beef on Toast 🐖 ⊘ ⍟

Preparation: **8 minutes**   Cooking: **7 minutes**   Serves **4**   Calories per serving: **315**

5 tablespoons butter or margarine

1 medium-size sweet green pepper, cored, seeded, and chopped

1 medium-size yellow onion, peeled and chopped

1/4 pound mushrooms, sliced

1/4 cup all-purpose flour

1 3/4 cups milk

2 jars (2 1/2 ounces each) dried beef slices, chopped

Here is a pepped-up version of the traditional recipe. Serve it for breakfast, lunch, or a light dinner.

1. Melt the **butter** in a 12-inch skillet over moderate heat. Add the **green pepper** and **onion,** and cook, uncovered, for 5 minutes, or until the onion is tender. Add the **mushrooms** and cook for 3 minutes. Blend in the **flour.**

2. Gradually add the **milk,** stirring constantly until the mixture is smooth and thick—about 3 minutes. Stir in the **beef** and simmer, uncovered, for 1 minute. Serve over hot buttered toast, split biscuits, cornbread, or buttered noodles.

Tip: This recipe can be halved.

BEEF

PORK

Pork is both nutritious and good to eat—especially when prepared in the pleasing ways you will find here. Try the versatile ham steak, for example. Fully cooked, it needs only a bit of spice or a glistening lemon-raisin sauce to make it exciting. In a really big rush? Stir-fry strips of pork with cucumbers in just 17 minutes. Or cook pork chops or sausages in new and different ways. Note that names and availability of cuts of meat vary. If you cannot find the pork sirloin cutlets called for in some recipes, use blade shoulder chops or a similar cut.

Casserole-Roasted Pork with Vegetable Sauce

Preparation: **20 minutes**   Cooking: **1³/₄ hours**   Serves **6**   Calories per serving: **820**

Although this pork takes a while to cook, it needs little attention during that time and will serve 6 from a bargain cut of meat. Leftovers can be used for sandwiches or in a recipe that calls for cooked pork. If you are feeding 6 and want leftovers for later use, roast a larger cut of pork, allowing about 30 minutes' roasting time per pound. An even simpler way to cook this cut of meat is to sprinkle it with about ¹/₂ teaspoon of salt and ¹/₄ teaspoon of black pepper, place the pork on a rack in the roasting pan, and roast it, uncovered, at 35 minutes per pound until a meat thermometer registers 170°F.

3 tablespoons vegetable oil

1 boned and rolled lean shoulder pork roast (about 3 pounds)

1 large yellow onion, peeled and chopped

1 large carrot, peeled and chopped

3 cloves garlic, peeled

1 teaspoon salt

¹/₂ teaspoon black pepper

³/₄ teaspoon dried rosemary, crumbled

¹/₂ cup dry white wine or chicken broth

¹/₂ cup half-and-half

1. Preheat the oven to 325°F. In a large roasting pan with a cover, heat the **oil** over moderately high heat for about 1 minute. Add the **pork roast** and brown it on all sides, turning it frequently—about 10 minutes. Remove the roast to a platter.

2. Lower the heat to moderate. Put the **onion, carrot,** and the whole cloves of **garlic** into the roasting pan, and cook, covered, for 5 minutes, or until the vegetables are tender. Remove the pan from the heat, and add the **salt, pepper,** and **rosemary.**

3. Return the roast to the pan. Insert a meat thermometer into the center of the roast, and cover the pan. Cook the meat, basting it several times with the pan juices, until the thermometer registers 170°F—about 90 minutes. Remove the meat to a platter, and keep it warm.

4. Set the roasting pan on the stove over moderate heat. Add the **wine** and simmer for 2 minutes, scraping up any brown bits stuck to the pan. Tilt the pan and skim off all but about 1 tablespoon of the fat from the pan juices. Mash the vegetables with a fork, and boil the sauce for 1 minute. Strain it through a sieve. Discard the vegetables.

5. Return the sauce to the pan and add the **half-and-half.** Warm the sauce over moderate heat until heated through—about 1 minute.

6. Cut the strings from the pork and carve the meat into ¹/₄-inch slices. Serve with the sauce and with French Green Peas, page 72.

Spicy Pork Tacos ⏵

Preparation: **10 minutes**   Cooking: **6 minutes**   Serves **4**   Calories per serving: **605**

12 taco shells

1 tablespoon vegetable oil

2 medium-size yellow onions, peeled and chopped

1 large stalk celery, chopped

1 clove garlic, peeled and minced

1 can (8 ounces) tomato sauce

2 canned whole green chilies, rinsed, seeded, and chopped

1/2 teaspoon dried oregano

1/4 teaspoon salt

1 1/2 cups chopped cooked pork

1 medium-size avocado, peeled, pitted, and sliced thin

3 tablespoons lemon juice

1 1/2 cups shredded lettuce

1/2 cup sour cream

Give the family a treat using leftover pork to make these zesty, fun-to-eat tacos.

1. Heat the **taco shells** according to package directions.

2. Meanwhile, heat the **oil** in a 9- or 10-inch skillet over moderate heat. Add the **onions, celery,** and **garlic.** Cook, uncovered, for 5 minutes, or until the onions are soft. Stir in the **tomato sauce, chilies, oregano,** and **salt.** Cover and simmer for 5 minutes, then add the **pork** and heat through—about 1 minute.

3. Toss the **avocado** slices with the **lemon juice.** Fill the taco shells with some of the meat mixture and some avocado slices and shredded **lettuce,** and top each with a dab of **sour cream.**

> *Tips: 1. You can substitute sliced cooked chicken or beef for the pork. 2. If you like, reserve 1/4 cup of the chopped raw onion to sprinkle over the filled tacos before serving.*

Hungarian Pork and Peppers ⏵ ◑

Preparation: **20 minutes**   Cooking: **7 minutes**   Serves **4**   Calories per serving: **345**

2 tablespoons vegetable oil

1 medium-size yellow onion, peeled and thinly sliced

3 medium-size sweet green peppers, cored, seeded, and cut into 1/4-inch strips

1 clove garlic, peeled and minced

1 tablespoon paprika

1/2 teaspoon salt

1/2 teaspoon sugar

3/4 pound pork sirloin cutlets, cut into 1/4-inch strips

1. Heat 1 tablespoon of the **oil** in a 12-inch skillet over moderately high heat. Add the **onion, green peppers,** and **garlic,** and cook, covered, for 3 minutes.

2. Reduce the heat to moderate, and add the **paprika, salt,** and **sugar,** and cook, partially covered, for 10 minutes. Transfer the mixture to a warm bowl and set aside.

3. Heat the remaining oil in the skillet over high heat for about 1 minute. Add the **pork** strips and cook, uncovered, stirring frequently, for 5 minutes, or until browned and cooked through.

4. Return the onion and pepper mixture to the skillet, and toss until heated through—about 2 minutes. Serve with buttered noodles.

> *Tips: 1. This recipe can be halved, but you should use the same amount of oil. 2. If you reheat this dish, do so slowly, or the meat may toughen.*

PORK

Pork Stir-Fry with Vegetables and Peanuts ⊘ ⬮

Preparation: **10 minutes** Cooking: **16 minutes** Serves **4** Calories per serving: **705**

2 tablespoons cornstarch

3/4 pound pork sirloin cutlets or boned fresh ham steak, cut in 1/2-inch cubes

6 tablespoons vegetable oil

6 green onions, trimmed and chopped

2 stalks celery, cut on the diagonal into 1/2-inch slices

1/2 pound mushrooms, sliced

3 tablespoons sugar

3 tablespoons white vinegar

1/4 cup soy sauce

1/2 cup water

Pinch crushed dried red pepper

1/2 cup roasted, unsalted peanuts

1. Put the **cornstarch** into a large bowl and toss the **pork** cubes in it until coated. Heat 4 tablespoons of the **oil** in a heavy 12-inch skillet over moderately high heat for about 1 minute. Add half the pork and cook, stirring, for 5 minutes. Using a slotted spoon, remove the cooked pork to a platter. Heat the remaining 2 tablespoons of oil in the skillet and cook the remaining pork.

2. Add the **onions, celery,** and **mushrooms** to the skillet and cook, stirring, for 1 minute.

3. In a small bowl, combine the **sugar, vinegar, soy sauce, water,** and **dried red pepper.** Pour the mixture into the skillet and cook, scraping up any brown bits stuck to the skillet, for 1 minute, or until the liquid thickens slightly.

4. Return the pork to the skillet, add the **peanuts,** and toss until heated through.

Tip: This recipe can be halved.

Cucumber Pork ⊘

Preparation: **10 minutes** Cooking: **7 minutes** Serves **4** Calories per serving: **395**

3 tablespoons vegetable oil

1 clove garlic, peeled and minced

1/4 teaspoon crushed dried red pepper

1 teaspoon salt

4 green onions, trimmed and cut into 2-inch lengths

3/4 pound pork sirloin cutlets, cut into 1/4-inch strips

16 fresh or frozen snow peas

1 tablespoon sugar

1 tablespoon cider vinegar

2 tablespoons beef broth

2 medium-size cucumbers, peeled, seeded, and cut into thin, 2-inch-long strips

You can prepare the ingredients for this dish a short while beforehand, and cook them at the last minute.

1. Heat the **oil** in a 9- or 10-inch skillet over moderately high heat. Add the **garlic, dried red pepper,** and **salt,** and cook, stirring, for 30 seconds.

2. Add the **green onions, pork,** and **snow peas.** Cook, stirring, for 5 minutes, or until the pork is no longer pink.

3. Combine the **sugar, vinegar,** and **broth,** and add the mixture to the skillet along with the **cucumbers.** Cook, tossing the ingredients, until heated through. Do not overcook or the pork will toughen. Serve with rice and Dry-Sautéed Broccoli, page 62.

Tip: As a variation, use 2 boneless, skinless chicken breasts (4 halves) instead of the pork.

Sweet and Sour Pork ⬡ ⬡

Preparation: **10 minutes**   Cooking: **7 minutes**   Serves **4**   Calories per serving: **425**

This popular Chinese-style dish is extra quick and easy to make.

2 teaspoons vegetable or peanut oil

3/4 pound pork sirloin cutlets, cut into 1/4-inch strips

2 cans (8 ounces each) pineapple chunks, undrained

2 tablespoons cornstarch

3 tablespoons cider vinegar

2 tablespoons lemon juice

3 tablespoons soy sauce

1/4 teaspoon salt

2 tablespoons firmly packed light brown sugar

1 large sweet green pepper, cored, seeded, and chopped

1 small yellow onion, peeled and thinly sliced

1. Heat the **oil** in a heavy 12-inch skillet over moderately high heat for about 1 minute. Add the **pork** strips and cook, uncovered, stirring frequently, for 5 minutes, or until browned.

2. Meanwhile, drain the juice from the **pineapple chunks** into a small bowl. Blend in the **cornstarch, vinegar, lemon juice, soy sauce, salt,** and **sugar,** and set aside.

3. Add the **green pepper** and **onion** to the skillet, and cook until the onion begins to soften—about 3 minutes.

4. Add the pineapple juice mixture to the skillet, reduce the heat to moderate, and cook, stirring, for 3 minutes, or until the liquid thickens slightly.

5. Add the pineapple chunks and heat through—about 1 minute. Serve over rice or crisp Chinese noodles and accompany with Cucumber Salad with Soy and Sesame Dressing, page 46.

Tip: This recipe can be halved; use a 10-inch skillet.

Quick Pork Stew with Oranges and Wine ⬡

Preparation: **25 minutes**   Cooking: **15 minutes**   Serves **6**   Calories per serving: **605**

3 tablespoons olive or vegetable oil

2 pounds boneless pork shoulder, trimmed of fat and cut into 1/2-inch cubes

1 large yellow onion, peeled and chopped

3 cloves garlic, peeled and minced

2/3 cup dry white wine

2/3 cup orange juice

1/4 teaspoon ground cumin

1/4 teaspoon cayenne pepper

1/2 teaspoon salt

2 small navel oranges, peeled and cut into 1-inch sections

1. Heat the **oil** in a heavy 12-inch skillet over moderately high heat for about 1 minute. Add the **pork** cubes and cook, uncovered, stirring frequently, for 5 minutes, or until browned.

2. Push the pork to one side of the skillet, add the **onion** and **garlic** to the cleared space, and cook, uncovered, for 5 minutes, or until the onion is soft.

3. Add the **wine** and boil, uncovered, for 2 minutes. Reduce the heat, and add the **orange juice, cumin, cayenne pepper,** and **salt.** Cover and simmer for 15 minutes, until the pork is tender and cooked through. Add the **oranges** during the last 5 minutes of cooking. Serve over buttered rice or noodles.

Tip: This recipe can be halved, or leftovers can be refrigerated for 1 or 2 days or frozen. If you freeze the dish, do not add the orange sections until after thawing.

PORK

Pork and Zucchini Skillet 🐷 ▷ ◑

Preparation: **13 minutes**   Cooking: **10 minutes**   Serves **4**   Calories per serving: **400**

3 tablespoons olive or vegetable oil

3/4 pound pork sirloin cutlets or boned fresh ham steak, cut into 1/2-inch cubes

1 large yellow onion, peeled and chopped

2 cloves garlic, peeled and minced

1 can (12 ounces) tomato juice

1/2 teaspoon salt

1/8 teaspoon black pepper

1/2 teaspoon dried rosemary, crumbled

1 teaspoon dried oregano, crumbled

3 medium-size zucchini (about 1 pound), cut into 1/2-inch slices

Practically a meal in itself, this dish need only be accompanied by buttered rice or noodles, bread, and a salad or fruit. To put this dish on the table in 23 minutes, peel and chop the onion and garlic while the pork browns, then while they are cooking, slice the zucchini.

1. Heat the **oil** in a heavy 12-inch skillet over moderately high heat for about 1 minute. Add the **pork** cubes and cook, uncovered, tossing frequently, for 5 minutes, or until browned.

2. Lower the heat to moderate, add the **onion** and **garlic,** and cook, uncovered, for 5 more minutes, or until the onion is soft.

3. Add the **tomato juice, salt, pepper, rosemary,** and **oregano.** Simmer, uncovered, for 5 minutes, stirring once or twice.

4. Add the **zucchini,** and cook, uncovered, for 5 minutes, or until the zucchini is crisp-tender, the juice has thickened, and the pork is well done.

> *Tip: This recipe can be halved, or leftovers can be refrigerated for 1 or 2 days. Reheat in a covered skillet over moderately low heat.*

Pork Chops with Orange Sauce ◑

Preparation: **9 minutes**   Cooking: **40 minutes**   Serves **4**   Calories per serving: **390**

1 tablespoon vegetable oil

4 pork chops, about 3/4 inch thick

1/2 teaspoon salt

1/4 cup water

1 1/4 teaspoons cornstarch

1/4 teaspoon ground cinnamon

1 cup orange juice

1 small navel orange

10 whole cloves

> *Tip: This recipe can be halved, or leftovers can be refrigerated for 1 or 2 days or frozen.*

1. Heat the **oil** in a heavy 12-inch skillet over moderately high heat for about 1 minute. Add the **pork chops** and cook, uncovered, for 4 minutes on each side. Add the **salt** and **water,** cover, reduce the heat, and simmer for 35 minutes.

2. Meanwhile, in a small bowl, combine the **cornstarch, cinnamon,** and 1/2 cup of the **orange juice.** Grate the rind of half the **orange** and add it to the bowl. Peel the orange, cut it into 1/2-inch slices, and add it to the mixture.

3. Remove the chops to a warm platter. Add the remaining 1/2 cup of orange juice and the **cloves** to the skillet and boil, stirring, for 4 or 5 minutes, or until only about 1/4 cup of juice remains. Remove the cloves with a slotted spoon.

4. Add the cornstarch mixture to the skillet and boil for 1 or 2 minutes, stirring until thickened. Pour the sauce over the chops and serve.

Breaded Pork Chops with Herbs ◫

Preparation: **15 minutes**   Cooking: **40 minutes**   Serves **4**   Calories per serving: **495**

While these pork chops bake, prepare a side dish, such as Romaine Salad with Blue Cheese and Walnuts, page 53, or Sweet Potato Pancakes, page 75. You'll have a meal fit for company.

3/4 cup fine dry bread crumbs

1/2 teaspoon salt

1/8 teaspoon black pepper

3/4 teaspoon dried rosemary, crumbled, or 1 tablespoon chopped parsley

2 tablespoons all-purpose flour

1 egg

4 pork chops, about 3/4 inch thick

3 tablespoons vegetable oil

1 tablespoon butter

1. Preheat the oven to 350°F. In a shallow bowl or pie plate, combine the **bread crumbs, salt, pepper,** and **rosemary.** Put the **flour** into another shallow bowl, and lightly beat the **egg** in a third shallow bowl. Coat the **pork chops** with the flour, dip them into the beaten egg, and then coat them with the bread-crumb mixture.

2. In a heavy 12-inch skillet with an ovenproof handle, heat the **oil** and **butter** over moderate heat for about 1 minute. Add the chops, and cook, uncovered, for 3 minutes on each side.

3. Spoon off all but 2 tablespoons of the drippings. Cover tightly, and bake for 40 minutes, or until the chops are tender and cooked through, turning once.

Tips: 1. This recipe can be halved—save the unused half egg for tomorrow morning's scrambled eggs. 2. If you do not have a skillet with an ovenproof handle, spoon 2 tablespoons of drippings into a baking dish, transfer the pork chops to it, cover, and bake.

Pork Chops in Spicy Tomato Sauce ◫

Preparation: **14 minutes**   Cooking: **30 minutes**   Serves **4**   Calories per serving: **455**

1 tablespoon butter or margarine

2 tablespoons olive or vegetable oil

4 pork chops, about 3/4 inch thick

1/2 cup dry red or white wine

2 cans (8 ounces each) tomato sauce

1/4 cup water

3 tablespoons chopped parsley

2 cloves garlic, peeled and minced

1/2 teaspoon dried rosemary, crumbled

1/2 teaspoon dried basil, crumbled

Tired of meatballs and spaghetti? Try these pork chops with pasta. Spoon the tomato sauce over noodles or linguine, and sprinkle with grated Parmesan cheese. Serve with a green salad.

1. Heat the **butter** and **oil** in a heavy 12-inch skillet over moderately high heat for about 1 minute. Add the **pork chops.** Cook, uncovered, for 4 minutes on each side, or until browned. Pour off all but 1 tablespoon of the drippings.

2. Add the **wine** and boil, uncovered, for 1 minute, or until only 4 tablespoonsful remain.

3. Stir in the **tomato sauce, water, parsley, garlic, rosemary,** and **basil.** Reduce the heat, cover, and simmer for 30 minutes, or until the chops are tender and cooked through; check occasionally and add a bit of water if the sauce seems too thick.

Tips: 1. This recipe can be halved. 2. You can cook this dish ahead and refrigerate it for 1 or 2 days, or freeze it.

Country Pork Chops with Gravy ⓓ

Preparation: 3 minutes   Cooking: 38 minutes   **Serves 4   Calories per serving: 505**

A staple in the Southern States, pork chops with gravy will be appreciated by discerning diners everywhere.

1 tablespoon vegetable oil

8 pork chops, about ½ inch thick

1 teaspoon salt

¼ teaspoon black pepper

2 tablespoons all-purpose flour

1 cup milk

Tips: 1. This recipe can be halved. 2. If you are really in a hurry, use 2 skillets and cut the cooking time in half.

1. Heat the **oil** in a 12-inch skillet over moderately high heat for about 1 minute. Add 4 of the **pork chops** and cook, uncovered, for 8 minutes on each side, or until the juices run clear when the chops are pierced near the bone. Remove the chops to a warm platter. Cook the remaining chops the same way. Sprinkle the chops with ½ teaspoon of the **salt** and ⅛ teaspoon of the **pepper.**

2. Pour off all but 2 tablespoons of the drippings from the skillet. Reduce the heat to moderate, add the **flour,** and cook, stirring constantly, until light brown—about 2 minutes.

3. Gradually stir in the **milk** and cook, stirring constantly, for 1 or 2 minutes, or until smooth and thickened. Add the remaining ½ teaspoon of salt and ⅛ teaspoon of pepper. Return the chops to the sauce in the skillet and reheat briefly. Spoon the sauce over the chops and serve with Baked Winter Squash, page 80.

Pork Chop Rice Skillet ⓓ

Preparation: 12 minutes   Cooking: 25 minutes   **Serves 4   Calories per serving: 555**

This skillet dinner is practically a meal in itself. Save time by preparing the onion, green pepper, and tomatoes while the chops are browning.

1 tablespoon vegetable oil

4 pork chops, ¾ inch thick

1 small yellow onion, peeled and chopped

1 cup uncooked rice

1 medium-size sweet green pepper, cored, seeded, and chopped

2¼ cups water

3 medium-size tomatoes, peeled and chopped, or 1 can (1 pound) tomatoes, chopped, with their juice

⅛ teaspoon black pepper

1½ teaspoons salt

1. Heat the **oil** in a heavy 12-inch skillet over moderately high heat for about 1 minute. Add the **pork chops** and cook, uncovered, for 4 minutes on each side, or until browned. Remove the chops to a platter and set aside.

2. Reduce the heat to moderately low, add the **onion** and **rice** to the skillet, and cook, stirring, for 1 minute.

3. Add the **green pepper, water, tomatoes, black pepper,** and 1 teaspoon of the **salt.** Bring the liquid to a boil and place the pork chops on top of the rice. Sprinkle the remaining ½ teaspoon of salt on the chops and cover the skillet.

4. Reduce the heat and simmer for 25 minutes, or until the rice is tender and the pork chops are cooked through. Check after 15 minutes and add ¼ to ½ cup of water if the mixture seems dry.

Tip: This recipe can be halved.

PORK

Braised Pork Chops with Pears and Onions ⊕

Preparation: **17 minutes**   Cooking: **40 minutes**   Serves **4**   Calories per serving: **500**

1 tablespoon butter or margarine

2 tablespoons vegetable oil

4 pork chops, about 3/4 inch thick

2 medium-size yellow onions, peeled and sliced

1/2 cup dry white wine

1/2 cup chicken broth

1/4 teaspoon salt

1/8 teaspoon black pepper

2 medium-size firm, ripe pears, peeled, cored, and cut into 1/4-inch slices

Tip: This recipe can be halved, or leftovers can be refrigerated for 1 or 2 days, but they should not be frozen, as frozen pears tend to get spongy.

1. Preheat the oven to 350°F. In a heavy 12-inch skillet with an ovenproof handle and a cover, heat the **butter** and **oil** over moderately high heat for about 1 minute. Add the **pork chops** and cook, uncovered, for 4 minutes on each side, or until browned. Remove the chops to a platter and set aside.

2. Reduce the heat to moderate, add the **onions** to the skillet, and cook, uncovered, for 5 minutes, or until soft. Spoon the onions over the chops. Add the **wine** and boil for 1 minute, scraping up any brown bits stuck to the skillet. Stir in the **chicken broth, salt,** and **pepper.**

3. Return the chops and onions to the skillet, and arrange the sliced **pears** on top. Bake, covered, for 40 minutes, or until the chops are tender and cooked through. Check occasionally and add a bit of water if the liquid is evaporating. Serve with sweet potatoes or winter squash and with Zucchini Patties, page 78.

Pork Chop Supper ⊕

Preparation: **10 minutes**   Cooking: **35 minutes**   Serves **4**   Calories per serving: **505**

1 tablespoon vegetable oil

4 pork chops, about 3/4 inch thick

2 1/4 cups beef broth

1 cup water

1/2 teaspoon salt

1/8 teaspoon black pepper

4 medium-size all-purpose potatoes, scrubbed (but not peeled) and cut into 1/2-inch slices

8 medium-size carrots (about 1 pound), peeled and coarsely chopped

1/2 teaspoon dried thyme, crumbled

1 tablespoon chopped parsley

This no-fuss, one-dish dinner has everything—meat, potatoes, and vegetables—but you may want to serve it with a salad such as Apple Salad with Sour Cream Dressing, page 57.

1. Heat the **oil** in a heavy 12-inch skillet over moderately high heat for about 1 minute. Add the **pork chops** and cook, uncovered, for 4 minutes on each side, or until browned.

2. Tilt the skillet and spoon off all but 3 tablespoons of the drippings. Add the **beef broth, water, salt, pepper, potatoes, carrots, thyme,** and **parsley.** Cover and cook over moderately low heat for 35 minutes or until the chops are tender and cooked through.

*Tips: **1.** This recipe can be halved. **2.** You can make this dish ahead and freeze it. **3.** You can substitute sweet potatoes for the white potatoes, but peel them before slicing.*

PORK

French-Canadian Pork Pie 🐖

Preparation: 15 minutes   Cooking: 15 minutes   Serves 4   Calories per serving: 465

Pork pie, or tourtière, is perhaps the most typical of French-Canadian fare. Traditionally, it is served after Christmas Eve midnight mass.

1 pound ground pork

1/4 cup chopped yellow onion

1/2 teaspoon salt

1/4 teaspoon black pepper

1/4 teaspoon dried savory or marjoram, crumbled

1/4 teaspoon dried thyme or sage, crumbled

Dash ground cloves

1/2 cup boiling water

2 tablespoons all-purpose flour

1 cup fine dry bread crumbs

1. Preheat the oven to 400°F. In a 9- or 10-inch skillet, combine the **pork, onion, salt, pepper, savory, thyme,** and **cloves.** Add the **boiling water,** bring to a simmer, and cook, uncovered, for 10 minutes, stirring occasionally. Tilt the skillet and skim off the fat from the liquid, then blend in the **flour.**

2. Transfer the mixture to an 8-inch pie plate and cover with the **bread crumbs.** Bake for about 15 minutes, or until lightly browned. Serve with baked beans or red kidney beans.

> **Tip:** *If you have time, use your favorite pie crust instead of the bread crumbs. Use 2 crusts: line the pie plate with 1 crust, add the filling, and cover the pie with the other. Seal the edges together, cut several small slits in the top crust, and bake until the pie is slightly browned—about 30 minutes.*

Pork Curry with Apples and Cream ◎ ◍

Preparation: 11 minutes   Cooking: 12 minutes   Serves 4   Calories per serving: 710

3 tablespoons vegetable oil

2 medium-size yellow onions, peeled and chopped

2 cloves garlic, peeled and minced

2 stalks celery, diced

1 pound lean ground pork

1 cup apple juice

2 teaspoons curry powder

1 teaspoon salt

1/4 teaspoon ground ginger

1 teaspoon ground cumin

1 medium-size tart red apple, cored and diced

1/2 cup raisins

1 cup sour cream

1. Heat the **oil** in a heavy 12-inch skillet over moderate heat. Add the **onions, garlic,** and **celery,** and cook, uncovered, for 5 minutes. Raise the heat to moderately high, add the **pork,** and cook, stirring, for 5 minutes, or until no pink remains.

2. Add the **apple juice, curry powder, salt, ginger, cumin, apple,** and **raisins.** Stir, then reduce the heat and simmer, uncovered, for 5 to 8 minutes, or until most of the apple juice has evaporated but the mixture is not yet dry.

3. Remove the skillet from the heat and stir in the **sour cream.** Return to the heat just long enough to heat through. Do not let the mixture boil or the sour cream will curdle. Serve with rice and a cucumber salad.

> **Tips: 1.** *You can substitute plain yogurt for the sour cream.* **2.** *This recipe can be halved.* **3.** *You can make this dish ahead, but do not add the sour cream until just before serving.*

Pork Balls with Mushrooms ◖◗

Preparation: 17 minutes Cooking: **15 minutes**   Serves **4** Calories per serving: **610**

This rich dish is made from thrifty ground pork, but the mushrooms make it elegant enough to serve to guests.

1 pound lean ground pork

1 egg, lightly beaten

1/2 teaspoon dried thyme, crumbled

1/2 teaspoon dried oregano, crumbled

1/2 teaspoon salt

1/4 cup fine dry bread crumbs

1 teaspoon Dijon or prepared spicy brown mustard

2 tablespoons butter or margarine

1 tablespoon vegetable oil

1/2 pound mushrooms, sliced

1/4 cup dry white wine

1/2 cup chicken broth

3/4 cup sour cream

1. In a mixing bowl, combine the **pork, egg, thyme, oregano, salt, bread crumbs,** and **mustard.** Shape the mixture into 1½-inch balls.

2. Heat the **butter** and **oil** in a heavy 12-inch skillet over moderately high heat for about 1 minute. Cook the meatballs, uncovered, turning frequently, until browned on all sides—about 5 minutes.

3. Reduce the heat to low, add the **mushrooms,** and cook gently about 2 minutes.

4. Add the **wine** and **chicken broth,** and simmer, uncovered, for 10 minutes. Blend in the **sour cream** and simmer 5 minutes longer, until the sauce has thickened and the pork balls are cooked through. Serve hot over buttered rice or noodles with Shredded Carrots with Herbs and Lemon, page 46, or steamed broccoli with butter and lemon.

Tips: 1. This recipe can be halved, or leftovers can be refrigerated for 1 or 2 days. Reheat in a covered skillet over low heat. When reheating, add more sour cream if needed. 2. You can substitute ground beef for the pork.

Hot and Spicy Ham Steak ◉

Preparation: 7 minutes Cooking: **10 minutes**   Serves **4** Calories per serving: **465**

1 tablespoon vegetable oil

1 pound fully cooked ham steak, about 1/2 inch thick

1/3 cup water or pineapple or orange juice

1/2 cup ketchup

2 tablespoons light brown or granulated sugar

1/4 cup cider vinegar

1 tablespoon prepared spicy brown mustard

1 tablespoon Worcestershire sauce

1/4 teaspoon crushed dried red pepper (optional)

1. Heat the **oil** in a heavy 12-inch skillet over moderately high heat for about 1 minute. Add the **ham steak** and cook, uncovered, for 3 minutes on each side, or until browned.

2. In a small bowl, combine the **water, ketchup, sugar, vinegar, mustard,** and **Worcestershire sauce,** and the **dried red pepper** if used. Add the mixture to the skillet and simmer, uncovered, for 10 minutes. Serve with Glorious Mashed Potatoes, page 74.

Tip: Add any leftovers to baked beans and heat them.

PORK

Ham Steak with Lemon-Raisin Sauce ⊡ ⌒

Preparation: **7 minutes**   Cooking: **6 minutes**   Serves **4**   Calories per serving: **605**

The tangy sauce for this dish is easy to make and is a perfect foil for the richness of the ham steaks.

4 tablespoons (½ stick) butter or margarine

1 pound fully cooked ham steak, about ½ inch thick

1 cup beef broth

½ cup dry white wine

2 tablespoons cider vinegar or white wine vinegar

4 teaspoons firmly packed light brown sugar

Grated rind and juice of 1 lemon

¾ cup raisins

1. Heat 1 tablespoon of the **butter** in a heavy 12-inch skillet over moderately high heat until bubbly. Add the **ham steak** and cook, uncovered, for 3 minutes on each side, or until browned. Remove the ham to a warm platter, cover with aluminum foil, and set aside.

2. Add the **beef broth, wine, vinegar, sugar, lemon rind, lemon juice,** and **raisins** to the skillet, and cook, stirring, over moderately high heat for 4 or 5 minutes, or until about ¾ cup of liquid remains.

3. Remove the sauce from the heat and stir in the remaining 3 tablespoons of butter. Pour the sauce over the ham, and serve with mashed sweet potatoes or Sweet Potato Pancakes, page 75.

> **Tip:** *This recipe can be halved, or leftovers can be refrigerated for 1 or 2 days or frozen.*

Ham Steak with Glazed Apple Rings ⊡ ⌒

Preparation: **7 minutes**   Cooking: **5 minutes**   Serves **4**   Calories per serving: **465**

3 tablespoons butter or margarine

1 pound fully cooked ham steak, about ½ inch thick

1 teaspoon light or dark brown sugar

¼ teaspoon ground cinnamon

1 medium-size tart apple, cored and cut into 6 rings

⅓ cup apple cider or juice

> **Tips: 1.** *This recipe can be halved, or leftovers can be refrigerated for up to 3 days.* **2.** *As a variation, use sliced firm pears instead of the apple rings.*

1. Heat 1 tablespoon of the **butter** in a heavy 12-inch skillet over moderately high heat until bubbly. Add the **ham steak** and cook, uncovered, for 3 minutes on each side, or until browned. Remove the ham to a platter and set aside.

2. Pour off and discard the drippings from the skillet, then add the remaining 2 tablespoons of butter and the **sugar** and **cinnamon.** Heat until the butter is bubbly, then add the **apple** rings and cook, uncovered, for 1 minute on each side, or until they just begin to soften. Arrange the apple rings on top of the ham steak.

3. Add the **apple cider** to the skillet and boil for 1 minute, scraping up any brown bits stuck to the pan. Return the ham and apple rings to the skillet to reheat briefly. Spoon the cider over the ham and apple, and serve with Baked Winter Squash, page 80, or Brussels Sprouts with Walnuts, page 63.

Baked Ham Steak 🐷 ◑

Preparation: **22 minutes**   Cooking: **20 minutes**   Serves **4**   Calories per serving: **425**

If you are short on time, bake the ham as soon as you pour the marinade over it. Or you can use the marinating time to prepare the rest of the meal.

1 pound fully cooked ham steak, about 1/2 inch thick

3 tablespoons lemon juice

1 tablespoon firmly packed light or dark brown sugar

1/4 teaspoon curry powder

1/2 teaspoon prepared spicy brown mustard

2 tablespoons butter or margarine, softened

1. Preheat the oven to 375°F. Place the **ham steak** in a nonaluminum 9"x 9"x 2" buttered baking dish and set aside. In a small saucepan, combine the **lemon juice, sugar, curry powder,** and **mustard.** Bring the mixture to a boil and pour over the ham. Let the ham marinate, uncovered, for 20 minutes at room temperature.

2. Bake the ham, uncovered, for 20 minutes, or until bubbly. Remove the ham to a warm platter. Add the **butter** to the juices in the baking dish and stir until blended. Pour the sauce over the ham, and serve with winter squash.

> *Tip: This recipe can be halved, or leftovers can be refrigerated for 1 or 2 days, or frozen.*

Ham Steak Florentine ◑

Preparation: **17 minutes**   Cooking: **8 minutes**   Serves **4**   Calories per serving: **565**

1 package (10 ounces) fresh spinach or 1 package (10 ounces) frozen chopped spinach

4 tablespoons (1/2 stick) butter or margarine

1 pound fully cooked ham steak, about 1/2 inch thick

1/2 cup chicken broth

1/2 cup sour cream or plain yogurt

1/8 teaspoon ground nutmeg

1/4 teaspoon salt

1/8 teaspoon black pepper

1/4 cup grated Parmesan cheese

> *Tip: You can use this spinach mixture on top of poached or broiled fish, chicken, or eggs—all very good combinations.*

1. Preheat the broiler. Trim the fresh **spinach** of coarse stems and blemished leaves, and wash it. Place the spinach in a 3- or 4-quart pot with just the water that clings to the leaves, and cook, covered, for 5 minutes, or until just limp. If you are using frozen spinach, cook according to package directions, drain well, and press out as much liquid as you can. Set aside.

2. Heat 2 tablespoons of the **butter** in a heavy 12-inch skillet over moderately high heat until bubbly. Add the **ham steak.** Cook, uncovered, for 3 minutes on each side, or until browned. Transfer to a 9"x 9"x 2" flameproof baking dish.

3. Add the **chicken broth** to the skillet, and cook, stirring, for 3 minutes, or until 2 tablespoons of broth remain. Reduce the heat to moderate, add the **sour cream,** and heat through but do not boil—about 2 minutes. Add the spinach, **nutmeg, salt, pepper,** and the remaining butter. Heat, stirring, for 1 minute.

4. Spread the spinach mixture over the ham steak and sprinkle with the **cheese.** Broil 3 inches from the heat for 2 or 3 minutes, or until the cheese is browned and bubbly. Serve with rice and Sautéed Green Peppers, page 73.

PORK

Ham with Mushrooms and Cream Sauce ▣ ⬲

Preparation: 15 minutes   Cooking: 3 minutes   **Serves 4   Calories per serving: 295**

Here is an elegant way to use leftover ham. You can serve it over toasted French bread as a luncheon main course or have it for dinner over buttered noodles or rice.

2 tablespoons butter or margarine

1 small yellow onion, peeled and chopped

1/2 teaspoon cornstarch

1 cup half-and-half

2 teaspoons sherry (optional)

1/2 pound mushrooms, sliced

2 cups cubed cooked ham (about 1/2 pound)

1. Melt the **butter** in a 12-inch skillet over moderate heat. Add the **onion** and cook, uncovered, for 5 minutes, or until soft.

2. Meanwhile, in a bowl, blend the **cornstarch** with 1 tablespoon of the **half-and-half** until smooth. Add the remaining half-and-half and the **sherry** if used. Set aside.

3. Add the **mushrooms** to the skillet and cook, uncovered, stirring frequently, for 3 minutes.

4. Add the **ham** and the half-and-half mixture to the skillet. Cook, uncovered, stirring frequently, over moderately high heat for 3 minutes, or until the sauce thickens.

> *Tips: 1. This recipe can be halved. 2. You can substitute cooked chicken or turkey for the ham.*

Smothered Ham and Pork Cutlets 🐷

Preparation: 15 minutes   Cooking: 20 minutes   **Serves 4   Calories per serving: 690**

Here is a thrifty and satisfying way to use up leftovers. You can use all ham or all pork.

2 cups minced cooked ham (about 1/2 pound)

2 cups minced cooked pork

1 medium-size yellow onion, peeled and grated

1 egg, lightly beaten

1 cup fine dry bread crumbs

1/4 teaspoon dried marjoram or rosemary, crumbled

1/4 teaspoon salt

1/8 teaspoon black pepper

1/4 cup vegetable oil

1 medium-size yellow onion, peeled and thinly sliced

5 tablespoons all-purpose flour

1 cup beef or chicken broth

1 tablespoon Dijon mustard

1. In a large bowl, combine the **ham, pork, grated onion, egg,** 3/4 cup of the **bread crumbs,** the **marjoram, salt, pepper,** and 1 tablespoon of the **oil.** You should be able to shape the mixture easily. If it is too sticky, add more bread crumbs; if it is too dry, add a bit of water.

2. Divide the mixture into 4 balls. Put the remaining 1/4 cup of bread crumbs in a shallow dish or pie plate. Roll the balls into the crumbs, flattening them into oval cutlets 1/4 inch thick.

3. In a heavy 10-inch skillet over moderate heat, heat the remaining oil for 1 minute. Add the cutlets, and cook, uncovered, for 6 minutes on each side. Using a slotted spoon, remove the cutlets to a platter and set aside.

4. Reduce the heat to moderately low. Add the **sliced onion** and cook, uncovered, for 5 minutes, or until soft. Blend in the **flour,** stirring constantly, then slowly add the **broth.** Cook, stirring constantly, until thickened—about 3 minutes. Blend in the **mustard.** Return the cutlets along with any accumulated juices to the gravy in the saucepan and reheat briefly. Spoon the gravy over the cutlets and serve.

PORK

Individual Ham Loaves with Sweet and Sour Sauce

Preparation: **10 minutes** Cooking: **35 minutes**   Serves **4**   Calories per serving: **530**

For a different way to use leftover ham, try these mildly spiced loaves baked in a muffin pan.

2 cups minced cooked ham (about 1/2 pound)

1/2 pound ground pork

1/2 cup fine dry bread crumbs

1 small yellow onion, peeled and chopped

1 egg, lightly beaten

3/4 cup milk

1/4 teaspoon salt

Pinch black pepper

1/2 cup firmly packed light brown sugar

2 tablespoons cider vinegar

2 teaspoons prepared yellow mustard

1. Preheat the oven to 375°F. In a large bowl, combine the **ham, pork, bread crumbs, onion, egg, milk, salt,** and **pepper.**

2. Butter eight 2-inch muffin pan cups and pack the mixture into the cups, mounding it slightly in the centers but not letting it touch the top edges of the cups. Bake for 20 minutes.

3. Meanwhile, in a small saucepan, combine the **sugar, vinegar,** and **mustard.** Bring to a boil over moderately high heat, then cook, stirring, for 1 minute, or until the sugar dissolves. Taste for seasoning, adding another tablespoon of vinegar and teaspoon of mustard if desired.

4. Pour the sauce evenly onto the ham mixture in the cups and bake an additional 15 minutes. Remove the loaves from the muffin pan, and serve hot with prepared horseradish or mustard on the side.

Ham and Cheese Strata

Preparation: **10 minutes** Cooking: **20 minutes**   Serves **4**   Calories per serving: **445**

Elevate a simple ham and cheese sandwich to main-course status by following this recipe.

8 slices firm-textured whole wheat or white bread

1 cup shredded sharp Cheddar cheese (about 4 ounces)

1 cup minced cooked ham (about 4 ounces)

4 eggs, lightly beaten

1 cup milk or half-and-half

1/4 teaspoon salt

Pinch cayenne pepper

1/2 teaspoon prepared yellow mustard

1 tablespoon butter or margarine

1. Preheat the oven to 400°F. Butter an 8"x 8"x 2" baking dish and arrange 4 slices of the **bread** on the bottom. If the bread will not fit neatly, trim off the crusts. Sprinkle the slices with half the **cheese** and all the **ham.** Top with the remaining 4 slices of bread.

2. Beat the **eggs, milk, salt, cayenne pepper,** and **mustard** together, and pour the mixture evenly over the bread to the edges of the pan. Top with the remaining cheese and dot with the **butter.** Bake for 20 to 25 minutes, or until the egg mixture is set. Serve hot with Red Cabbage with Apples, page 65, or Spinach Dressed with Oil and Vinegar, page 76.

Tips: 1. This recipe can be halved. 2. Try rye bread and Swiss cheese instead of whole wheat or white bread and Cheddar cheese.

PORK

138

Oriental Ham and Beef Balls ⊘

Preparation: **15 minutes**   Cooking: **10 minutes**   Serves **6**   Calories per serving: **620**

¾ pound cooked ham, finely chopped

¾ pound lean ground beef

½ cup finely chopped green onions

1½ cups fine dry bread crumbs

1 egg, lightly beaten

6 tablespoons milk

3 tablespoons vegetable oil

¾ cup firmly packed light brown sugar

6 tablespoons water

6 tablespoons cider vinegar

1 teaspoon dry mustard

1 tablespoon soy sauce

1. In a large bowl, combine the **ham, beef, green onions, bread crumbs, egg,** and **milk.** Shape the mixture into 1½-inch balls.

2. Heat the **oil** in a heavy 12-inch skillet over moderately high heat for about 1 minute. Cook the meatballs, uncovered, turning frequently, until browned on all sides—about 5 minutes.

3. Meanwhile, in a small bowl, combine the **brown sugar, water, vinegar,** and **mustard.** Pour this mixture over the meatballs, reduce the heat to moderate, cover, and simmer for 10 minutes, stirring occasionally. If the sauce seems too thick, add 1 or 2 tablespoons of water. Stir in the **soy sauce.** Serve with rice and Asparagus Chinese Style, page 58.

> *Tips:* **1.** *You can substitute pork for the beef, but simmer the meatballs 5 minutes longer.* **2.** *Make the balls smaller and serve them hot with toothpicks as hors d'oeuvres.*

Ham Jambalaya 🐖 ⊘

Preparation: **15 minutes**   Cooking: **20 minutes**   Serves **4**   Calories per serving: **470**

3 tablespoons vegetable oil

2 large yellow onions, peeled and chopped

1 large sweet green pepper, cored, seeded, and chopped

2 or 3 cloves garlic, peeled and minced

2 cups cubed cooked ham (about ½ pound)

1 cup uncooked rice

½ teaspoon dried thyme, crumbled

½ teaspoon salt

4 drops liquid hot red pepper seasoning

3 medium-size fresh tomatoes, peeled and chopped, or 1 can (1 pound) tomatoes, chopped, with their juice

¾ cup chicken broth

1. Heat the **oil** in a heavy 12-inch skillet over moderate heat. Add the **onions, green pepper,** and **garlic,** and cook, uncovered, for 5 minutes, or until the onions are soft.

2. Add the **ham** and **rice,** and stir until the rice is well coated with oil—about 1 minute.

3. Add the **thyme, salt, red pepper seasoning, tomatoes,** and **broth.** Cover and simmer for 20 to 25 minutes, or until the rice is tender and all the liquid has been absorbed; check after 15 minutes and add ¼ cup of water if the mixture seems dry. Serve jambalaya with a green salad and crusty bread.

> *Tips:* **1.** *This recipe can be halved. Use 1 can (8 ounces) tomato sauce instead of the tomatoes.* **2.** *You can substitute cooked chicken or turkey for the ham.* **3.** *For an elaborate company meal, add 1 pound shelled shrimp, crabmeat, or chopped lobster meat, or 1 pint shucked oysters during the last 10 minutes of cooking.* **4.** *Reheat leftovers in a double boiler or in an aluminum-foil–lined colander set over boiling water.*

PORK

Egg and Sausage Cake 🐷 ⟢ ⬭

Preparation: **4 minutes**   Cooking: **18 minutes**   Serves **4**   Calories per serving: **680**

Known as a frittata in Italy, this omeletlike dish is easy to prepare and is superb for brunch or supper. It is also easy on the budget.

4 hot or sweet Italian sausages or 8 breakfast sausages (about ½ pound)

6 tablespoons butter or margarine

3 tablespoons olive or vegetable oil

2 medium-size all-purpose potatoes, scrubbed (but not peeled) and cut into ⅛-inch slices

1½ teaspoons salt

1 medium-size yellow onion, peeled and chopped

6 eggs

Tips: 1. This recipe can be halved. 2. You can substitute cubed cooked ham for the sausages.

1. Preheat the broiler. Prick the **sausages** all over with a fork. Place them on the broiler rack 4 inches from the heat. Broil for 10 minutes, turning once. Remove from the broiler and slice into ¼-inch rounds.

2. While the sausages are broiling, heat 4 tablespoons of the **butter** and 2 tablespoons of the **oil** in a heavy 12-inch skillet over moderately high heat for about 1 minute. Add the **potatoes**, sprinkle with 1 teaspoon of the **salt**, and toss several times to coat with the butter and oil. Cook, uncovered, tossing frequently, for 10 minutes, or until the potatoes are golden brown and lightly crisped.

3. Push the potatoes to one side of the skillet, add the sausages and **onion** to the cleared space, lower the heat to moderate, and cook, uncovered, for 3 minutes.

4. In a small bowl, beat the **eggs** with the remaining ½ teaspoon of salt. Toss the potatoes, sausages, and onions together in the skillet. Add the remaining 2 tablespoons of butter and 1 tablespoon of oil, coating the sides of the skillet. Pour the eggs over the mixture, cover, and cook for 3 or 4 minutes, or until the eggs begin to set. Shake the skillet from time to time to prevent sticking.

5. Leaving the broiler door open, place the skillet (but not the handle) under the broiler 2 inches from the heat. Broil for 2 minutes, or until the mixture has browned slightly and the eggs are fully set. Cut into wedges, and serve hot or at room temperature. Serve with Skillet Asparagus, page 58.

PORK

Sausage Patties with Cream Gravy ⊘ ⊘

Preparation: **3 minutes**   Cooking: **20 minutes**   Serves **6**   Calories per serving: **590**

In the Southern States, this hearty dish is usually served over buttered biscuits, but try it also with English muffins or hamburger buns, making the patties 4 inches in diameter instead of 2 inches.

1½ pounds mild or hot sausage meat

1 large yellow onion, peeled and chopped

3 tablespoons all-purpose flour

⅓ cup water

1 cup half-and-half or milk

¾ teaspoon salt

¼ teaspoon black pepper

> **Tip:** *This recipe can be halved, or leftovers can be refrigerated for 1 or 2 days.*

1. Shape the **sausage meat** into 8 patties, each about 2 inches in diameter and ¼ inch thick. Cook the patties in a heavy 12-inch skillet, uncovered, over moderately high heat for 5 minutes on each side. Drain on paper toweling and set aside.

2. Pour off all but about ⅓ cup of the drippings from the skillet. Reduce the heat to moderate, add the **onion,** and cook, uncovered, for 5 minutes, or until soft.

3. Raise the heat to moderately high, add the **flour,** and stir until blended. Add the **water** and boil for about 2 minutes, scraping up any brown bits stuck to the skillet.

4. Add the **half-and-half, salt,** and **pepper,** and stir until smooth. Return the patties to the skillet and heat through—about 2 or 3 minutes.

Sausages and Apples ⊘

Preparation: **1 minute**   Cooking: **20 minutes**   Serves **4**   Calories per serving: **645**

The combination of pork and apples is traditional in the cooking of many countries. Try this French-Canadian recipe from Quebec.

1 pound pork sausage links

2 large apples

½ cup milk

½ cup all-purpose flour

¼ teaspoon ground cinnamon

2 tablespoons firmly packed light or dark brown sugar

½ cup water

¼ teaspoon salt

¼ teaspoon black pepper

> **Tip:** *As a variation, use sliced firm pears instead of the apples.* ·

1. Cook the **sausages** in a heavy 12-inch skillet, uncovered, over moderate heat for 10 minutes. Remove the sausages to a platter. Do not discard the drippings in the skillet.

2. Meanwhile, core the **apples,** but do not peel, and cut them into ½-inch rings.

3. Place the **milk** and **flour** in separate small shallow bowls or saucers. Dip the apple rings into the milk, coat them with the flour, then place them in the skillet. Reduce the heat to moderately low. Sprinkle the rings with the **cinnamon** and **brown sugar,** and cook, uncovered, for 3 minutes on each side. Remove the apples to the platter.

4. Add the **water, salt,** and **pepper.** Raise the heat and bring to a boil, scraping up any brown bits stuck to the skillet. Cook, uncovered, until only about ¼ cup of liquid remains—about 4 minutes. Return the apples and sausages to the skillet to reheat briefly.

PORK

Sausage Pilaf ◍

Preparation: **12 minutes** Cooking: **22 minutes** Serves **6** Calories per serving: **650**

For a Near Eastern taste, try this sausage, rice, and eggplant dish. Serve it with a side dish of chilled plain yogurt to spoon over the top, if desired.

1 small eggplant (about ¹/₂ pound)

¹/₂ cup vegetable oil

¹/₂ pound mushrooms, sliced

1 cup uncooked rice

1¹/₂ cups water

¹/₂ teaspoon ground cumin

2 teaspoons salt

¹/₂ teaspoon black pepper

1 pound pork sausage links, cut into 1-inch pieces

Tips: 1. This recipe can be halved. 2. You can omit the eggplant and use a whole pound of mushrooms or substitute cubed cooked chicken, ham, or lamb for the sausage.

1. Cut the **eggplant,** unpeeled, into ¹/₄-inch slices, then cut the slices into ¹/₄-inch strips.

2. Heat the **oil** in a heavy 3-quart saucepan over moderate heat. Add the eggplant strips and **mushrooms.** Cook, uncovered, for 5 minutes, or until the vegetables are soft and golden.

3. Add the **rice** and stir until it is well coated with oil—about 1 minute. Add the **water, cumin, salt,** and **pepper.** Reduce the heat, cover, and simmer for 20 minutes, or until the rice is tender and all the liquid has been absorbed. Check after 10 minutes and add ¹/₄ cup of water if the mixture seems dry.

4. Meanwhile, cook the **sausages** in a heavy 12-inch skillet, uncovered, over moderate heat for 10 minutes, or until browned. Drain the sausages on paper toweling and stir them into the rice mixture when the rice is done. Cover and heat through—about 2 or 3 minutes.

Sausages, Tomatoes, and Peppers ▷ ◍

Preparation: **15 minutes** Cooking: **10 minutes** Serves **4** Calories per serving: **660**

If you like traditional Italian sausages and peppers, try this version. To save time, prepare the onions and peppers while the sausage is cooking.

1 pound mild or hot pork sausage links, cut into 1-inch pieces

3 tablespoons vegetable oil

2 large yellow onions, peeled and chopped

2 large sweet green peppers, cored, seeded, and cut into ¹/₂-inch strips

3 medium-size tomatoes, peeled and chopped, or 1 can (1 pound) tomatoes, drained and chopped

¹/₄ teaspoon salt

1. Cook the **sausages** in a heavy 12-inch skillet, uncovered, over moderate heat for 10 minutes, or until browned. Remove the sausages to a platter and set aside. Pour off and discard the drippings from the skillet.

2. Heat the **oil** in the skillet over moderate heat, add the **onions,** and cook, stirring occasionally, for 5 minutes, or until soft.

3. Add the **peppers, tomatoes,** and **salt.** Return the sausages to the pan, cover, and cook over moderate heat for 10 minutes. Tilt the skillet and spoon the fat from the sauce. Serve hot with pasta, crusty bread, and a green salad with Oil and Vinegar Dressing for Green Salads, page 51.

Tip: This recipe can be halved; substitute 1 can (8 ounces) tomato sauce for the fresh or canned tomatoes.

PORK

LAMB

Years ago, lamb was almost always cooked well done. But today, perhaps because more people are traveling to places where lamb is often served pink, more rose-colored meat is showing up on tables across the country. When overcooked, lamb is frequently tough, dry, and grayish, but when taken from the heat slightly underdone, it is moist, tender, flavorful, and attractive. Recipes in this chapter—such as Roast Leg of Lamb, Lamb Chops with Mushrooms and Wine, Honey-Orange Lamb Chops, and Parsley Lamb Chops—give you a choice of how the meat should be cooked.

If you have always eaten your lamb well done, the next time you have it, try removing it from the heat when it is medium or medium rare. You will discover why lamb prepared this way has become so popular.

Roast Leg of Lamb

Preparation: **12 minutes**   Cooking: **1¼ hours**   Serves **6**   Calories per serving: **420**

The roasting times given in this recipe are based on lamb taken directly from the refrigerator.

1 half leg of lamb (about 3 pounds), shank or sirloin half

1 large clove garlic, peeled and cut into 6 slivers

¹⁄₂ teaspoon dried rosemary, crumbled

¹⁄₂ teaspoon dried thyme, crumbled

1 teaspoon salt

1 tablespoon olive or vegetable oil

Tips: 1. The shank half of the lamb is usually meatier and easier to carve. The sirloin half is cheaper, but it has less meat and more bone. 2. A 3-pound piece serves 4 with enough leftovers for another meal. 3. The price per pound may be less if you buy the whole leg—ask the butcher at the supermarket to cut the leg in half, then freeze one half to cook another time.

1. Preheat the oven to 325°F. With a sharp knife, remove all the fat and fell (the thin, tough, papery membrane) from the **lamb**. To remove the fell, loosen it from the flesh with the knife and cut it off in sections.

2. With the point of a small knife, make 6 incisions about ¹⁄₂ inch wide and ¹⁄₂ inch deep all over the lamb. Insert a **garlic** sliver and a pinch of the **rosemary** and **thyme** into each slit. Sprinkle the lamb with the **salt,** and rub it all over with the **oil**.

3. Place the lamb on a rack in an 8″x 8″x 2″ baking pan. Insert a meat thermometer, if you have one, into the thickest part of the lamb, not touching the bone.

4. If you are using the shank half, roast, uncovered, for 1¼ hours for medium rare (140°F on the meat thermometer), 1¹⁄₂ hours for medium well (160°F), and 1³⁄₄ hours for well done (170°F). If you are using the sirloin half, roast for 1 hour for medium rare (140°F), 1¼ hours for medium well (160°F), and 1¹⁄₂ hours for well done (170°F). Note: The sirloin half cooks more quickly than the shank half because it has more bone.

5. When the lamb is done the way you like it, remove it to a platter, and let it rest for 10 minutes before carving.

Shepherd's Stew ◑

Preparation: **16 minutes** Cooking: **20 minutes** Serves **4** Calories per serving: **450**

3 tablespoons vegetable oil

1 large yellow onion, peeled and coarsely chopped

3 small all-purpose potatoes, peeled and cut into 1-inch cubes

4 medium-size carrots, peeled and cut into ½-inch cubes

2 tablespoons all-purpose flour

1¼ cups beef broth

½ teaspoon dried rosemary, crumbled

2 cups cubed cooked lamb

1 package (10 ounces) frozen baby green peas, thawed

1 teaspoon salt

¼ teaspoon black pepper

1. Heat the **oil** in a 2-quart saucepan over moderate heat. Add the **onion, potatoes,** and **carrots,** and cook, uncovered, for 5 minutes, or until the onion is soft. Sprinkle the vegetables with the **flour,** and cook, stirring, for 1 minute.

2. Gradually add the **beef broth,** stirring constantly, then the **rosemary.** Bring to a boil, partially cover the saucepan, lower the heat, and simmer, stirring occasionally, for 15 minutes, or until the carrots and potatoes are almost tender.

3. Uncover, add the **lamb, peas, salt,** and **pepper,** and mix well. Simmer for 5 more minutes. Serve with a fresh green salad and some crusty bread.

> **Tips: 1.** This recipe can be halved. **2.** You can substitute leftover beef or pork for the lamb. **3.** Add 2 or more cups of beef broth and serve as a soup.

Armenian Pilaf 🐷 ◑

Preparation: **10 minutes** Cooking: **30 minutes** Serves **6** Calories per serving: **425**

2 tablespoons vegetable oil

1 small yellow onion, peeled and thinly sliced

¾ cup uncooked fine noodles

2 cups cubed cooked lamb

¾ cup uncooked rice

½ cup raisins

3 cups beef broth

1 teaspoon dried mint, crumbled

½ teaspoon salt

¼ teaspoon black pepper

¼ cup slivered almonds

Not only does this recipe offer a flavorful way to use leftover lamb, but it stretches 2 cups of meat to serve 6.

1. In a 2-quart flameproof casserole or a saucepan with a cover, heat the **oil** over moderate heat. Add the **onion** and **noodles,** and cook, stirring, until the noodles are golden— about 5 minutes.

2. Stir in the **lamb, rice, raisins, beef broth, mint, salt,** and **pepper.** Bring to a boil, lower the heat, cover, and simmer for 30 minutes. Sprinkle with the **almonds.** Serve with Orange-Ginger Carrots, page 66.

> **Tips: 1.** This recipe can be halved **2.** As a variation, omit the mint, decrease the broth to 2 cups, and add 1 cup of chopped tomatoes. **3.** You can substitute cooked beef for the lamb.

LAMB

Lamb with Green Onions ▷ ⬭

Preparation: **15 minutes**   Cooking: **5 minutes**   Serves **4**   Calories per serving: **715**

2 tablespoons cold water

4 teaspoons cornstarch

1 teaspoon sugar

1/4 cup soy sauce

1 1/2 pounds boneless lamb shoulder, cut into 2"x 2"x 1/4" slices

2 tablespoons dry sherry

2 teaspoons cider vinegar

1/4 cup vegetable oil

1 clove garlic, peeled and minced

6 green onions, trimmed and sliced

Tip: This recipe can be halved.

1. In a mixing bowl, combine the **water, cornstarch, sugar**, and 2 tablespoons of the **soy sauce**. Add the **lamb**, and toss to coat. Marinate for 10 to 15 minutes at room temperature.

2. In a small bowl, combine the remaining 2 tablespoons of soy sauce, the **sherry, vinegar,** and 1 tablespoon of the **oil**. Place this sauce near the stove along with the **garlic** and **green onions**.

3. Heat the remaining 3 tablespoons of oil in a heavy 12-inch skillet. When the oil is very hot, add the garlic and cook, stirring, for 30 seconds. Add the lamb and any marinade remaining in the bowl, and continue to cook, stirring, until no pink remains—about 3 minutes.

4. Add the green onions and stir for a few seconds. Add the sauce and continue to stir until smooth—about 1 minute. Serve over or with rice.

Lamb Chops with Mushrooms and Wine ▷ ⬭

Preparation: **5 minutes**   Cooking: **18 minutes**   Serves **4**   Calories per serving: **495**

Use the time while the lamb chops are cooking to prepare the mushrooms, onion, and garlic.

4 tablespoons (1/2 stick) butter or margarine

4 shoulder lamb chops, about 3/4 inch thick, trimmed of excess fat

1/4 pound mushrooms, sliced

1 medium-size yellow onion, peeled and chopped

4 large cloves garlic, peeled and minced

1/2 cup dry red wine

1/2 cup beef broth

1/4 teaspoon salt

1/4 teaspoon black pepper

Tip: This recipe can be halved.

1. Heat 2 tablespoons of the **butter** in a heavy 12-inch skillet over moderately high heat until bubbly. Add the **lamb chops** and cook, uncovered, for 3 minutes on each side for medium rare, 5 minutes for medium, and 6 minutes for well done. Remove the chops to a serving platter and keep warm.

2. Add the **mushrooms, onion,** and **garlic** to the skillet, and cook for 3 minutes, or until the onion begins to color slightly. Add the **wine** and **beef broth,** and scrape up any brown bits stuck to the skillet. Bring to a boil and cook, uncovered, until only about 1/2 cup of liquid remains—about 5 minutes.

3. Remove from the heat, and stir in the **salt, pepper,** and the remaining 2 tablespoons of butter. Return the chops and any accumulated juices to the skillet to reheat briefly. Spoon the sauce over the chops, and serve with boiled or mashed potatoes.

LAMB

Lamb Chops Provençal ⊕

Preparation: **10 minutes**   Cooking: **15 minutes**   Serves **4**   Calories per serving: **440**

1 tablespoon olive or
vegetable oil

1 medium-size yellow onion,
peeled and chopped

2 cloves garlic, peeled and
minced

1 medium-size sweet green
pepper, cored, seeded, and
cut into ¼-inch strips

3 medium-size fresh tomatoes,
peeled and chopped, or 1 can
(1 pound) tomatoes, drained
and chopped

¾ cup dry red wine

1 teaspoon salt

¼ teaspoon black pepper

4 shoulder lamb chops, about
¾ inch thick, trimmed of
excess fat

*The French country sauce that accompanies these chops
may also be served with pork or chicken or as a topping
for pasta or omelets. If you have time, double the
sauce and freeze half for future use.*

1. Preheat the broiler. Heat the **oil** in a 2-quart
saucepan over moderate heat. Add the **onion,
garlic,** and **green pepper,** and cook for
2 minutes. Add the **tomatoes,** and cook for
1 minute. Stir in the **wine, salt,** and **black
pepper,** and simmer, uncovered, for 15 minutes.

2. During the last 10 minutes that the sauce is
cooking, place the **lamb chops** on the rack of the
broiler pan, and broil 4 inches from the heat for
3 to 4 minutes on each side for medium, and
4 to 5 minutes on each side for well done.
Remove the chops to a platter, and top with the
sauce. Serve with Potato Pancakes, page 74, or
Zucchini Patties, page 78.

*Tips: 1. Add ¼ cup of chopped black olives (preferably
oil-cured) along with the tomatoes, and cook as directed
above. 2. The sauce can be made 1 or 2 days ahead,
refrigerated, and reheated, but cook the chops at the last
minute. 3. Substitute pork chops for the lamb, if you like,
but cook them until well done. 4. This recipe can be halved.*

Cheese-Glazed Lamb Chops ⊕

Preparation: **5 minutes**   Cooking: **37 minutes**   Serves **4**   Calories per serving: **410**

4 shoulder lamb chops, about
¾ inch thick, trimmed of
excess fat

¼ teaspoon salt

⅛ teaspoon black pepper

¼ cup dry white wine, beer,
or water

¼ cup shredded Gruyère or
Swiss cheese

1 tablespoon Dijon or prepared
spicy brown mustard

1½ tablespoons milk

Tip: This recipe can be halved.

1. Heat a heavy 12-inch skillet over high heat for
about 1 minute, add the **lamb chops,** and brown
for 1 minute on each side. (You will not need
any oil.) Sprinkle with the **salt** and **pepper.** Add
the **wine,** cover, reduce the heat, and simmer for
35 to 40 minutes, or until the lamb chops are
tender. About 10 minutes before the chops are
done, preheat the broiler.

2. Meanwhile, cream the **cheese, mustard,** and
milk together with a spoon until smooth.
Transfer the chops to the rack of the broiler pan.
Spread the cheese mixture evenly over the chops,
and broil 3 inches from the heat for 2 to 3 minutes
until the glaze is speckled with brown.

Honey-Orange Lamb Chops ⊚ ⊕

Preparation: **3 minutes**   Cooking: **12 minutes**   Serves **4**   Calories per serving: **430**

1 tablespoon vegetable oil

4 shoulder lamb chops, about
³/4 inch thick, trimmed of
excess fat

¹/2 cup orange juice

1 tablespoon lemon juice

¹/2 teaspoon dried tarragon,
crumbled

1 tablespoon honey

¹/2 teaspoon salt

¹/4 teaspoon black pepper

1 teaspoon Dijon or prepared
spicy brown mustard

1 tablespoon butter or
margarine

1. Heat the **oil** in a heavy 12-inch skillet over moderately high heat for about 1 minute. Add the **lamb chops** and cook, uncovered, for 3 minutes on each side for medium rare, 5 minutes for medium, and 6 minutes for well done. Remove the chops to a platter.

2. Add the **orange juice, lemon juice,** and **tarragon** to the skillet, and scrape up any brown bits stuck to the pan. Bring to a boil and cook, uncovered, until only about ¹/4 cup of liquid remains—about 3 minutes. Reduce the heat to low.

3. Add the **honey, salt, pepper,** and **mustard.** Mix thoroughly, then swirl in the **butter.** Return the chops and any accumulated juices to the skillet, and heat through—about 1 minute. Serve with buttered noodles.

> *Tip: This recipe can be halved.*

Parsley Lamb Patties ⊚ ⊕

Preparation: **5 minutes**   Cooking: **10 minutes**   Serves **4**   Calories per serving: **270**

1 pound ground lamb

¹/2 teaspoon salt

¹/4 teaspoon black pepper

¹/2 cup chopped parsley

1 teaspoon grated lemon rind

1. Preheat the broiler. Combine the **lamb, salt, pepper, parsley,** and **lemon rind,** and shape the mixture into 4 patties.

2. Broil for 5 minutes on each side for rare, 7 minutes for medium, and 8 to 9 minutes for well done. Serve with Confetti Corn, page 68.

> *Tips: **1.** You can panbroil the patties: sprinkle ¹/4 teaspoon of salt in a heavy 10-inch skillet, heat over moderately high heat, add the patties, and cook for 5 minutes on each side for rare, 6 for medium, and 7 for well done. **2.** As a variation, omit the lemon rind and add ¹/2 teaspoon of ground allspice to the lamb mixture. **3.** This recipe can be halved.*

Curried Lamb and Vegetables ⏐⏐

Preparation: **17 minutes**   Cooking: **8 minutes**   Serves **4**   Calories per serving: **535**

4 tablespoons (½ stick) butter or margarine

1 to 3 tablespoons curry powder

¼ teaspoon ground ginger

2 or 3 cloves garlic, peeled and minced

1 medium-size yellow onion, peeled and chopped

½ pound mushrooms, sliced

½ medium-size sweet green pepper, cored, seeded, and chopped

1 stalk celery, diced

1 pound ground lamb

1 teaspoon salt

¼ teaspoon cayenne pepper (optional)

½ cup half-and-half

1. Melt the **butter** in a heavy 12-inch skillet over moderate heat. Add the **curry powder, ginger, garlic, onion, mushrooms, green pepper,** and **celery.** Cook, uncovered, stirring, for 1 minute, then cover and cook for 5 more minutes, or until the onion is soft.

2. Turn the heat to high, add the **lamb** and **salt,** and the **cayenne pepper** if used, and cook, tossing the lamb and vegetables constantly for 3 minutes. Reduce the heat, add the **half-and-half,** and simmer, uncovered, for 5 minutes. Serve with Shredded Cabbage with Garlic, page 64.

> **Tip:** *This recipe can be halved.*

Herbed Lamb Patties ▷ ⏐⏐

Preparation: **8 minutes**   Cooking: **10 minutes**   Serves **6**   Calories per serving: **300**

1 tablespoon olive or vegetable oil

8 green onions, trimmed and sliced

1½ pounds ground lamb

¼ teaspoon black pepper

½ teaspoon salt

½ teaspoon dried thyme or basil, crumbled

1 teaspoon dried rosemary, crumbled

1 tablespoon minced parsley

2 teaspoons lemon juice

1. Heat the **oil** in a heavy 12-inch skillet over moderate heat, add the **green onions,** and cook for 1½ minutes, or until crisp-tender.

2. Preheat the broiler. In a small bowl, combine the cooked green onions, the **lamb, pepper, salt, thyme, rosemary, parsley,** and **lemon juice.** Shape the mixture into 6 patties, and broil about 3 inches from the heat for 5 minutes on each side for rare, 6 for medium, and 7 for well done. Serve with Lima Beans in Sour Cream, page 60, and a sliced tomato salad.

> **Tips: 1.** *This recipe can be halved.* **2.** *For a change in taste, broil the patties for 5 minutes, then turn and broil for 3 more minutes. Top each patty with a thin slice of sharp Cheddar cheese, and broil for 2 minutes, or until the cheese has melted.* **3.** *To panbroil, sprinkle ¼ teaspoon of salt in a heavy 12-inch skillet, heat over moderately high heat, and cook the patties for 5 minutes on each side for rare, 6 for medium, and 7 for well done.*

LAMB

VARIETY MEAT

This section has recipes for beef liver and chicken livers only. Other variety meats, such as calf's liver and tripe, were excluded because they are too expensive or time-consuming. All the liver recipes here are inexpensive and extra quick. All can be halved.

Beef Liver in Basil Tomato Sauce

Preparation: **5 minutes**   Cooking: **10 minutes**   Serves **4**   Calories per serving: **345**

1 pound beef liver, cut into 4 serving-size pieces

1/4 teaspoon salt

1/4 teaspoon black pepper

1/2 cup all-purpose flour

2 tablespoons vegetable oil

3 tablespoons butter

4 anchovy fillets, chopped

2 cloves garlic, peeled and minced

1 large tomato, peeled and finely chopped

1 teaspoon dried basil

1. Sprinkle the **liver** with the **salt** and **pepper.** Put the **flour** on a plate or a sheet of wax paper and press the liver into the flour to coat.

2. Heat the **oil** and 1 tablespoon of the **butter** in a heavy 9- or 10-inch skillet over high heat for about 1 minute. Add the liver and cook, uncovered, for 3 minutes on each side, or until browned on the outside but still pink inside. Remove the liver and keep warm.

3. Add the **anchovy fillets** and **garlic** to the skillet, and cook, stirring, over moderate heat for 30 seconds. Add the **tomato** and **basil,** stir, and let the mixture boil, uncovered, for 2 minutes. Swirl in the remaining 2 tablespoons of butter. Pour the sauce over the liver, and serve.

Beef Liver in Mustard Tarragon Cream

Preparation: **6 minutes**   Cooking: **11 minutes**   Serves **4**   Calories per serving: **385**

4 tablespoons (1/2 stick) butter or margarine

1 pound beef liver, cut into strips 1/2 inch wide and 2 inches long

1/2 teaspoon salt

1/3 cup dry white wine or beef broth

1 tablespoon Dijon or prepared spicy brown mustard

1 teaspoon dried tarragon, crumbled

1/2 cup heavy cream or half-and-half

1. Heat the **butter** in a heavy 9- or 10-inch skillet over high heat until bubbly. Add the **liver** strips and cook, uncovered, for 3 minutes on each side, or until browned on the outside but still pink inside. Sprinkle with the **salt,** remove the liver to a warm platter, and set aside.

2. Add the **wine** to the skillet and stir for 1 minute, scraping up any brown bits stuck to the skillet. Lower the heat to moderately high, stir in the **mustard** and **tarragon,** and cook, stirring constantly, for 2 minutes, or until the liquid has boiled down to a thick glaze.

3. Reduce the heat to low, stir in the **heavy cream,** and cook 1 minute longer. Return the liver to the skillet along with any accumulated juices, and toss to coat with the sauce.

VARIETY MEAT

Chicken Livers with Sage 🐷 ▷ ⊘

Preparation: **3 minutes**   Cooking: **10 minutes**   Serves **4**   Calories per serving: **285**

4 tablespoons (½ stick) butter or margarine

1 pound chicken livers, drained

1 small yellow onion, peeled and finely chopped

1 teaspoon dried sage, crumbled

½ cup each dry white wine and chicken broth or 1 cup chicken broth

1 teaspoon salt

¼ teaspoon black pepper

Tips: 1. As a variation, use beef liver, cut into strips, in place of the chicken livers, and swirl in 1 tablespoon of butter at the end of the cooking. 2. Leftovers can be refrigerated overnight and rewarmed over low heat.

1. Heat the **butter** in a heavy 9- or 10-inch skillet over moderately high heat until bubbly. Add the **chicken livers, onion,** and **sage,** and cook, stirring, until the livers are browned but still pink inside—about 5 minutes. Remove the livers to a platter and set aside.

2. Raise the heat to high, and add the **wine** and **chicken broth** to the skillet. Cook, stirring and scraping up any brown bits stuck to the skillet, until only about ½ cup of liquid remains—about 3 minutes.

3. Lower the heat to moderate. Return the livers and any accumulated juices to the skillet, heat the livers for 1 minute, and season with the **salt** and **pepper.** Spoon the sauce over the livers, and serve with buttered noodles and French Green Peas, page 72, Stuffed Zucchini, page 79, or Baked Stuffed Tomatoes, page 81.

Chicken Livers in Sherry 🐷 ▷ ⊘

Preparation: **5 minutes**   Cooking: **10 minutes**   Serves **4**   Calories per serving: **325**

3 tablespoons all-purpose flour

1 teaspoon salt

¼ teaspoon black pepper

1 pound chicken livers, drained

3 tablespoons butter or margarine

1 clove garlic, peeled and minced

1 cup dry sherry

Tips: 1. You can substitute ½ cup Marsala and ½ cup chicken broth for the sherry, and beef liver, cut into strips, for the chicken livers. 2. Leftovers can be refrigerated overnight or frozen. Rewarm over low heat.

1. Mix the **flour** with the **salt** and **pepper** on a plate or a sheet of wax paper. Press the **chicken livers** into the mixture, coating them on all sides. Shake off any excess flour.

2. Heat 2 tablespoons of the **butter** in a heavy 9- or 10-inch skillet over moderately high heat until bubbly. Add the livers and the **garlic,** and cook, stirring, until the livers are browned but still pink inside—about 5 minutes. Remove the livers to a platter and set aside.

3. Raise the heat to high and add the **sherry** to the skillet. Cook, stirring and scraping up any brown bits from the skillet, until only about ½ cup of sherry remains—about 3 minutes. Remove from the heat and swirl in the remaining tablespoon of butter. Return the livers and any accumulated juices to the skillet and heat the livers for 1 minute, basting them with the sauce. Serve over rice or toast and accompany with Peas with Orange and Mint, page 71.

VARIETY MEAT

Chicken Livers in Vinegar Sauce 🐷 ▷ ⫸

Preparation: **2 minutes**   Cooking: **12 minutes**   Serves **4**   Calories per serving: **270**

This method of cooking chicken livers is from France. If you prefer, you can substitute beef liver, cut into strips, for the chicken livers.

2 tablespoons vegetable oil

1 tablespoon plus 1 teaspoon butter or margarine, softened

1 pound chicken livers, drained

1 teaspoon salt

1/2 teaspoon black pepper

1 medium-size yellow onion, peeled and finely chopped

1/3 cup red wine vinegar

1 small tomato, peeled and chopped

1/2 cup chicken broth

1 teaspoon all-purpose flour

2 tablespoons minced parsley

1. Heat the **oil** and 1 tablespoon of the **butter** in a heavy 9- or 10-inch skillet over moderately high heat for about 1 minute. Add the **chicken livers, salt,** and **pepper,** and cook, stirring, until the livers are browned but still pink inside—about 5 minutes. Remove the livers to a platter; set aside.

2. Lower the heat to moderate, add the **onion** to the skillet, and cook, uncovered, for 2 minutes, or until slightly browned.

3. Add the **vinegar** and cook, uncovered, until only about 1 tablespoon of vinegar remains—about 3 minutes. Add the **tomato** and **chicken broth,** and bring to a boil.

4. Combine the **flour** and the remaining teaspoon of butter with a fork, then add to the skillet. Stir the mixture into the sauce, and boil gently, stirring, for 1 minute.

5. Reduce the heat to low, return the livers to the skillet along with any accumulated juices, and simmer for 1 minute, or until the livers are heated through. Sprinkle with the **parsley,** and serve with potatoes and Sautéed Summer Squash, page 77.

Deviled Chicken Livers 🐷 ▷ ⫸

Preparation: **5 minutes**   Cooking: **7 minutes**   Serves **4**   Calories per serving: **320**

1/4 cup all-purpose flour

2 teaspoons paprika

1 pound chicken livers, drained

4 tablespoons (1/2 stick) butter or margarine or 1/4 cup vegetable oil

1/4 cup chopped yellow onion

1/4 teaspoon salt

Pinch black pepper

Pinch cayenne pepper

1/2 teaspoon dry mustard

1 teaspoon Worcestershire sauce

1/2 cup ketchup or chili sauce

1/2 cup water

1. Mix the **flour** and **paprika** on a plate or a sheet of wax paper. Press the **chicken livers** into the mixture, coating them on all sides. Shake off any excess flour.

2. Heat the **butter** in a heavy 9- or 10-inch skillet over moderately high heat until bubbly. Add the livers and **onion,** and cook, stirring, until the livers are browned but still pink inside—about 5 minutes.

3. Lower the heat to moderate and stir in the **salt, black pepper, cayenne pepper, mustard, Worcestershire sauce, ketchup,** and **water.** Simmer, uncovered, for 2 minutes. Serve over toast or steamed rice with Cauliflower Fritters, page 67, and a green salad.

FISH AND SHELLFISH

In this section you will find recipes for both fish fillets and whole fish, including the delicate, but often neglected, whiting (silver hake); new ways to dress up canned tuna and salmon; a French fish stew; garlic-flavored mussels; and an oyster pie. Because fish can be costly, choices are given in most recipes so that you can select one that is reasonably priced.

Broiled Flounder ⌖ ⌘

Preparation: **5 minutes**　Cooking: **8 minutes**　　　Serves **4**　Calories per serving: **255**

4 tablespoons (¹/₂ stick) butter or margarine

1 teaspoon Worcestershire sauce

¹/₄ teaspoon celery salt

4 bay leaves

¹/₈ teaspoon black pepper

¹/₂ cup grated Parmesan cheese

4 whole (about ¹/₂ pound each) flounder or whitings (silver hake), dressed

1. Preheat the broiler. Melt the **butter** in a 1-quart saucepan over low heat. Add the **Worcestershire sauce, celery salt, bay leaves, pepper,** and **cheese.** Stir to mix. Pour half the mixture into the bottom of the broiler pan while the mixture is hot. Place the **flounder,** dark skin down, in the pan. Pour the remaining mixture over the flounder.

2. Broil 3 to 4 inches from the heat, without turning, for 8 minutes or longer, depending on the thickness of the fish. When the fish flakes easily when tested with a fork, it is done. Serve with Coleslaw, page 45, and French fried potatoes.

Tip: This recipe can be halved.

Broiled Deviled Fish Fillets ⌖

Preparation: **5 minutes**　Cooking: **5 minutes**　　　Serves **4**　Calories per serving: **185**

1¹/₂ pounds flounder, sole, halibut, cod, or haddock fillets

¹/₄ cup tomato juice

4 or more drops liquid hot red pepper seasoning

4 teaspoons vegetable oil

4 teaspoons Dijon or prepared spicy brown mustard

4 teaspoons prepared horseradish

1 tablespoon Worcestershire sauce

1. Preheat the broiler. Butter the rack of the broiler pan and place the **fish fillets** on it. Combine the **tomato juice, red pepper seasoning, oil, mustard, horseradish,** and **Worcestershire sauce.** Spread the mixture evenly over the fish.

2. Broil 3 to 4 inches from the heat, without turning, for 5 minutes or longer, depending on the thickness of the fish. When the fish flakes easily when tested with a fork, it is done.

Tip: For a milder version, substitute ¹/₄ cup of chili sauce for the tomato juice and hot red pepper seasoning.

Broiled Fish with Peppery Almond Butter ◯ ◑

Preparation: **5 minutes**   Cooking: **5 minutes**   Serves **4**   Calories per serving: **400**

1½ pounds flounder, sole, halibut, cod, or haddock fillets

¼ cup all-purpose flour

½ teaspoon salt

½ teaspoon paprika

4 tablespoons (½ stick) butter or margarine

5 teaspoons vegetable oil

½ cup slivered blanched almonds

2 tablespoons lemon or lime juice

5 or more drops liquid hot red pepper seasoning

Tip: This recipe can be halved.

1. Preheat the broiler. Pat the **fish** dry with paper toweling. Combine the **flour, salt,** and **paprika** in a shallow dish or plate. Coat the fish fillets with the flour mixture. Shake off any excess flour.

2. In a 7-inch skillet, melt 1½ tablespoons of the **butter,** stir in the **oil,** and brush the rack of the broiler pan with some of the mixture. Place the fish on the rack, and brush the fish with the remaining butter-oil mixture. Broil 3 to 4 inches from the heat, without turning, for 5 minutes or longer, depending on the thickness of the fish. When the fish flakes easily when tested with a fork, it is done. Remove to a warm platter.

3. While the fish is broiling, melt the remaining 2½ tablespoons of butter in the skillet over moderate heat. Add the **almonds,** and cook, stirring constantly, until lightly browned. Using a slotted spoon, remove the almonds from the skillet, and scatter them over the fish.

4. Add the **lemon juice** and **red pepper seasoning** to the skillet, heat, and pour over the fish. Serve with Carrots Amana Style, page 67, or French Green Peas, page 72.

Chinese Baked Fish with Green Onions and Ginger

Preparation: **5 minutes**   Cooking: **20 minutes**   Serves **4**   Calories per serving: **245**

1 whole (about 2½ pounds) sea trout (weakfish), sea bass, haddock, or red snapper, dressed

3 tablespoons soy sauce

3 tablespoons dry sherry

3 green onions, trimmed and cut into ¼-inch slices

1 teaspoon minced fresh ginger root or ¼ teaspoon ground ginger

1 clove garlic, peeled and minced

¼ teaspoon sugar

1. Preheat the oven to 350°F. Make cuts in the **fish,** about 1 inch apart, through the flesh and down to the bone, from the gills to the tail. Do this on both sides of the fish.

2. In a small bowl, combine the **soy sauce, sherry, green onions, ginger, garlic,** and **sugar.** Place the fish in a buttered 8"x 8"x 2" baking dish, and sprinkle the mixture evenly over the fish. Bake, uncovered, for 20 minutes or longer, depending on the thickness of the fish. When the fish flakes easily when tested with a fork, it is done. Serve with Brussels Sprouts with Walnuts, page 63.

Baked Stuffed Sea Trout

Preparation: 5 minutes   Cooking: 20 minutes   Serves 4   Calories per serving: **320**

1 cup soft fresh bread crumbs (2 slices bread)

3 tablespoons butter or margarine, melted

1/4 teaspoon black pepper

1 small yellow onion, peeled and chopped

1/4 cup chopped sweet green pepper

1/8 teaspoon dried thyme, crumbled

1 1/4 teaspoons salt

3/4 cup chopped mushrooms

1 whole (about 2 1/2 pounds) sea trout (weakfish), sea bass, or red snapper, dressed

1. Preheat the oven to 375°F. In a mixing bowl, combine the **bread crumbs**, 2 tablespoons of the melted **butter**, the **black pepper, onion, green pepper, thyme,** 1/4 teaspoon of the **salt**, and the **mushrooms.** Set aside.

2. Sprinkle the **sea trout** inside and out with the remaining teaspoon of salt. Stuff the fish loosely with the bread crumb mixture, and close the opening with skewers, or sew the opening with a needle and kitchen string.

3. Place the fish in a buttered 13"x 9"x 2" baking dish. Brush the fish with the remaining tablespoon of melted butter. Bake, uncovered, for 20 minutes or longer, depending on the thickness of the fish. When the fish flakes easily when tested with a fork, it is done. Serve with New Potatoes with Green Onions, page 73.

Baked Whitings with Cucumbers, Dill, and Cream ⓓ

Preparation: 20 minutes   Cooking: 20 minutes   Serves 4   Calories per serving: **290**

Crisp-tender cucumbers, a touch of dill, and a bit of rich cream are ideal accompaniments for delicate whitings (also known as silver hake).

4 whole whitings (about 1/2 pound each), dressed

3/4 teaspoon salt

1/4 teaspoon black pepper

1 small yellow onion, peeled and finely chopped

2 large cucumbers, peeled

2 tablespoons snipped fresh dill or 1/2 teaspoon dried dillweed

2 tablespoons butter or margarine

1/2 cup heavy cream

1. Preheat the oven to 375°F. Wash the **whitings,** dry them with paper toweling, and sprinkle with the **salt** and **pepper.** Place them in a buttered 13"x 9"x 2" baking dish and cover with the **onion.**

2. Slice the **cucumbers** in half lengthwise, scoop out the seeds with a spoon, then cut the halves into 1/2-inch slices. Scatter the cucumbers around the fish. Sprinkle the fish and cucumbers with the **dill,** and dot with the **butter.**

3. Bake, uncovered, for 10 minutes. Pour the **cream** around the fish, and continue to bake, uncovered, for 10 more minutes, or until done. To check for doneness, insert a knife along the backbone at the thickest part of the fish. When the flesh separates easily from the bone, it is done. Remove the fish to a warm platter, surround with the cucumbers, and pour the sauce over all. Serve with buttered rice.

> **Tips: 1.** *This recipe can be halved.*
> **2.** *Substitute sole, flounder, halibut, cod, or haddock fillets for the whiting.*

Curried Flounder Madras

Preparation: **10 minutes**   Cooking: **10 minutes**   Serves **4**   Calories per serving: **305**

6 tablespoons (³/₄ stick) butter or margarine

1 teaspoon minced fresh ginger root or ¹/₄ teaspoon ground ginger

1 medium-size yellow onion, peeled and chopped

4 green onions, trimmed and chopped

1 clove garlic, peeled and minced

2 teaspoons curry powder

1¹/₂ pounds flounder, sole, halibut, cod, or haddock fillets

¹/₄ cup water

¹/₄ cup dry sherry or dry white wine (optional)

¹/₂ teaspoon salt

1. Preheat the oven to 350°F. In a 9- or 10-inch skillet with an ovenproof handle, melt the **butter** over moderate heat. Add the **ginger, yellow onion, green onions, garlic,** and **curry powder,** and cook, uncovered, for 5 minutes. Remove the skillet from the heat.

2. Push the onion mixture to one side of the skillet. If the **flounder fillets** are very thin, fold them in half. They should be about 1 inch thick when folded. Place the fillets in the skillet in one layer and spread the onion mixture evenly over them. Pour the **water,** and the **sherry** if used, evenly over the fillets, and sprinkle with the **salt.** Bake, uncovered, for 10 minutes or longer, depending on the thickness of the fish. If the fish flakes easily when tested with a fork, it is done. Serve with Shredded Cabbage with Garlic, page 64.

Tip: If you do not have a skillet with an ovenproof handle, place the fillets in an 8"x 8"x 2" buttered baking dish, add the cooked onion-garlic mixture and the remaining ingredients as directed, and bake.

Baked Bluefish with Olives and Tomatoes ◖◗

Preparation: **35 minutes**   Cooking: **10 minutes**   Serves **4**   Calories per serving: **335**

2 tablespoons olive or vegetable oil

1 small yellow onion, peeled and chopped

¹/₄ cup chopped green olives

¹/₂ small sweet green pepper, cored, seeded, and chopped

3 medium-size fresh tomatoes, peeled and chopped, or 1 can (1 pound) tomatoes, drained and chopped

¹/₂ cup dry white wine

¹/₄ cup tomato paste

¹/₂ teaspoon salt

¹/₄ teaspoon black pepper

1¹/₂ pounds bluefish or mackerel fillets

1. Heat the **oil** in a 2-quart saucepan over moderate heat. Add the **onion, olives,** and **green pepper,** and cook, uncovered, for 3 minutes. Add the **tomatoes,** and cook 5 minutes longer. Add the **wine, tomato paste, salt,** and **black pepper,** and simmer, uncovered, for 20 minutes.

2. About 10 minutes before the sauce is done, preheat the oven to 350°F. Place the **bluefish fillets** in an ungreased 8"x 8"x 2" baking dish, and spoon the sauce over them. Bake, uncovered, for 10 minutes or longer, depending on the thickness of the fish. When the fish flakes easily when tested with a fork, it is done.

Tips: 1. This recipe can be halved; use half a small onion and 1 large or 2 small tomatoes. 2. Leftovers can be served cold. 3. You can make the sauce ahead and reheat it, then proceed with Step 2.

Crumbed Oven-Fried Fish ⊘

Preparation: **3 minutes**   Cooking: **5 minutes**   Serves **4**   Calories per serving: **290**

½ **cup milk**

½ **teaspoon salt**

½ **cup fine dry bread crumbs**

1 **teaspoon paprika**

1½ **pounds flounder, sole, halibut, cod, or haddock fillets**

4 **tablespoons (½ stick) butter or margarine, melted**

1 **lemon, cut into 4 wedges (optional)**

1. Adjust the oven rack to slightly above the middle of the oven, and preheat the oven to 500°F. Put the **milk** into a shallow bowl or pie plate, and stir in the **salt**. Mix the **bread crumbs** with the **paprika** on a plate or a sheet of wax paper. Dip the **fish fillets** into the milk, then coat with the bread crumb mixture. Place the fillets in a single layer in a buttered 8"x 8"x 2" baking dish.

2. Pour the melted **butter** over the fillets. Bake, uncovered, for 5 minutes or longer, depending on the thickness of the fish. When the fish flakes easily when tested with a fork, it is done. Garnish with the **lemon wedges** if desired. Serve with Coleslaw, page 45, or Spinach-Bacon Salad with Warm Dressing, page 48.

Panfried Whitings with Lemon Butter Sauce ⊘⊘

Preparation: **15 minutes**   Cooking: **11 minutes**   Serves **4**   Calories per serving: **300**

The whiting, also known as silver hake, is not only easy to prepare, it is easy to eat. It has only one central bone, and no small ones to watch out for.

4 **whole whitings (about ½ pound each), dressed**

½ **teaspoon dried rosemary, crumbled**

½ **teaspoon salt**

¼ **teaspoon black pepper**

¼ **cup all-purpose flour**

½ **cup vegetable oil**

3 **tablespoons butter or margarine**

2 **tablespoons lemon juice**

2 **tablespoons minced parsley**

Tip: This recipe can be halved.

1. Wash the **whitings** and dry them with paper toweling. Sprinkle them inside with the **rosemary,** and outside with the **salt** and **pepper.** Place the **flour** on a plate or a sheet of wax paper, and coat the fish with the flour. Shake off any excess flour.

2. Heat the **oil** in a heavy 12-inch skillet over moderately high heat for about 1 minute. Carefully place the fish in the oil, and cook for 5 minutes on each side, or until golden brown. To check for doneness, insert a knife along the backbone at the thickest part of the fish. When the flesh separates easily from the bone, it is done. Remove the fish to a warm platter.

3. Discard the oil in the skillet. Reduce the heat to low, and add the **butter, lemon juice,** and **parsley.** Cook about 30 seconds, scraping up any brown bits stuck to the skillet. Pour the sauce over the fish, and serve with Baked Zucchini with Tomatoes, page 79.

156

New England Codfish Hash

Preparation: **12 minutes**   Cooking: **7 minutes**   Serves **4**   Calories per serving: **320**

4 medium-size all-purpose potatoes (about 1 pound), peeled and cut into ½-inch dice

¾ cup half-and-half

4 tablespoons (½ stick) butter or margarine

1 pound cod or haddock fillets, finely chopped

1 teaspoon salt

⅛ teaspoon black pepper

1 tablespoon snipped fresh dill or ¼ teaspoon dried dillweed

Here is one of those simple, old-fashioned recipes too few people make anymore. It is subtle in flavor and satisfying. Try it.

1. Place the **potatoes** in a 3-quart saucepan, add water to cover, and boil, uncovered, for 5 minutes, or until the potatoes are tender but not too soft. Drain and set aside.

2. Heat the **half-and-half** and **butter** in a heavy 9- or 10-inch skillet over moderate heat until the butter melts. Add the **cod fillets,** and cook, uncovered, for 2 to 3 minutes, or just until the cod turns opaque—do not allow the mixture to boil.

3. Add the potatoes, **salt,** and **pepper,** and continue to cook, stirring, 3 to 4 minutes longer, until heated through; the mixture should not brown. Sprinkle with the **dill.**

French Fish Stew with Carrots and Potatoes ⏺

Preparation: **10 minutes** Cooking: **26 minutes**   Serves **4**   Calories per serving: **325**

4 tablespoons (½ stick) butter or margarine

2 medium-size yellow onions, peeled and chopped

2 medium-size all-purpose potatoes, peeled and diced

2 medium-size carrots, peeled and cut into ½-inch slices

3 cups chicken broth

¾ cup dry white wine or dry vermouth

1 bay leaf

¼ teaspoon dried thyme, crumbled

½ teaspoon salt

¼ teaspoon black pepper

1 pound cod, haddock, or halibut fillets, cut into 2-inch pieces

1 tablespoon finely chopped parsley

Serve this one-dish meal in soup bowls with plenty of crusty bread to mop up the juices.

1. Melt the **butter** in a 3-quart saucepan over moderate heat. Add the **onions, potatoes,** and **carrots,** and cook, covered, for 10 minutes. Add the **chicken broth, wine, bay leaf, thyme, salt,** and **pepper,** and bring to a boil—about 3 minutes. Cover and simmer for 10 minutes, or until the vegetables are almost tender.

2. Add the **fish fillets,** and continue to simmer, covered, for 3 to 5 minutes, or until the fish flakes easily when tested with a fork. Sprinkle with the **parsley.**

> *Tips: 1. Add ½ cup of heavy cream just before serving.*
> *2. This recipe can be halved.*

FISH AND SHELLFISH

Acadian Cod and Potato Pancake 🐷 ◐

Preparation: **12 minutes**   Cooking: **16 minutes**   Serves **4**   Calories per serving: **230**

¾ pound cod or haddock fillets, finely chopped

2 eggs, lightly beaten

1½ cups finely grated raw, peeled all-purpose potatoes (about 3 medium-size potatoes or ¾ pound)

2 tablespoons all-purpose flour

1 small yellow onion, peeled and finely chopped

1 tablespoon chopped parsley

⅛ teaspoon ground nutmeg

1 teaspoon salt

¼ teaspoon black pepper

2 tablespoons butter or margarine

This cod and potato dish is an example of the traditional fare of Canada's Maritime Provinces.

1. In a large bowl, combine the **cod fillets, eggs, potatoes, flour, onion, parsley, nutmeg, salt,** and **pepper.**

2. Melt 1 tablespoon of the **butter** in a heavy 9- or 10-inch skillet over moderate heat. Using a large spoon, drop enough of the mixture into the skillet to make 4 pancakes, flatten each slightly with a pancake turner, and cook, uncovered, for 4 minutes, or until the bottoms are brown. Turn carefully with the pancake turner, and cook for 4 minutes on the other side. Drain on paper toweling placed on a serving platter. Set in a keep-warm (250°F) oven. Melt the remaining tablespoon of butter, and cook the remaining mixture the same way. Serve with applesauce.

> *Tip: This recipe can be halved.*

Baked Deviled Tuna 🐷 ◐

Preparation: **15 minutes**   Cooking: **10 minutes**   Serves **4**   Calories per serving: **375**

3 tablespoons butter or margarine

1 medium-size yellow onion, peeled and chopped

¾ cup sliced mushrooms

2 teaspoons dry mustard

1 teaspoon chili powder

½ teaspoon salt

2 tablespoons saltine crumbs

1 cup half-and-half

1 can (12½ ounces) or 2 cans (6½ or 7 ounces each) tuna, drained and flaked

1 teaspoon Worcestershire sauce

Pinch cayenne pepper (optional)

2 eggs, lightly beaten

1. Preheat the oven to 400°F. Heat 2 tablespoons of the **butter** in a heavy 9- or 10-inch skillet over moderate heat. Add the **onion,** and cook, uncovered, for 3 minutes, then add the **mushrooms** and cook 3 minutes longer.

2. Stir in the **mustard, chili powder, salt, saltine crumbs, half-and-half, tuna,** and **Worcestershire sauce,** and the **cayenne pepper** if used. Bring the mixture to a simmer and cook for 2 minutes. Remove the skillet from the heat, and stir in the **eggs.**

3. Spoon the mixture into 4 buttered 6-ounce (¾ cup) individual baking dishes or custard cups. Melt the remaining tablespoon of butter and pour some over the top of each. Place the dishes on a baking sheet, and bake for 10 minutes.

> *Tips: 1. This recipe can be halved. 2. Serve this dish cold or as an hors d'oeuvre spread on thin slices of French or Italian bread.*

Salmon Loaf with Cucumber-Dill Sauce

Preparation: 15 minutes Cooking: **30 minutes** Serves **4** Calories per serving: **600**

1 can (15½ ounces) salmon

½ cup milk (approximately)

3 tablespoons butter or margarine

1 small yellow onion, peeled and chopped

3 tablespoons all-purpose flour

½ medium-size sweet green pepper, cored, seeded, and chopped

1 cup fine dry bread crumbs

2 eggs, lightly beaten

½ teaspoon salt

¼ teaspoon black pepper

¼ cup snipped fresh dill or 1 teaspoon dried dillweed

1 cup sour cream

1 tablespoon cider vinegar

½ cup diced cucumber

1. Preheat the oven to 350°F. Drain the **salmon,** saving the liquid. Combine the salmon liquid with enough **milk** to make 1 cup. Set aside.

2. Melt the **butter** in a 2-quart saucepan over moderate heat. Add the **onion,** and cook, uncovered, for 3 minutes. Blend in the **flour,** and cook for 1 minute, stirring constantly.

3. Gradually add the salmon liquid and milk mixture, and cook, stirring constantly, until very thick—about 3 minutes. Remove from the heat. Add the salmon, **green pepper, bread crumbs, eggs, salt, black pepper,** and 2 tablespoons of the **dill,** and mix well.

4. Transfer the salmon mixture to a buttered 8"x 8"x 2" baking dish, and form the mixture into a loaf. Bake, uncovered, for 30 minutes.

5. Meanwhile, in a small serving bowl, combine the **sour cream, vinegar, cucumber,** and the remaining 2 tablespoons of dill. Serve this sauce on the side with the salmon loaf, accompanied by Skillet Asparagus, page 58.

Steamed Mussels with Garlic and Butter Sauce

Preparation: 25 minutes Cooking: **10 minutes** Serves **4** Calories per serving: **385**

Serve these mussels as a first course for 8 or a main course for 4. Have plenty of crusty bread on the table to dip into the delicious broth.

4 pounds mussels (about 3½ quarts)

½ cup (1 stick) butter at room temperature

2 green onions, trimmed and chopped

6 cloves garlic, peeled and minced

1 cup dry white wine or dry vermouth

½ teaspoon salt

⅛ teaspoon black pepper

½ cup chopped parsley

1. Scrub the **mussels** thoroughly with a stiff brush under cold running water, discarding any with open or broken shells. With scissors or a small, sharp knife, cut off and discard the "beard" that extends from the side of the mussel.

2. Melt 2 tablespoons of the **butter** in a 6-quart, nonaluminum pot over low heat. Add the **green onions** and 2 teaspoons of the **garlic,** and cook, uncovered, for 2 minutes. Add the mussels, **wine, salt,** and **pepper.** Cover, bring to a boil, and cook, shaking the pot occasionally, for 3 minutes, or until the mussels open (throw away any that do not open). Using a slotted spoon, place the mussels in individual serving bowls.

3. Mix together the remaining butter and garlic and the **parsley.** Stir the mixture into the broth in the pot, and pour over the mussels.

Hangtown Fry ⊙ ⊕

Preparation: **5 minutes** Cooking: **7 minutes**   Serves **4** Calories per serving: **245**

This legendary dish was invented, it is said, during the days of the California Gold Rush to satisfy a wealthy miner who desired the most expensive food in the camp of Hangtown. Fortunately, oysters are not so costly today.

5 eggs

3 tablespoons milk

1/2 teaspoon salt

1/4 teaspoon black pepper

12 medium-size shucked oysters, drained (about 1 cup)

1/2 cup soda cracker crumbs

2 tablespoons butter or margarine

1. In a small bowl, beat the **eggs** with the **milk, salt,** and **pepper.** Roll the **oysters** in the **cracker crumbs,** then dip them into the egg mixture and coat again with the cracker crumbs. Reserve the egg mixture that remains.

2. Melt the **butter** in a heavy 9-inch skillet over moderate heat. Add the oysters and cook, uncovered, for 30 seconds, or until golden brown on one side. Turn them over, reduce the heat, and pour the remaining egg mixture over the oysters.

3. Cook until the eggs are set and lightly browned. During the cooking, lift the cooked egg mixture with a pancake turner to let the uncooked part run underneath. Remove the eggs and oysters to a warm platter and serve.

> *Tip: This recipe can be halved.*

Oyster and Mushroom Pie ⊕

Preparation: **15 minutes** Cooking: **10 minutes**   Serves **4** Calories per serving: **320**

1 pint shucked oysters

1 cup (approximately) half-and-half or heavy cream

4 tablespoons (1/2 stick) butter or margarine

1/4 pound mushrooms, thinly sliced

2 tablespoons all-purpose flour

1/4 teaspoon Worcestershire sauce

1 teaspoon lemon juice

Pinch cayenne pepper

3/4 teaspoon salt

1/4 teaspoon black pepper

1 cup soft fresh bread crumbs (2 slices bread)

> *Tip: This recipe can be halved.*

1. Preheat the oven to 425°F. Drain the **oysters,** saving the liquor. Combine the oyster liquor with enough **half-and-half** to make 1 1/2 cups. Set aside.

2. Melt 2 tablespoons of the **butter** in a heavy 9- or 10-inch skillet over moderate heat. Add the **mushrooms,** and cook, uncovered, for 3 minutes, or until lightly browned. Remove the mushrooms to a platter and set aside.

3. Reduce the heat to low and melt 1 tablespoon of the remaining butter in the skillet. Blend in the **flour,** and cook for 1 minute, stirring constantly. Gradually add the oyster liquor and half-and-half mixture, and cook, stirring constantly, until the mixture thickens—about 3 minutes. Remove from the heat.

4. Add the oysters, the cooked mushrooms and any accumulated liquid, and the **Worcestershire sauce, lemon juice, cayenne pepper, salt,** and **black pepper.** Pour the mixture into a buttered 8-inch glass or ceramic pie plate.

5. Sprinkle with the **bread crumbs,** and dot with the last tablespoon of butter. Bake, uncovered, until the crumbs are browned—about 10 minutes.

SAUCES

These sauces have been selected not only for ease and speed of preparation (all but 2 take less than 12 minutes) but because they can be used to enhance many kinds of foods from vegetables, eggs, and pasta to poultry, meats, and seafood.

Blender Mayonnaise

Preparation: 4 minutes   Yield: **1 cup**   Calories per tablespoon: **130**

Why not make your own mayonnaise for a change? It takes only 4 minutes in an electric blender, it is cheaper than the store-bought dressing, and its taste is far superior. You can make this recipe ahead and refrigerate it for 1 week.

1 egg

1/2 teaspoon salt

1/2 teaspoon Dijon or prepared spicy brown mustard

1 tablespoon lemon juice or cider vinegar

1 cup vegetable oil at room temperature

1. Put the **egg, salt, mustard, lemon juice,** and 1/4 cup of the **oil** into the jar of an electric blender. Cover and whirl at top speed for 30 seconds. Uncover, and add the remaining oil, pouring it in a very slow, thin, steady stream with the blender running at moderately high speed.

2. Turn off the blender occasionally and clean the sides of the jar with a rubber spatula. Taste and add more lemon juice and salt if necessary.

> *Tips: 1. To make a Béarnaise sauce, substitute tarragon vinegar for the lemon juice and add 1 teaspoon crumbled dried tarragon to the finished sauce. Serve with cold chicken and seafood. 2. Use one of the following variations on the finished sauce. Horseradish: Mix in 1 to 2 tablespoons prepared horseradish. For meat and seafood salads. Dill: Fold in 1/2 teaspoon dried dillweed. For seafood. Curry: Blend in 1 teaspoon or more curry powder. For chicken, meat, and egg salads.*

Easy White Sauce

Preparation and cooking: 8 minutes   Yield: **1 cup**   Calories per tablespoon: **25**

Try this easy method of making white sauce without lumps. Use it in casseroles, over vegetables, and for making creamed soups or creamed chicken or tuna.

1 cup milk or half-and-half

2 tablespoons butter or margarine, softened

2 tablespoons all-purpose flour

1/4 teaspoon salt

1/8 teaspoon black pepper

1. Bring the **milk** to a simmer in a 2-quart saucepan over moderate heat. Meanwhile, in a small bowl, blend the **butter** and **flour** together with a spoon to form a smooth paste.

2. Using a wire whisk, vigorously beat the butter-flour mixture, 1 rounded teaspoonful at a time, into the hot milk. Cook, stirring constantly, over moderate heat for 2 to 3 minutes, or until the sauce is smooth and thick. Season with the **salt** and **pepper.**

> *Tip: For a thinner sauce, reduce the butter and flour to 1 tablespoon each; for a thicker sauce, increase to 3 tablespoons each.*

Mock Hollandaise Sauce

Preparation: 5 minutes   Cooking: **4 minutes**   Yield: **²/₃ cup**   Calories per tablespoon: **60**

This sauce tastes almost as good as an authentic hollandaise, but it has fewer calories, is less expensive, and is much simpler to make.

¹/₂ cup mayonnaise

2 tablespoons lemon juice

4 tablespoons (¹/₂ stick) butter or margarine

2 egg yolks

Pinch cayenne pepper

Pinch salt

1. Combine the **mayonnaise** and **lemon juice** in the top of a double boiler. Place over barely simmering water and cook, stirring constantly, for 3 minutes, or until warm but not hot.

2. Add the **butter** and **egg yolks,** and cook, stirring constantly, for 1 minute, or until the mixture becomes thick enough to coat a spoon. Watch carefully; if the mixture gets too hot, the eggs will curdle. Remove the top of the double boiler from the water, and stir in the **cayenne pepper** and **salt.** Serve over broccoli, cauliflower, green beans, asparagus, globe artichokes, poached eggs, and poached or baked fish.

> *Tip: For a sauce that is faster (4 minutes) and more foolproof, but not as authentic-tasting or low in calories as the one above, melt 4 tablespoons of butter or margarine in a small saucepan over low heat. Gradually whisk in 5 teaspoons of lemon juice and 1¹/₄ cups of mayonnaise. Beat for 2 minutes. Remove from the heat and serve. Makes about 1¹/₂ cups; about 100 calories per tablespoon.*

Jiffy Cheese Sauce

Preparation: 4 minutes   Cooking: **4 minutes**   Yield: **1¹/₂ cups**   Calories per tablespoon: **35**

Serve this sauce over cooked vegetables, eggs, pasta, or buttered toast.

1 cup milk or half-and-half

1 cup shredded sharp or extra sharp Cheddar cheese (about 4 ounces)

2 tablespoons all-purpose flour

¹/₄ teaspoon salt

¹/₈ teaspoon black pepper

A few grains cayenne pepper or paprika

2 tablespoons butter or margarine, cut into small pieces

Bring the **milk** to a simmer in a 2-quart saucepan over moderate heat. Reduce the heat to low, add the **cheese,** and cook, stirring occasionally, until the cheese melts. Do not let the milk boil, and do not stir too much after the cheese melts or the cheese may become stringy. Blend in the **flour** with a wire whisk and stir until smooth. Season with the **salt, black pepper,** and **cayenne pepper.** Add the **butter,** and stir until it melts.

> *Tips: 1. When the cheese melts, the mixture may seem curdled, but it will become smooth again when the flour is whisked in. 2. To vary the sauce, substitute ¹/₂ cup blue cheese for ¹/₂ cup of the Cheddar cheese, or add 2 teaspoons Dijon or prepared spicy brown mustard, 1 teaspoon Worcestershire sauce, and 3 to 4 drops liquid hot red pepper seasoning after whisking in the flour. 3. This recipe can be halved.*

Easy Sour Cream Sauces ⊗

All of these sauces can be served hot or cold. For best results when preparing heated sauces, bring the sour cream to room temperature, then heat gently, preferably in the top of a double boiler so that the sour cream does not curdle. Unless otherwise indicated, heat the sour cream before adding the remaining ingredients. As a general rule, serve hot sauces with hot food, cold sauces with cold food.

You can substitute plain yogurt for the sour cream in all of the recipes below except the Sour Cream–Cheese Sauce.

Sour Cream–Cheese Sauce

Melt 1 cup finely shredded sharp or extra sharp Cheddar cheese with 1/4 cup milk and 1 teaspoon bottled steak sauce in the top of a double boiler over simmering water. Blend in 1 cup sour cream. Serve with fish, baked potatoes, and green vegetables. Yield: 1 3/4 cups; 35 calories per tablespoon.

Sour Cream–Cucumber Sauce

Combine 1 cup sour cream with 1 cup peeled, seeded, and diced cucumber, 2 tablespoons white wine vinegar, 1 tablespoon snipped fresh dill or 1/2 teaspoon dried dillweed, and salt and pepper to taste. Serve with fish or ham. Yield: 2 cups; 17 calories per tablespoon (6 calories if made with yogurt).

Sour Cream–Curry Sauce

In a small saucepan over low heat, melt 1 tablespoon butter with 1 teaspoon curry powder and 1 tablespoon finely grated yellow onion for 2 to 3 minutes. Blend in 1 cup sour cream, and add salt and pepper to taste. Serve with meat or fish. Yield: 1 cup; 35 calories per tablespoon (14 calories if made with yogurt).

Sour Cream–Horseradish Sauce

Combine 1 cup sour cream with 2 tablespoons cider vinegar and 2 tablespoons prepared horseradish. Serve with beef, ham, or pork. Yield: 1 1/4 cups; 30 calories per tablespoon (13 calories if made with yogurt).

Sour Cream–Mustard Sauce

Combine 1 cup sour cream with 2 to 3 tablespoons of any type of prepared mustard and 1 tablespoon cider vinegar. Serve with beef, ham, or pork. Yield: 1 cup; 30 calories per tablespoon (9 calories if made with yogurt).

Creole Sauce

Preparation: **15 minutes** Cooking: **25 minutes** Yield: **1 1/2 cups** Calories per tablespoon: **20**

3 tablespoons vegetable oil

1 medium-size yellow onion, peeled and chopped

1 clove garlic, peeled and chopped

1/2 medium-size sweet green pepper, cored, seeded, and chopped

3 medium-size mushrooms, thinly sliced

3 medium-size fresh tomatoes, peeled and chopped, or 1 can (1 pound) tomatoes, chopped, with their juice

1/4 teaspoon salt

Here is a versatile tomato-based sauce. Serve it with fish, shellfish, meat, poultry, omelets, rice, or spaghetti.

Heat the **oil** in a 2-quart saucepan over moderate heat, add the **onion**, and cook, uncovered, for 2 minutes. Add the **garlic, green pepper,** and **mushrooms,** and cook, uncovered, for 2 more minutes. Add the **tomatoes** and **salt** and simmer, uncovered, for 25 minutes.

> **Tip:** You can make this sauce ahead and refrigerate it for 1 or 2 days or freeze it.

Low-Calorie Lemon Sauce for Vegetables ⬭

Preparation: **5 minutes**   Cooking: **7 minutes**   Yield: **1¼ cups**   Calories per tablespoon: **15**

1 cup chicken broth

1 tablespoon butter or margarine

1 tablespoon cornstarch

¼ cup cold water

2 egg yolks

Juice and grated rind of 1 medium-size lemon

1. Heat the **chicken broth** and **butter** in a 1-quart saucepan over moderate heat. Meanwhile, in a small bowl, combine the **cornstarch** and **water,** and stir into the heated broth. Cook for 3 minutes, stirring constantly.

2. Using the same bowl, beat together the **egg yolks, lemon juice,** and **lemon rind** until frothy. Gradually stir ¼ cup of the hot broth into the egg-yolk mixture, then pour slowly back into the hot broth, stirring constantly. Be careful not to let the sauce boil or the eggs will curdle. Serve over cauliflower, broccoli, spinach, zucchini, and other vegetables.

> *Tips:* **1.** *This recipe can be halved.* **2.** *You can make this sauce ahead and refrigerate it for 1 or 2 days.* **3.** *Freeze the egg whites in ice cube trays (one egg white per cup); when frozen, transfer the egg whites to a plastic bag and return to the freezer. Use the whites to make angel food cakes, macaroons, meringues, and frosting.*

All-Purpose Barbecue Sauce 🐷 ⬭

Preparation: **5 minutes**   Cooking: **20 minutes**   Yield: **1¼ cups**   Calories per tablespoon: **35**

¼ cup cider vinegar

½ cup water

2 tablespoons sugar

1 tablespoon prepared yellow mustard

½ teaspoon black pepper

1½ teaspoons salt

¼ teaspoon paprika

1 slice lemon, about ½ inch thick

1 small yellow onion, peeled and thinly sliced

4 tablespoons (½ stick) butter or margarine

½ cup ketchup or chili sauce

2 tablespoons Worcestershire sauce

1. Combine the **vinegar, water, sugar, mustard, pepper, salt, paprika, lemon, onion,** and **butter** in a 1-quart saucepan. Simmer, uncovered, for 20 minutes, stirring occasionally.

2. Remove the saucepan from the heat, and stir in the **ketchup** and **Worcestershire sauce.** Remove and discard the lemon slice. Use as a brush-on basting for beef, veal, lamb, chicken, or fish.

> *Tips:* **1.** *This recipe can be halved.* **2.** *You can make this sauce ahead and refrigerate it for 1 week or freeze it.*

CASSEROLES

Casseroles often take longer to cook than other dishes, but most of the cooking time is unattended baking. In addition, many of the recipes in this section are for one-dish meals that need be accompanied by only a tossed salad and some fruit.

Garden Casserole

Preparation: **15 minutes**   Cooking: **35 minutes**   Serves **4**   Calories per serving: **205**

2 zucchini (about 1/2 pound)

1 small eggplant
(about 1/2 pound), unpeeled

1 medium-size yellow onion,
peeled

2 large, very ripe tomatoes

1 medium-size sweet green
pepper, cored and seeded

1 teaspoon each dried basil
and thyme, crumbled

2 cloves garlic, peeled and
minced

2 teaspoons salt

1/4 teaspoon black pepper

1/4 cup chopped parsley

5 tablespoons vegetable oil

Here is a simplified version of that famed Mediterranean creation ratatouille. A treasure for the busy cook, it takes only minutes to prepare for baking, it can be made ahead and reheated or served cold, and it is nourishing.

1. Preheat the oven to 400°F. Slice the **zucchini, eggplant, onion, tomatoes,** and **green pepper** as thin as you can. In a dish, combine the **basil, thyme, garlic, salt, black pepper,** and **parsley.**

2. Grease the bottom of a 2-quart casserole with 2 tablespoons of the **oil.** Layer the zucchini, then the eggplant, onion, tomatoes, and green pepper in the casserole, sprinkling each layer with the herb and garlic mixture. Sprinkle the remaining oil over the top, and bake, covered, for 35 minutes, or until the vegetables are tender.

Tip: You can substitute 1 can (1 pound) Italian plum tomatoes, drained, for the fresh tomatoes.

Asparagus with Pimiento and Cheese

Preparation: **15 minutes**   Cooking: **30 minutes**   Serves **4**   Calories per serving: **375**

1 1/2 pounds asparagus

1 teaspoon salt

1/4 teaspoon black pepper

1 pimiento, chopped

3 eggs, lightly beaten

1 cup shredded sharp Cheddar
cheese (about 4 ounces)

1 cup fine dry bread crumbs

1 cup milk

2 tablespoons butter

1. Preheat the oven to 375°F. Bring about 1 inch of lightly salted water to a boil in a 2-quart saucepan. Break off the tough stem ends of the **asparagus** as far down as the stalks snap easily. Cut the stalks into 1-inch pieces, add to the boiling water, and cook, uncovered, for 5 minutes. Drain.

2. In an ungreased 1 1/2-quart casserole, mix the asparagus, **salt, pepper, pimiento, eggs, cheese,** 3/4 cup of the **bread crumbs,** and the **milk.** Dot with the **butter,** sprinkle with the remaining 1/4 cup of bread crumbs, and bake, uncovered, for 30 minutes, or until almost firm.

Green Beans with Mushrooms and Water Chestnuts

Preparation: **15 minutes**   Cooking: **20 minutes**   Serves **4**   Calories per serving: **415**

3/4 pound green beans

6 tablespoons (3/4 stick) butter or margarine

1 large yellow onion, peeled and chopped

1 1/2 cups thinly sliced mushrooms (about 4 ounces)

2 tablespoons all-purpose flour

1 cup milk

1/2 cup shredded Cheddar cheese (about 2 ounces)

1/2 teaspoon salt

1/4 teaspoon black pepper

1 can (4 ounces) water chestnuts, drained and sliced

1/4 cup blanched slivered almonds

1/2 cup fine dry bread crumbs

1. Preheat the oven to 350°F. Wash the **beans** and cut off the ends. Bring about 1 inch of lightly salted water to a boil in a 1-quart saucepan and add the beans. Cook, covered, for 5 to 7 minutes, or until just tender. Drain the beans and set aside.

2. Meanwhile, melt 5 tablespoons of the **butter** in a heavy 8-inch skillet over moderate heat. Add the **onion** and **mushrooms,** and cook, uncovered, for 5 minutes, or until the onion is soft. Blend in the **flour,** add the **milk, cheese, salt,** and **pepper,** and cook, stirring, until the cheese melts and the sauce thickens—about 5 minutes.

3. In a buttered 1-quart casserole or 8"x 8"x 2" baking dish, combine the cheese mixture, the beans, and the **water chestnuts.** Top with the **almonds** and **bread crumbs,** and dot with the remaining tablespoon of butter. Bake, uncovered, for 20 minutes, or until bubbly.

Tips: 1. You can use frozen beans instead of fresh; thaw but do not cook them. 2. You can also substitute broccoli spears for the beans. 3. As another variation, omit the Cheddar cheese and almonds, and use 1/2 cup shredded Swiss cheese instead. Mix 1/4 cup grated Parmesan cheese with the bread crumbs.

Holiday Carrots and Sweet Potatoes

Preparation: **20 minutes**   Cooking: **25 minutes**   Serves **4**   Calories per serving: **250**

This Eastern European dish goes well with roast pork, chicken, or turkey—it tastes even better when made ahead and reheated.

3 medium-size carrots, peeled and diced

1 large sweet potato, peeled and diced

1 orange

2 tablespoons butter or margarine

1/4 teaspoon black pepper

1/2 cup pitted prunes

1/4 cup honey

1. Preheat the oven to 400°F. Bring 1 inch of lightly salted water to a boil in a 2-quart saucepan. Add the **carrots** and **sweet potato,** and cook, covered, for 15 minutes. Drain.

2. Meanwhile, grate the rind from the **orange,** then juice the orange. Place the rind and juice in a buttered 1 1/2-quart casserole.

3. Add the drained carrots and potato, 1 tablespoon of the **butter,** the **pepper** and **prunes,** and mix well. Drizzle the **honey** over the top, and dot with the remaining tablespoon of butter. Cover and bake for 25 minutes.

Mexican Corn and Cheese Casserole 🐷

Preparation: 20 minutes Cooking: **30 minutes** Serves **4** Calories per serving: **350**

2 cups fresh sweet corn (cut from 4 medium-size ears) or 1 package (10 ounces) frozen whole-kernel corn, thawed

1 can (4 ounces) whole green chilies, rinsed, seeded, and chopped

3/4 cup shredded sharp Cheddar cheese (about 3 ounces)

1 cup sour cream or plain yogurt

1 egg, lightly beaten

1/2 teaspoon salt

2 tablespoons butter or margarine, melted

Serve this as a side dish with roast beef, lamb, pork, chicken, or baked ham, or as a main course for a light lunch with a lettuce and tomato salad.

1. Preheat the oven to 400°F. In a mixing bowl, combine the **corn, chilies, cheese, sour cream, egg, salt,** and **butter.**

2. Pour the mixture into a buttered 8"x 8"x 2" baking dish, and bake, uncovered, for 30 to 35 minutes, or until a knife inserted in the center of the casserole comes out clean.

Tip: This dish is also good served at room temperature or cold.

Eggplant with Cheese and Tomatoes 🐷

Preparation: 20 minutes Cooking: **15 minutes** Serves **4** Calories per serving: **250**

1 small eggplant (about 1/2 pound), peeled and cut into 1-inch slices

1 teaspoon salt

3/4 teaspoon black pepper

3 tablespoons vegetable oil

1 large yellow onion, peeled and chopped

1 clove garlic, peeled and minced

2 medium-size fresh tomatoes, peeled and chopped, or 1 can (8 ounces) stewed tomatoes

Pinch dried thyme

1/4 cup minced parsley

1/2 cup soft fresh bread crumbs (1 slice bread)

1 cup shredded Swiss, sharp Cheddar, or Monterey Jack cheese (about 4 ounces)

Here is a thrifty main course casserole that can be made ahead. Cook the recipe through Step 2, refrigerate overnight, and bake just before serving.

1. Preheat the broiler. Place the **eggplant** slices on a greased 8"x 8"x 2" baking pan. Sprinkle with 1/2 teaspoon of the **salt** and 1/2 teaspoon of the **pepper,** and brush with 1 tablespoon of the **oil.** Broil for 5 minutes on each side and remove from the broiler.

2. While the eggplant is broiling, heat the remaining 2 tablespoons of oil in a heavy 9-inch skillet over moderate heat. Add the **onion,** and cook, uncovered, until soft—about 5 minutes. Add the **garlic,** and cook for 1 minute longer, then add the **tomatoes** and cook, stirring, until the mixture thickens slightly—about 8 minutes. Stir in the **thyme, parsley,** and **bread crumbs,** and the remaining 1/2 teaspoon of salt and 1/4 teaspoon of pepper.

3. Reduce the oven heat to 350°F. Spoon the tomato mixture over the eggplant, top with the **cheese,** and bake, uncovered, until the cheese has melted—about 15 minutes.

Mushroom and Barley Casserole 🐷

Preparation: **15 minutes**   Cooking: **35 minutes**   Serves **4**   Calories per serving: **295**

While you prepare the main course, bake this tasty side dish. It is a thrifty substitute for wild rice.

5 tablespoons butter or margarine

1 large yellow onion, peeled and finely chopped

1/4 pound mushrooms, thinly sliced

3/4 cup medium pearl barley

1/2 teaspoon salt

1/4 teaspoon black pepper

2 cups chicken or beef broth

1. Preheat the oven to 350°F. Melt the **butter** in a heavy 9- or 10-inch skillet over moderate heat. Add the **onion**, and cook, uncovered, for 3 minutes. Add the **mushrooms** and **barley**, and cook, uncovered, for 4 minutes, stirring occasionally.

2. Add the **salt, pepper**, and **chicken broth**, and bring to a boil. Pour the mixture into an ungreased 1½-quart casserole, and bake, covered, for 35 minutes.

*Tips: **1.** You can eliminate one cooking utensil if you use a flameproof casserole or a skillet with an ovenproof handle. **2.** Try adding 1/4 cup of currants and 1/4 teaspoon of allspice before adding the broth.*

Spinach, Noodles, and Cheese in Casserole 🐷

Preparation: **15 minutes**   Cooking: **30 minutes**   Serves **4**   Calories per serving: **505**

4 ounces medium egg noodles

1 package (10 ounces) fresh spinach or 1 package (10 ounces) frozen chopped spinach

4 tablespoons (1/2 stick) butter or margarine

1 small yellow onion, peeled and chopped

2 eggs

1 cup sour cream

3/4 teaspoon salt

1/8 teaspoon black pepper

1 cup shredded extra sharp Cheddar cheese

Tip: This dish can be prepared ahead. Simply cook the noodles, spinach, and onions, mix the ingredients as directed, then cover and refrigerate. Before serving, mix again lightly, pour into the buttered dish, and bake.

1. Preheat the oven to 375°F. Cook the **noodles** according to package directions, drain thoroughly in a colander, and set aside.

2. Meanwhile, trim the fresh **spinach** of coarse stems and blemished leaves, and wash it. Place the spinach in a large saucepan with just the water that clings to the leaves, and cook, covered, for 5 minutes, or until the spinach is just limp. If you are using frozen spinach, cook according to package directions, drain well, and press out as much liquid as you can.

3. In a mixing bowl, combine the noodles and spinach. Melt the **butter** in an 8- or 9-inch skillet over moderate heat. Add the **onion**, and cook, uncovered, until soft—about 5 minutes. Stir the onion and butter into the noodle mixture.

4. Beat the **eggs** with the **sour cream, salt**, and **pepper**. Add to the noodle mixture along with the **cheese**. Mix well.

5. Pour into a buttered 1-quart casserole or 8"x 8"x 2" baking dish, and bake, uncovered, for 30 minutes.

Yellow Squash with Bacon 🐷

Preparation: **20 minutes**   Cooking: **20 minutes**   Serves **4**   Calories per serving: **220**

2 slices bacon, cut into 1-inch strips

3 medium-size yellow squash (about 1 pound), chopped

1 medium-size yellow onion, peeled and chopped

⅓ cup water

2 tablespoons butter or margarine, softened

½ teaspoon salt

2 teaspoons sugar

1 egg, lightly beaten

1 cup corn bread crumbs or soft fresh bread crumbs (2 slices bread)

1. Cook the **bacon** in a heavy 8-inch skillet over moderately high heat until crisp—about 5 minutes. Using a slotted spoon, remove the bacon to drain on paper toweling and set aside.

2. Preheat the oven to 350°F. Add the **squash** and **onion** to the drippings in the skillet, and cook, uncovered, for 2 minutes. Add the **water,** cover, and cook until the vegetables are tender—about 5 minutes.

3. Remove the skillet from the heat and mash the vegetables with a potato masher. Add the **butter, salt, sugar, egg,** and **bread crumbs,** and mix well. Pour into a buttered 1½-quart casserole. Crumble the reserved bacon, sprinkle it over the squash mixture, and bake, uncovered, for 20 minutes.

> *Tip: You can make this dish a day ahead and refrigerate it.*

Chicken and Broccoli Bake

Preparation: **20 minutes**   Cooking: **15 minutes**   Serves **4**   Calories per serving: **380**

Here is a good way to use leftover chicken—or turkey, if you prefer.

1 pound broccoli

3 tablespoons butter or margarine

2 tablespoons finely chopped yellow onion

3 tablespoons all-purpose flour

½ teaspoon salt

Pinch black pepper

⅛ teaspoon poultry seasoning (optional)

2 cups milk

1½ cups cubed cooked chicken

1 cup shredded Cheddar cheese (about 4 ounces)

1. Preheat the oven to 350°F. Trim the leaves and coarse stem ends from the **broccoli,** and cut the remaining stems and florets into bite-size pieces. Bring about 1 inch of lightly salted water to a boil in a 2-quart saucepan. Add the broccoli and boil, covered, for 5 minutes, or until crisp-tender. Drain thoroughly in a colander, then transfer to an ungreased 1-quart casserole or 8"x 8"x 2" baking dish.

2. Meanwhile, melt the **butter** in a 1-quart saucepan over moderate heat. Add the **onion,** and cook, uncovered, until soft—about 5 minutes.

3. Blend in the **flour, salt,** and **pepper,** and the **poultry seasoning** if used, to form a smooth paste. Gradually add the **milk,** and cook over moderate heat, stirring, until thickened—about 5 minutes.

4. Add the **chicken,** then pour the mixture over the broccoli. Sprinkle the **cheese** over the top and bake, uncovered, for 15 minutes. Serve with Cherry Tomatoes in Brown-Butter Sauce, page 80.

Hot Chicken Salad ⊘

Preparation: 15 minutes   **Cooking: 15 minutes**   **Serves 4**   **Calories per serving: 770**

2 cups cubed cooked chicken

¹/₂ cup chopped almonds

1 cup mayonnaise

2 tablespoons lemon juice

2 large stalks celery, thinly sliced

1 tablespoon minced yellow onion

1 teaspoon salt

¹/₄ teaspoon black pepper

1 cup soft fresh bread crumbs (2 slices bread)

1 tablespoon butter or margarine, melted

¹/₂ cup shredded Swiss cheese (about 2 ounces)

1. Preheat the oven to 350°F. In a mixing bowl, combine the **chicken, almonds, mayonnaise, lemon juice, celery, onion, salt,** and **pepper.** Place the mixture in an ungreased 1-quart casserole or 8"x 8"x 2" baking dish.

2. Combine the **bread crumbs** with the melted **butter.** Top the casserole with the buttered bread crumbs, and sprinkle with the **cheese.** Bake, uncovered, for 15 minutes.

Tips: 1. As a variation, use cooked turkey instead of the chicken and add 2 tablespoons of snipped fresh dill. 2. You can make this dish a day ahead and refrigerate it, or reheat any leftovers.

Chicken Risotto 🐷 ⊘

Preparation: 12 minutes   **Cooking: 15 minutes**   **Serves 4**   **Calories per serving: 495**

4 tablespoons (¹/₂ stick) butter or margarine

1 medium-size yellow onion, peeled and chopped

1 clove garlic, peeled and minced

1 large stalk celery, chopped

1 cup uncooked rice

1 cup cubed cooked chicken

2 cups chicken broth

¹/₂ teaspoon salt

¹/₄ teaspoon black pepper

¹/₈ teaspoon dried rosemary, crumbled

1 cup frozen baby peas, thawed

³/₄ cup grated Parmesan cheese (about 3 ounces)

1. Preheat the oven to 400°F. Melt the **butter** over moderately high heat in a 2-quart saucepan with an ovenproof handle. Add the **onion, garlic,** and **celery,** and cook, uncovered, for 3 minutes.

2. Add the **rice** and **chicken,** and cook for another 2 minutes. Add the **chicken broth, salt, pepper,** and **rosemary,** and bring to a boil. Cover and set in the oven.

3. Bake for 10 minutes, then add the **peas** and **cheese,** cover again, and bake 5 minutes longer. When done, the rice should be firm, not soft.

Tips: 1. If you do not have a covered saucepan with an ovenproof handle, use a regular 9-inch skillet until you are ready to bake the dish. Then transfer to a 1¹/₂-quart casserole and cover. 2. You can make this dish a day ahead and refrigerate it, or reheat any leftovers.

Curried Chicken and Rice ⊙

Preparation: 7 minutes   Cooking: 15 minutes   Serves 4   Calories per serving: 480

Here is a fast way to give leftover chicken and rice a freshly made taste.

1½ cups half-and-half

4 tablespoons (½ stick) butter or margarine

1 tablespoon cornstarch

6 tablespoons dry sherry

1 teaspoon curry powder

¾ teaspoon salt

⅛ teaspoon cayenne pepper (optional)

2 cups cubed cooked chicken

1½ cups cooked rice

1. Preheat the oven to 350°F. Put the **half-and-half** and **butter** into a 1-quart saucepan over moderate heat and bring to a boil.

2. In a small bowl, combine the **cornstarch** and **sherry,** and slowly add to the saucepan, stirring vigorously to prevent lumping. Add the **curry powder** and **salt,** and the **cayenne pepper** if used, and cook until the sauce has boiled and thickened—about 3 minutes. Add the **chicken,** stir, and remove from the heat.

3. Cover the bottom of a buttered 8″x 8″x 2″ baking dish with the **rice,** and pour in the chicken mixture. Bake, uncovered, for 15 minutes.

Tip: If you like foods spicy, increase the cayenne pepper to ¼ teaspoon and add 3 chopped green onions.

Brazilian Beef Bake 🐷

Preparation: 15 minutes   Cooking: 20 minutes   Serves 4   Calories per serving: 320

2 tablespoons olive or vegetable oil

1 medium-size yellow onion, peeled and finely chopped

1 clove garlic, peeled and crushed

1 pound lean ground beef

½ teaspoon ground coriander

¼ teaspoon ground ginger

2 medium-size tomatoes, peeled and chopped, or ½ cup tomato sauce (half an 8-ounce can)

1 teaspoon light brown sugar

2 tablespoons minced parsley

⅓ cup chopped pimiento-stuffed olives

½ teaspoon salt

⅛ teaspoon black pepper

1. Preheat the oven to 375°F. Heat the **oil** in a heavy 12-inch skillet over moderate heat. Add the **onion** and **garlic,** and cook, uncovered, for 5 minutes, or until the onion is soft. Push to one side, add the **beef,** and cook, uncovered, stirring occasionally, until browned—about 5 minutes.

2. Add the **coriander, ginger, tomatoes, brown sugar, parsley, olives, salt,** and **pepper,** and mix well. Transfer to an ungreased 1-quart casserole, and bake, uncovered, for 20 minutes. Serve with rice and a green salad.

Tips: 1. You can also bake the mixture in an unbaked 9-inch pie crust. 2. This dish can be made 1 or 2 days ahead and refrigerated, or leftovers can be reheated.

Indonesian Beef 🐷

Preparation: **15 minutes**   Cooking: **20 minutes**   Serves **4**   Calories per serving: **300**

2 tablespoons vegetable oil

1 medium-size yellow onion, peeled and chopped

1 clove garlic, peeled and minced

1 teaspoon minced fresh ginger root or ¼ teaspoon ground ginger

1 pound lean ground beef

¼ teaspoon crushed dried red pepper

1 medium-size sweet green or red pepper, cored, seeded, and cut into ¼-inch strips

3 green onions, trimmed and cut into 1-inch pieces

1 teaspoon salt

Pinch paprika

1. Preheat the oven to 400°F. Heat the **oil** in a heavy 9- or 10-inch skillet over moderate heat. Add the **yellow onion, garlic,** and **ginger,** and cook, uncovered, until the onion is golden—about 6 minutes.

2. Add the **beef** and **dried red pepper,** and cook, uncovered, stirring occasionally, until the beef has browned—about 5 minutes. Add the **green pepper, green onions, salt,** and **paprika,** stir, and transfer the mixture to an ungreased 8"x 8"x 2" baking dish. Cover with aluminum foil and bake for 20 minutes. Before serving, tilt the dish and skim off the fat. Serve with steamed rice and Asparagus Chinese Style, page 58.

> **Tips: 1.** *You can substitute ground lamb or pork for the beef.* **2.** *Add ½ cup sliced mushrooms to the beef while it is browning.*

Copenhagen Cabbage Casserole 🐷

Preparation: **10 minutes**   Cooking: **35 minutes**   Serves **4**   Calories per serving: **315**

1 pound lean ground beef

¼ cup finely chopped yellow onion

1 can (8 ounces) tomato sauce

½ cup beef broth

⅛ teaspoon ground cinnamon

⅛ teaspoon ground cloves

1 teaspoon salt

½ small head cabbage, shredded (about 3 cups)

1. Preheat the oven to 350°F. Place the **beef** and **onion** in a heavy 9- or 10-inch skillet over moderate heat. Cook, uncovered, stirring occasionally, until the beef has browned—about 5 minutes. Pour off and discard the drippings from the skillet. Add the **tomato sauce, beef broth, cinnamon, cloves,** and **salt** to the beef, and stir to blend.

2. Place half the **cabbage** in an ungreased 2-quart casserole, and top with half the beef mixture. Repeat the layers. Cover and bake for 35 minutes. Serve with buttered noodles and Green Beans with Garlic and Cheese, page 59.

> **Tips: 1.** *You can make this dish a day ahead and refrigerate it or reheat leftovers.* **2.** *As a variation, use ground pork instead of the beef.*

Curried Beef Casserole

Preparation: **12 minutes**   Cooking: **20 minutes**   Serves **4**   Calories per serving: **590**

4 tablespoons (½ stick) butter or margarine

1 large yellow onion, peeled and finely chopped

2 slices white bread

¾ cup milk

1 pound lean ground beef

⅓ cup raisins

½ cup chopped almonds

2 tablespoons apricot preserves

3 tablespoons lemon juice

1 tablespoon curry powder

⅛ teaspoon dried oregano, crumbled

¼ teaspoon salt

⅛ teaspoon black pepper

1 egg

Here's a versatile casserole for the extra busy cook. You can serve it hot from the oven or refrigerate it and serve it cold the next day.

1. Preheat the oven to 325°F. Melt the **butter** in a heavy 9- or 10-inch skillet over moderate heat. Add the **onion,** and cook, uncovered, for 5 minutes, or until soft. Meanwhile, soak the **bread** in ¼ cup of the **milk.**

2. When the onion is done, add the bread, **beef, raisins, almonds, preserves, lemon juice, curry powder, oregano, salt,** and **pepper.** Cook for 5 minutes, stirring constantly. Transfer the mixture to a buttered 8″ x 8″ x 2″ baking dish.

3. In a small bowl, beat the remaining ½ cup of milk with the **egg,** and pour over the beef mixture in the baking dish. Bake, uncovered, for 20 minutes. Spoon the fat from the top of the dish and serve.

> ***Tip:*** *You can substitute ground pork or lamb for the beef.*

Beef and Noodles with Two Cheeses

Preparation: **15 minutes**   Cooking: **30 minutes**   Serves **6**   Calories per serving: **415**

Make this casserole at your leisure, and reheat and serve it when you're ready.

6 ounces broad egg noodles

1 pound lean ground beef

1 small yellow onion, peeled and chopped

1 teaspoon salt

¼ teaspoon black pepper

1 can (8 ounces) tomato sauce

¾ cup large-curd cottage cheese

6 ounces cream cheese (¾ of an 8-ounce package)

3 tablespoons sour cream

⅓ cup chopped sweet green pepper

⅓ cup chopped green onions

1. Preheat the oven to 350°F. Cook the **noodles** according to package directions, drain thoroughly in a colander, and set aside.

2. Meanwhile, heat a heavy 9- or 10-inch skillet over moderate heat. Add the **beef** and **yellow onion,** and cook, uncovered, stirring occasionally, until the beef has browned—about 5 minutes. Add the **salt, black pepper,** and **tomato sauce,** stir, and simmer the mixture slowly while preparing the remaining ingredients.

3. In a mixing bowl, combine the **cottage cheese, cream cheese, sour cream, green pepper,** and **green onions.**

4. Place half the noodles in a buttered 1½-quart casserole or 9″ x 9″ x 2″ baking dish. Cover with the cheese mixture, then with the remaining noodles. Pour the meat mixture over the top. Bake, uncovered, for 30 minutes. Serve with Sautéed Summer Squash, page 77.

Baked Cheeseburger Casserole

Preparation: **15 minutes**   Cooking: **25 minutes**   Serves **4**   Calories per serving: **535**

2 tablespoons butter

6 slices white bread, toasted

1 pound lean ground beef

1 small yellow onion, peeled and chopped

1/4 cup chopped celery

1 tablespoon prepared yellow mustard

1 teaspoon salt

1 cup shredded sharp Cheddar cheese (about 4 ounces)

1 egg

3/4 cup milk

1/8 teaspoon dry mustard

1/4 teaspoon paprika

1. Preheat the oven to 350°F. Spread the **butter** on both sides of the **bread,** cut the slices in half diagonally, and set aside.

2. Heat a heavy 9- or 10-inch skillet over moderate heat. Add the **beef, onion, celery, prepared mustard,** and 1/2 teaspoon of the **salt,** and cook, uncovered, stirring occasionally, until the beef has browned—about 5 minutes.

3. In a buttered 9"x 9"x 2" baking dish, place alternate layers of toast, beef mixture, and **cheese.**

4. In a small bowl, beat the **egg,** then stir in the **milk, dry mustard,** and the remaining salt. Pour the mixture over the cheese, sprinkle with the **paprika,** and bake, uncovered, for 25 minutes.

Tip: This dish can be made ahead and refrigerated overnight or frozen.

South American Pork and Corn Pie

Preparation: **20 minutes**   Cooking: **20 minutes**   Serves **4**   Calories per serving: **575**

1/4 cup vegetable oil

1 medium-size yellow onion, peeled and chopped

1 cup cubed cooked pork

1/3 cup plus 1 tablespoon all-purpose flour

1 tablespoon chili powder

1 cup chicken broth

1 package (10 ounces) frozen whole-kernel corn, thawed

1/4 cup raisins

1/4 cup chopped black olives

1/2 teaspoon salt

1 tablespoon lemon juice

1 cup milk

2/3 cup cornmeal

1 egg, lightly beaten

2 teaspoons baking powder

1/2 teaspoon baking soda

1. Heat 3 tablespoons of the **oil** in a 9-inch ovenproof skillet or 1-quart flameproof casserole over moderate heat. Add the **onion,** and cook, uncovered, for 5 minutes. Add the **pork,** and cook until lightly browned—about 2 minutes.

2. Blend in 1 tablespoon of the **flour,** the **chili powder,** and the **chicken broth.** Add the **corn, raisins, olives,** and 1/4 teaspoon of the **salt.** Stir until the mixture thickens—about 4 minutes.

3. Preheat the oven to 450°F. In a small bowl, stir the **lemon juice** into the **milk,** and let stand for a few minutes. In a mixing bowl, combine the **cornmeal** with the remaining flour and salt. In the order listed, gradually stir in the milk mixture, **egg, baking powder, baking soda,** and remaining oil.

4. Reheat the pork mixture. Stir the topping mixture and pour over the pork. Bake, uncovered, for 20 minutes, or until the topping is firm.

Tip: If you do not have an ovenproof skillet or flameproof casserole, use a regular skillet to make the pork mixture and transfer it to a casserole just before baking.

Golden Ham Casserole

Preparation: 15 minutes · Cooking: **20 minutes**   Serves **4**   Calories per serving: **430**

4 ounces broad egg noodles

1 tablespoon cider vinegar or lemon juice

1 cup milk

1 cup cubed cooked ham

2 eggs, lightly beaten

1/2 teaspoon salt

1/4 teaspoon black pepper

1 cup shredded Cheddar cheese (about 4 ounces)

1 tablespoon minced yellow onion

1/4 cup sliced celery

1/4 cup chopped sweet green pepper

1 cup cooked peas (optional)

1 cup soft fresh bread crumbs (2 slices bread)

1 tablespoon butter or margarine

You can use leftover ham for this casserole or a 1/2-pound slice of fully cooked ham.

1. Preheat the oven to 375°F. Cook the **noodles** according to package directions and drain thoroughly in a colander. Meanwhile, stir the **vinegar** into the **milk,** and let stand for a few minutes. The milk will sour.

2. In a mixing bowl, combine the milk, **ham, eggs, salt, black pepper, cheese,** and the noodles. Add the **onion, celery,** and **green pepper,** and the **peas** if used, and mix well. Pour the mixture into a buttered 1½-quart casserole.

3. Sprinkle the **bread crumbs** over the casserole, and dot with the **butter.** Bake, uncovered, for 20 minutes. Serve with French Cream of Tomato Soup, page 33, and a green salad.

Ham and Egg Casserole 🐷

Preparation: 17 minutes   Cooking: **20 minutes**   Serves **4**   Calories per serving: **295**

If you don't have hard-cooked eggs on hand, allow 15 minutes for cooking them. Start cooking them about 5 minutes before you turn on the oven.

2 tablespoons butter or margarine

1 medium-size yellow onion, peeled and thinly sliced

2 tablespoons all-purpose flour

1 cup milk

1 tablespoon prepared spicy brown mustard

1/4 teaspoon black pepper

2 cups cubed cooked ham

2 hard-cooked eggs, sliced

1. Preheat the oven to 350°F. Melt the **butter** in a 1-quart saucepan over moderate heat. Add the **onion,** and cook, uncovered, for 5 minutes, or until soft.

2. Reduce the heat to low. Blend in the **flour,** slowly add the **milk,** and cook, stirring constantly, until the mixture is thickened and smooth—about 3 minutes. Remove the pan from the heat, and stir in the **mustard** and **pepper.**

3. Pour half the sauce into an ungreased 1-quart casserole. Add a layer of the **ham,** then a layer of half the sliced **eggs.** Repeat the layers of ham and eggs, then pour the remaining sauce over all. Bake, uncovered, for 20 minutes, or until the sauce is bubbly.

Sausage Casserole

Preparation: **15 minutes**   Cooking: **45 minutes**   Serves **4**   Calories per serving: **530**

1 pound sweet Italian sausage, with the casing removed

2 medium-size all-purpose potatoes, peeled and thinly sliced

1 medium-size yellow onion, peeled and thinly sliced

1 large carrot, peeled and thinly sliced

1 teaspoon dried basil, crumbled

3 medium-size fresh tomatoes, peeled and chopped, or 1 can (1 pound) tomatoes, chopped, with their juice

1 teaspoon salt

1/8 teaspoon black pepper

1. Preheat the oven to 400°F. Place the **sausage** in a heavy 9- or 10-inch skillet over moderate heat, and cook, uncovered, stirring frequently, until browned—about 5 minutes. Pour off and discard the drippings from the skillet.

2. Layer an ungreased 2-quart casserole with the sausage, **potatoes, onion,** and **carrot.** Repeat the layers. Add the **basil, tomatoes, salt,** and **pepper,** and bake, covered, for 45 minutes.

Tips: **1.** *You can use link sausage instead of the Italian sausage, but omit the basil if you do.* **2.** *You can make this dish a day ahead and refrigerate it or reheat the leftovers.*

Corn and Sausage Casserole

Preparation: **12 minutes**   Cooking: **20 minutes**   Serves **4**   Calories per serving: **670**

1 pound bulk sausage or mild link sausages, with the casing removed

2 cups fresh sweet corn (cut from 4 medium-size ears) or 1 package (10 ounces) frozen whole-kernel corn, thawed

2 eggs, lightly beaten

1/4 teaspoon salt

1/8 teaspoon black pepper

1 1/2 cups soft fresh bread crumbs (3 slices bread)

1. Preheat the oven to 400°F. Place the **sausage** in a heavy 9- or 10-inch skillet over moderate heat, and cook, uncovered, stirring frequently, until browned—about 5 minutes.

2. Meanwhile, in a small bowl, combine the **corn, eggs, salt,** and **pepper,** and place half the mixture in an ungreased 1-quart casserole.

3. Using a slotted spoon, transfer the sausage from the skillet to the casserole, and arrange evenly on the corn mixture. Top with the remaining mixture.

4. Add the **bread crumbs** to the skillet, stir to coat them with the drippings, and spread over the top of the casserole. Bake, uncovered, for 20 minutes, or until the mixture has set and browned. Serve with a lettuce and tomato salad.

Lentil and Sausage Stew 🐷

Preparation: **25 minutes**   Cooking: **25 minutes**   Serves **4**   Calories per serving: **765**

Ingredients

1 pound dried lentils

1 teaspoon salt

2 tablespoons vegetable oil

1 medium-size yellow onion, peeled and chopped

1 clove garlic, peeled and minced

3 medium-size fresh tomatoes, peeled and chopped, or 1 can (1 pound) tomatoes, chopped, with their juice

¾ pound kielbasa (with the casing removed), knockwurst, smoked sausage, or frankfurters, cut into 1-inch pieces

1 bay leaf

¼ teaspoon dried thyme, crumbled

¼ teaspoon dried marjoram, crumbled

¼ teaspoon black pepper

This is a very thrifty and satisfying main dish. It tastes even better when reheated.

1. Preheat the oven to 400°F. Rinse and sort the **lentils,** and put them into a 2-quart saucepan. Cover the lentils with water and add the **salt.** Bring to a boil, cover, and simmer for 20 minutes, or until the lentils are tender. Do not drain.

2. Meanwhile, heat the **oil** in a heavy 10-inch skillet over moderate heat. Add the **onion** and **garlic,** and cook, uncovered, until the onion is soft—about 5 minutes. Stir in the **tomatoes.**

3. Pour the lentils and their cooking liquid into a 3-quart ungreased casserole. Stir in the **kielbasa,** the tomato mixture, and the **bay leaf, thyme, marjoram,** and **pepper.** Cover and bake for 20 minutes. Uncover and continue baking for 5 more minutes.

Tip: Instead of the kielbasa or other smoked sausage, use 1 pound of Italian sausage, with the casing removed, and brown along with the onion and garlic.

New England Fish Casserole ⊘

Preparation: **20 minutes**   Cooking: **8 minutes**   Serves **4**   Calories per serving: **320**

4 slices bacon, cut into 1-inch strips

3 medium-size all-purpose potatoes, peeled and cut into ¼-inch dice

1 medium-size sweet green pepper, cored, seeded, and cut into ¼-inch dice

1 pound cod or scrod fillets, cut into 1-inch pieces

½ cup water

1 teaspoon salt

¼ teaspoon black pepper

You will need only one cooking dish if you use a flameproof casserole.

1. Preheat the oven to 450°F. Cook the **bacon** in a 1-quart saucepan over moderate heat for 3 minutes. Add the **potatoes** and **green pepper,** and cook, uncovered, for 5 minutes, stirring often.

2. Transfer the mixture to an ungreased 1½-quart casserole, and stir in the **fish fillets, water, salt,** and **black pepper.** Bake, covered, for 8 to 10 minutes, depending on the thickness of the fish. When the fish flakes easily when tested with a fork, it is done.

Chilean Fish Casserole ⊙

Preparation: **20 minutes**   Cooking: **10 minutes**   Serves **4**   Calories per serving: **435**

1 pound mackerel fillets, with the skin

⅓ cup all-purpose flour

4 tablespoons olive or vegetable oil

1 large yellow onion, peeled and thinly sliced

2 medium-size carrots, peeled and thinly sliced

¼ cup lime or lemon juice

1 bay leaf, crumbled

¾ teaspoon salt

¼ teaspoon black pepper

1. Slice the **mackerel fillets** crosswise into 1-inch strips. Put the **flour** on a plate or a sheet of wax paper, and coat the strips completely. Shake off any excess flour.

2. Heat 2 tablespoons of the **oil** in a 1½-quart flameproof casserole over moderately high heat. Cook the fish strips for 1 minute on each side. Using a slotted spoon, remove the fish to a platter and set aside.

3. Preheat the oven to 450°F. Add the remaining 2 tablespoons of oil and the **onion** and **carrots** to the casserole, and cook, stirring, for 2 minutes. Reduce the heat to moderate, cover, and cook for 5 minutes.

4. Remove the casserole from the heat, and add the fish, **lime juice, bay leaf, salt,** and **pepper.** Stir. Bake, covered, for about 10 minutes. When the fish flakes easily when tested with a fork, it is done. Serve hot with steamed rice.

Greek Fish and Potato Bake

Preparation: **15 minutes**   Cooking: **30 minutes**   Serves **4**   Calories per serving: **360**

Grated rind of 1 lemon

1 clove garlic, peeled and minced

1 teaspoon dried oregano, crumbled

1 teaspoon salt

¼ teaspoon black pepper

4 medium-size potatoes (about 1 pound), peeled and very thinly sliced

5 tablespoons olive or vegetable oil

1 pound red snapper, sea trout (weakfish), sea bass, bluefish, or tilefish fillets, with the skin

1 tablespoon chopped parsley

1. Preheat the oven to 450°F. In a small bowl, combine the **lemon rind, garlic, oregano, salt,** and **pepper.**

2. Place half the mixture in a greased 13"x 9"x 2" baking dish. Add the **potatoes** and 3 tablespoons of the **oil,** and mix to coat the potatoes well. Spread the potatoes flat in the dish. Bake, uncovered, for 25 minutes, stirring once. The potatoes should be almost tender.

3. Place the **fish fillets** skin side down over the potatoes. Sprinkle with the remaining half of the lemon rind mixture and the remaining 2 tablespoons of oil. Bake, uncovered, basting with the oil in the dish, for 5 to 7 minutes, depending on the thickness of the fish. When the fish flakes easily when tested with a fork, it is done. Sprinkle with the **parsley** and serve.

Salmon and Mushroom Casserole

Preparation: **15 minutes**   Cooking: **20 minutes**   Serves **4**   Calories per serving: **430**

4 ounces broad egg noodles

5 tablespoons butter or margarine

1/4 cup chopped yellow onion

1/4 pound mushrooms, thinly sliced

2 tablespoons all-purpose flour

1 can (7 3/4 ounces) salmon

1 cup milk

2 tablespoons water or chicken broth

1/4 teaspoon salt

1/8 teaspoon black pepper

1/3 cup fine dry bread crumbs

Tip: You can substitute tuna for the salmon.

1. Preheat the oven to 425°F. Cook the **noodles** according to package directions, drain thoroughly in a colander, and set aside.

2. Meanwhile, melt 4 tablespoons of the **butter** in a heavy 9- or 10-inch skillet over moderate heat. Add the **onion** and **mushrooms,** and cook, uncovered, until the onion is soft—about 5 minutes. Blend in the **flour** and set aside.

3. Drain the **salmon,** reserving the liquor. Remove any skin and bone, mash, and set aside. Add the reserved salmon liquor and the **milk** and **water** to the onion-mushroom mixture, and cook, stirring constantly, until thickened—about 3 minutes. Season with the **salt** and **pepper.**

4. In a buttered 1 1/2-quart casserole, combine the sauce, salmon, and noodles. Top with the **bread crumbs,** and dot with the remaining tablespoon of butter. Bake, uncovered, for 20 minutes. Serve with a green salad.

Upside-Down Tuna Pie with Corn Bread Crust

Preparation: **20 minutes**   Cooking: **20 minutes**   Serves **4**   Calories per serving: **585**

1 lemon, very thinly sliced

2 tablespoons butter or margarine

1/4 cup plus 2 tablespoons all-purpose flour

2 cups milk

3/4 teaspoon salt

1/8 teaspoon black pepper

2 cans (6 1/2 or 7 ounces each) tuna, drained and flaked

1/4 cup finely chopped yellow onion

1/2 cup soft fresh bread crumbs (1 slice bread)

3/4 cup cornmeal

1 1/2 teaspoons baking powder

1 egg

1/4 cup vegetable oil

1. Preheat the oven to 425°F. Line an ungreased 8"x 8"x 2" baking dish or deep 8-inch pie plate with the **lemon** slices. Set aside.

2. Melt the **butter** in a 2-quart saucepan over moderate heat. Stir in 2 tablespoons of the **flour,** then add 1 1/2 cups of the **milk,** 1/4 teaspoon of the **salt,** and the **pepper.** Cook, stirring constantly, until the mixture thickens—about 3 minutes. Fold in the **tuna, onion,** and **bread crumbs.** Pour over the lemon slices.

3. Into a mixing bowl, sift together the **cornmeal,** the remaining flour and salt, and the **baking powder.** Beat the **egg,** the remaining milk, and the **oil** with a rotary beater, and blend thoroughly into the dry ingredients.

4. Spoon over the tuna mixture. Bake, uncovered, for 20 minutes. Remove from the oven and let cool for 10 minutes. Loosen the edges with a knife, cover with a 12-inch plate, and turn over onto the plate.

Clam and Corn Soufflé ⊘

Preparation: **10 minutes** Cooking: **20 minutes** Serves **4** Calories per serving: **355**

1 cup crumbled saltines

½ cup milk

2 eggs, lightly beaten

1 can (6½ ounces) minced clams, undrained

2 cups fresh sweet corn (cut from 4 medium-size ears) or 1 package (10 ounces) frozen whole-kernel corn, thawed

2 tablespoons minced parsley

2 tablespoons butter or margarine, melted

2 tablespoons finely chopped yellow onion

½ teaspoon Worcestershire sauce

½ cup shredded Cheddar or grated Parmesan cheese

1. Preheat the oven to 425°F. In a mixing bowl, combine the **saltines, milk, eggs, clams, corn, parsley, butter, onion,** and **Worcestershire sauce.**

2. Transfer the mixture to an ungreased 1-quart casserole, and top with the **cheese.** Bake, uncovered, for 20 minutes. Serve with Coleslaw, page 45, or Shredded Carrots with Herbs and Lemon, page 46.

> *Tip: Substitute ¾ cup shucked, undrained oysters for the clams.*

Oyster Noodle Casserole ⊘

Preparation: **15 minutes** Cooking: **15 minutes** Serves **4** Calories per serving: **440**

4 ounces broad egg noodles

1 pint shucked oysters

6 tablespoons (¾ stick) butter or margarine

3 tablespoons finely chopped yellow onion

2 tablespoons finely chopped sweet green pepper

2 tablespoons all-purpose flour

1 cup milk

1 teaspoon salt

⅛ teaspoon black pepper

Pinch cayenne pepper

½ cup fine dry bread crumbs

> *Tip: You can make this dish a day ahead.*

1. Preheat the oven to 425°F. Cook the **noodles** according to package directions, drain thoroughly in a colander, and set aside.

2. Meanwhile, drain the **oysters,** reserving the liquor, and set both aside. Melt 3 tablespoons of the **butter** in a 1-quart saucepan over moderate heat. Add the **onion** and **green pepper,** and cook, uncovered, for 5 minutes, or until the onion is soft.

3. Blend in the **flour** with a wire whisk, then add the **milk,** and stir vigorously until the mixture is thickened and smooth—about 3 minutes. Add the oyster liquor, **salt, black pepper,** and **cayenne pepper.**

4. Place half the noodles in a buttered 1½-quart casserole, cover with the oysters, then add the remaining noodles. Pour the sauce over all, top with the **bread crumbs,** dot with the remaining 3 tablespoons of butter, and bake, uncovered, for 15 minutes, or until brown and bubbly.

Sunday Eggs and Bacon

Preparation: 10 minutes   **Cooking: 25 minutes**   **Serves 4**   **Calories per serving: 505**

Serve this for a hearty Sunday brunch or a light supper.

½ pound bacon, cut into 1-inch strips

4 tablespoons (½ stick) butter or margarine

2 cups cubed firm-textured bread

1 cup shredded extra sharp Cheddar cheese (about 4 ounces)

4 eggs

1 cup milk

4 teaspoons dry mustard

¼ teaspoon salt

1. Preheat the oven to 425°F. Cook the **bacon** in a heavy 12-inch skillet over moderately high heat until crisp—about 5 minutes. Drain on paper toweling and set aside.

2. Melt the **butter** in the oven in a 1-quart casserole. Add the **bread** cubes to the casserole, sprinkle with the **cheese,** and toss well.

3. In a small bowl, beat the **eggs** with the **milk, mustard,** and **salt.** Pour the egg mixture over the cheese and bread, and sprinkle with the bacon. Bake, uncovered, for 25 minutes. Let stand for 5 minutes before serving.

Noodles with Sour Cream and Cottage Cheese

Preparation: 10 minutes   **Cooking: 30 minutes**   **Serves 4**   **Calories per serving: 320**

4 ounces medium egg noodles

1 cup cream-style cottage cheese

1 cup sour cream

½ teaspoon salt

⅛ teaspoon black pepper

¼ cup chopped fresh or freeze-dried chives

1 tablespoon butter or margarine

You can prepare this dish in the morning, cover and refrigerate it, and bake it for the evening meal.

1. Preheat the oven to 375°F. Cook the **noodles** according to package directions and drain thoroughly in a colander.

2. In a buttered 1-quart casserole or 8"x 8"x 2" baking dish, combine the noodles with the **cottage cheese, sour cream, salt, pepper,** and **chives.** Dot with the **butter,** and bake, uncovered, for 30 minutes, or until the top starts to brown. Serve with a mixed green salad tossed with Oil and Vinegar Dressing for Green Salads, page 51.

Tips: 1. *For a savory variation, add ¼ teaspoon each dried basil and thyme, crumbled, and 1 tablespoon chopped parsley.* **2.** *For a sweet variation, omit the pepper and chives, and add 1 teaspoon ground cinnamon, 1 grated apple, ¼ cup raisins, and 2 lightly beaten eggs.*

EGGS AND CHEESE

Why not try one of these egg and cheese dishes in place of meat? They are inexpensive and suitable as main courses for dinner or supper. Some, such as Mexican Eggs and Crustless Swiss Cheese and Onion Quiche, are good for brunch, too. Because eggs and cheese are staples found in most refrigerators, many of the recipes make excellent pickup meals.

Mexican Eggs

Preparation: **15 minutes**   Cooking: **10 minutes**   Serves **4**   Calories per serving: **410**

If you like, fry the tortillas lightly on both sides in a bit of oil and keep them warm while the eggs are cooking.

1/4 **cup vegetable oil**

1 medium-size yellow onion, peeled and finely chopped

1 medium-size sweet green pepper, cored, seeded, and finely chopped

3 medium-size fresh tomatoes, peeled and chopped, or 1 can (1 pound) tomatoes, drained and chopped

1 whole canned jalapeño pepper, rinsed, seeded, and chopped, or 1/4 **teaspoon crushed dried red pepper**

2 cloves garlic, peeled and minced

1/2 **teaspoon salt**

1/2 **teaspoon ground cumin**

2 teaspoons chili powder

1/4 **teaspoon dried oregano, crumbled**

4 corn tortillas

4 eggs

1 cup shredded Monterey Jack cheese (about 4 ounces)

1. Preheat the broiler. Heat 2 tablespoons of the **oil** in a heavy 2-quart saucepan over moderate heat. Add the **onion** and **green pepper,** and cook, uncovered, for 5 minutes, or until the onion is soft.

2. Raise the heat to moderately high. Add the **tomatoes, jalapeño pepper, garlic,** and **salt,** and cook, uncovered, for 5 minutes, or until slightly thickened. Stir in the **cumin, chili powder,** and **oregano,** and remove the sauce from the heat.

3. While the sauce is cooking, arrange the **tortillas** on an ungreased baking sheet.

4. About 2 minutes before the sauce is done, heat the remaining 2 tablespoons of oil in a heavy 12-inch skillet over moderate heat. Break the **eggs** into the skillet, spacing them so that they do not overlap. Lower the heat slightly, and cook, uncovered, for 1 minute, or just until the whites are set. Using a pancake turner, carefully remove the eggs from the skillet, and place an egg on each tortilla.

5. Pour the sauce over the eggs, sprinkle with the **cheese,** and place under the broiler for 1 minute, or until the cheese begins to melt. Serve with a green salad or a salad of sliced oranges and avocados.

Tips: 1. If you want to get a head start on this dish, make the sauce in advance, then reheat it while the eggs are cooking. 2. Several brands of tortillas are available frozen or canned in most supermarkets.

Potato Eggs with Lemon 🐷

Preparation: **25 minutes**   Cooking: **20 minutes**   Serves **4**   Calories per serving: **210**

In this elegant but hearty dish, the eggs are separated, the whites are whipped and spread over a bed of mashed potatoes, and the yolks are cooked in pockets made in the whipped whites.

3 large all-purpose potatoes (about 1½ pounds), peeled and cut into ¼-inch slices

¼ cup milk

2 tablespoons butter or margarine, softened

¾ teaspoon salt

¼ teaspoon black pepper

1 tablespoon snipped fresh dill or ½ teaspoon dried dillweed

2 tablespoons grated yellow onion

2 tablespoons minced parsley

4 eggs

1 tablespoon grated lemon rind

1. Preheat the oven to 350°F. Place the **potatoes** in a 3-quart saucepan, add water to cover, set the lid on the pan askew, and boil for 15 minutes, or until tender.

2. Drain and mash the potatoes, adding the **milk** to moisten them. Stir in the **butter,** and season with ½ teaspoon of the **salt** and the **pepper.**

3. Mix the **dill, onion,** and **parsley** into the potatoes, transfer the mixture to a buttered shallow 1-quart casserole, and set aside.

4. Separate the **eggs.** Beat the whites until stiff, beat in the remaining ¼ teaspoon of salt, then gradually beat in the **lemon rind.**

5. Spread the beaten egg whites lightly over the potatoes, shaping them into peaks as you would a meringue. With half an eggshell, make 4 depressions in the egg whites, then slide an egg yolk into each depression. Bake, uncovered, for 20 minutes, or until the eggs are set.

> *Tip: You can make the mashed potatoes ahead (Steps 1 and 2) or use 3 cups of leftover mashed potatoes.*

Zesty Baked Eggs 🍳

Preparation: **10 minutes**   Cooking: **17 minutes**   Serves **4**   Calories per serving: **425**

⅓ cup mayonnaise

¼ teaspoon salt

⅛ teaspoon black pepper

¼ teaspoon paprika

¼ teaspoon Worcestershire sauce

1 tablespoon chopped fresh or freeze-dried chives (optional)

½ cup milk

1 cup shredded sharp Cheddar cheese (about 4 ounces)

8 eggs

1. Preheat the oven to 350°F. In a 1-quart saucepan, combine the **mayonnaise, salt, pepper, paprika,** and **Worcestershire sauce,** and the **chives** if used.

2. Gradually add the **milk,** stirring constantly, and continue to stir until smooth. Add the **cheese,** and cook over low heat, stirring, until the cheese is melted—about 5 minutes.

3. Butter 4 individual 6-ounce baking dishes and pour 2 tablespoons of sauce into each one. Break 2 **eggs** into each dish and top with the rest of the sauce. Place the baking dishes in a pan filled with about ½ inch of hot water and bake, uncovered, for 17 to 20 minutes, or until the eggs are of the desired consistency.

> *Tip: This recipe can be halved; use a scant 3 tablespoons of mayonnaise.*

Eggs with Chicken Livers 🐷 ⊙

Preparation: 7 minutes   Cooking: 13 minutes   Serves 4   Calories per serving: **355**

Speed up this dish by preparing the onion and green peppers while the chicken livers are cooking. Then, while the onion and peppers cook, peel and chop the tomatoes, and chop the parsley.

4 tablespoons (½ stick) butter or margarine

1 pound chicken livers, drained

½ teaspoon salt

¼ teaspoon black pepper

1 medium-size yellow onion, peeled and thinly sliced

2 medium-size sweet green peppers, cored, seeded, and cut into strips

2 medium-size tomatoes, peeled and chopped

1 tablespoon chopped parsley

4 eggs

1. Melt 2 tablespoons of the **butter** in a heavy 8- or 9-inch skillet over moderately high heat until bubbly. Add the **livers, salt,** and **black pepper,** and cook, stirring, until the livers are browned on the outside but still pink inside—about 5 minutes. Remove to a platter and set aside.

2. Reduce the heat to moderately low, and melt the remaining 2 tablespoons of butter in the skillet. Add the **onion** and **green peppers,** and cook, uncovered, stirring occasionally, for 5 minutes, or until the vegetables are limp.

3. Add the **tomatoes** and 2 teaspoons of the **parsley,** and simmer, uncovered, for 5 minutes. Return the livers to the pan for 1 minute to heat through.

4. Break the **eggs** over the mixture, being careful not to break the yolks. Cover and simmer just until the whites of the eggs are set—about 3 minutes. Sprinkle with the remaining teaspoon of parsley, and serve with a green salad and crusty bread.

Tip: For a meatless version of this dish, omit the chicken livers, cook the eggs in the vegetable mixture, sprinkle 1 cup of grated Parmesan cheese over the top, and put under the broiler until the cheese browns slightly. (Unless the skillet has a flameproof handle, leave the broiler door open and do not place the skillet handle under the flames.)

Creamed Curried Eggs 🐷 ◑

Preparation: 17 minutes   Cooking: 10 minutes   Serves 4   Calories per serving: **320**

The preparation time includes 15 minutes for cooking the eggs.

3 tablespoons butter or margarine

1 medium-size yellow onion, peeled and chopped

2 tablespoons all-purpose flour

1½ teaspoons curry powder

¾ teaspoon salt

1½ cups milk

8 hard-cooked eggs

1. Melt the **butter** in a 1-quart saucepan over moderate heat. Add the **onion,** and cook, uncovered, for 5 minutes, or until soft.

2. Remove the pan from the heat and stir in the **flour, curry powder,** and **salt,** and then the **milk.** Cook, stirring constantly, for 1 minute, or until the sauce thickens. Peel the **eggs,** quarter them lengthwise, and add them to the sauce. Serve on buttered toast or English muffins.

Tips: 1. This recipe can be halved. 2. If you are using cold hard-cooked eggs, warm them in the sauce for about 1 minute before serving.

Egg Croquettes with Chicken

Preparation: 35 minutes   Cooking: **5 minutes** | Serves **4**   Calories per serving: **395**

You can use leftover chicken (or turkey) in these croquettes. It takes 15 minutes to hard-cook eggs; use this time to chop the chicken, olives, and parsley and to make the sauce.

3 tablespoons butter or margarine

1/2 cup plus 2 tablespoons unsifted all-purpose flour

2/3 cup milk

1/2 cup finely chopped cooked chicken

1 tablespoon finely chopped pimiento-stuffed olives

1 tablespoon minced parsley

4 hard-cooked eggs, minced

1/2 teaspoon salt

1/4 teaspoon black pepper

1/2 cup fine dry bread crumbs

2 tablespoons vegetable oil

1 egg, lightly beaten

1. Melt 2 tablespoons of the **butter** in a 1-quart saucepan over moderate heat. Blend in the 2 tablespoons of **flour,** and cook, uncovered, for 1 minute. Add the **milk,** and cook, stirring constantly with a wire whisk, until the sauce is very thick—about 5 minutes. Remove from the heat.

2. Add the **chicken, olives, parsley, hard-cooked eggs, salt,** and **pepper.** Mix well, then place the saucepan in the freezer for 12 minutes, or until the mixture is stiff enough to shape.

3. Place the remaining 1/2 cup of flour on a plate or a sheet of wax paper and the **bread crumbs** on another. Shape the chilled egg and chicken mixture into 8 oval patties about 1 inch thick.

4. Heat the **oil** and the remaining 1 tablespoon of butter in a heavy 9- or 10-inch skillet over moderately high heat. Coat each patty with the flour, then dip into the **beaten egg,** and finally coat with the bread crumbs. Shake off any excess crumbs. Cook the patties for 2 minutes on each side. Serve immediately.

Baked Eggs with Onions and Cheese 🐷

Preparation: 17 minutes   Cooking: **14 minutes** | Serves **4**   Calories per serving: **315**

The ingredients for this dish are almost always on hand, making it ideal for unexpected guests. To save time, make the sauce and shred the cheese while the eggs are cooking.

2 tablespoons butter or margarine

2 medium-size yellow onions, peeled and sliced

5 teaspoons all-purpose flour

1 1/2 cups milk

1/2 teaspoon salt

1/4 teaspoon black pepper

6 hard-cooked eggs, sliced

1/2 cup shredded mild Cheddar cheese (about 2 ounces)

1. Preheat the oven to 400°F. Melt the **butter** in a 1-quart saucepan over moderately high heat. Add the **onions,** and cook, stirring occasionally, for 3 minutes, or until they begin to soften.

2. Blend in the **flour,** and cook, stirring, for 30 seconds. Add the **milk, salt,** and **pepper,** stirring constantly. Bring to a boil, lower the heat, and simmer for 1 minute, stirring frequently.

3. Arrange the **eggs** in an ungreased 9-inch pie pan. Pour the sauce over the eggs and mix gently. Sprinkle the **cheese** over the top and bake, uncovered, for 10 minutes. Place under the broiler about 3 inches from the heat. Broil for 4 to 5 minutes to brown.

> **Tip:** *If you omit the eggs, you can use the sauce over cooked cauliflower, zucchini, or carrots.*

Egg Foo Yung

Preparation: **5 minutes**   Cooking: **17 minutes**   Serves **4**   Calories per serving: **315**

This traditional Chinese dish is one of the staples of Cantonese cooking.

1 tablespoon soy sauce

1 tablespoon cider vinegar

1 teaspoon sugar

1 cup chicken broth

2 teaspoons cornstarch

3 tablespoons vegetable oil

1 clove garlic, peeled and minced

1/2 cup finely chopped green onions

1 1/2 cups bean sprouts, drained, or thinly sliced celery

1 cup shredded cooked pork or chicken, or 1/2 pound raw shrimp, shelled and deveined

4 eggs

1/2 teaspoon salt

1. In a 1-quart saucepan, combine the **soy sauce, vinegar, sugar,** and 3/4 cup of the **chicken broth.** Bring the mixture to a boil.

2. Mix the **cornstarch** with the remaining 1/4 cup of broth. Add the mixture to the saucepan and continue to boil, stirring constantly, for 2 minutes. Keep the sauce warm over very low heat.

3. Heat the **oil** in a heavy 9- or 10-inch skillet over high heat. Add the **garlic** and **green onions,** and toss for 30 seconds. Add the **bean sprouts** and toss for 30 seconds. Add the **pork** and toss for 2 minutes.

4. Beat the **eggs** with the **salt,** and add to the skillet. Reduce the heat to low. Cook, uncovered, for 3 minutes, then cover and cook for 5 more minutes, or until the eggs are set.

5. Loosen the bottom of the eggs from the skillet with a spatula and invert the omelet onto a serving platter. Cut into 4 wedges. Heat the reserved sauce to boiling and pour over the eggs. Serve with Fried Rice, page 204.

Country Supper Omelet

Preparation: **9 minutes**   Cooking: **14 minutes**   Serves **4**   Calories per serving: **325**

A favorite in the Southern States, this hearty omelet is made with bacon, potatoes, and onions.

4 slices bacon, cut into 1-inch strips, or 1/4 pound crumbled pork sausage

1 medium-size yellow onion, peeled and chopped

2 small all-purpose potatoes, peeled and cut into 1/4-inch dice

1 medium-size sweet green pepper, cored, seeded, and chopped (optional)

1/2 teaspoon salt

1/4 teaspoon black pepper

8 eggs, lightly beaten

1. Cook the **bacon** in a heavy 9- or 10-inch skillet, preferably nonstick, over moderate heat for 3 minutes. Leaving the bacon in the skillet, pour off all but 2 tablespoons of the drippings.

2. Add the **onion** and **potatoes** to the skillet, and the **green pepper** if used. Cook, uncovered, stirring occasionally, for 10 minutes, or until the vegetables are tender. Sprinkle with the **salt** and **black pepper.**

3. Pour the **eggs** over the vegetables and bacon, and as the eggs cook, push the edges toward the center with a pancake turner to allow any uncooked portion to run underneath. When the bottom is firm—in about 3 to 4 minutes—cover and cook for 1 minute, or until firm but not dry. Cut into 4 wedges and serve.

Tip: This recipe can be halved.

Sicilian Pasta Omelet with Anchovies 🐷 ▷ ⏸

Preparation: **8 minutes**   Cooking: **6 minutes**   Serves **4**   Calories per serving: **320**

3 tablespoons olive or vegetable oil

2 cups cooked pasta or 4 ounces vermicelli or fine egg noodles, cooked according to package directions and drained

4 eggs

1/3 cup grated Parmesan cheese

6 anchovy fillets, rinsed and chopped, or 1 can (6 1/2 or 7 ounces) tuna, drained and flaked

1/4 teaspoon black pepper

2 tablespoons chopped basil or parsley

1. Preheat the broiler. Heat the **oil** over moderate heat in a heavy 8- or 9-inch skillet. Add the **pasta,** and cook, uncovered, for 8 minutes, or until golden and crisp on the bottom.

2. Meanwhile, in a small bowl, beat the **eggs** with the **cheese, anchovy fillets, pepper,** and **basil.** Pour the mixture over the pasta, tilting the skillet from side to side over the heat until the eggs are just set—about 3 minutes.

3. Place the skillet (but not the handle) under the broiler about 3 inches from the heat. Broil until the top of the omelet has puffed and browned—about 3 minutes. Remove from the broiler, cut into 4 wedges, and serve.

Tip: This recipe can be halved.

Vegetable Frittata

Preparation: **13 minutes**   Cooking: **9 minutes**   Serves **4**   Calories per serving: **265**

2 tablespoons butter or margarine

1 tablespoon olive or vegetable oil

1/2 medium-size yellow onion, peeled and chopped

1 clove garlic, peeled and minced

1/4 pound mushrooms, thinly sliced

1 cup chopped cooked spinach, zucchini, or broccoli

4 eggs, lightly beaten

3/4 cup grated Parmesan cheese

1/4 teaspoon dried marjoram, crumbled

1 teaspoon dried basil, crumbled

1/2 teaspoon salt

1/4 teaspoon black pepper

Here is a good way to use leftover spinach, zucchini, or broccoli. Or use 1 package (10 ounces) of frozen spinach, thawed, drained, and squeezed dry.

1. Preheat the broiler. Heat the **butter** and **oil** in a heavy 8-inch skillet over moderately high heat. Add the **onion** and **garlic,** and cook, uncovered, for 5 minutes, or until the onion is soft. Add the **mushrooms** and cook, tossing, for 1 minute, then add the **spinach** and cook, tossing, for 1 more minute.

2. In a small bowl, combine the **eggs, cheese, marjoram, basil, salt,** and **pepper.** Pour over the vegetables in the skillet, reduce the heat to low, and cook, uncovered, until the eggs are almost set—about 7 minutes.

3. Place the skillet (but not the handle) under the broiler about 3 inches from the heat. Broil for 2 to 3 minutes, or until the frittata is lightly browned. Cut into 4 wedges and serve.

Tip: In place of the cooked vegetables, brown 1/2 pound of crumbled Italian sausage with 1 cored, seeded, and sliced sweet red pepper. Slice the onion instead of chopping it, then cook as above.

187

Cheddar Egg Cups ⊕

Preparation: **10 minutes**   Cooking: **15 minutes**   Serves **4**   Calories per serving: **315**

2 tablespoons butter or margarine

2 tablespoons all-purpose flour

1 cup milk

Few drops liquid hot red pepper seasoning (optional)

¹/₂ cup shredded sharp Cheddar cheese (about 2 ounces)

1 cup chopped cooked ham

4 eggs

¹/₄ cup soft fresh bread crumbs (¹/₂ slice bread)

Tips: 1. *This recipe can be halved.* 2. *As a variation, you can use Swiss cheese instead of the Cheddar, but add 1 small yellow onion, peeled, chopped, and cooked in 1 tablespoon of butter until golden.*

1. Preheat the oven to 350°F. Melt the **butter** in a 1-quart saucepan over low heat. Blend in the **flour,** and cook, stirring constantly, until just bubbly—about 1 minute.

2. Stir in the **milk** and the **red pepper seasoning** if used. Raise the heat to moderate and cook, stirring, until the mixture thickens—about 3 minutes. Continue cooking and stirring for 1 minute, then remove from the heat.

3. Add all but 2 tablespoons of the **cheese,** and cook, stirring constantly, until the cheese melts.

4. Divide the **ham** evenly among 4 ungreased individual 6-ounce baking dishes and top with the cheese sauce. Break the **eggs,** 1 into each dish. Sprinkle the **bread crumbs** and the remaining 2 tablespoons of cheese evenly over the eggs. Bake, uncovered, for 15 minutes, or until the eggs are set as you like them.

Crustless Swiss Cheese and Onion Quiche

Preparation: **12 minutes**   Cooking: **25 minutes**   Serves **4**   Calories per serving: **510**

Take the fuss out of making a quiche simply by eliminating the crust.

6 tablespoons (³/₄ stick) butter or margarine

2 medium-size yellow onions, peeled and sliced

2 eggs, lightly beaten

2 egg yolks

1 cup shredded Swiss cheese (about 4 ounces)

1¹/₂ cups half-and-half

¹/₈ teaspoon ground nutmeg

1 teaspoon salt

¹/₄ teaspoon black pepper

¹/₂ cup fine dry bread crumbs

1. Preheat the oven to 350°F. Melt 4 tablespoons of the **butter** in a 1-quart saucepan over moderately low heat. Add the **onions,** and cook, covered, for 10 minutes, or until very soft.

2. Meanwhile, in a mixing bowl, combine the **eggs, egg yolks, cheese, half-and-half, nutmeg, salt,** and **pepper.**

3. When the onions are cooked, spread them out in a buttered 9-inch pie plate. Melt the remaining 2 tablespoons of butter in the saucepan. Add the egg mixture to the pie plate, and sprinkle the **bread crumbs** and melted butter over the top. Bake, uncovered, for 25 minutes, or until puffed and set.

Tips: 1. *Leftovers can be refrigerated and reheated in a 325°F oven, but do not freeze the quiche or it will turn rubbery.* 2. *You can substitute 2 bunches of green onions, chopped, for the yellow onions, but cook them for only 5 minutes before adding them to the pie plate.*

Cheese Soufflé Pudding

Preparation: 5 minutes   **Cooking: 25 minutes**   Serves 4   Calories per serving: **345**

This tasty cheese pudding is easy to make and is almost as light and airy as a true soufflé.

2 eggs

²/₃ cup heavy cream

³/₄ cup shredded Cheddar cheese (about 3 ounces)

³/₄ cup grated Parmesan cheese

¹/₄ teaspoon salt

¹/₈ teaspoon black pepper

1. Preheat the oven to 450°F. Break the **eggs** into a mixing bowl, add the **cream,** and beat lightly. Add the **Cheddar cheese, Parmesan cheese, salt,** and **pepper,** and beat again until combined.

2. Pour the mixture into an ungreased 1-quart baking dish and bake, uncovered, for 25 minutes, or until golden brown.

Tip: *You can substitute Swiss cheese for the Cheddar.*

Cheese and Potato Soufflé

Preparation: 20 minutes   **Cooking: 20 minutes**   Serves 4   Calories per serving: **330**

3 large all-purpose potatoes (about 1¹/₂ pounds), peeled and cut into ¹/₄-inch slices

1 teaspoon salt

2 tablespoons butter or margarine

2 tablespoons chopped yellow onion

2 tablespoons chopped sweet green pepper

¹/₂ cup half-and-half

¹/₄ teaspoon black pepper

3 eggs, separated

1 cup shredded sharp Cheddar cheese (about 4 ounces)

1. Preheat the oven to 400°F. Place the **potatoes** in a 3-quart saucepan, add the **salt** and enough water to cover. Set the lid on the pan askew and boil for 15 minutes, or until tender.

2. Meanwhile, melt the **butter** in a heavy 8- or 9-inch skillet over moderate heat. Add the **onion** and **green pepper,** and cook, uncovered, for 5 minutes, or until the onion is soft. Remove from the heat and set aside.

3. Drain the potatoes and mash with a potato masher or fork, adding the **half-and-half** to moisten them. Beat in the **black pepper** and the cooked onion and green pepper. Taste, and add more salt or pepper if needed.

4. Add the yolks of the **eggs** and the **cheese** to the potatoes, and mix well. Beat the egg whites until soft peaks can be formed, and fold the whites into the potatoes with a rubber spatula.

5. Spoon the mixture into a buttered 1- or 1¹/₂-quart casserole. Bake, uncovered, until the top has puffed and browned—about 20 to 25 minutes. Serve immediately.

Tip: *Try using turnips instead of the potatoes.*

Cottage Cheese Soufflé

Preparation: **12 minutes**   Cooking: **20 minutes** | Serves **4**   Calories per serving: **290**

4 tablespoons (1/2 stick) butter or margarine

1 tablespoon finely chopped yellow onion

4 tablespoons all-purpose flour

3/4 cup milk

1 cup small-curd cottage cheese

2 whole pimientos, coarsely chopped

4 eggs, separated

1/4 teaspoon salt

1/8 teaspoon black pepper

1. Preheat the oven to 425°F. Melt the **butter** in a 1-quart saucepan over moderate heat. Add the **onion,** and cook, uncovered, for 3 minutes, or until pale gold.

2. Blend in the **flour.** Add the **milk** gradually, and cook, stirring constantly, until the mixture is smooth and very thick—about 3 minutes.

3. Remove from the heat and add the **cottage cheese, pimientos,** the yolks of the **eggs,** and the **salt** and **pepper.** Mix thoroughly.

4. Beat the egg whites until soft peaks can be formed, then fold into the mixture with a rubber spatula. Pour into an unbuttered straight-sided 1-quart casserole. Bake, uncovered, for 20 minutes, or until the soufflé is puffed and brown and quivers gently when you nudge the dish.

Tip: Leftovers can be served cold.

Cheese Soufflé Baked in Tomatoes

Preparation: **15 minutes**   Cooking: **15 minutes** | Serves **4**   Calories per serving: **285**

Bring a bit of elegance to your table with these soufflé-stuffed tomatoes. Use them as a main course, allowing 2 tomatoes for each person. Serve with a green salad and crusty bread and with apple pie for dessert. Or, if you prefer, serve them as a side dish for 8.

8 medium-size firm, ripe tomatoes

4 1/2 teaspoons butter or margarine

1 tablespoon all-purpose flour

1/3 cup half-and-half

1/2 teaspoon salt

1/4 teaspoon black pepper

1 cup shredded Swiss or sharp Cheddar cheese (about 4 ounces)

3 eggs, separated

1. Preheat the oven to 350°F. Slice off the tops of the **tomatoes** and scoop out the tomato pulp with a spoon. Discard the tops and save the pulp for another use. Set the tomato shells aside.

2. Melt the **butter** in a 1-quart saucepan over low heat. Blend in the **flour,** and gradually stir in the **half-and-half, salt,** and **pepper.** Cook, stirring constantly, until smooth and thick—about 3 minutes.

3. Remove from the heat and beat in the **cheese** and the yolks of the **eggs.** Beat the egg whites until soft peaks can be formed, then fold into the egg and cheese mixture with a rubber spatula.

4. Spoon the mixture into the tomatoes, filling each about three-quarters full. Place the tomatoes in a buttered 9-inch pie plate. Bake, uncovered, until the soufflé has puffed and browned—about 15 minutes. Serve immediately.

Tip: The tomato pulp can be used to add to a soup or to mix with a vegetable dish.

Peppers Stuffed with Ricotta Cheese

Preparation: **15 minutes**   Cooking: **20 minutes**   Serves **4**   Calories per serving: **330**

4 medium-size sweet green peppers, halved lengthwise, cored, and seeded

4½ teaspoons vegetable oil

1 medium-size yellow onion, peeled and chopped

1 clove garlic, peeled and minced

1 cup ricotta cheese

¼ cup grated Parmesan cheese

½ cup fine dry bread crumbs

3 eggs

3 tablespoons sour cream

¼ teaspoon each dried thyme, and rosemary, crumbled

Pinch ground nutmeg

2 tablespoons minced parsley

½ teaspoon salt

¼ teaspoon black pepper

1. Preheat the oven to 400°F. Bring about 2 inches of lightly salted water to a boil in a 1-quart saucepan over moderately high heat. Add the **green peppers,** and cook, uncovered, for 5 minutes. Drain.

2. Meanwhile, heat the **oil** in a heavy 8- or 9-inch skillet over moderate heat. Add the **onion** and **garlic,** and cook, uncovered, for 3 minutes. Remove from the heat and set aside.

3. In a mixing bowl, combine the **ricotta cheese, Parmesan cheese, bread crumbs, eggs, sour cream, thyme, rosemary, nutmeg, parsley, salt,** and **black pepper.** Mix in the onion and garlic.

4. Place the green pepper halves close together in a buttered 10-inch pie plate, and spoon the filling into them. Add ¼ cup of water to the pie plate and bake, uncovered, for 20 minutes.

Tips: 1. As a variation, use cottage cheese instead of the ricotta. Or substitute ½ cup of feta cheese for ½ cup of the ricotta cheese, and use 2 tablespoons of snipped dill in place of the rosemary. 2. Cover leftovers with tomato sauce and reheat in a 350°F oven.

Rink Tum Ditty ⊙

Preparation: **10 minutes**   Cooking: **7 minutes**   Serves **4**   Calories per serving: **530**

2 tablespoons butter

1 medium-size yellow onion, peeled and chopped

3 medium-size tomatoes, peeled and chopped

1 teaspoon salt

¼ teaspoon black pepper

1 tablespoon sugar

½ cup half-and-half

3 cups shredded sharp Cheddar cheese (¾ pound)

2 eggs, lightly beaten

4 thick slices crusty bread, lightly toasted

Rink Tum Ditty is a name Colonial Americans gave to Welsh rarebit. To speed preparation, peel and chop the tomatoes before you start the recipe. Shred the cheese during the cooking in Steps 1 and 2.

1. Melt the **butter** in a 1-quart saucepan over moderate heat. Add the **onion,** and cook, uncovered, for 5 minutes, or until soft.

2. Add the **tomatoes, salt, pepper, sugar,** and **half-and-half,** and simmer for 3 minutes.

3. Add the **cheese** gradually, stirring constantly. Be careful to keep the mixture cooking at a slow simmer. Do not let it boil. When all the cheese has melted, stir in the **eggs,** and pour over the **bread.**

Tip: Try Rink Tum Ditty over croquettes instead of toast.

EGGS AND CHEESE

Mexican Rarebit ⟩

Preparation: **15 minutes**   Cooking: **5 minutes**   Serves **4**   Calories per serving: **575**

1 tablespoon butter or margarine

3 tablespoons chopped sweet green pepper

1 medium-size tomato, peeled and chopped

1 cup fresh sweet corn (cut from 2 medium-size ears) or ½ package (5 ounces) frozen whole-kernel corn

2 whole canned green chilies, rinsed, seeded, and chopped

¼ teaspoon salt

4 cups shredded sharp Cheddar or Monterey Jack cheese or a combination of the two (about 1 pound)

4 slices toast

1 pimiento, sliced (optional)

1 tablespoon minced parsley (optional)

The Welsh are not the only ones who can make rarebit. Try this Mexican rarebit for brunch or Sunday supper. You can shred the cheese while the green pepper is cooking, but you must prepare the remaining ingredients before you start the recipe.

1. Melt the **butter** in the top of a double boiler set directly over moderate heat. Add the **green pepper,** and cook, uncovered, until soft—about 5 minutes. Meanwhile, bring about 1 inch of water to a simmer in the bottom of the double boiler.

2. Place the top of the double boiler over the hot water, and add the **tomato, corn, chilies, salt,** and **cheese.** Stir until the mixture is well blended and the cheese has melted—about 5 minutes. Serve over the **toast,** and garnish with the **pimiento** and **parsley** if desired.

> *Tip: Instead of serving the rarebit on toast, try it with tortillas that have been warmed in the oven, or over toasted English muffins.*

Feta and Ricotta Cheese Fondue 🐷 ⟩

Preparation: **5 minutes**   Cooking: **5 minutes**   Serves **4**   Calories per serving: **260**

Set this dish in the center of the table and let everyone dip chunks of crusty bread into it. It is both tasty and fun. Serve it as the centerpiece of a light lunch or supper.

3 tablespoons butter or margarine

1 cup feta cheese, cut into ½-inch cubes (about 4 ounces)

1 cup ricotta cheese

⅛ teaspoon black pepper

Juice of 1 lemon

1 tablespoon minced parsley (optional)

1. Melt the **butter** in a heavy 8-inch skillet or a 1-quart saucepan over low heat. Add the **feta cheese, ricotta cheese,** and **pepper.** Cook, stirring constantly, and mashing the cheeses slightly, until they soften and begin to bubble—about 5 minutes.

2. Stir in the **lemon juice,** and garnish with the **parsley** if desired. Serve at once; as the fondue cools, it loses flavor.

> *Tip: As a variation, substitute shredded Fontina cheese for the feta, or large- or small-curd cottage cheese for the ricotta or feta or both.*

192

PASTA, RICE, AND CEREALS

Pasta deserves a special place at mealtime. It is inexpensive, quick and easy to prepare, and extremely versatile, combining well with almost any meat, seafood, or vegetable. Many of the dishes here are substantial enough for a main course, requiring only a vegetable or a green salad to round out the meal.

The pasta in the following recipes should be cooked according to package directions in water that has been brought to a rolling boil, then tossed with the sauce as described in the recipes. The preparation times given include 10 minutes for bringing the water to a boil, but this time may vary depending on your stove and the temperature of the water you start with. (To save time, begin with hot tap water.) Once the pasta has cooked, it should not wait, so be sure to start the sauce in time to have it ready when the pasta is done.

Also included in this section are recipes for rice, bulgur, cornmeal, and hominy grits. Bulgur, or cracked wheat, is a nutritious alternative to rice. Grits can be a real treat when flavored with garlic and cheese.

Spaghetti Carbonara

Preparation and cooking: **22 minutes**   Serves **4**   Calories per serving: **890**

1 pound thin spaghetti

8 slices bacon, cut into 1-inch strips

¼ cup olive or vegetable oil

1 medium-size yellow onion, peeled and chopped

4 tablespoons (½ stick) butter or margarine, cut into small pieces

½ cup chicken broth

⅛ teaspoon salt

¼ teaspoon black pepper

2 eggs, at room temperature, lightly beaten

¼ cup chopped parsley

1 cup grated Parmesan cheese

A favorite in Rome, this spaghetti dish made with bacon and eggs is thrifty and easy to make. There are various theories about the origin of the name. One says that it comes from the fact that the dish was once cooked over coals (carbone) *and another that it was popular among coal miners and other workers.*

1. Cook the **spaghetti** according to package directions.

2. Meanwhile, cook the **bacon** in a 12-inch skillet over moderate heat for 5 minutes, or until crisp. Using a slotted spoon, remove the bacon to paper toweling to drain. Discard the drippings and wipe the skillet with paper toweling.

3. Heat the **oil** in the skillet over moderate heat. Add the **onion,** and cook, uncovered, for 5 minutes, or until soft. Add the **butter, chicken broth, salt,** and **pepper,** and heat through but do not boil—about 2 minutes. Remove from the heat.

4. Drain the spaghetti thoroughly in a colander, and toss with the sauce in the skillet. Add the **eggs,** and continue tossing for about 1 minute, or until the sauce thickens. Add the **parsley,** then the **cheese,** and toss again. Crumble the reserved bacon over the spaghetti and stir it in.

Spaghetti with Oil, Garlic, and Cheese

Preparation and cooking: **20 minutes**   Serves **4**   Calories per serving: **808**

1 pound thin spaghetti

6 tablespoons olive oil

6 cloves garlic, peeled and minced

6 tablespoons (3/4 stick) butter or margarine, cut into small pieces

1/4 teaspoon salt

1/4 teaspoon black pepper

1/2 cup grated Parmesan cheese

1. Cook the **spaghetti** according to package directions.

2. About 5 minutes before the spaghetti is done, heat the **oil** in a 10-inch skillet over low heat. Add the **garlic,** and cook, uncovered, for 3 minutes. Stir in the **butter** until melted. Remove from heat.

3. Drain the spaghetti thoroughly in a colander, place in a warm serving bowl, and toss with the sauce. Season with the **salt** and **pepper.** Sprinkle with the **cheese,** and serve with Spinach-Bacon Salad with Warm Dressing, page 48.

> **Tip:** *This recipe can be halved.*

Spaghetti Florentine

Preparation and cooking: **25 minutes**   Serves **4**   Calories per serving: **640**

3/4 pound thin spaghetti

2 tablespoons vegetable oil

3/4 pound lean ground beef

1 medium-size yellow onion, peeled and chopped

2 cloves garlic, peeled and minced

2 stalks celery, chopped

3 medium-size fresh tomatoes, peeled and chopped, or
1 can (1 pound) tomatoes, drained and chopped

1 teaspoon salt

1/4 teaspoon black pepper

1/2 teaspoon each dried basil and oregano

1 package (10 ounces) fresh spinach, rinsed and with the stems removed, or
1 package (10 ounces) frozen spinach, thawed

1/2 cup grated Parmesan cheese

Here is an extra-thrifty, nutritious one-dish meal.

1. Cook the **spaghetti** according to package directions.

2. Meanwhile, heat the **oil** in a heavy 12-inch skillet over moderately high heat for about 1 minute. Add the **beef,** and cook, uncovered, stirring occasionally, for 5 minutes, or until browned.

3. Push the beef to one side of the skillet and add the **onion, garlic,** and **celery.** Reduce the heat to moderate, and cook, uncovered, for 5 minutes, or until the onion is soft. Add the **tomatoes, salt, pepper, basil, oregano,** and **spinach.** Cover and simmer for 10 minutes.

4. Drain the spaghetti thoroughly in a colander, and toss with the sauce in the skillet. Sprinkle with the **cheese,** and serve hot with a green salad.

> **Tips: 1.** *This recipe can be halved.* **2.** *If you have the time, baking will make this dish even better. Cook the beef, tomato, and spinach mixture for 5 minutes, then stir in 2 lightly beaten eggs, and toss with the pasta. Spoon into a lightly buttered 9"x 9"x 2" baking dish, sprinkle with the cheese, and bake, uncovered, in a preheated 400°F oven for 20 minutes, or until golden. This baked version freezes well.*

Spaghetti with Shredded Zucchini and Cheese ▷ ⬤

Preparation and cooking: **20 minutes**   Serves **4**   Calories per serving: **710**

1 pound thin spaghetti

4 tablespoons (½ stick) butter or margarine

3 cloves garlic, peeled and minced

2 medium-size zucchini (about ¾ pound), coarsely shredded

2 large carrots, peeled and shredded

½ teaspoon dried oregano or marjoram, crumbled

½ teaspoon dried rosemary, crumbled

¾ cup sour cream

¾ cup plain yogurt

¼ teaspoon salt

⅛ teaspoon black pepper

½ cup grated Parmesan cheese

1. Cook the **spaghetti** according to package directions.

2. Meanwhile, melt the **butter** in a heavy 12-inch skillet over moderate heat. Add the **garlic,** and cook, uncovered, for 30 seconds. Add the **zucchini** and **carrots,** and cook, uncovered, stirring frequently, for 4 or 5 minutes, or until crisp-tender. Reduce the heat to low, stir in the **oregano** and **rosemary,** and remove from the heat.

3. Add the **sour cream** and **yogurt** to the skillet, and mix thoroughly. Return to low heat for 1 minute to heat through, but do not boil or the sour cream and yogurt will curdle. Season with the **salt** and **pepper.**

4. Drain the spaghetti thoroughly in a colander, place in a warm serving bowl, and pour the sauce over it. Serve the **cheese** separately.

> **Tips: 1.** If you like, use 1½ cups plain yogurt and omit the sour cream. **2.** This recipe can be halved, or leftovers can be refrigerated for 1 or 2 days. Reheat, covered, in a double boiler. **3.** Add 1 cup of cubed cooked ham.

Spaghetti with Tuna and Tomatoes 🐷 ▷

Preparation and cooking: **20 minutes**   Serves **4**   Calories per serving: **615**

1 pound spaghetti

4 tablespoons (½ stick) butter or margarine

2 cloves garlic, peeled and minced

3 medium-size fresh tomatoes, peeled and chopped, or 1 can (1 pound) tomatoes, chopped, with their juice

1 can (6½ or 7 ounces) tuna, drained

¼ teaspoon black pepper

¼ cup minced parsley

> **Tip:** You can make the sauce ahead and refrigerate it overnight. Add the second 2 tablespoons of butter just after the sauce is reheated.

1. Cook the **spaghetti** according to package directions.

2. Meanwhile, melt 2 tablespoons of the **butter** in a 12-inch skillet over low heat. Add the **garlic,** and cook, uncovered, for 3 minutes, or until golden. Add the **tomatoes,** and cook, uncovered, for 10 minutes, stirring occasionally.

3. Add the **tuna** to the skillet, breaking up the chunks with the side of a spoon. Stir to mix, and cook for 5 minutes, uncovered, over moderate heat. Remove from the heat, and stir in the **pepper, parsley,** and the remaining 2 tablespoons of butter.

4. Drain the spaghetti thoroughly in a colander, and toss with the sauce in the skillet.

Spaghetti Tetrazzini ⟩ ⬮

Preparation and cooking: **20 minutes**   Serves **4**   Calories per serving: **745**

1 pound spaghetti

4 tablespoons (1/2 stick) butter or margarine

1 small yellow onion, peeled and chopped

1 small sweet green pepper, cored, seeded, and chopped

2 stalks celery, chopped

1/2 pound mushrooms, chopped

1 1/2 cups half-and-half

1 cup cubed cooked chicken or turkey

1/4 teaspoon salt

1/4 teaspoon black pepper

1. Cook the **spaghetti** according to package directions.

2. Meanwhile, melt the **butter** in a heavy 12-inch skillet over moderate heat. Add the **onion, green pepper,** and **celery,** and cook, uncovered, for 3 minutes. Add the **mushrooms,** and cook 2 or 3 minutes longer, or until they are just tender.

3. Add the **half-and-half** to the skillet, raise the heat to high, and boil for 6 to 8 minutes, or until the sauce thickens. Stir in the **chicken, salt,** and **black pepper,** and cook for another minute, or until the chicken is heated through.

4. Drain the spaghetti thoroughly in a colander, and toss with the sauce in the skillet.

Tip: This recipe can be halved.

Spaghetti Bolognese

Preparation: **15 minutes**   Cooking: **20 minutes**   Serves **6**   Calories per serving: **805**

1 tablespoon butter

1 tablespoon vegetable oil

3 cloves garlic, peeled and minced

1 medium-size yellow onion, peeled and chopped

1/2 pound lean ground beef

1/2 pound ground pork

1/2 cup dry red or white wine

3 medium-size fresh tomatoes, peeled and chopped, or 1 can (1 pound) tomatoes, chopped, with their juice

1 tablespoon chopped parsley

1 bay leaf

1/2 teaspoon each dried oregano and basil, crumbled

1 teaspoon salt

1/4 teaspoon black pepper

1 pound thin spaghetti

Serve this classic meat-and-tomato dish in less than 40 minutes; there is no need to simmer the sauce for hours. Cut preparation time by peeling and chopping the tomatoes, chopping the parsley, and measuring the herbs while the onion, garlic, and meat are cooking.

1. Heat the **butter** and **oil** in a 12-inch skillet over moderately high heat for about 1 minute. Add the **garlic** and **onion** to one side of the skillet and the **beef** and **pork** to the other. Cook, uncovered, for 6 minutes, or until the onion is soft and the meat has browned. Stir the meat occasionally, but keep it separate from the garlic and onion.

2. Add the **wine** to the skillet, bring to a boil, and let it boil for 3 minutes. Add the **tomatoes, parsley, bay leaf, oregano, basil, salt,** and **pepper.** Stir to mix, cover, reduce the heat, and simmer for 20 minutes, stirring occasionally.

3. While the sauce is simmering, cook the **spaghetti** according to package directions.

4. Remove the sauce from the heat, skim off all but about 1 tablespoon of the surface fat, and keep warm until the spaghetti is done. Drain the spaghetti thoroughly in a colander, and toss with the sauce in the skillet.

Spaghetti with Sausages and Peas ⊘ ⟳

Preparation and cooking: **20 minutes**   Serves **4**   Calories per serving: **1245**

1 pound spaghetti

³/₄ pound sweet Italian sausages

¹/₂ cup olive or vegetable oil

¹/₂ teaspoon dried rosemary, crumbled

¹/₂ cup chopped green onions

1 package (10 ounces) frozen peas

¹/₂ cup dry white wine

3 tablespoons butter or margarine, cut into small pieces

¹/₃ cup grated Parmesan cheese

1. Cook the **spaghetti** according to package directions.

2. Meanwhile, bring about 1 inch of water to a boil in a 2-quart saucepan. Prick the **sausages** in several places with a fork, drop them into the boiling water, and cook, uncovered, for 5 minutes. Drain.

3. Heat the **oil** in a 12-inch skillet over moderate heat. Cut the sausages into ¹/₄-inch slices, add them to the skillet, and cook, stirring frequently, for 5 minutes, or until browned.

4. Add the **rosemary, green onions,** and **peas,** cover, and cook for 4 minutes. Raise the heat to moderately high, add the **wine,** and boil for 3 minutes. Stir in the **butter** and **cheese** until melted. Drain the spaghetti thoroughly in a colander, and toss with the sauce in the skillet.

> *Tips: 1. This recipe can be halved. 2. You can substitute breakfast sausages for the Italian sausages. If you do, you may add ¹/₂ teaspoon of fennel seeds.*

Spaghetti with Chicken Livers ⊘ ⟳

Preparation and cooking: **20 minutes**   Serves **4**   Calories per serving: **725**

1 pound spaghetti

3 tablespoons olive or vegetable oil

¹/₂ cup finely chopped green onions

³/₄ cup dry white wine

¹/₂ pound chicken livers, drained and chopped

3 tablespoons butter or margarine

¹/₄ teaspoon dried sage, crumbled

¹/₂ teaspoon salt

¹/₈ teaspoon black pepper

¹/₄ cup grated Parmesan cheese

2 tablespoons minced parsley

1. Cook the **spaghetti** according to package directions.

2. Meanwhile, heat the **oil** in a 10-inch skillet over moderate heat. Add the **green onions,** and cook, uncovered, for 5 minutes, or until soft.

3. Add the **wine** to the skillet, and simmer, uncovered, for 2 minutes. Add the **chicken livers, butter, sage, salt,** and **pepper,** and simmer for 10 more minutes.

4. Drain the spaghetti thoroughly in a colander, and place in a warm serving bowl. Toss the chicken liver mixture with the spaghetti, and sprinkle with the **cheese** and **parsley.** Serve with a green salad or with Baked Zucchini with Tomatoes, page 79.

> *Tips: 1. You can substitute chicken broth for the wine. If you do, omit the salt. 2. This recipe can be halved.*

Linguine in Marinara Sauce

Preparation and cooking: **25 minutes**   Serves **4**   Calories per serving: **680**

1 pound linguine

1/4 cup olive or vegetable oil

1 medium-size yellow onion, peeled and chopped

3 cloves garlic, peeled and minced

2 large carrots, peeled and cut into 1/4-inch slices

6 medium-size fresh tomatoes, peeled and chopped, or 1 can (2 pounds 3 ounces) tomatoes, chopped, with their juice

1 teaspoon dried oregano, crumbled

1 teaspoon dried basil, crumbled

2 tablespoons chopped parsley

1 teaspoon salt

1/4 teaspoon black pepper

3 tablespoons butter or margarine, cut into small pieces

This recipe makes a meatless main course for 4 or a side dish for 6. Before you put the linguine water on to boil, prepare the onion, garlic, and carrots; while they cook, peel and chop the tomatoes.

1. Cook the **linguine** according to package directions.

2. Meanwhile, heat the **oil** in a 12-inch skillet over moderate heat. Add the **onion, garlic,** and **carrots,** and cook, uncovered, for 5 minutes, or until the onion is soft. Add the **tomatoes, oregano, basil, parsley, salt,** and **pepper,** and simmer, partially covered, for 12 minutes, or until the sauce thickens slightly. Remove from the heat and stir in the **butter** until it melts.

3. Drain the linguine thoroughly in a colander, and toss with the sauce in the skillet. Serve with Sautéed Green Peppers, page 72, or steamed broccoli tossed with butter.

> **Tips: 1.** *Stir in 1/2 pound of sliced mushrooms during the last 5 minutes of cooking.* **2.** *Marinara sauce can be served over chicken, fish, or steamed vegetables as well as pasta, so if you need only half this recipe for your meal, cook 8 ounces of pasta but the entire amount of sauce. Refrigerate or freeze the remaining sauce for later use.*

Linguine with Clam Sauce

Preparation and cooking: **20 minutes**   Serves **4**   Calories per serving: **785**

1 pound linguine

2/3 cup olive oil or 1/3 cup each olive oil and vegetable oil

4 cloves garlic, peeled and minced

1/2 pint shucked fresh clams, minced, with their liquor, or 1 can (7 ounces) minced clams, undrained

3/4 teaspoon dried oregano, crumbled

1/2 teaspoon salt

1/4 teaspoon black pepper

1/4 cup chopped parsley

1. Cook the **linguine** according to package directions.

2. Meanwhile, heat the **oil** in a 10-inch skillet over low heat. Add the **garlic,** and cook, uncovered, for 3 minutes, or until golden. Add the **clams** and their liquor, the **oregano, salt,** and **pepper.** Simmer, uncovered, for 5 minutes. Stir in the **parsley.**

3. Drain the linguine thoroughly in a colander, and divide among 4 soup bowls. Pour equal amounts of the sauce over each serving, making sure the clams are distributed evenly. Serve with Scalloped Eggplant, page 70, or steamed zucchini with butter.

Linguine with Green Sauce 🐷 ▷

Preparation and cooking: 20 minutes   Serves **4**   Calories per serving: **565**

1 pound linguine

1 package (10 ounces) fresh spinach or 1 package (10 ounces) frozen chopped spinach

3 tablespoons olive or vegetable oil

4 cloves garlic, peeled and minced

⅓ cup Parmesan cheese

1 teaspoon dried basil, crumbled

½ teaspoon salt

⅛ teaspoon black pepper

Tip: Make an extra batch of sauce and freeze it.

1. Cook the **linguine** according to package directions.

2. Meanwhile, trim the fresh **spinach** of coarse stems and blemished leaves, and wash it. Place the spinach in a 12-inch skillet with just the water that clings to the leaves, and cook, covered, for 3 to 5 minutes, or until it is just limp. If you are using frozen spinach, cook according to package directions. Drain the cooked spinach in a sieve or colander, pressing out most of the liquid from the spinach with the back of a large spoon. Chop the spinach fine.

3. Wipe the skillet dry. Heat the **oil** in the skillet over low heat. Add the **garlic,** and cook, uncovered, for 3 minutes, or until golden. Remove from the heat, and add the spinach, **cheese, basil, salt,** and **pepper.**

4. Drain the linguine thoroughly in a colander, and toss with the sauce in the skillet.

Fettucini Alfredo ▷ ◫

Preparation and cooking: 20 minutes   Serves **4**   Calories per serving: **735**

Serve this as a main course for 4 or as the first course of a special dinner for 6.

1 pound fettucini

1½ cups half-and-half

5 tablespoons butter, cut into small pieces

Pinch ground nutmeg

¼ teaspoon black pepper

¾ cup grated Parmesan cheese

Tips: 1. This recipe can be halved. 2. For extra richness, substitute heavy cream for the half-and-half.

1. Cook the **fettucini** according to package directions.

2. During the last 6 minutes of cooking, bring the **half-and-half** to a boil in a 12-inch skillet. Reduce the heat and simmer, stirring constantly, for 5 minutes. Remove from the heat.

3. Drain the fettucini thoroughly in a colander, and add to the half-and-half in the skillet. Toss well, then add the **butter, nutmeg, pepper,** and ½ cup of the **cheese.** Toss again to distribute the cheese evenly. Serve hot and pass the remaining ¼ cup of cheese separately.

Ziti with Onions and Garlic 🐷 ◐

Preparation and cooking: **22 minutes**   Serves **6**   Calories per serving: **600**

1 pound ziti

2 tablespoons butter or margarine

6 tablespoons olive or vegetable oil

6 medium-size yellow onions, peeled, halved, and thinly sliced

3 cloves garlic, peeled and minced

8 ounces mozzarella cheese, diced

1/4 teaspoon salt

1/8 teaspoon black pepper

The ingredients are simple, but this is a special dish.

1. Cook the **ziti** according to package directions.

2. Meanwhile, heat the **butter** and **oil** in a heavy 12-inch skillet over moderately low heat. Add the **onions,** and cook, uncovered, for 15 minutes, stirring frequently. Add the **garlic,** and cook 1 minute longer.

3. Drain the ziti thoroughly in a colander, then toss with the onions in the skillet. Add the **cheese,** and toss again. Season with the **salt** and **pepper.**

> ***Tips: 1.*** *This recipe can be halved.* ***2.*** *You can make this dish ahead, or refrigerate leftovers for 1 or 2 days. Reheat, covered, in a double boiler.*

Ziti with Bacon, Tomatoes, and Hot Pepper 🐷 ◐

Preparation and cooking: **23 minutes**   Serves **4**   Calories per serving: **690**

1 pound ziti

8 slices bacon, cut into 1-inch strips

1 large yellow onion, peeled and chopped

2 cloves garlic, peeled and minced

3 medium-size fresh tomatoes, peeled and chopped, or 1 can (1 pound) tomatoes, chopped, with their juice

1/2 teaspoon crushed dried red pepper

1/2 teaspoon dried basil, crumbled

1/4 teaspoon salt

1/2 cup grated Parmesan cheese

1. Cook the **ziti** according to package directions.

2. Meanwhile, cook the **bacon** in a heavy 14-inch skillet over moderate heat for 5 minutes, or until crisp. Using a slotted spoon, remove the bacon to paper toweling to drain.

3. Pour off all but 3 tablespoons of the bacon drippings. Add the **onion** to the skillet, and cook, uncovered, for 5 minutes, or until soft. Add the **garlic,** and cook 1 minute longer.

4. Add the **tomatoes, dried red pepper, basil,** and **salt.** Simmer, uncovered, until the sauce has thickened slightly—about 12 minutes.

5. Drain the ziti thoroughly in a colander, and toss with the sauce in the skillet. Sprinkle with the **cheese,** crumble the reserved bacon over the top, and serve hot.

> ***Tips: 1.*** *This recipe can be halved.* ***2.*** *Reheat leftovers, covered, in a double boiler.*

PASTA, RICE, AND CEREALS

200

Macaroni with Sweet Peppers ⬡ ⬭

Preparation and cooking: **20 minutes**   Serves **4**   Calories per serving: **640**

1 pound small shell macaroni

1 cup chicken or beef broth

¼ cup olive or vegetable oil or 2 tablespoons each olive oil and vegetable oil

1 large sweet green pepper, cored, seeded, and cut into ¼-inch strips

1 large sweet red pepper, cored, seeded, and cut into ¼-inch strips

3 cloves garlic, peeled and minced

2 tablespoons butter or margarine

1 teaspoon dried marjoram or rosemary, crumbled

1 teaspoon dried basil, crumbled

¼ cup grated Parmesan cheese

This light sauce is excellent with shell macaroni because it clings easily to the shells. You can also use spirals. Serve as a main course for 4 or a side dish for 6.

1. Cook the **macaroni** according to package directions.

2. Meanwhile, boil the **chicken broth** in a 1-quart saucepan, uncovered, until only about ½ cup remains—about 5 minutes.

3. Heat the **oil** in a 10-inch skillet over moderate heat. Add the **green pepper** and **red pepper**, and cook, uncovered, for 3 or 4 minutes, or until crisp-tender. Add the **garlic,** and cook about 15 seconds. Stir in the **butter, marjoram, basil,** and the reduced broth.

4. Drain the macaroni thoroughly in a colander, place it in a warm serving bowl, and pour the sauce over it. Sprinkle with the **cheese,** and serve with a green salad, steamed broccoli, or green beans with butter and lemon.

> **Tip:** *This recipe can be halved, or leftovers can be refrigerated for 1 or 2 days. Reheat, covered, in a double-boiler.*

Macaroni with Chilies and Pimientos 🐷 ⬡ ⬭

Preparation and cooking: **20 minutes**   Serves **4**   Calories per serving: **630**

1 pound small elbow or shell macaroni

2 canned whole green chilies, rinsed, seeded, and chopped

1 jar (2 ounces) pimientos, drained

1 cup sour cream

¼ teaspoon salt

¼ teaspoon dried oregano, crumbled

⅛ teaspoon chili powder

¾ cup shredded sharp Cheddar or Monterey Jack cheese (about 3 ounces)

1. Cook the **macaroni** according to package directions.

2. Meanwhile, place the **chilies, pimientos, sour cream, salt, oregano,** and **chili powder** in a 12-inch skillet, and stir.

3. About 1 minute before the macaroni is done, heat the sauce mixture in the skillet over moderate heat. Drain the macaroni thoroughly in a colander. Add the macaroni and the **cheese** to the skillet, and toss thoroughly. Serve with orange and avocado slices with Oil and Vinegar Dressing for Fruit Salads, page 55.

> **Tips: 1.** *This recipe can be halved.* **2.** *To reduce calories, use yogurt instead of the sour cream, but be sure to heat the sauce gently and to rinse the chilies, or the sauce may curdle.*

Deluxe Macaroni and Cheese

Preparation: 20 minutes   **Cooking: 30 minutes**   Serves **4**   Calories per serving: **730**

8 ounces small elbow macaroni

2 cups large-curd cottage cheese

1 cup sour cream

1 egg, lightly beaten

3/4 teaspoon salt

1/8 teaspoon black pepper

2 teaspoons Dijon or prepared spicy brown mustard

2 1/2 cups shredded sharp Cheddar cheese (about 10 ounces)

1. Preheat the oven to 400°F. Cook the **macaroni** according to package directions.

2. Meanwhile, in a large bowl, combine the **cottage cheese, sour cream, egg, salt, pepper, mustard,** and 2 cups of the **Cheddar cheese.**

3. Drain the macaroni thoroughly in a colander, and toss with the cheese mixture in the bowl. Spread the mixture evenly in a buttered 8"x 8"x 2" baking dish. Top with the remaining 1/2 cup of Cheddar cheese, and bake, uncovered, for 30 to 35 minutes, or until set. If the macaroni and cheese are browning too quickly, cover with aluminum foil after 20 minutes of baking.

Macaroni with Tomato and Mozzarella Sauce 🄊

Preparation and cooking: 25 minutes   Serves **4**   Calories per serving: **950**

1 pound large elbow macaroni, rigatoni, or ziti

6 medium-size fresh tomatoes, chopped, or 1 can (2 pounds, 3 ounces) tomatoes, drained and chopped

1 small red onion, peeled and chopped

2 cloves garlic, peeled and minced

1/2 teaspoon salt

2 tablespoons red wine vinegar

6 tablespoons olive oil or 3 tablespoons each olive oil and vegetable oil

1/4 teaspoon black pepper

1 tablespoon dried basil, crumbled

1 1/2 cups pitted small ripe olives

8 ounces mozzarella cheese, cut into 1/4-inch dice

1/2 cup grated Parmesan cheese

Here is a pasta dish with an uncooked sauce that is perfect for warm weather and picnics. While the macaroni is cooking, you will be able to prepare the tomatoes, onion, and garlic, and combine them with the other ingredients as directed.

1. Cook the **macaroni** according to package directions.

2. Meanwhile, in a mixing bowl, combine the **tomatoes, onion, garlic, salt, vinegar, oil, pepper, basil,** and **olives.**

3. Drain the macaroni thoroughly in a colander, and return it to the pot. Add the **mozzarella** and **Parmesan cheese,** and toss until just combined. Then add the tomato mixture and toss well. Serve hot, at room temperature, or cold.

> **Tips: 1.** You can substitute Muenster for the mozzarella cheese. **2.** This recipe can be halved, or leftovers can be refrigerated overnight and eaten cold, or reheated, covered, in a double boiler. **3.** To reduce the calories per serving, use only 3 tablespoons of oil and 1 tablespoon of vinegar.

Macaroni with Green Peppers and Pimientos ⅋

Preparation: **15 minutes**   Cooking: **35 minutes**   Serves **4**   Calories per serving: **480**

½ pound medium-size shell or elbow macaroni

4 tablespoons (½ stick) butter or margarine

1 large yellow onion, peeled and chopped

1 medium-size sweet green pepper, cored, seeded, and chopped

1 jar (2 ounces) pimientos, drained and chopped

2 tablespoons minced parsley

4 eggs, lightly beaten

1 cup milk

3 tablespoons grated Parmesan cheese

½ teaspoon salt

¼ teaspoon black pepper

3 tablespoons fine dry bread crumbs

This recipe takes only 15 minutes of your time because the 35 minutes of cooking time is unattended.

1. Preheat the oven to 350°F. Cook the **macaroni** according to package directions.

2. Meanwhile, melt 2 tablespoons of the **butter** in a 10-inch skillet over moderate heat. Add the **onion,** and cook, uncovered, for 5 minutes, or until soft. Add the **green pepper, pimientos,** and **parsley,** and mix well.

3. Drain the macaroni thoroughly in a colander, and toss with the vegetables in the skillet. Place the macaroni and vegetables in a buttered 2-quart baking dish.

4. In a small bowl, beat together the **eggs, milk, cheese, salt,** and **black pepper.** Pour the mixture over the pasta, sprinkle with the **bread crumbs,** dot with the remaining 2 tablespoons of butter, and bake, uncovered, for 35 minutes, or until set.

> *Tip: This recipe can be halved.*

Texas Rice ⅋

Preparation: **10 minutes**   Cooking: **20 minutes**   Serves **6**   Calories per serving: **255**

3 tablespoons butter or margarine

1 medium-size yellow onion, peeled and chopped

1½ cups uncooked rice

1 medium-size sweet green pepper, cored, seeded, and chopped

1 teaspoon chili powder

1 teaspoon dried oregano, crumbled

1 cup tomato juice

½ cup tomato sauce

1½ cups water

1½ teaspoons salt

1. Melt the **butter** in a heavy 3-quart saucepan over moderate heat. Add the **onion,** and cook, uncovered, for 5 minutes, or until soft.

2. Stir in the **rice, green pepper, chili powder, oregano, tomato juice,** and **tomato sauce,** then add the **water** and **salt.** Stir once, cover, and bring to a boil. Reduce the heat and simmer for 20 minutes, or until the rice is tender and the liquid has been absorbed.

> *Tips: 1. This recipe can be halved. 2. For a heartier dish, stir 1 cup of warm cubed cooked pork or ham into the cooked rice and sprinkle with shredded Cheddar cheese.*

Singapore Rice 🐷 ◑

Preparation: **10 minutes**   Cooking: **20 minutes**   Serves **4**   Calories per serving: **385**

3 tablespoons butter or margarine

1 small yellow onion, peeled and chopped

3 cups chicken broth

1/4 teaspoon ground cardamom

1/4 teaspoon ground nutmeg

1/4 teaspoon ground ginger

1/2 teaspoon ground cinnamon

1 tablespoon grated orange rind

1/2 teaspoon salt

1/8 teaspoon black pepper

1 1/2 cups uncooked rice

1. Melt the **butter** in a heavy 2-quart saucepan over moderate heat. Add the **onion**, and cook, uncovered, for 5 minutes, or until soft.

2. Add the **chicken broth, cardamom, nutmeg, ginger, cinnamon, orange rind, salt,** and **pepper,** and bring to a boil. Add the **rice,** stir once, cover, and return to a boil. Reduce the heat and simmer for 20 minutes, or until the rice is tender and the liquid has been absorbed.

> *Tip: This recipe can be halved, or leftovers can be refrigerated for up to 3 days.*

Fried Rice ◑

Preparation: **12 minutes**   Cooking: **14 minutes**   Serves **6**   Calories per serving: **370**

If you have leftover cooked rice, here is a perfect way to use it. If you do not have any cooked rice on hand, cook 2 cups of raw rice according to package directions to obtain the amount needed for this dish.

6 tablespoons vegetable oil

3 eggs, lightly beaten

1 large yellow onion, peeled and chopped

1 can (5 ounces) bamboo shoots, drained and thinly sliced, or 2 stalks celery, thinly sliced

1 large sweet green pepper, cored, seeded, and chopped

1/2 pound mushrooms, thinly sliced

6 cups cold cooked rice

Soy sauce

1. Heat 1 tablespoon of the **oil** in a heavy 12-inch skillet or a wok over moderate heat. Add the **eggs,** and swirl the pan so that the eggs coat the bottom to form a thin omelet. Cook, uncovered, for 4 minutes, or until set (do not flip). Remove the omelet to a plate and let cool.

2. Heat the remaining 5 tablespoons of oil in the skillet over moderate heat. Add the **onion, bamboo shoots,** and **green pepper,** and cook, uncovered, for 3 minutes, or until the onion just begins to soften. Add the **mushrooms,** and cook 3 minutes longer.

3. Reduce the heat to low, add the **rice,** and cook, stirring frequently, until heated through— about 4 minutes. Cut the omelet into thin strips and toss into the rice mixture. Serve with the **soy sauce.**

> *Tips: 1. This recipe can be halved, or leftovers can be refrigerated for 1 or 2 days. 2. For a heartier main-course dish, add 1 to 2 cups of cubed cooked chicken, ham, or pork.*

Curried Rice 🐷 🍽

Preparation: **8 minutes**　Cooking: **20 minutes**　　　Serves **4**　Calories per serving: **315**

3 tablespoons butter or margarine

1 small yellow onion, peeled and chopped

1 cup uncooked rice

2 cups chicken or beef broth

1/4 cup raisins

1 teaspoon curry powder

1/4 cup sour cream or plain yogurt (optional)

1/4 cup chutney (optional)

1. Melt the **butter** in a heavy 2-quart saucepan over moderate heat. Add the **onion**, and cook, uncovered, for 5 minutes, or until soft. Add the **rice**, and stir to coat with the butter.

2. Add the **chicken broth, raisins**, and **curry powder**. Stir once, cover, and bring to a boil. Reduce the heat and simmer for 20 minutes, or until the rice is tender and the liquid has been absorbed. Serve hot or cold with the **sour cream** and **chutney** if desired.

> *Tips:* **1.** *For a light lunch or supper dish, stir in 1 to 2 cups of cubed cooked meat.* **2.** *This recipe can be halved, or leftovers can be refrigerated for up to 3 days.*

Brown Rice with Chicken and Herbs

Preparation: **5 minutes**　Cooking: **40 minutes**　　　Serves **4**　Calories per serving: **425**

2 1/4 cups water

3/4 teaspoon salt

1 cup uncooked brown rice

2 whole chicken breasts, (4 halves), skinned and boned

2 tablespoons minced parsley

1/4 teaspoon dried tarragon, crumbled

1/4 teaspoon dried basil, crumbled

1/4 teaspoon dried thyme, crumbled

1/4 teaspoon dried rosemary, crumbled

2 tablespoons all-purpose flour

3 tablespoons butter or margarine

2 medium-size yellow onions, peeled and thinly sliced

1 1/2 cups chicken broth

3 tablespoons tomato paste or ketchup

1. Bring the **water** to a boil with 1/2 teaspoon of the **salt** in a 2-quart saucepan. Add the **rice**, lower the heat, cover, and simmer for 40 minutes. The rice will be chewy.

2. While the rice is cooking, cut the **chicken breast** halves crosswise into 1/2-inch strips and set aside. In a small bowl, combine the **parsley, tarragon, basil, thyme, rosemary, flour**, and the remaining 1/4 teaspoon of salt. Set aside.

3. About 15 minutes before the rice is done, melt the **butter** in a heavy 12-inch skillet over moderate heat. Add the **onions**, and cook, uncovered, for 5 minutes, or until soft.

4. Push the onions to one side of the skillet. Add the chicken, and cook, stirring, for 3 minutes. The chicken will be pink. Add the herb mixture, stir thoroughly, and cook, uncovered, for 1 minute.

5. Add the **chicken broth** and **tomato paste**. Bring to a boil, and cook, stirring, for 3 minutes, or until the sauce has thickened. Pour the chicken and sauce over the rice, and serve.

> *Tip: Leftovers can be reheated the next day in a double boiler.*

Bulgur Pilaf 🐷

Preparation: **10 minutes**   Cooking: **15 minutes**   Serves **4**   Calories per serving: **280**

Serve this nutritious cracked wheat dish with chicken or lamb in place of rice for a change of pace. Bulgur is available in health food stores and in some supermarkets.

2 tablespoons butter or margarine

1 small yellow onion, peeled and chopped

1 clove garlic, peeled and minced

1 cup uncooked bulgur (cracked wheat)

2 cups chicken or beef broth

1/4 teaspoon salt

1/8 teaspoon black pepper

1/4 teaspoon dried sage, crumbled (optional)

1. Melt the **butter** in a 2-quart saucepan over moderate heat. Add the **onion** and **garlic,** and cook, uncovered, for 1 minute.

2. Add the **bulgur,** and cook, stirring, for 1 minute to coat the bulgur with the butter. Stir in the **chicken broth, salt,** and **pepper,** and the **sage** if used. Bring to a boil, lower the heat, cover, and simmer for 15 minutes. The bulgur will be chewy.

Tip: Leftovers can be reheated the next day; add a few tablespoons of water and heat, covered, in a double boiler.

Bulgur with Bacon

Preparation: **12 minutes**   Cooking: **15 minutes**   Serves **4**   Calories per serving: **345**

Here is a new twist on a Middle Eastern side dish.

4 slices bacon, cut into 1-inch strips

6 green onions, trimmed and thinly sliced

1 cup uncooked bulgur (cracked wheat)

2 cups chicken broth

Tip: Try one of the following variations. 1. Add 1 chopped small sweet green pepper or 1/4 pound chopped mushrooms along with the green onions. 2. Stir in 1/4 teaspoon Dijon mustard and 1/4 teaspoon Worcestershire sauce or 1/4 cup raisins before serving. 3. Top with 1/4 cup chopped almonds or walnuts sautéed in 1 tablespoon butter or margarine.

1. Cook the **bacon** in a heavy 10-inch skillet over moderately high heat for 5 minutes, or until crisp. Using a slotted spoon, remove the bacon to paper toweling to drain. Pour off all but 2 tablespoons of the drippings.

2. Reduce the heat to moderate. Add the **green onions** to the skillet, and cook, uncovered, for 3 to 4 minutes, or until they just begin to soften.

3. Add the **bulgur** and **chicken broth,** stir once, cover, reduce the heat, and simmer for 15 to 20 minutes, or until the bulgur is tender and the broth has been absorbed. Crumble the reserved bacon over the top and serve.

Baked Cornmeal and Cheese 🐷 ◑

Preparation: **13 minutes**   Cooking: **30 minutes**   Serves **4**   Calories per serving: **600**

3 3/4 cups milk

1 1/2 cups yellow cornmeal

3 eggs, lightly beaten

1/8 teaspoon cayenne pepper

1/2 teaspoon salt

Pinch black pepper

1 cup grated Parmesan cheese

4 tablespoons (1/2 stick) butter or margarine

Tip: This recipe can be halved; save the extra 1/2 beaten egg for the next morning's scrambled eggs.

1. Preheat the oven to 425°F. Heat the **milk** in a heavy 3-quart saucepan over moderately high heat to just below the boiling point. Reduce the heat to moderate, and gradually stir in the **cornmeal.** Cook, stirring constantly to avoid lumping, for 5 minutes, or until the mixture is thick. Remove from the heat.

2. Using a wire whisk, beat the **eggs** into the mixture, whisking vigorously. Add the **cayenne pepper, salt, black pepper,** and 1/2 cup of the **cheese.** Pour the mixture into a buttered 13"x 9"x 2" baking dish. Dot with the **butter,** and sprinkle with the remaining 1/2 cup of cheese. Bake, uncovered, for 30 to 35 minutes, or until set. Cut into squares and serve with a tomato sauce.

Crispy Fried Hominy-Cheese Squares 🐷 ◑

Preparation: **30 minutes**   Cooking: **6 minutes**   Serves **4**   Calories per serving: **305**

Serve this as a side dish with chicken, roast beef, or eggs, or topped with a tomato sauce for a light lunch or supper accompanied by hot biscuits and a green salad.

2 1/2 cups water

1/2 teaspoon salt

1/2 cup quick-cooking hominy grits

2 cloves garlic, peeled and minced

2/3 cup shredded extra sharp Cheddar cheese (about 3 ounces)

1/8 teaspoon black pepper

Pinch cayenne pepper

1 egg, lightly beaten

1/2 cup fine dry bread crumbs

3 tablespoons bacon drippings or vegetable oil

1. Bring the **water** and **salt** to a boil in a 2-quart saucepan. Slowly add the **grits** while stirring constantly. Return to a boil, reduce the heat, and simmer, uncovered, for 4 to 5 minutes, or until the mixture is very thick.

2. Stir in the **garlic, cheese, black pepper,** and **cayenne pepper.** Spread in a buttered 8"x 8"x 2" pan and chill in the freezer for 20 minutes, or until firm.

3. Meanwhile, place the **egg** and **bread crumbs** in separate shallow dishes. Cut the chilled mixture into 2-inch squares, and dip into the beaten egg, then press into the bread crumbs to coat.

4. Heat the **bacon drippings** in a heavy 12-inch skillet over moderately high heat. Add the squares, and cook, uncovered, for 3 to 4 minutes on each side, or until hot and crisp.

Tips: 1. Save some of the preparation time by using leftover grits, or prepare the grits the night before and refrigerate. 2. This recipe can be halved.

COOKING FOR ONE

When you eat alone, you want to get out of the kitchen fast. Most of these dishes take less than 20 minutes to prepare, and any of them can be doubled for another serving.

Peas with Watercress Butter Sauce 🐷 ▷

Preparation: **3 minutes**   Cooking: **7 minutes**   Calories: **425**

3 tablespoons butter	Melt the **butter** in a 1-quart saucepan over moderate heat. Add the **watercress, onion,** and **salt.** Cover, and cook for 5 minutes. Add the **peas** and **vinegar,** and stir. Cover, and cook for 2 minutes.
1/2 cup minced watercress	
1 tablespoon grated onion	
1/8 teaspoon salt	
5 ounces (half a 10-ounce package) frozen green peas	
1 teaspoon cider vinegar	

Tip: Prepare a salad the next day with any unused watercress and an oil and vinegar dressing.

Savory Squash 🐷 ▷

Preparation: **8 minutes**   Cooking: **6 minutes**   Calories: **450**

2 slices bacon, cut into 1-inch strips	**1.** Cook the **bacon** in a heavy 8-inch skillet over moderately high heat for 3 minutes. Pour off all but 2 tablespoons of the drippings. Add the **onion** and **squash,** and cook, uncovered, for 3 minutes.
2 tablespoons finely chopped yellow onion	
1 yellow squash (about 1/2 pound), cut into 1/2-inch dice	**2.** Add the **walnuts, basil,** and **salt,** and cook, uncovered, stirring occasionally, for 3 minutes, or until the squash is crisp-tender.
1 tablespoon chopped walnuts	
1/2 teaspoon dried basil	
1/8 teaspoon salt	

Tip: You can omit the bacon and use 2 tablespoons of butter or margarine and 1/4 cup of chopped cooked ham.

Curried Tomato 🐷 ▷

Preparation: **3 minutes**   Cooking: **4 minutes**   Calories: **230**

1 medium-size tomato, halved	**1.** Preheat the broiler. Sprinkle the **tomato** halves with the **salt.** Combine the **butter, curry powder,** and **onion,** and spread the tops of the tomato halves with this mixture.
Pinch salt	
2 tablespoons butter or margarine, softened	**2.** Place the tomato halves on the rack of the broiler pan or in an individual baking pan. Broil 5 inches from the heat for 4 or 5 minutes, or until tender but not mushy.
1/2 teaspoon curry powder	
1 teaspoon grated yellow onion	

Chicken Breast Parmesan

Preparation: **10 minutes**   Cooking: **8 minutes**   Calories: **820**

1 small whole chicken breast
(2 halves), skinned and boned

1/8 teaspoon black pepper

3 tablespoons fine dry bread
crumbs

3 tablespoons grated
Parmesan cheese

1/2 teaspoon dried oregano,
crumbled

1 egg, lightly beaten

2 tablespoons butter or
margarine

1/2 cup tomato sauce

4 thin slices mozzarella,
Muenster, or Swiss cheese

Tip: Two turkey cutlets (about 4 or 5 ounces each) can be used in place of the chicken breasts.

1. Preheat the broiler. Pound the **chicken breast** halves between 2 sheets of wax paper to a thickness of about 1/4 inch. Season with the **pepper.** Note: Salt is not needed in this dish because of the saltiness of the cheeses.

2. Combine the **bread crumbs, Parmesan cheese,** and **oregano** on a sheet of wax paper. Dip the chicken breast halves into the **egg,** then press them into the bread crumb mixture to coat well on both sides.

3. Heat the **butter** in a heavy 10-inch skillet over moderate heat until bubbly. Add the chicken and cook for 3 minutes on each side, or until no longer pink when pierced with a knife. Do not overcook.

4. Line the rack of the broiler pan with aluminum foil and place the chicken on it. Spoon the **tomato sauce** over the breast halves, and top each with 2 slices of the **mozzarella cheese,** trimmed to fit. Broil 3 inches from the heat for about 2 minutes, or until the cheese melts. Serve with Peas with Watercress Butter Sauce, page 208.

Hawaiian Hamburger

Preparation: **13 minutes**   Cooking: **6 minutes**   Calories: **540**

6 ounces ground beef

2 tablespoons finely chopped
yellow onion

1/2 clove garlic, peeled and
minced

2 tablespoons soy sauce

1/8 teaspoon ground ginger

1/2 teaspoon sugar

1 tablespoon vegetable oil

Tip: You can substitute ground lamb for the beef.

1. In a small bowl, combine the **beef** and **onion,** and shape the mixture into a 1-inch-thick patty. Place the patty on a small plate.

2. In the same bowl, combine the **garlic, soy sauce, ginger,** and **sugar,** and pour over the patty. Let stand for 10 minutes to marinate, then remove the patty from the marinade.

3. Heat the **oil** in a heavy 6-inch skillet over moderate heat for about 1 minute. Add the patty and cook, uncovered, about 3 minutes on each side for rare, 4 for medium, and 6 for well done.

Chinese Beef and Green Beans

Preparation: **12 minutes** Cooking: **9 minutes**   Calories: **535**

You will probably not be able to buy a 4-ounce piece of flank steak in the supermarket, but you can buy a larger piece, cut off what you need, and freeze the rest for later use.

4 ounces flank steak, cut crosswise into strips 1/4 inch thick and 2 inches long

1 1/2 teaspoons soy sauce

4 ounces green beans

2 tablespoons vegetable oil

1 clove garlic, peeled and minced

1/4 teaspoon salt

2 tablespoons water

1. Put the **steak** slices into a small bowl, add the **soy sauce,** and toss to mix. Let the steak stand for 10 minutes to marinate. Meanwhile, wash the **beans,** cut off the ends, and break into 2-inch lengths.

2. Heat the **oil** in a heavy 8-inch skillet over moderate heat for about 1 minute. Add the **garlic** and **salt,** and cook, stirring, for 30 seconds. Do not let the garlic brown. Add the beans to the skillet and cook, stirring, for 3 minutes. Add the **water,** cover, reduce the heat, and cook for 3 more minutes.

3. Raise the heat to moderately high, cook until the water has boiled away, then add the steak and marinade. Cook, uncovered, stirring constantly, for 2 minutes. The steak should be pink; do not overcook or it will be tough. Serve with rice.

Beef, Tomato, and Noodle Supper

Preparation: **12 minutes** Cooking: **20 minutes**   Calories: **785**

1 tablespoon butter or margarine

6 ounces ground beef

1 medium-size yellow onion, peeled and chopped

2 small fresh tomatoes, peeled and chopped, or 1 can (8 ounces) tomatoes, chopped, with their juice

1 stalk celery, finely chopped

1/2 teaspoon salt

1/8 teaspoon black pepper

1/4 teaspoon dried basil, crumbled

1/4 teaspoon dried oregano, crumbled

1/3 cup uncooked egg noodles, elbow macaroni, or ziti

Heat the **butter** in a heavy 8-inch skillet over moderate heat until bubbly. Add the **beef** and **onion,** and cook, uncovered, stirring occasionally, for 5 minutes, or until the beef has browned and the onion is soft. Add the **tomatoes, celery, salt, pepper, basil, oregano,** and **noodles.** Cover, and simmer for 20 minutes, or until the noodles are tender, stirring occasionally.

Tips: 1. You can substitute ground lamb for the beef. 2. You can make this dish a day ahead and refrigerate it. You may need to add a few tablespoons of water when reheating if the mixture seems too dry.

Chicken Livers with Mushrooms and Tomato

Preparation: 7 minutes   Cooking: 11 minutes   **Calories: 530**

Serve this dish with buttered noodles or rice and a green salad, and you will enjoy a tasty complete meal. To save time, prepare the tomato and mushrooms while the onion is cooking.

3 tablespoons butter or margarine

1 small yellow onion, peeled and chopped

1 medium-size tomato, peeled and chopped

4 medium-size mushrooms, chopped

1/4 teaspoon dried rosemary, crumbled

1/8 teaspoon salt

1/8 teaspoon black pepper

4 ounces chicken livers, drained

1. Melt 2 tablespoons of the **butter** in an 8-inch skillet over moderate heat until bubbly. Add the **onion,** and cook, uncovered, for 5 minutes, or until soft.

2. Add the **tomato, mushrooms, rosemary, salt,** and **pepper,** and cook, uncovered, for 3 minutes. Push the vegetables to one side of the skillet.

3. Add the remaining tablespoon of butter and the **chicken livers** to the skillet, and cook the livers for 2 minutes on each side. Stir the livers in with the vegetables, and cook, uncovered, for 4 more minutes.

Tip: Substitute 4 ounces of beef liver cut into 1/4-inch strips for the chicken livers.

Broiled Fish with Cucumber Sauce ⊘

Preparation: 5 minutes   Cooking: 10 minutes   **Calories: 355**

2 tablespoons butter or margarine, melted

2 tablespoons minced seeded cucumber

1/2 small yellow onion, peeled and grated

2 dashes liquid hot red pepper seasoning

1 tablespoon lemon juice

1 tablespoon chopped parsley

1 haddock, cod, or halibut fillet (about 6 ounces)

1/8 teaspoon salt

1/8 teaspoon black pepper

While you prepare this recipe, boil a few new potatoes to serve sprinkled with a bit of dried dillweed.

1. Preheat the broiler. In a small bowl, combine the **butter, cucumber, onion, red pepper seasoning, lemon juice,** and **parsley.** Spread about one third of this mixture on the bottom of an 8"x 8"x 2" baking pan. Place the **fish fillet** in the pan, and top with the remaining mixture. Sprinkle with the **salt** and **pepper.**

2. Broil 5 inches from the heat for 10 minutes or longer, depending on the thickness of the fish. Baste the fish twice with the liquid in the pan. When the fish flakes easily when tested with a fork, it is done.

Baked Fish with Tomatoes and Tarragon

Preparation: **7 minutes** Cooking: **15 minutes**   Calories: **320**

1 or 2 flounder, cod,
haddock, bluefish, or perch
fillets (about 6 ounces)

2 small fresh tomatoes,
peeled and chopped, or
1 can (8 ounces) tomatoes,
chopped, with their juice

1 small yellow onion, peeled
and chopped

2 tablespoons chopped sweet
green pepper

1/4 teaspoon dried tarragon,
crumbled

1/8 teaspoon salt

1 tablespoon butter

1. Preheat the oven to 400°F. Place the **fish fillet** in a buttered 8"x 8"x 2" baking dish. If the fillet is very thin, fold it in half.

2. In a small bowl, combine the **tomatoes, onion, green pepper, tarragon,** and **salt.** Sprinkle the mixture over the fish, then dot with the **butter.**

3. Bake, uncovered, for 15 minutes or longer, depending on the thickness of the fish. When the fish flakes easily when tested with a fork, it is done. Serve with rice and Peas with Watercress Butter Sauce, page 208.

Sausage Fried Rice 🐷

Preparation: **10 minutes** Cooking: **20 minutes**   Calories: **860**

4 ounces mild or hot sausage
meat

1/3 cup uncooked rice

1 small yellow onion, peeled
and finely chopped

4 medium-size mushrooms,
thinly sliced

1/2 clove garlic, peeled and
minced

2 small fresh tomatoes,
peeled and chopped, or
1 can (8 ounces) tomatoes,
chopped, with their juice

1/4 cup water

1/2 teaspoon salt

1/8 teaspoon black pepper

1/8 teaspoon liquid hot red
pepper seasoning

1 tablespoon chopped parsley

To complete the meal, serve this with a green salad, which you can prepare while the sausage and rice are cooking.

1. Cook the **sausage meat,** uncovered, in a heavy 8-inch skillet over moderate heat for 3 minutes, stirring occasionally. Add the **rice, onion,** and **mushrooms,** and cook for 3 minutes, stirring frequently.

2. Add the **garlic, tomatoes, water, salt,** and **pepper.** Cover, and simmer for 20 minutes, or until the rice is tender. Stir in the **red pepper seasoning** and **parsley,** and serve.

Macaroni with Bacon, Tomato, and Sweet Pepper 🐷

Preparation and cooking: **17 minutes**   Calories: **1040**

4 ounces elbow macaroni

3 slices bacon, cut into 1-inch strips

3 green onions, trimmed and cut into 1/2-inch slices

1 small sweet green pepper, cored, seeded, and chopped

3 medium-size tomatoes, peeled and chopped

2 tablespoons chopped parsley

Pinch dried basil, crumbled

1/8 teaspoon salt

1/8 teaspoon black pepper

1/4 cup grated Parmesan cheese

Prepare the onions, green pepper, tomatoes, and parsley before you start the recipe. If the sauce is done before the macaroni, keep the sauce warm over very low heat.

1. Cook the **macaroni** according to package directions. Meanwhile, cook the **bacon** in a 10-inch skillet over moderately high heat for 3 minutes, or until almost crisp. Pour off all but 2 tablespoons of the drippings. Add the **green onions** and **green pepper,** and cook for 2 minutes. Add the **tomatoes, parsley, basil, salt,** and **black pepper,** and cook for 3 more minutes. Remove from the heat and set aside.

2. When the macaroni is done, drain it thoroughly in a colander and add it to the skillet with the bacon and vegetables. Toss to mix over low heat. Add the **cheese,** and toss again.

Green Grapes in Snow 🐷 ▷

Preparation: **4 minutes**   Calories: **170**

1/3 cup plain yogurt or sour cream

1 tablespoon confectioners' sugar

1 teaspoon grated orange rind

1 cup seedless green grapes

Fresh mint sprigs (optional)

Combine the **yogurt, sugar,** and **orange rind.** Mound the **grapes** in an individual serving bowl, and spoon the yogurt mixture over the grapes. Garnish with the **mint sprigs** if used.

Butterscotch Peach Crisp 🐷

Preparation: **5 minutes**   Cooking: **15 minutes**   Calories: **365**

1 large ripe peach, peeled, halved, pitted, and sliced

2 tablespoons firmly packed light or dark brown sugar

1 tablespoon all-purpose flour

1/8 teaspoon ground cinnamon

A few grains ground nutmeg

2 tablespoons butter or margarine

1. Preheat the oven to 350°F. Place the sliced **peach** in a buttered individual baking dish.

2. In a small bowl, combine the **sugar, flour, cinnamon,** and **nutmeg.** Cut in the **butter** with a fork until the mixture resembles coarse meal. Sprinkle over the peach slices, and bake, uncovered, for 15 minutes.

> **Tip:** *This dish may be baked in a toaster oven.*

BREAKFAST

Since breakfast sets the pace for the day, it should be good. If you are tired of cereal or ham and eggs, vary your breakfasts with some of the recipes in this section. Make your own nutritious granola, try one of the 4 egg recipes, or branch out with a spectacular Giant Pancake, Grandma's French Toast, or Ginger Waffles, or add a fresh fruit dish. If you have to eat on the run, try one of the Seven Jiffy Breakfast Shakes. If these are not enough, you will find additional breakfast recipes in the Breads chapter, beginning on page 227.

Granola ⊙

Preparation: 5 minutes   Yield: **6¹/₂ cups**   Calories per ¹/₂ cup: **270**

2 cups uncooked oatmeal

1 cup wheat germ

1 cup bran or bran cereal

1 cup raisins

1 cup diced dried fruit, such as apricots, apples, prunes, figs, or a mixture

¹/₂ cup chopped nuts, such as walnuts, pecans, cashews, hazelnuts, or almonds

¹/₂ cup sunflower seeds

¹/₄ cup sesame seeds

¹/₄ cup flaked coconut

Make your own granola, and enjoy a fast and nutritious breakfast. All the ingredients should be available in your local supermarket.

Combine all the ingredients and store in an airtight container in the refrigerator. (It will keep for at least 2 weeks.) Serve with milk and, if desired, sugar or honey.

Tip: If you like, you can cook the granola. For each serving, bring ³/₄ cup of water to a boil, add ¹/₂ cup of granola and a pinch of salt, and cook, uncovered, over moderate heat for 5 minutes. Turn off the heat, cover, and let the granola stand for 3 minutes. Serve with butter and brown sugar or honey.

Apples in Brown Sugar Sauce 🐷 ◑

Preparation: 5 minutes   Cooking: **7 minutes**   Serves **4**   Calories per serving: **205**

4 tablespoons (¹/₂ stick) butter or margarine

4 medium-size tart apples, cored, peeled, and cut into ¹/₄-inch slices

2 tablespoons firmly packed light or dark brown sugar

¹/₄ teaspoon ground nutmeg

¹/₄ cup apple juice

These glazed apples go perfectly with ham and eggs or with pancakes or waffles. If you prefer, substitute firm pears for the apples.

1. Melt the **butter** in a heavy 9- or 10-inch skillet over moderate heat. Add the **apples,** and cook, stirring frequently, for 5 minutes.

2. Sprinkle the apples with the **sugar, nutmeg,** and **apple juice.** Continue to cook, shaking the pan, until the sugar melts and the mixture comes to a boil.

Tip: This recipe can be halved, or leftovers can be refrigerated and reheated over low heat.

BREAKFAST

Baked Bananas 🐷 ◑

Preparation: **3 minutes**   Cooking: **15 minutes**   Serves **4**   Calories per serving: **160**

4 medium-size bananas, peeled and halved lengthwise

1 tablespoon lemon juice

2 tablespoons butter or margarine, melted

2 tablespoons firmly packed light or dark brown sugar

Preheat the oven to 350°F. Arrange the **bananas** in 1 layer in a buttered 9"x 9"x 2" baking dish. Sprinkle with the **lemon juice,** and brush with the **butter,** then sprinkle with the **sugar.** Bake, uncovered, for 15 minutes, turning the bananas once about halfway through the cooking.

> **Tip:** *This recipe can be halved.*

Peach Ambrosia ◎ ◑

Preparation: **7 minutes**   Serves **4**   Calories per serving: **160**

1 medium-size grapefruit

2 medium-size peaches

1 can (8 ounces) unsweetened pineapple chunks, drained

1/2 cup seedless green grapes

1 tablespoon lemon juice

1/4 cup flaked coconut

1/4 cup sour cream or plain yogurt

2 tablespoons chopped toasted almonds

Commonly thought of as a side dish or dessert, ambrosia makes a nutritious, appetizing breakfast. Allow time to chill the ambrosia after assembling it, or start with cold ingredients.

1. Peel and section the **grapefruit,** and remove all the white pith. Peel and slice the **peaches,** and remove the pits.

2. In a mixing bowl, gently mix together the grapefruit sections, peaches, **pineapple, grapes, lemon juice, coconut,** and **sour cream.** Just before serving, sprinkle the fruit and sour cream mixture with the **almonds.**

> **Tip:** *This recipe can be halved, doubled, or made in any amount desired.*

Egg in a Hole 🐷 ◎ ◑

Preparation: **6 minutes**   Cooking: **4 minutes**   Serves **4**   Calories per serving: **240**

Cook your egg and toast together for a breakfast treat. You can substitute whole wheat, cinnamon-raisin, or pumpernickel for the white bread.

4 slices white bread

4 tablespoons (1/2 stick) butter or margarine

4 eggs

1/4 teaspoon salt

1/8 teaspoon black pepper

> **Tip:** *This recipe can be reduced proportionally to serve 1, 2, or 3.*

1. Using a 2½-inch round cookie cutter or the rim of a glass, cut a hole into the center of each slice of **bread.** Melt 2 tablespoons of the **butter** in a heavy 12- or 14-inch skillet over moderately high heat. Add the bread (including the cut-out centers) and cook, uncovered, until browned lightly—about 3 minutes.

2. Turn the bread over, add the remaining 2 tablespoons of butter, and reduce the heat to moderately low. Break an **egg** into each hole, and season with the **salt** and **pepper.** Cover, and cook until the eggs are set—about 4 minutes. Serve with the cut-out toast centers on the side.

Eggs in Sausage Rings ⏀

Preparation: **5 minutes**   Cooking: **8 minutes**   Serves **4**   Calories per serving: **595**

Here is a novel way of cooking sausage and eggs that makes an attractive dish you can serve for lunch or supper as well as breakfast. Try it with potatoes and Baked Stuffed Tomatoes, page 81.

1 pound bulk pork sausage meat, cut into 4 equal pieces and flattened slightly

4 eggs

1 tablespoon chopped fresh or freeze-dried chives

⅛ teaspoon black pepper

> **Tips: 1.** *If you do not have a cookie cutter, use the rim of a glass.* **2.** *This recipe can be halved or doubled.*

1. Place the pieces of **sausage meat** 4 inches apart on a sheet of wax paper. Cover with a second sheet of wax paper and, using a rolling pin, roll the meat out into circles about 4 inches in diameter. They will be about ⅜ inch thick.

2. Remove the top sheet of wax paper. Using a 2½-inch round cookie cutter, cut a hole in the center of each patty, and remove the center circles. Place the sausage rings and the circles in a 10- or 12-inch skillet.

3. Turn the heat to moderately high and cook the sausage, uncovered, for 3 minutes. Flip the sausage rings and circles with a pancake turner, then break an **egg** into the center of each ring. Sprinkle with the **chives** and **pepper**.

4. Cook, uncovered, for 5 to 8 minutes, depending on how firm you want the eggs to be. Top with the sausage circles and serve.

Quick Eggs Benedict ⏀

Preparation: **15 minutes**   Cooking: **5 minutes**   Serves **4**   Calories per serving: **870**

Eggs Benedict is a popular dish for company breakfast or brunch. Try this quick, simple version using a foolproof mock hollandaise sauce.

6 tablespoons (¾ stick) butter or margarine

4 thin slices cooked ham

2 English muffins, split

1 quart water

2 tablespoons cider vinegar

½ teaspoon salt

4 eggs

2 tablespoons lemon juice

1¼ cups mayonnaise

> **Tip:** *You can halve this recipe, or you may want to allow 2 eggs per serving.*

1. Melt 1 tablespoon of the **butter** in a heavy 9-inch skillet over moderate heat. Add the **ham,** and cook, uncovered, for 1 minute on each side, or until lightly browned. Meanwhile, toast the **muffins** and butter them with 1 tablespoon of the butter. Arrange the muffins on serving plates and top with the ham. Set aside and keep warm.

2. Combine the **water, vinegar,** and **salt** in a 9-inch skillet, and bring to a boil, then reduce the heat until the water simmers. Break the **eggs** one at a time into a saucer and carefully slide each egg into the water. Cook, uncovered, until the eggs are done as you like them—3 to 5 minutes. Remove the eggs with a slotted spoon, let them drain, then place them on the muffins.

3. While the eggs cook, melt the remaining butter in a 1-quart saucepan over low heat. Gradually beat in the **lemon juice** and **mayonnaise** with a wire whisk. Continue to beat for 2 minutes. Remove from the heat and spoon over the eggs.

Spanish Scrambled Eggs ◑

Preparation: **8 minutes**   Cooking: **6 minutes**   Serves **4**   Calories per serving: **270**

Spice up scrambled eggs for a change. You can add more chilies, if you like, or you can leave them out completely. To save time, chop the pimientos, chilies, green onions, and tomato while the bacon is cooking.

6 slices bacon, cut into 1-inch strips

6 eggs, lightly beaten

1 jar (2 ounces) pimientos, drained and chopped

1 or 2 canned whole green chilies, rinsed, seeded, and chopped

2 tablespoons butter or margarine

1 bunch (6 to 8) green onions, trimmed and finely chopped

1 large tomato, peeled and chopped

1. Cook the **bacon** in an 8-inch skillet over moderately high heat for 5 minutes, or until crisp. Using a slotted spoon, remove the bacon from the skillet and drain on paper toweling. Discard the drippings.

2. In a small bowl, combine the **eggs, pimientos,** and **chilies,** and set aside.

3. Melt the **butter** in the skillet over moderate heat. Add the **green onions** and **tomato,** and cook, uncovered, for 3 minutes, or until the green onions are tender.

4. Add the egg mixture and continue to cook, stirring, for 3 to 4 minutes, or until the eggs are firm but still moist. Spoon onto a serving platter and crumble the bacon over the top.

> *Tips: **1.** This recipe can be halved. **2.** As a variation, omit the bacon and add 1/4 pound of pork sausage to the onions to brown. **3.** Instead of scrambling the eggs, let them set into a pancake; when it has browned on the bottom, cut into wedges and serve.*

Blintz Pancakes 🐷 ◑

Preparation: **5 minutes**   Cooking: **24 minutes**   Serves **4**   Calories per serving: **395**

Blintzes are pancakes that are usually stuffed with soft cheese and topped with sour cream. In this variation, the cheese and sour cream are added to the batter.

1 cup unsifted all-purpose flour

1 tablespoon sugar

1/2 teaspoon salt

1 cup sour cream or plain yogurt

1 cup large-curd cottage cheese

4 eggs, lightly beaten

1 tablespoon vegetable oil

1. Mix the **flour, sugar,** and **salt** together in a mixing bowl. Add the **sour cream, cottage cheese,** and **eggs.** Fold the ingredients together until the flour is barely moistened.

2. Heat the **oil** in a heavy 12-inch skillet over moderate heat. Drop enough batter into the skillet to form 4 pancakes—about 1/4 cup of batter per pancake. Cook, uncovered, for 3 or 4 minutes, until browned on the bottom, then turn the pancakes and cook for another 3 or 4 minutes.

3. Remove the pancakes to a platter and set, uncovered, in a keep-warm (250°F) oven, while you make 3 more batches of pancakes in the same way. Add more oil to the skillet if necessary.

> *Tips: **1.** You can cut the cooking time in half if you use 2 skillets. **2.** Making these pancakes with plain yogurt instead of sour cream reduces the calories per serving to 305. **3.** This recipe can be halved.*

Giant Pancake 🐷

Preparation: **5 minutes**   Cooking: **16 minutes**   Serves **4**   Calories per serving: **255**

This pancake serves 4, but after you try it, you may want to double the recipe to serve the same 4. If you do, use 2 skillets, and put the second one into the oven as you take out and serve the first. If you do not have a skillet with a heatproof handle, melt the butter in a small saucepan and pour into a 13"x 9"x 2" baking dish; then pour in the batter and bake as described.

2 eggs

½ cup unsifted all-purpose flour

½ cup milk

¼ teaspoon ground nutmeg

5 tablespoons butter or margarine, cut into small pieces

2 tablespoons confectioners' sugar

2 tablespoons lemon juice

1. Preheat the oven to 425°F. In a mixing bowl, beat the **eggs** lightly with a rotary beater, then beat in the **flour, milk,** and **nutmeg.**

2. Melt the **butter** over moderate heat in a heavy 12-inch skillet with a heatproof handle. When the butter is hot, immediately pour in all the batter. Bake for 15 to 20 minutes, or until golden brown and puffed.

3. Sift the **sugar** over the pancake and return it to the oven for 1 or 2 minutes. Remove the pancake from the oven and sprinkle it with the **lemon juice.** Cut into wedges, and serve with fruit syrup, preserves, honey, or maple syrup.

Tips: 1. The pancake will puff while baking, but when taken from the oven it will fall, resembling a large crêpe. 2. As a variation, after heating the butter, add 1 apple that has been cored, peeled, and sliced tissue thin, and cook, uncovered, for 1 minute. Spread the apple slices out to cover the bottom of the pan, then pour the batter over the apples and bake for 15 minutes. Eliminate the confectioners' sugar and lemon juice, but sprinkle the finished pancake with a mixture of 2 tablespoons of granulated sugar and 1½ teaspoons of ground cinnamon.

Grandma's French Toast 🐷 🍳

Preparation: **15 minutes**   Cooking: **8 minutes**   Serves **4**   Calories per serving: **425**

Use up day-old bread and give the family a treat at the same time.

1 cup milk

2 tablespoons sugar

1 teaspoon vanilla extract

½ teaspoon grated lemon rind

¼ teaspoon ground nutmeg

8 slices day-old French bread, cut ¾ inch thick

1 tablespoon butter or margarine

1 tablespoon vegetable oil

4 eggs

Pinch salt

1. In a large bowl, combine the **milk, sugar, vanilla, lemon rind,** and **nutmeg.** Soak the **bread** in the mixture for 10 minutes, or until all the mixture is absorbed.

2. Meanwhile, heat the **butter** with the **oil** in a heavy 12- or 14-inch skillet over moderately high heat. Beat the **eggs** with the **salt.**

3. Dip each slice of bread into the beaten eggs, then place in the skillet and cook, uncovered, for 4 minutes on each side, or until golden brown.

Tips: 1. This recipe can be halved. 2. You can use sliced hard rolls, raisin bread, or firm-textured white bread instead of the French bread. (The average supermarket sliced white bread should not be used, as it may fall apart.) If you use raisin bread, substitute cinnamon for the nutmeg. 3. If the bread will not fit into the skillet in 1 batch, cook in 2 batches, adding another tablespoon each of butter and oil to the pan for the second batch.

BREAKFAST

Ginger Waffles 🐷 ◑

Preparation: **5 minutes**   Cooking: **20 minutes**   Serves **4**   Calories per serving: **390**

1½ **cups unsifted all-purpose flour**

1½ **teaspoons baking powder**

½ **teaspoon baking soda**

1 **teaspoon ground ginger**

1 **teaspoon ground cinnamon**

¼ **teaspoon ground nutmeg**

1 **cup buttermilk**

2 **eggs, lightly beaten**

¼ **cup melted butter or margarine**

1 **tablespoon molasses**

¼ **cup firmly packed dark brown sugar**

1. In a mixing bowl, combine the **flour, baking powder, baking soda, ginger, cinnamon,** and **nutmeg.** Stir in the **buttermilk, eggs, butter, molasses,** and **brown sugar,** and mix until smooth.

2. Cook the waffles in a waffle iron according to manufacturer's directions. You should get 4 large (8″x 8″) waffles, and they should take about 5 minutes each to cook.

> **Tips: 1.** *This recipe can be halved.* **2.** *You can use this batter to make large pancakes instead of waffles. Simply spoon one quarter of the batter at a time into a buttered 12-inch skillet and cook over moderate heat for 4 minutes on each side, or until browned.*

Seven Jiffy Breakfast Shakes 🐷 ▷

For an extra quick yet healthful breakfast, try one of these jiffy shakes. None will take you more than 3 minutes to prepare, and no cooking is required. Each shake makes one tall glassful—enough to serve 1 person generously.

General Directions

To make any of the shakes described below, put all the ingredients into the jar of an electric blender or a mixing bowl. If you are using a blender, blend for 1 minute at high speed. If you are not using a blender, beat with an electric mixer until all the ingredients are well mixed and the shake is smooth.

Banananog

1 egg, ½ cup cold milk, 1 tablespoon firmly packed light or dark brown sugar, 2 teaspoons instant coffee, and 1 ripe banana, sliced. 295 calories.

Cheese Zip

1 cup chilled tomato juice, ¼ cup large- or small-curd cottage cheese, 1 egg, a pinch each black pepper and celery salt, and a dash Worcestershire sauce. 190 calories.

Maple Graham Shake

1 cup cold milk, 1 tablespoon maple syrup, and 4 graham crackers, crumbled, or ¼ cup graham cracker crumbs. 320 calories.

Golden Flip

¾ cup chilled apricot nectar, ¼ cup chilled pineapple juice, ½ cup plain yogurt, 1 egg, and 1 tablespoon sugar. 335 calories.

Strawberry Cream

1 cup cold milk, 1 egg, 1 tablespoon sugar, and 6 strawberries, sliced. Or you can use ⅓ package frozen sliced strawberries and omit the sugar. 305 calories.

Low-Calorie Frosted Coffee

1 cup cold skim milk, 1 teaspoon instant coffee, 1 teaspoon vanilla extract, 1 teaspoon sugar, and a pinch ground cinnamon. 150 calories.

Blueberry Swirl

½ cup blueberries, ½ cup chilled orange juice, ½ cup chilled buttermilk or plain yogurt, 1 egg, and 1 tablespoon sugar. 265 calories.

BREAKFAST

SANDWICHES AND BROWN BAG LUNCHES

Don't fall into the sandwich doldrums—a BLT today and a ham on rye tomorrow—but break that routine with the recipes in this section. To save time, keep a few hard-cooked eggs on hand for the recipes that call for them. All the recipes can be halved or doubled.

High-Protein Vegetarian Salad 🐷 ▷ ◫

Preparation: 8 minutes   Serves **4**   Calories per serving: **445**

1/4 cup plain yogurt

3 tablespoons vegetable oil

1/8 teaspoon salt

1/4 teaspoon ground cumin

1 can (20 ounces) chick peas, rinsed and drained

2 medium-size sweet green or red peppers, cored, seeded, and chopped

1 small yellow onion, peeled and chopped

1/4 cup sunflower seeds

Put this salad in plastic containers and pack, along with fresh fruit, for a school or office lunch.

In a mixing bowl, combine the **yogurt, oil, salt, and cumin.** Add the **chick peas, peppers, onion,** and **sunflower seeds,** and toss to mix. Taste for seasoning, and add more salt and cumin if desired.

> *Tips: 1. Use chopped walnuts in place of the sunflower seeds if you like. 2. You can substitute sour cream for the yogurt, but in so doing you will increase the number of calories per serving to 465.*

Chinese Chicken Salad ◫

Preparation and cooking: **20 minutes**   Serves **6**   Calories per serving: **165**

Pack this salad in plastic containers for an office or school lunch.

3 whole chicken breasts (6 halves), skinned and boned

1/2 teaspoon salt

1 can (8 ounces) pineapple, drained and coarsely chopped

2 stalks celery, chopped

2 green onions, trimmed and finely chopped

1 tablespoon vegetable oil

2 tablespoons soy sauce

2 teaspoons white wine vinegar

1. Place the **chicken breasts** in a 3-quart saucepan with just enough water to cover. Add the **salt.** Bring to a boil, lower the heat, cover, and simmer about 12 minutes, or until the chicken is no longer pink when pierced with a fork. Remove the chicken to a platter to cool. Save the chicken broth for another use.

2. Meanwhile, in a large mixing bowl, combine the **pineapple, celery, onions, oil, soy sauce,** and **vinegar.** Set the mixture aside.

3. When the chicken is cool enough to handle (in about 5 minutes), cut it into 3/4-inch cubes. Add the cubed chicken to the pineapple mixture, and toss to mix thoroughly.

Liverwurst Salad Sandwiches ⏺

Preparation: **12 minutes**   Serves **4**   Calories per serving: **465**

1/2 **pound liverwurst, cut into** 1/2-**inch cubes**

3 **tablespoons drained sweet pickle relish**

3 **tablespoons finely chopped yellow onion**

2 **teaspoons Dijon or prepared spicy brown mustard**

2 **tablespoons mayonnaise**

8 **slices rye or pumpernickel bread**

In a mixing bowl, combine the **liverwurst, relish, onion, mustard,** and **mayonnaise**. Taste for seasoning, and add more relish, onion, or mustard if desired. Divide the liverwurst mixture among 4 slices of the **bread,** and top with the remaining bread.

> **Tips: 1.** Add tomato slices and lettuce to the sandwiches if you wish. **2.** You can substitute chopped cooked ham for the liverwurst.

Grilled Ham Salad Sandwiches ⏺

Preparation: **22 minutes**   Cooking: **8 minutes**   Serves **4**   Calories per serving: **465**

1 **cup finely chopped or ground cooked ham**

2 **hard-cooked eggs, chopped**

1 **teaspoon lemon juice**

1 **teaspoon prepared spicy brown mustard**

1/4 **teaspoon Worcestershire sauce**

1/2 **teaspoon salt**

2 **tablespoons finely chopped sweet green pepper**

4 **tablespoons mayonnaise**

2 **tablespoons finely chopped sour or dill pickle (optional)**

8 **slices bread**

1 **raw egg**

1/4 **cup milk**

4 **tablespoons (**1/2 **stick) butter or margarine**

If you like, serve this as a salad on lettuce leaves instead of bread, and omit Steps 2 and 3. The preparation time includes 15 minutes for hard-cooking the eggs.

1. In a mixing bowl, combine the **ham, hard-cooked eggs, lemon juice, mustard, Worcestershire sauce, salt, green pepper,** and **mayonnaise,** and the **pickle** if used. Spread the ham mixture on 4 slices of the **bread,** and top with the remaining bread.

2. In a shallow bowl or pie plate, beat together the **raw egg** and **milk.** Carefully holding each sandwich to keep the filling intact, dip it quickly on each side into the egg and milk mixture.

3. Melt the **butter** in a heavy 12-inch skillet over moderate heat. Place the sandwiches in the skillet, and cook, uncovered, for 4 or 5 minutes on each side, or until golden brown.

> **Tips: 1.** The ham mixture can be made ahead and refrigerated for 1 or 2 days. **2.** You can substitute leftover cooked pork, beef, lamb, or chicken for the ham.

Open-Face Hot Sausage Sandwiches ⊕

Preparation: **15 minutes**   Cooking: **4 minutes**   Serves **4**   Calories per serving: **555**

Sausage and sauerkraut sandwiches as filling as these should satisfy the heartiest appetites.

12 breakfast sausage links

4 slices rye or pumpernickel bread

3 tablespoons butter or margarine, softened

1 teaspoon prepared spicy brown mustard

1 medium-size tart apple, peeled

1 can (8 ounces) sauerkraut, drained

1 cup shredded Swiss cheese (about 4 ounces)

1. Cook the **sausages** in a 10-inch skillet according to package directions. Meanwhile, toast the **bread,** spread it with the **butter,** then the **mustard,** and set aside. Preheat the broiler.

2. Using the coarsest side of a four-sided grater, shred the **apple** into a small bowl, add the **sauerkraut,** and mix. Place ¼ of the mixture on each slice of toast.

3. Split each sausage link in half lengthwise and place 3 split sausages on each sandwich. Top with the **cheese,** and broil 4 inches from the heat for 4 minutes, or until the cheese melts.

> **Tips: 1.** *Serve the sauerkraut and apple mixture on the side if you wish.* **2.** *You can substitute 4 bratwurst or 4 knockwurst for the breakfast sausage.*

Sardine Stacks ⊕

Preparation: **22 minutes**   Serves **6**   Calories per serving: **450**

¾ cup mayonnaise

2 tablespoons lemon juice

2 tablespoons chili sauce or ketchup

12 slices rye, pumpernickel, or whole wheat bread

6 hard-cooked eggs, sliced

2 cans (4½ to 5 ounces each) skinless, boneless sardines, drained

12 lettuce leaves

If you have hard-cooked eggs in the refrigerator, you can eliminate 15 minutes of the preparation time.

In a small mixing bowl, combine the **mayonnaise, lemon juice,** and **chili sauce.** Spread this mixture on 6 slices of the **bread,** then evenly distribute the **eggs, sardines,** and **lettuce leaves** in layers over the slices. Top with the remaining bread.

Tuna Melt ◑

Preparation: **12 minutes**   Cooking: **3 minutes**   Serves **4**   Calories per serving: **665**

4 English muffins, split, or 8 slices whole wheat bread

2 cans (6½ or 7 ounces each) tuna, drained and flaked

¼ cup finely chopped sweet green pepper

1 tablespoon grated yellow onion

6 tablespoons mayonnaise

1 teaspoon Dijon or prepared spicy brown mustard

4 teaspoons Worcestershire sauce

¼ teaspoon black pepper

8 ounces extra sharp Cheddar cheese, thinly sliced

1 pimiento, cut into 8 strips (optional)

Melted cheese on tuna salad may seem unusual, but the combination is a good one.

1. Preheat the broiler. Toast the **muffins,** and set aside.

2. Meanwhile, in a mixing bowl, combine the **tuna, green pepper, onion, mayonnaise, mustard, Worcestershire sauce,** and **black pepper.** Spread the tuna mixture on the 8 muffin halves, and top with the **cheese** slices.

3. Broil 4 inches from the heat for 3 minutes, or until the cheese melts and browns lightly. Top each half with a **pimiento** strip if desired. Serve with a lettuce and tomato salad.

> *Tips: 1. The tuna mixture can be made a day ahead, but do not spread it on the muffins until just before broiling. 2. Cut each muffin into 8 wedges and serve as hors d'oeuvres.*

Scrambled Egg and Onion Sandwiches 🐷 ▷ ◑

Preparation: **6 minutes**   Cooking: **2 minutes**   Serves **4**   Calories per serving: **400**

Vary a plain scrambled egg sandwich with mayonnaise and a slice of Bermuda onion.

8 slices white, whole wheat, or rye bread

6 tablespoons mayonnaise

2 tablespoons butter or margarine

4 eggs

½ teaspoon salt

¼ teaspoon black pepper

4 very thin slices Bermuda or Spanish onion

1. Toast the **bread,** let it cool, then spread with the **mayonnaise,** and set aside.

2. Melt the **butter** in a 10-inch skillet over moderate heat. In a small bowl, beat the **eggs** with the **salt** and **pepper,** and add them to the skillet. Scramble for 2 to 4 minutes, to the desired consistency.

3. Divide the scrambled eggs among 4 slices of the toast. Top each with a slice of **onion** and the remaining toast.

> *Tips: 1. Spread the toast with butter or margarine instead of the mayonnaise. 2. If you like, before scrambling the eggs, cook the onion slices in 2 tablespoons of butter or margarine in a small skillet for 5 minutes and eliminate the mayonnaise. 3. Omit the onion and add a thin slice of tomato, or use both onion and tomato.*

Deviled Egg Sandwiches 🐷 ◑

Preparation: **27 minutes**   Serves **4**   Calories per serving: **260**

1/4 cup drained sweet pickle relish

6 hard-cooked eggs, chopped

2 tablespoons minced yellow onion

1 teaspoon Dijon or prepared spicy brown mustard

3 tablespoons milk

1/2 teaspoon salt

1/4 teaspoon black pepper

8 slices plain or toasted bread

If a refrigerator or cool storage place is available, you can pack these sandwiches for a brown bag lunch. Cut the preparation time by 15 minutes if you have hard-cooked eggs on hand.

In a mixing bowl, combine the **relish, eggs, onion, mustard, milk, salt,** and **pepper.** Spread the egg mixture on 4 slices of the **bread.** Top with the remaining bread.

Creole Cheese Sandwiches ◑

Preparation: **8 minutes**   Cooking: **8 minutes**   Serves **4**   Calories per serving: **320**

4 slices bacon, cut into 1-inch strips

1 1/4 cups shredded Muenster or Swiss cheese (about 5 ounces)

1/2 cup chopped sweet green pepper

1/4 cup chili sauce or ketchup

1/2 teaspoon Worcestershire sauce

8 slices bread

1. Preheat the oven to 425°F. Cook the **bacon** in a heavy 10-inch skillet over moderately high heat for 5 minutes, or until crisp. Using a slotted spoon, remove the bacon to paper toweling to drain.

2. In a mixing bowl, combine the **cheese, green pepper, chili sauce, Worcestershire sauce,** and bacon. Spread the mixture on 4 slices of the **bread,** and top with the remaining bread. Place the sandwiches on a baking sheet and bake, uncovered, for 8 minutes.

Chili-Cheddar Sandwiches 🐷 ▷ ◑

Preparation: **10 minutes**   Serves **4**   Calories per serving: **620**

3 cups shredded sharp Cheddar cheese (about 3/4 pound)

6 tablespoons (3/4 stick) butter or margarine, softened

1 can (4 ounces) whole green chilies, rinsed, seeded, and chopped

1 small yellow onion, peeled and grated

1/2 teaspoon ground cumin

8 slices whole wheat bread

Moderately hot and decidedly tasty, these sandwiches will add zest to a brown bag lunch.

In a mixing bowl, combine the **cheese** and **butter,** then mix in the **chilies, onion,** and **cumin.** Spread the cheese mixture on 4 slices of the **bread,** and top with the remaining bread.

> *Tips:* **1.** *Add tomato and lettuce to each sandwich if you like.* **2.** *The cheese mixture can be made ahead; it will keep for a week in the refrigerator.*

Apple–Cream Cheese Sandwiches 🐷 ▷ ⬭

Preparation: **10 minutes**   Serves **4**   Calories per serving: **255**

1 medium-size tart apple, cored and cut into ¼-inch slices

1 tablespoon lemon juice

4 ounces cream cheese, softened

4 teaspoons honey

8 slices plain or toasted pumpernickel or raisin bread

Fruit sandwiches? Yes, and they are nutritious and fresh tasting. Pack these sandwiches into a brown bag lunch if you have access to a refrigerator or cool storage space.

1. In a mixing bowl, toss the **apple** slices with the **lemon juice,** and set aside.

2. Mix the **cream cheese** with the **honey** in a small bowl, and spread the mixture on 4 slices of the **bread.** Drain the apples, and place them on the cream cheese. Top with the remaining bread.

Cranberry–Cream Cheese Sandwiches 🐷 ▷ ⬭

Preparation: **8 minutes**   Serves **4**   Calories per serving: **350**

8 slices pumpernickel, whole wheat, or raisin bread

4 ounces cream cheese, softened

¼ cup chopped walnuts or pecans

1 can (8 ounces) whole or jellied cranberry sauce

Pack these sandwiches into your lunch box if you have a cool place to keep them.

Spread the **bread** with the **cream cheese.** Top 4 of the slices with the **walnuts** and **cranberry sauce** and the remaining bread.

> **Tips: 1.** For a heartier sandwich, omit the nuts and add a slice of turkey, chicken, ham, or crisp bacon to each sandwich. **2.** Add lettuce to each sandwich if you like. **3.** In place of the cranberry sauce, use 1 tablespoon apricot preserves or orange marmalade for each sandwich.

West Coast Hero ⬭

Preparation: **15 minutes**   Serves **4**   Calories per portion: **655**

3 medium-size carrots, peeled and shredded (about 1 cup)

½ cup mayonnaise

½ teaspoon salt

4 teaspoons lemon juice

8 ounces alfalfa sprouts (optional)

1 large ripe avocado, peeled, halved lengthwise, and pitted

1 loaf Italian or French bread (about 18 inches long)

¼ pound thinly sliced cooked ham

8 ounces mozzarella or mild Cheddar cheese, thinly sliced

1. In a mixing bowl, combine the **carrots, mayonnaise, salt,** and 2 teaspoons of the **lemon juice,** and the **alfalfa sprouts** if used. Cut the **avocado** halves lengthwise into ¼-inch slices. In a small bowl, toss the slices with the remaining 2 teaspoons of lemon juice.

2. Cut the **bread** in half lengthwise and scoop out the center of the bottom half, leaving a shell 1 inch thick. Save the center for another use.

3. Place half the carrot mixture in the scooped-out half, and cover with the avocado slices, **ham,** and **cheese.** Top with the remaining carrot mixture and the other half of the bread. Cut into 4 portions.

Pizza Hero ⓓⓓ

Preparation: **10 minutes**   Cooking: **15 minutes**   Serves **4**   Calories per serving: **610**

2 tablespoons olive or vegetable oil

1 medium-size yellow onion, peeled and chopped

1 pound lean ground beef

2 cans (8 ounces each) tomato sauce

1/2 teaspoon dried oregano, crumbled

1/2 teaspoon dried basil, crumbled

1/4 teaspoon dried rosemary, crumbled

1/2 teaspoon salt

1/4 teaspoon black pepper

1 loaf Italian or French bread (about 18 inches long)

2 cups shredded mozzarella cheese (about 8 ounces)

1. Preheat the oven to 350°F. Heat the **oil** in a heavy 12-inch skillet over moderate heat for about 1 minute. Add the **onion** and **beef,** and cook, uncovered, stirring occasionally, for 5 minutes, or until the onion is soft and the beef has browned. Stir in the **tomato sauce, oregano, basil, rosemary, salt,** and **pepper.** Cook, uncovered, for 1 minute.

2. Cut the **bread** in half lengthwise and scoop out the center of each half, leaving a shell 1 inch thick. Save the center for another use.

3. Place half the beef mixture in each half loaf, then sprinkle with the **cheese.** Place on an ungreased baking sheet and bake, uncovered, for 15 minutes, or until the cheese melts. Cut into 4 portions and serve hot.

> *Tip:* You can substitute 1 jar (15 to 16 ounces) of spaghetti sauce for the tomato sauce.

Peanut Butter Sandwiches and Spreads ▷

Peanut butter goes well with many ingredients besides jelly. Try these interesting combinations.

BLT Sandwich with Peanut Butter

Mix 2 tablespoons of peanut butter with 1 teaspoon of prepared horseradish and 2 teaspoons of mayonnaise. Spread the mixture on 1 slice of toast and top with 2 slices of crisp bacon, a slice of tomato, lettuce, and a second slice of toast. 465 calories.

Cheese and Peanut Butter Sandwich

Preheat the broiler. Spread 1 slice of toast with 2 tablespoons of peanut butter and top with 2 slices of crisp bacon. Add a slice of tomato and a slice of sharp Cheddar cheese. Broil 3 inches from the heat for about 2 minutes, or until the cheese melts. 420 calories.

Ham and Peanut Butter Sandwich

Mix 2 tablespoons of peanut butter with 2 tablespoons of drained crushed pineapple and 1/4 teaspoon of grated orange rind. Spread the mixture on a slice of bread. Top with a slice of boiled ham and a second slice of bread. Spread the outside of the sandwich with soft butter or margarine, and cook, uncovered, in an 8-inch skillet over moderate heat for 2 minutes on each side, or until lightly browned. 585 calories.

Peanut Butter Spreads

Peanut butter spreads are a boon when you need quick snacks. Spread one of the following combinations on bread, toast, or crackers:

● Mix together 2 tablespoons each peanut butter, drained crushed pineapple, and shredded coconut. 40 calories per tablespoon.
● Mix together 2 tablespoons each peanut butter and mashed banana and a few drops lemon juice. 50 calories per tablespoon.
● Mix together 2 tablespoons each peanut butter and deviled ham, 1 tablespoon grated yellow onion, and 1 teaspoon mayonnaise. 80 calories per tablespoon.

BREADS

Did you know that with only a little extra time you can make pancakes, biscuits, corn bread, muffins, and even coffee cake from scratch rather than from a packaged mix? Follow the recipes on these pages, and you will find that homemade quick breads (breads that do not require a preliminary rising) are not only easy to make but far better tasting than breads made from packaged ingredients. Using the Magic Mix recipe, for example, you can get drop biscuits ready for the oven in less than 5 minutes; the use of heavy cream speeds preparation time. The other breads take no more than 15 minutes to assemble, while the cooking period is unattended baking time that leaves you free to prepare the rest of the meal.

Magic Mix

Preparation: **5 minutes**   Yield: **7 cups**   Calories per cup: **375**

Keep this mix on hand for making a quick batch of pancakes for breakfast or feather-light drop biscuits for dinner. (Follow the recipes given below.)

6 cups sifted all-purpose flour

2 tablespoons plus 1¹/₂ teaspoons baking powder

1 cup instant nonfat dry milk powder

2¹/₂ teaspoons salt

In a large mixing bowl, thoroughly combine the **flour, baking powder, dry milk,** and **salt.** Spoon the mixture into a 2-quart glass or plastic container. Cover tightly and store in the refrigerator. Magic Mix will keep for about a month.

Baking Powder Drop Biscuits:
Preheat the oven to 450°F. In a mixing bowl, stir 2 cups Magic Mix and 1¹/₄ cups heavy cream (or 1 cup heavy cream plus ¹/₄ cup milk) with a fork just enough to moisten the mix. The dough will be slightly sticky; do not overmix or the biscuits will be tough. Drop the dough by heaping tablespoons onto a lightly greased baking sheet, spacing the biscuits about 1 inch apart. Bake for 8 to 10 minutes, or until lightly browned.

To add a different accent to these biscuits, stir one of the following into the Magic Mix before pouring in the cream: 1. ¹/₂ to 1 teaspoon caraway seeds or crumbled dried oregano, thyme, or sage; 2. ¹/₃ cup shredded extra sharp Cheddar cheese or grated Parmesan cheese; 3. 3 slices crisp bacon, crumbled; 4. ¹/₄ cup chopped chives; 5. ¹/₄ to ¹/₂ teaspoon curry powder.

Pancakes: In a mixing bowl, beat 1 egg lightly with a fork, then add 1 cup Magic Mix, ³/₄ cup cold water, and 2 tablespoons melted butter or margarine or vegetable oil. Stir just enough to moisten the mix—the batter should be lumpy. Lightly grease a griddle or 12-inch skillet and heat it over moderate heat until a drop of water dances when sprinkled on it. Using about 3 tablespoons of batter for each pancake, pour the batter onto the griddle, allowing plenty of space between pancakes. Cook until bubbles form and then break on the tops of the pancakes, then turn and cook on the other side until golden. Serve with butter and syrup.

You may also want to try one of the following pancake variations: 1. Just before cooking, stir in ¹/₂ cup blueberries, washed and drained, or ¹/₂ cup chopped banana. 2. Stir ¹/₄ teaspoon each ground cinnamon and ground nutmeg into the dry ingredients, then just before cooking stir in 1 peeled, cored, and finely chopped tart apple. 3. Substitute unsifted buckwheat flour for ¹/₂ cup of the Magic Mix, and increase the milk to 1 cup. 4. Substitute unsifted whole wheat flour for ¹/₂ cup of the Magic Mix. 5. When cooking, before turning the pancakes, dot them with ¹/₂ cup crumbled cooked mild or hot sausage meat or thin slices of cooked sausage links.

Johnnycakes

Preparation: 5 minutes   Cooking: **8 minutes**   Yield: **12**   Calories each: **80**

Some authorities believe that this thin, flat bread was originally called journey cake because it was the staple of circuit riders as they preached the Gospel from settlement to settlement.

1 cup white cornmeal

1/2 teaspoon salt

2 teaspoons sugar (optional)

1 cup boiling water

1/4 cup milk

3 tablespoons vegetable oil

1. In a mixing bowl, combine the **cornmeal** and **salt,** and the **sugar** if used. Add the boiling **water,** mix well, then stir in the **milk.**

2. Heat the **oil** in a heavy 12-inch skillet over moderate heat. Drop in the batter by heaping tablespoons to form cakes about 3 inches in diameter. Cook, uncovered, for 4 or 5 minutes on each side, or until crisp and golden brown. Serve hot with butter and maple syrup.

Tip: This recipe can be halved.

Hush Puppies

Preparation: 10 minutes   Cooking: **12 minutes**   Yield: **24**   Calories each: **70**

These crisp cornmeal morsels supposedly got their name because they were often thrown to hunting dogs to keep them quiet. They go perfectly with fried fish, crab cakes, or other seafood.

1 cup yellow cornmeal

1 cup unsifted all-purpose flour

2 1/2 teaspoons salt

1/8 teaspoon black pepper

Pinch cayenne pepper

1 tablespoon baking powder

1 egg

About 1 cup water

1 medium-size yellow onion, peeled and finely chopped

About 1/2 cup vegetable oil

1. In a mixing bowl, combine the **cornmeal, flour, salt, black pepper, cayenne pepper,** and **baking powder.**

2. In a small bowl, beat the **egg** with 1/2 cup of the **water,** and stir it into the cornmeal mixture. Stir in the **onion** and just enough of the remaining water to make a thick batter. The batter should drop, not pour, from the spoon.

3. Pour enough **oil** into a heavy 12-inch skillet to measure about 1/4 inch deep. Heat until the oil is very hot—ripples should be clearly visible on the bottom of the skillet. Drop the batter by heaping tablespoons into the oil, and cook, uncovered, over moderately high heat for about 3 minutes on each side. Drain briefly on paper toweling, then place on an ovenproof platter in a keep-warm (250°F) oven while you cook the remaining batch of hush puppies in the same way. Serve hot.

Tip: This recipe can be halved.

Maritime Oatcakes 🐖 ◖◗

Preparation: **12 minutes**   Cooking: **15 minutes**   Yield: **24**   Calories each: **105**

Hailing from the Maritime Provinces of Canada, these crisp biscuits can be served in place of bread at dinner, with soup and a salad, or as a snack.

1¹/₂ cups unsifted all-purpose flour

¹/₂ teaspoon salt

¹/₂ teaspoon baking soda

1¹/₂ cups uncooked quick-cooking rolled oats

2 tablespoons sugar

¹/₂ cup vegetable shortening

4 tablespoons (¹/₂ stick) butter or margarine, cut into small pieces

3 to 4 tablespoons water

1. Preheat the oven to 350°F. In a mixing bowl, combine the **flour, salt,** and **baking soda,** then stir in the **oats** and **sugar.** Cut in the **shortening** and **butter** with a pastry blender or fork until the mixture resembles coarse meal. Mix in just enough **water** to make a firm but not dry dough.

2. Roll the dough into 1¹/₂-inch balls. Place the balls on ungreased baking sheets, pressing each ball with the heel of your hand to a thickness of about ¹/₄ inch. Bake for 15 to 20 minutes, or until lightly browned. Serve warm or at room temperature with butter.

> *Tip: This recipe can be halved, or leftover cakes can be stored in an airtight container.*

Buttermilk Corn Bread 🐖 ◖◗

Preparation: **5 minutes**   Cooking: **20 minutes**   Serves **8**   Calories per serving: **190**

Here is a basic corn bread that is quick and easy to make. If you like corn bread sweet, increase the amount of sugar to 1 tablespoon. If you prefer a spicier corn bread, prepare as directed, but add a pinch each of cayenne pepper and black pepper.

4 tablespoons (¹/₂ stick) butter or margarine

³/₄ cup unsifted all-purpose flour

1¹/₂ teaspoons baking powder

¹/₂ teaspoon baking soda

³/₄ teaspoon salt

1 teaspoon sugar

1 cup white or yellow cornmeal

1 cup buttermilk

2 eggs

1. Preheat the oven to 425°F. Melt the **butter** in a small saucepan over low heat and set aside to cool. In a mixing bowl, combine the **flour, baking powder, baking soda, salt,** and **sugar.** Stir in the **cornmeal.**

2. In a separate bowl, beat the **buttermilk** and **eggs** together until mixed. Add the melted butter, then pour the buttermilk mixture into the cornmeal and flour mixture. Stir just until the dry ingredients are moistened.

3. Spread the batter evenly in a greased 9"x 9"x 2" baking pan. Bake for 20 minutes, or until the center of the cornbread springs back when touched.

> *Tips: 1. This recipe can be halved. Divide the baking pan in half with aluminum foil. 2. You can substitute plain yogurt for the buttermilk. 3. Corn bread freezes well; reheat in a 350°F oven.*

High-Fiber Muffins ⓓ

Preparation: **10 minutes**   Cooking: **15 minutes**   Yield: **20**   Calories each: **130**

2 cups unsifted all-purpose flour

⅓ cup sugar

1 teaspoon salt

1 teaspoon baking soda

1½ cups uncooked quick-cooking rolled oats

1 cup whole bran cereal, bran, or wheat germ

½ cup raisins or chopped dried prunes or apricots

2 eggs, lightly beaten

1⅓ cups buttermilk

½ cup light molasses

These flavorful muffins are high in fiber, B vitamins, protein, and minerals. Serve them as a snack with peanut butter and a crisp apple.

1. Preheat the oven to 350°F. In a mixing bowl, combine the **flour, sugar, salt,** and **baking soda.** Stir in the **oats, bran cereal,** and **raisins.**

2. Combine the **eggs, buttermilk,** and **molasses.** Add them to the dry ingredients and stir just until the dry ingredients are moistened.

3. Spoon the batter into greased 2-inch muffin cups, filling each cup two-thirds full. Bake for 15 to 20 minutes, or until a toothpick inserted into a muffin comes out clean.

Tips: 1. This recipe can be halved. 2. Leftover muffins can be frozen and reheated in a 350°F oven.

The Queen's Muffins ⓓ

Preparation: **15 minutes**   Cooking: **15 minutes**   Yield: **16**   Calories each: **210**

During one of Queen Elizabeth II's visits to Canada, chefs across the country prepared these muffins for Her Majesty's afternoon tea. On many occasions, the press corps assigned to cover the royal visit ate the muffins so fast that it was necessary to reserve a few for the Queen.

1⅔ cups unsifted all-purpose flour

2½ teaspoons baking powder

½ teaspoon salt

½ cup (1 stick) plus 2 tablespoons butter or margarine, softened

½ cup sugar

2 eggs, lightly beaten

1¼ cups milk

¾ cup wheat germ

1 cup raisins, dried currants, or finely chopped dried apricots

1. Preheat the oven to 375°F. In a mixing bowl, combine the **flour, baking powder,** and **salt,** and set aside.

2. In a large bowl, beat the **butter** with a rotary hand or electric beater until light and fluffy. Gradually blend in the **sugar,** then the **eggs.** Beat well.

3. Alternately mix in a little of the flour mixture and a little of the **milk** until all have been added. Stir in the **wheat germ** and **raisins.**

4. Spoon the batter into greased 2-inch muffin cups, filling each cup two-thirds full. Bake for 15 to 20 minutes, or until a toothpick inserted into a muffin comes out clean.

Tips: 1. This recipe can be halved; use ⅓ cup of wheat germ. 2. Leftover muffins can be frozen and reheated in a 350°F oven.

Apple-Nut Muffins ⏀

Preparation: **15 minutes**   Cooking: **20 minutes**   Yield: **12**   Calories each: **195**

Sweet and rich, these muffins make a good snack. Butter them and serve warm with coffee or tea.

2 cups unsifted all-purpose flour

1½ teaspoons baking powder

1½ teaspoons salt

1 teaspoon ground cinnamon

⅓ cup plus 4 tablespoons sugar

1 medium-size apple, peeled, cored, and chopped into ¼-inch dice

½ cup chopped walnuts or pecans

1 cup sour cream

1 egg, lightly beaten

½ cup milk

1. Preheat the oven to 425°F. Sift together the **flour, baking powder, salt, cinnamon,** and ⅓ cup of the **sugar** into a mixing bowl. Stir in the **apple** and **walnuts.**

2. In a small bowl, blend ¾ cup of the **sour cream** with the **egg** and **milk.** Add the mixture to the dry ingredients and stir just until the dry ingredients are moistened.

3. Spoon the batter into greased 2-inch muffin cups, filling each cup two-thirds full. Drop 1 teaspoon of the remaining sour cream into the center of each muffin. Sprinkle the top of each muffin with 1 teaspoon of the remaining sugar. Bake for 20 to 25 minutes, or until a toothpick inserted into a muffin comes out clean.

Tips: 1. This recipe can be halved. Use the remaining ½ beaten egg in your next morning's scrambled eggs. 2. You can substitute 1 firm, ripe pear for the apple, or ¾ cup buttermilk or plain yogurt for ¾ cup of the sour cream. 3. Leftover muffins can be frozen and reheated in a 350°F oven.

Crumb Coffee Cake

Preparation: **12 minutes**   Cooking: **30 minutes**   Serves **8**   Calories per serving: **230**

For a special breakfast treat, bake this rich, tasty coffee cake. It smells as good as it tastes and is easy to make.

1¼ cups unsifted all-purpose flour

1 cup firmly packed light brown sugar

¼ teaspoon salt

4 tablespoons (½ stick) butter or margarine

½ teaspoon baking powder

¼ teaspoon baking soda

½ teaspoon ground cinnamon

1 egg, lightly beaten

½ cup buttermilk

½ cup raisins (optional)

1. Preheat the oven to 375°F. In a mixing bowl, combine the **flour, sugar,** and **salt.** Cut in the **butter** with a pastry blender or fork until the mixture resembles coarse meal. Reserve ½ cup of the mixture for the topping.

2. Stir the **baking powder, baking soda,** and **cinnamon** into the remaining mixture. In a small bowl, beat the **egg** and **buttermilk** together and add to the mixture. Stir just until the dry ingredients are moistened. Stir in the **raisins** if desired.

3. Pour the batter into a greased 8"x 8"x 2" baking pan and scatter the reserved topping mixture over the batter. Bake for 30 to 35 minutes, or until a toothpick inserted into the center of the cake comes out clean.

Tip: Leftovers can be frozen and reheated in a 350°F oven.

DESSERTS

If you have been leaving desserts off your daily menus because you have no time to make them or because high-quality bakery goods and other ready-made desserts are expensive, use these recipes to end your meals with soul-satisfying sweetness. Except for the Glazed Strawberry Pie and the Very Best Cheese Cake, all of these desserts can be assembled in 15 minutes or less, then cooked on top of the stove or baked. And, just as helpful, most of them can be made ahead of time—you don't have to rush to prepare them at the last moment.

Glazed Strawberry Pie

Preparation and cooking: **35 minutes**   Serves **6**   Calories per serving: **320**

Here is an ideal warm-weather dessert that requires almost no cooking. Because the pie should be chilled for at least 2 hours before serving, make it before you prepare the rest of your meal.

1¼ cups vanilla wafer crumbs (about 24 vanilla wafers)

5 tablespoons butter or margarine, melted

3 pints (6 cups) strawberries, washed and hulled

1¼ cups cold water

1 teaspoon lemon juice

¾ cup sugar

3 tablespoons cornstarch

¼ teaspoon salt

1 cup heavy cream, whipped (optional)

Tips: 1. The crust can be made ahead and frozen until needed. 2. To cool the glaze more quickly, place the saucepan containing it in cold water. 3. If you wish, whip a little sugar and vanilla extract with the cream.

1. In a mixing bowl, combine the **vanilla wafer crumbs** with the **butter.** Turn the mixture into an 8-inch pie plate, and press the crumbs firmly and evenly over the bottom and sides (but not the rim) of the plate. Chill in the freezer for 30 minutes.

2. While the crust is chilling, chop 1 cup of the **strawberries,** and put them into a 1-quart saucepan with the **water** and **lemon juice.** Mix together the **sugar, cornstarch,** and **salt,** and blend into the mixture in the saucepan. Bring to a boil over medium heat, stirring constantly, and cook until the glaze is thick and clear—about 3 minutes. (For a more professional-looking pie, press the glaze through a sieve at this point.) Cool.

3. Dry the remaining 5 cups of strawberries with paper toweling, and line the bottom of the crust with the berries, stem ends down. Spoon the cooled glaze evenly over the whole berries. Chill the pie for at least 2 hours. Serve topped with the **whipped cream** if desired.

Pecan Pie

Preparation: **15 minutes**   Cooking: **30 minutes**   Serves **6**   Calories per serving: **510**

1 cup graham cracker crumbs (about 16 2½-inch squares)

7 tablespoons butter or margarine, melted

2 eggs

⅓ cup heavy cream

⅓ cup dark corn syrup

Pinch salt

¼ teaspoon ground cinnamon

½ cup firmly packed light brown sugar

½ teaspoon vanilla extract

1 cup chopped pecans

1 cup heavy cream, whipped (optional)

1. Preheat the oven to 350°F. In a mixing bowl, combine the **graham cracker crumbs** with 5 tablespoons of the **butter.** Turn the mixture into an 8-inch pie plate, and press the crumbs firmly and evenly over the bottom and sides (but not the rim) of the plate. Set aside.

2. In a mixing bowl, combine the **eggs, cream, corn syrup, salt, cinnamon, sugar,** and **vanilla,** and the remaining 2 tablespoons of butter, and mix well. Add the **pecans** and stir.

3. Pour the mixture into the crust, and place the pie plate on a baking sheet. Bake for 30 minutes, or until the top of the pie is brown and puffy. Watch carefully toward the end of the baking to prevent burning. The filling will set as it cools. Serve topped with the **whipped cream** if desired.

> *Tips: **1.** When baking the pie, line the baking sheet with aluminum foil to catch any spills. **2.** If you wish, whip a little sugar and vanilla extract with the cream.*

Lazy Day Yellow Cake 🐷

Preparation: **8 minutes**   Cooking: **35 minutes**   Serves **4**   Calories per serving: **535**

1½ cups sifted all-purpose flour

1 cup sugar

2 teaspoons baking powder

½ teaspoon salt

¾ cup milk

⅓ cup butter or margarine, cut into small pieces

1 egg

2 teaspoons vanilla extract

1. Preheat the oven to 350°F. Grease and flour an 8″x 8″x 2″ baking pan. Put the **flour, sugar, baking powder, salt, milk, butter, egg,** and **vanilla** into a mixing bowl. With an electric mixer at medium speed, beat the ingredients together for 3 minutes, or until well blended.

2. Pour the mixture into the pan and bake, uncovered, for 35 minutes. Cool in the pan on a wire rack for 10 minutes, then remove the cake from the pan to the rack and let cool completely. If you wish, frost the cake with Cream Cheese Frosting, page 236, or Butter Cream Frosting, page 236.

> *Tip: This cake can be frozen, frosted or unfrosted.*

Carrot Cake

Preparation: **12 minutes**   Cooking: **30 minutes**   Serves **6**   Calories per serving: **525**

½ **cup firmly packed light or dark brown sugar**

2 **eggs**

¾ **cup vegetable oil**

¾ **teaspoon salt**

1 **cup sifted all-purpose flour**

1 **teaspoon baking soda**

1 **teaspoon ground cinnamon**

2 **large carrots, peeled and grated on the second-coarsest side of a four-sided grater (about 1½ cups)**

¾ **cup chopped walnuts or pecans**

1 **teaspoon grated orange rind**

1 **teaspoon grated lemon rind**

1. Preheat the oven to 350°F. Grease and flour a 9-inch round cake pan. Place the **sugar, eggs,** and **oil** in a mixing bowl, and with an electric mixer at medium speed, beat the ingredients together for 2 minutes.

2. In a small bowl, combine the **salt, flour, baking soda,** and **cinnamon,** and add to the sugar mixture. Beat at slow speed for 1 minute, then fold in the **carrots, walnuts, orange rind,** and **lemon rind.**

3. Pour the batter into the pan and spread evenly. Bake, uncovered, for 30 minutes, or until a toothpick inserted into the center of the cake comes out clean. Cool in the pan on a wire rack for 10 minutes, then remove the cake from the pan to the rack and let cool completely. If you wish, frost with Cream Cheese Frosting, page 236, or Butter Cream Frosting, page 236.

> *Tips: 1. Transform this recipe into an apple cake by substituting 2 large peeled, cored, and grated apples for the carrots. 2. This recipe can be doubled. Use a 13"x 9"x 2" pan and bake in a 300°F oven for 50 minutes to 1 hour. 3. This cake can be frozen, frosted or unfrosted.*

Sour Cream Spice Cake

Preparation: **6 minutes**   Cooking: **30 minutes**   Serves **6**   Calories per serving: **370**

1 **cup sour cream**

1 **cup sugar**

2 **eggs, lightly beaten**

1½ **cups sifted all-purpose flour**

1 **teaspoon baking soda**

1 **teaspoon baking powder**

½ **teaspoon salt**

1 **teaspoon ground cinnamon**

½ **teaspoon ground cloves**

½ **teaspoon ground nutmeg**

¼ **cup chopped nuts or dates, or** ½ **cup chopped raisins**

1. Preheat the oven to 350°F. Grease and flour an 8"x 8"x 2" baking pan. In a mixing bowl, combine the **sour cream, sugar,** and **eggs.**

2. In a separate bowl, combine the **flour, baking soda, baking powder, salt, cinnamon, cloves,** and **nutmeg.** Stir into the sour cream mixture, then stir in the **nuts.**

3. Pour the batter into the pan and bake, uncovered, for 30 minutes, or until a toothpick inserted into the center of the cake comes out clean. Cool in the pan on a wire rack for 10 minutes, then remove the cake from the pan to the rack to cool completely. If you wish, frost the cake with Cream Cheese Frosting, page 236, or Butter Cream Frosting, page 236.

> *Tip: This cake can be frozen, frosted or unfrosted.*

Chocolate Cake Express 🐷

Preparation: 7 minutes   Cooking: **25 minutes**   Serves **6**   Calories per serving: **420**

This dark, moist cake is almost as fast to make as a cake from a mix, and is better, too.

1½ cups unsifted all-purpose flour

1 cup granulated sugar

⅓ cup unsweetened cocoa

1 teaspoon baking soda

½ teaspoon salt

1 tablespoon vanilla extract

1 tablespoon cider vinegar

½ cup vegetable oil

1 cup water

1 tablespoon confectioners' sugar

1. Preheat the oven to 375°F. Grease and flour an 8"x 8"x 2" baking pan. In a mixing bowl, combine the **flour, granulated sugar, cocoa, baking soda,** and **salt.** Make a well in the center of the mixture, and add the **vanilla, vinegar,** and **oil,** then gradually stir in the **water.** Continue stirring until thoroughly blended, but do not overmix.

2. Pour the batter into the baking pan and bake, uncovered, for 25 to 30 minutes, or until a toothpick inserted into the center of the cake comes out clean. Do not overbake; the secret of this cake is moistness. Cool in the pan on a wire rack for 10 minutes, then remove the cake from the pan to the rack to cool completely. Sift the **confectioners' sugar** over the top, and serve.

Tip: This cake can be frozen.

Very Best Cheese Cake

Preparation: 25 minutes   Cooking: **30 minutes**   Serves **8**   Calories per serving: **465**

You must allow at least 6 hours or overnight for chilling this cake, but you can make it as far ahead as a week and refrigerate it. A fine company dessert!

1 cup graham cracker crumbs (about 16 2½-inch squares)

5 tablespoons butter or margarine, melted

2 packages (8 ounces each) cream cheese, softened

2 eggs

1 teaspoon grated lemon rind

1 teaspoon lemon juice

¾ cup sugar

1 cup sour cream

1 teaspoon vanilla extract

Tip: If you use a glass pie plate, bake the cake at 350°F for 20 minutes, then at 450°F for 10 minutes.

1. Preheat the oven to 375°F. In a mixing bowl, combine the **graham cracker crumbs** with the **butter.** Turn the mixture into a 9-inch deep-dish pie pan, and press the crumbs firmly over the bottom and a third of the way up the sides.

2. Put the **cream cheese, eggs, lemon rind, lemon juice,** and ½ cup of the **sugar** into a mixing bowl. With an electric mixer at medium speed, beat the ingredients together until satiny.

3. Pour the mixture into the crust, and bake, uncovered, for 20 minutes. Cool in the pan on a wire rack for 15 minutes.

4. While the cheese cake is cooling, raise the oven temperature to 450°F. Blend the **sour cream,** the remaining ¼ cup of sugar, and the **vanilla,** and spread the mixture gently over the cheese filling. Return the cheese cake to the oven, and bake, uncovered, 10 minutes longer.

5. Cool the cheese cake in the pan on a wire rack until it reaches room temperature, then cover with aluminum foil and chill for 6 hours or overnight. Cut into slim wedges and serve.

Cream Cheese Frosting ⊙

Preparation: **4 minutes**   Yield: **2 cups**   Calories per tablespoon: **40**

1 package (3 ounces) cream cheese, softened

2 tablespoons butter or margarine, softened

1/2 teaspoon vanilla extract

2 cups confectioners' sugar, sifted

Wonderfully rich and creamy, this frosting never has any lumps. The recipe will cover an 8- or 9-inch round or square cake or 12 cupcakes. To fill and frost a 2-layer 8- or 9-inch cake or a 9"x 13" cake, double the recipe.

In a mixing bowl, beat the **cream cheese, butter,** and **vanilla** with a large spoon or an electric mixer at medium speed until smooth. Gradually beat in the **sugar** until well blended.

> *Tip: You can use the same variations for Cream Cheese Frosting as given below for Butter Cream Frosting.*

Butter Cream Frosting ⊙

Preparation: **5 minutes**   Yield: **2 cups**   Calories per tablespoon: **35**

This recipe will cover an 8- or 9-inch round or square cake or 12 cupcakes. To fill and frost a 2-layer 8- or 9-inch cake or a 9"x 13" cake, double the recipe and the amounts in the variations, if used.

3 tablespoons butter or margarine, softened

2 cups confectioners' sugar, sifted

1 1/2 to 2 tablespoons milk or heavy cream

1/2 teaspoon vanilla extract

In a mixing bowl, cream the **butter** with a large spoon or an electric mixer at medium speed until light and fluffy. Gradually beat in about half the **sugar** until well blended. Beat in the **milk** and **vanilla.** Gradually beat in the remaining sugar. If necessary, add a few drops more milk to make the frosting more spreadable.

> *Tip: Try one of these variations:*
> ***Chocolate Frosting.*** *Blend 2 melted squares (1 ounce each) unsweetened chocolate into the butter or 1/4 cup sifted unsweetened cocoa into the sugar.*
> ***Mocha Frosting.*** *Stir 2 tablespoons sifted unsweetened cocoa and 1 1/2 teaspoons instant coffee powder into the confectioners' sugar.*
> ***Peppermint Frosting.*** *Mix in 1 tablespoon crushed peppermint candy.*
> ***Nut Frosting.*** *Mix in 1/4 cup chopped pecans or walnuts.*
> ***Pineapple Frosting.*** *Mix in 1/2 cup well-drained crushed pineapple.*
> ***Almond Frosting.*** *Mix in 1/4 teaspoon almond extract.*
> ***Banana Frosting.*** *Mix in 1/2 cup mashed ripe banana.*
> ***Coconut Frosting.*** *Mix in 1/2 cup shredded coconut or 1/4 cup each shredded coconut and well-drained crushed pineapple.*
> ***Peanut Frosting.*** *Mix in 3 tablespoons peanut butter.*
> ***Orange Frosting.*** *Omit the milk and vanilla, and add the grated rind of 1/2 orange and 2 tablespoons orange juice.*

Bananas Foster ⊙ ⊕

Preparation: **4 minutes**   Cooking: **6 minutes**   Serves **4**   Calories per serving: **435**

The famous original version of this dessert was created at Brennan's restaurant in New Orleans. Measure out all the ingredients before you start.

4 tablespoons (¹/₂ stick) butter, cut into small pieces

¹/₄ cup firmly packed light brown sugar

¹/₂ teaspoon ground cinnamon

4 firm, ripe bananas, peeled and cut in half lengthwise

1 tablespoon lemon juice

1 pint very hard vanilla ice cream

2 tablespoons banana or orange liqueur such as Cointreau or curaçao

¹/₂ cup dark rum

1. Melt the **butter** in a 12-inch skillet over moderate heat, then stir in the **sugar** and **cinnamon.** When the mixture is bubbly, add the **bananas** and **lemon juice.** Cook for 3 or 4 minutes, spooning the syrup over the bananas. The bananas should not overcook and become mushy.

2. Spoon the **ice cream** into 4 dessert dishes.

3. Add the **banana liqueur** and **rum** to the skillet, and heat for about 5 seconds. Avert your face, and light the syrup with a match. When the flame dies, serve the bananas over the ice cream.

Tips: 1. This makes a dramatic dessert to serve when cooked at the table in a chafing dish. 2. Make sure that the ice cream is very hard or it will melt too fast when you add the hot bananas and syrup. 3. The bananas may be served without the ice cream. 4. Substitute sliced fresh pineapple for the bananas. 5. This recipe can be halved.

Peaches in Macaroon Meringue 🐷 ⊕

Preparation: **5 minutes**   Cooking: **21 minutes**   Serves **4**   Calories per serving: **200**

2 tablespoons butter or margarine, softened

4 ripe peaches, halved and pitted

2 egg whites at room temperature

¹/₈ teaspoon cream of tartar

3 tablespoons sugar

¹/₂ cup crumbled coconut or almond macaroons

¹/₄ teaspoon almond extract

1 tablespoon dry sherry (optional)

Tips: 1. This recipe can be halved. 2. You can substitute ¹/₂ cup finely ground almonds for the macaroons.

1. Preheat the oven to 375°F. Grease an 8″x 8″x 2″ baking dish with 1 tablespoon of the **butter.** Place the **peaches** in the dish, pitted side up, and dot the centers with the remaining tablespoon of butter. Cover with aluminum foil and bake for 15 minutes.

2. Meanwhile, in a small bowl, use an electric mixer at medium speed to beat the **egg whites** and **cream of tartar** to soft peaks. Gradually add the **sugar,** beating until stiff. Fold in the crumbled **macaroons** and **almond extract,** and the **sherry** if used.

3. Remove the baking dish from the oven, uncover, and place a heaping tablespoon of meringue on each peach half. Return to the oven and bake, uncovered, for 6 to 8 minutes, or until the meringue is slightly browned. Serve at once.

Pears in Red Wine ◎ ⑪

Preparation: 7 minutes Cooking: **8 minutes**   Serves **4** Calories per serving: **345**

For a refreshingly cool dessert, make these pears ahead and serve them chilled.

2 cups red or white wine or 1 cup each red and white wine

Grated rind of 1 lemon

2 tablespoons lemon juice

³/₄ cup sugar

¹/₂ teaspoon ground cinnamon

4 firm, ripe pears, such as Anjou, Bosc, or Bartlett

1. Combine the **wine, lemon rind, lemon juice, sugar,** and **cinnamon** in a 2-quart saucepan. Bring to a boil, reduce the heat, and simmer, uncovered, until the sugar has melted.

2. Meanwhile, peel, halve, and core the **pears.** When the sugar has melted, drop the pears into the syrup. Add more wine or water, if necessary, to cover the pears. Simmer for 8 minutes, turning the pears once, until they are just tender. Let cool for 20 minutes, and serve with the syrup.

Tips: 1. This recipe can be halved. 2. Substitute peaches for the pears, if you like.

Strawberries with Raspberry Sauce ◎ ⑪

Preparation: 10 minutes   Serves **4** Calories per serving: **100**

1 package (10 ounces) quick-thaw frozen raspberries

1 pint strawberries, washed and hulled

Tips: 1. You may wish to sweeten the strawberries with a few teaspoons of sugar. 2. This recipe can be halved.

Try the raspberry sauce with fresh pineapple or peaches, too.

1. Thaw the **raspberries** according to package directions, or place the frozen berries in an electric blender and purée at low speed for 30 seconds. Press the raspberries and juice through a sieve. Discard the seeds.

2. Divide the **strawberries** among 4 dessert dishes, and spoon the raspberry sauce over them.

Banana Pudding 🐖

Preparation: 8 minutes Cooking: **25 minutes**   Serves **4** Calories per serving: **405**

4 medium-size ripe bananas, peeled and sliced ¹/₄ inch thick

2 tablespoons lemon juice

¹/₂ cup sour cream

¹/₂ cup firmly packed light brown sugar

Pinch ground nutmeg

¹/₂ cup soft fresh bread crumbs (1 slice bread)

2 tablespoons butter or margarine

¹/₄ cup chopped pecans

1. Preheat the oven to 350°F. Arrange a layer of sliced **bananas** on the bottom of a greased 8"x 8"x 2" baking pan or a shallow 1-quart casserole. Sprinkle with 1 tablespoon of the **lemon juice,** spread with ¹/₄ cup of the **sour cream,** then sprinkle with ¹/₄ cup of the **sugar,** a few grains of the **nutmeg,** and ¹/₄ cup of the **bread crumbs.**

2. Repeat with another layer, using the remaining ingredients. Dot with the **butter,** and bake, uncovered, for 25 minutes until golden. Sprinkle with the **pecans,** and serve warm or cold.

Tip: You can substitute shredded coconut for the pecans.

DESSERTS

Bread and Butter Pudding 🐷

Preparation: **8 minutes**   Cooking: **25 minutes**   Serves **4**   Calories per serving: **430**

Many of us have forgotten how good this old-fashioned dessert really is.

1/2 cup raisins

5 slices day-old white bread

3 tablespoons butter or margarine, softened

2 cups milk or half-and-half

1/2 cup sugar

1 teaspoon vanilla extract

2 eggs

> **Tips: 1.** *Sprinkle 1/8 to 1/4 teaspoon ground nutmeg or cinnamon over the top of the pudding after removing it from the oven.* **2.** *Use whole wheat or raisin bread instead of the white bread.* **3.** *If you don't have day-old bread, toast fresh bread very lightly.*

1. Preheat the oven to 350°F. Place the **raisins** in 1 cup of hot water, and let them soak for 5 minutes. Meanwhile, trim the crusts from the **bread**, spread one side of each slice with the **butter**, then cut the slices in half. Put the bread, buttered side up, into a greased 8"x 8"x 2" baking dish. Drain the raisins and sprinkle them over the bread.

2. Heat the **milk** and **sugar** until steaming. Remove from the heat and stir in the **vanilla**.

3. In a mixing bowl, beat the **eggs** lightly, then gradually stir the hot milk into the eggs. Pour the mixture over the bread slices. Bake, uncovered, for 25 minutes, or until the top is brown and a knife inserted into the center of the pudding comes out clean.

Right-Away Rice Pudding 🐷 🍥

Preparation: **5 minutes**   Cooking: **18 minutes**   Serves **6**   Calories per serving: **445**

You can do most of the preparation while the rice cooks. Or use about 3 cups leftover cooked rice, and assemble the pudding in 5 minutes.

1/2 teaspoon salt

2 cups water

1 cup uncooked rice

1 cup raisins

1/4 cup firmly packed light brown sugar

1 cup chopped walnuts

1 cup sour cream

1/4 teaspoon ground cinnamon

2 teaspoons lemon juice

1. Bring the **salt** and **water** to a boil in a 2-quart saucepan. Add the **rice**, stir once, reduce the heat, cover, and simmer for 18 to 20 minutes, or until all the water has been absorbed.

2. Meanwhile, in a mixing bowl, combine the **raisins, sugar, walnuts, sour cream, cinnamon,** and **lemon juice.** Add the warm rice, stir to mix, and serve warm or cold.

> **Tips: 1.** *You can substitute plain yogurt for the sour cream and chopped dried apricots or dried figs for the raisins.* **2.** *You can also substitute brown rice for the white rice, but it will take about 40 minutes for the brown rice to cook.* **3.** *This recipe can be halved.*

DESSERTS

Fudge Pudding

Preparation: **7 minutes**   Cooking: **30 minutes**   Serves **4**   Calories per serving: **330**

1/2 cup unsifted all-purpose flour

1 teaspoon baking powder

1/8 teaspoon salt

1/4 cup granulated sugar

1/4 cup unsweetened cocoa

1/4 cup milk

1 tablespoon vegetable oil

1/2 cup chopped walnuts or pecans

1/3 cup firmly packed light or dark brown sugar

3/4 cup hot water

1 cup heavy cream, whipped (optional)

Assemble this fudge pudding and let it bake while you prepare the rest of the meal, or make and refrigerate it a few hours ahead of time.

1. Preheat the oven to 350°F. In a mixing bowl, combine the **flour, baking powder, salt, granulated sugar,** and 2 tablespoons of the **cocoa.** Stir in the **milk, oil,** and **walnuts.** Spread the mixture into a greased 9-inch deep-dish pie plate.

2. In a small bowl, combine the **brown sugar** with the remaining 2 tablespoons of cocoa and sprinkle over the top. Pour the hot **water** evenly over the mixture. Bake, uncovered, for 30 minutes. Serve hot, warm, or cold with the **whipped cream** if desired.

Lemon Pudding Cake

Preparation: **15 minutes**   Cooking: **35 minutes**   Serves **4**   Calories per serving: **350**

While baking, the pudding sinks to the bottom and the cake rises to the top. The result is an outstanding dessert that resembles a lemon pie but is far easier to make. Note that the cooking time is unattended baking and that you can make the cake a day or two ahead and refrigerate it.

3 eggs, separated

3 tablespoons butter or margarine

3/4 cup sugar

Grated rind of 1 lemon

1/3 cup lemon juice

1 cup milk

1/4 cup unsifted all-purpose flour

1. Preheat the oven to 350°F. In a mixing bowl, beat the whites of the **eggs** with an electric mixer at medium speed until stiff, and set aside.

2. In a separate bowl, cream the **butter** and **sugar** with the mixer until light and fluffy. Beat in the **lemon rind, lemon juice,** and the egg yolks, one at a time, until well mixed. Beat in the **milk,** then the **flour** until blended.

3. Fold the beaten egg whites into the lemon mixture, then pour into a greased 8"x 8"x 2" baking dish. Set the dish into a larger pan; pour hot water into the pan to a level of about 1 inch. Bake, uncovered, for 35 minutes. Serve warm or cold.

Apple-Oatmeal Crunch

Preparation: **12 minutes**   Cooking: **30 minutes**   Serves **4**   Calories per serving: **530**

4 or 5 medium-size tart apples, cored, peeled, and thinly sliced

6 tablespoons firmly packed light brown sugar

6 tablespoons granulated sugar

1/2 cup unsifted all-purpose flour

3/4 cup uncooked quick-cooking rolled oats

1/2 cup (1 stick) butter, melted

1/2 cup water

1 cup heavy cream, whipped, or 1 pint vanilla ice cream (optional)

Simply prepared foods are often the most delicious, and this dessert is no exception.

1. Preheat the oven to 375°F. Spread the sliced **apples** over the bottom of a greased 8"x 8"x 2" baking dish.

2. In a mixing bowl, combine the **brown sugar, granulated sugar, flour,** and **oats,** then stir in the melted **butter.** Spread this mixture over the apples. Pour the **water** evenly over the top.

3. Bake, uncovered, until the apples are tender—about 30 minutes. Serve warm or at room temperature with the **whipped cream** if desired.

> **Tip:** *Prepare as directed, but mix in 1/2 teaspoon of ground cinnamon and 1/4 teaspoon of ground nutmeg with the sugar, flour, and oats.*

Italian Custard

Preparation: **4 minutes**   Cooking: **5 minutes**   Serves **4**   Calories per serving: **190**

This dessert, also called zabaglione, is quick to make. You can prepare it while the coffee is brewing.

6 large egg yolks

5 tablespoons sugar

1/2 cup Marsala wine

Pinch salt

> **Tips: 1.** *This recipe can be halved.* **2.** *You can substitute dry sherry or Madeira for the Marsala.* **3.** *This custard may be served over strawberries, peaches, puddings, or sliced cake.* **4.** *Freeze the egg whites for another use in ice cube trays, then transfer the cubes to a plastic bag and return to the freezer.*

Place the **egg yolks, sugar, wine,** and **salt** in the top of a double boiler set over gently boiling water. Beat constantly with a wire whisk or an electric beater at medium speed until the custard mounds slightly when dropped from the whisk. Do not overcook or the custard will curdle. Remove from the hot water immediately, and spoon the custard into 4 wineglasses or dessert dishes. Serve at once.

Blender Chocolate Mousse ⊘

Preparation: **10 minutes**   Serves **6**   Calories per serving: **205**

This chocolate mousse requires at least 50 minutes' chilling time, but you can prepare it as much as a day ahead and refrigerate it. If you like, serve it with heavy cream whipped just before serving or with Make-Ahead Whipped Cream, below.

4 eggs

1 package (6 ounces) semisweet chocolate bits

5 tablespoons boiling water or coffee

2 teaspoons vanilla extract or 2 tablespoons rum

1. Separate the **eggs,** placing the whites in a small mixing bowl and the yolks in a cup. Beat the egg whites until stiff but not dry. Set aside.

2. Place the **chocolate bits** into the jar of an electric blender. Whirl to break up the pieces. Add the boiling **water,** and whirl until smooth.

3. Add the egg yolks and **vanilla.** Whirl 1 minute, or until thoroughly blended. Pour the chocolate mixture slowly over the egg whites, and fold in gently until no white shows. Spoon into individual dessert dishes or a 1-quart serving dish. Refrigerate 50 minutes, or until firm and well chilled.

Make-Ahead Whipped Cream 🐷 ⊘

Preparation: **10 minutes**   Yield: **2½ cups**   Calories per tablespoon: **20**

Whip cream according to this recipe, and it will keep as long as 4 days in the refrigerator without separating. Just be sure the cream is very fresh.

½ teaspoon unflavored gelatin

1 tablespoon cold water

1 cup heavy cream

Pinch salt

½ teaspoon vanilla extract

1 tablespoon sugar (optional)

1. Sprinkle the **gelatin** over the **water** in a small ovenproof bowl or custard cup, then set the bowl into 1 inch of hot water in a saucepan. Let stand until the gelatin dissolves. Remove the bowl from the water, and let the mixture cool for about 1 minute.

2. Whip the **cream** until almost stiff, then add the dissolved gelatin mixture, the **salt** and **vanilla,** and the **sugar** if used, and continue to whip until the cream is stiff. Cover and refrigerate. Just before serving, beat with a spoon to blend.

> *Tips:* **1.** *Add 1 tablespoon whiskey or orange liqueur, or substitute ¼ teaspoon almond extract for the vanilla extract.* **2.** *As a variation, whip 1 cup of heavy cream with the gelatin as directed above, then add ⅓ cup sour cream, 1 tablespoon sugar, and ½ teaspoon vanilla extract. Blend well. Serve over fresh peaches or berries. The result is a mock crème fraîche, a French-style cream.* **3.** *This recipe can be doubled.*

Custard Sauce 🐷 ⏲ ◖

Preparation: **8 minutes**   Cooking: **5 minutes**   Yield: **2 cups**   Calories per tablespoon: **20**

Here is a sauce to serve over fresh or cooked fruit as well as cake, apple pie, cobblers, and puddings.

2 cups milk

3 tablespoons sugar

Pinch salt

4 egg yolks

1 teaspoon vanilla extract, dry sherry, or brandy

> *Tips: 1. This sauce will keep for up to 3 days in the refrigerator. 2. This recipe can be halved.*

1. In a heavy 2-quart saucepan over moderate heat, heat the **milk, sugar,** and **salt** until the sugar has dissolved and the milk is very hot.

2. In a small bowl, beat the **egg yolks** lightly, then stir in a few tablespoons of the hot milk mixture. Blend the egg yolk mixture with the hot mixture in the saucepan. Reduce the heat to low, and cook, stirring constantly, until the mixture coats the spoon—about 5 minutes. Do not boil or the sauce will curdle.

3. Remove the pan from the heat and place it in cold water. Stir the sauce constantly for 2 minutes, then blend in the **vanilla.** Cool, then cover and refrigerate until serving time.

Butterscotch Sauce 🐷 ⏲

Preparation: **1 minute**   Cooking: **5 minutes**   Yield: **1 cup**   Calories per tablespoon: **75**

Treat the family or guests to a sundae with homemade butterscotch sauce.

1 cup firmly packed light brown sugar

1/4 cup half-and-half

2 tablespoons butter or margarine

2 tablespoons light corn syrup

Heat the **sugar, half-and-half, butter,** and **corn syrup** to boiling in a heavy 1-quart saucepan over moderate heat, stirring occasionally. Serve warm over ice cream, cake, or frozen desserts.

> *Tip: This sauce will keep for several weeks in the refrigerator.*

Orange Cream Sauce 🐷 ⏲

Preparation: **5 minutes**   Cooking: **3 minutes**   Yield: **3/4 cup**   Calories per tablespoon: **40**

Serve this quick sauce warm or cold over plain cake, sponge cake, or simple puddings.

1 orange

1/4 cup sugar

2 teaspoons cornstarch

1/4 cup heavy cream or half-and-half

1. Grate enough rind from the **orange** to measure 1/2 teaspoon, and set aside. Squeeze the juice from the orange and strain into a measuring cup. Add enough water to yield 3/4 cup.

2. Pour the orange juice mixture into a 1-quart saucepan. Combine the **sugar** and **cornstarch,** and stir into the orange mixture. Cook over low heat, stirring frequently, until the sugar has dissolved and the mixture has thickened—about 3 minutes. Remove the pan from the heat, and stir in the reserved orange rind and **cream.**

Chocolate Sauce ⬚

Preparation: **2 minutes** Cooking: **4 minutes** Yield: **1¹⁄₃ cups** Calories per tablespoon: **70**

1 package (6 ounces) semisweet chocolate bits

¹⁄₂ cup light corn syrup

¹⁄₄ cup half-and-half

1 tablespoon butter or margarine

1 teaspoon vanilla extract

In a heavy 2-quart saucepan over low heat, melt the **chocolate** with the **corn syrup,** stirring constantly. Remove the pan from the heat, and stir in the **half-and-half, butter,** and **vanilla.** Serve warm over ice cream, pound cake, or angel food cake.

Tips: **1.** *As a variation, add ¹⁄₄ teaspoon of mint extract to the sauce.* **2.** *This sauce will keep for several weeks in the refrigerator.*

Soft Molasses Drop Cookies 🐷 ⬚

Preparation: **12 minutes** Cooking: **12 minutes** Yield: **48 cookies** Calories each: **50**

This is a recipe from Upper Canada Village in Morrisburg, Ontario, where life goes on in restored houses and shops as it did in the era from 1784 to 1867.

2 cups unsifted all-purpose flour

1 teaspoon ground ginger

1 teaspoon ground cinnamon

¹⁄₄ teaspoon ground nutmeg

¹⁄₈ teaspoon ground allspice

¹⁄₂ cup (1 stick) butter or margarine, softened

¹⁄₂ cup firmly packed light brown sugar

1 egg yolk

¹⁄₂ cup molasses

¹⁄₂ cup hot water

1 teaspoon baking soda

1. Preheat the oven to 350°F. In a mixing bowl, combine the **flour, ginger, cinnamon, nutmeg,** and **allspice,** and set aside.

2. In another mixing bowl, cream the **butter** and **sugar** with an electric mixer at medium speed until light and fluffy, then beat in the **egg yolk.** Add the **molasses, water, baking soda,** and the flour mixture. Mix thoroughly.

3. Drop the batter by rounded teaspoons onto greased baking sheets, leaving about 2 inches between cookies. Bake for 12 minutes. Remove the cookies to a wire rack to cool.

Tip: This recipe can be halved.

No-Bake Date Balls ⊘

Preparation: **15 minutes**   Yield: **24 pieces**   Calories each: **50**

2 cups corn, wheat, or bran flakes

³/₄ cup pitted dates

¹/₂ cup pecans or walnuts

2 tablespoons honey

1 tablespoon butter or margarine. softened

2 teaspoons lemon juice

3 tablespoons confectioners' sugar

1. Put the **corn flakes, dates,** and **pecans** into an electric blender or a food processor, and whirl just until well chopped. Or crush the cereal with your hands, and chop the dates and nuts with a knife.

2. In a mixing bowl, combine the cereal mixture with the **honey, butter,** and **lemon juice.** Knead until well mixed, then roll into 1-inch balls.

3. Sprinkle the **sugar** on a sheet of wax paper, and roll the balls in the sugar. Store in an airtight container.

Walnut Dreams

Preparation: **12 minutes**   Cooking: **20 minutes**   Yield: **18 cookies**   Calories each: **105**

¹/₂ cup (1 stick) butter, softened

¹/₄ cup confectioners' sugar, unsifted

1 teaspoon vanilla extract

1 cup sifted all-purpose flour

Pinch ground nutmeg

¹/₈ teaspoon salt

³/₄ cup finely chopped walnuts

1. Preheat the oven to 300°F. In a mixing bowl, cream the **butter** and **sugar** with an electric mixer at medium speed until light and fluffy. Stir in the **vanilla, flour, nutmeg, salt,** and **walnuts.**

2. Roll the dough into 1-inch balls. Place the balls about 1 inch apart on a lightly greased baking sheet, pressing each ball with the heel of your hand to a thickness of about ¹/₂ inch.

3. Bake, uncovered, for 20 minutes, or until the bottoms are golden brown. Cool on a wire rack.

Chewy Oatmeal Raisin Bars

Preparation: **15 minutes**   Cooking: **12 minutes**   Yield: **24 bars**   Calories each: **130**

¹/₂ cup (1 stick) butter

1 cup firmly packed light brown sugar

1 egg

1 teaspoon vanilla extract

1 cup sifted all-purpose flour

¹/₂ teaspoon baking soda

¹/₄ teaspoon salt

1 cup uncooked quick-cooking rolled oats

¹/₂ cup chopped walnuts

¹/₂ cup raisins

1. Preheat the oven to 400°F. In a mixing bowl, cream the **butter** and **sugar** with an electric mixer at medium speed until light and fluffy. Beat in the **egg, vanilla, flour, baking soda,** and **salt.** Stir in the **oats, walnuts,** and **raisins** until well mixed. The mixture will be very stiff.

2. Turn the mixture into a greased 9"x 9"x 2" baking pan and spread evenly. Bake, uncovered, for 12 minutes. Cool in the pan, then cut into 24 bars.

ACKNOWLEDGMENTS

Grateful acknowledgment is made for permission to use and adapt recipes from the following sources. Note that when the recipe title differs from the title under which the recipe originally appeared, the original title is given in parentheses. **Atheneum Publishers** Richard Olney, "Squash Soup" ("Bread and Squash Soup"), from *Simple French Food.* Copyright © 1974 by Richard Olney. Reprinted by permission of Atheneum Publishers and John Schaffner Associates Inc. **The Bach Cookbooks** "Lentil and Sausage Stew" ("Conductor's Stew"), from *Bach's Lunch—Picnic and Patio Classics.* "Egg Chutney Madras," from *Bach for More—Fireside Classics.* Reprinted by permission of the Junior Committee of the Cleveland Orchestra. **Better Homes & Gardens Books** "Spicy Pork Tacos," "Turkey Jambalaya," from *Better Homes and Gardens Pork, Sausage, and Ham Cookbook.* Reprinted by permission of Better Homes & Gardens Books. **Canadian Government Publishing Centre** "Maritime Oatcakes," "French-Canadian Pork Pie" ("Tourtière"), from *Food à La Canadienne.* Reproduced by permission of the Minister of Supply and Services—Canada. **The Canadian Home Economics Association** "Acadian Cod and Potato Pancake" ("Acadian Fish Pancake"), from *A Collage of Canadian Cooking.* Reprinted by permission of the Canadian Home Economics Association. **Chapel Hill Service League** "Spaghetti Carbonara," from *Chapel Hill's Favorites.* Reprinted by permission of the Chapel Hill Service League. **Contemporary Books, Inc.** "Spaghetti Florentine" ("Baked Spaghetti Florentine"), "Deluxe Macaroni and Cheese" ("Macaroni and Cheese Casserole"), "Mock Hollandaise Sauce," "Quick Hollandaise Sauce," "Spaghetti with Oil, Garlic, and Cheese" ("Spaghetti, Oil, and Garlic"), from *Shortcut Cooking* by Charlotte Erickson. Copyright © 1981 by Charlotte Erickson. Reprinted by permission of Contemporary Books, Inc. **Crown Publishers, Inc.** "Spicy Texas Beef Stew" ("Picadillo—Spicy Beef"), "Quick Chili Con Carne" ("Speedy Chili Con Carne"), from *Jane Butel's Tex-Mex Cookbook* by Jane Butel. Copyright © 1980 by Jane Butel. Used by permission of Harmony Books, a division of Crown Publishers, Inc. "Chicken and Sausage Fricassee with Sage" ("Chicken Fricassee"), from *The Talisman Italian Cookbook* by Ada Boni, translated by Matilde La Rosa. Copyright © 1950, 1977 by Crown Publishers. Used by permission of Crown Publishers, Inc. **David and Charles Limited** "Green Beans in Egg Sauce," from *Customs and Cookery in the Périgord and Quercy.* Reprinted by permission of David and Charles Limited. **Delair Publishing Co., Inc.** "Vegetable and Ground Beef Chowder" ("Vegetable and Hamburger Chowder"), from *250 Delicious Soups.* Reprinted by permission of Delair Publishing Co., Inc. **Dell Publishing Co., Inc.** "Mexican Chicken," excerpted from *Michele Evans' All Poultry Cookbook* by Michele Evans. Copyright © 1974 by Michele Evans. Reprinted by permission of Dell Publishing Co., Inc. **Doubleday & Company, Inc.** "Creole Cheese Sandwiches," from *Best Loved Recipes of the American People* by Ida Bailey Allen. Copyright © 1973 by Ruth Allen Castelli. "Macaroni Salad" ("Basic Macaroni Salad"), "Beef Croquettes," "Oven-Fried Chicken Parmesan" ("Chicken Parmesan"), "Confetti Corn," "Low-Calorie Fruit Dressing," "Spinach Dressed with Oil and Vinegar," "Very Best Cheese Cake" ("The Very Best Cheese Pie"), "All-Purpose Barbecue Sauce," "Easy Sour Cream Sauces" ("Some Easy Sour Cream Sauces"), from *The Doubleday Cookbook* by Jean Anderson and Elaine Hanna. Copyright © 1975 by Doubleday & Company, Inc. "Broiled Flounder" ("Flounders Flanagan"), from *Hook 'Em and Cook 'Em* by Bunny Day. Copyright © 1962 by Eleanor F. Day. "Braised Chinese Chicken" ("Three Cups Chicken"), from *The Joy of Wokking* by Martin Yan. Copyright © 1982 by Martin Yan. "Mexican Rarebit," from *San Francisco à la Carte* by the Junior League of San Francisco. Copyright © 1979 by the Junior League of San Francisco, Inc. Reprinted by permission of Doubleday & Company, Inc. "New England Cod Fish Hash" ("Codfish Hash"), "Haddock Chowder," "Sturbridge-Style Creamed Hashed Onions," from *Recipes from America's Restored Villages* by Jean Anderson. Copyright © 1975 by Jean Anderson. Reprinted by permission of Doubleday & Company, Inc., and McIntosh and Otis, Inc. "Chicken with Apples and Onions" ("Shaker Chicken Pudding"), from *365 Ways to Cook Chicken* by Carl Lyren. Copyright © 1974 by Carl Lyren. Reprinted by permission of Doubleday & Company, Inc., and JCA Literary Agency, Inc. **Dover Publications Inc.** "Curried Flounder Madras" ("Madras Fish, Gowanus Bay"), from *Long Island Seafood Cook Book* by J. George Frederick. Reprinted by permission of Dover Publications Inc. **E.P. Dutton Co., Inc.** "Chinese Noodle Salad," "Cucumber Salad" ("Pan Huang Kua"), from *Florence Lin's Chinese Regional Cookbook* by Florence Lin. Copyright © 1975 by Florence Lin. Reprinted by permission of E.P. Dutton, Inc. **The Entre Nous Club, Inc.** "Yellow Squash with Bacon" ("Bacon-Squash Casserole"), "Chicken and Broccoli Bake" ("Chicken Broccoli Bake"), from *Sunshine Sampler.* Reprinted by permission of the Entre Nous Club. **M. Evans and Company, Inc.** "Fried Rice," "Singapore Rice," from *American Home All-Purpose Cook Book,* edited by the Food Staff of American Home. Copyright © 1966 by the Curtis Publishing Company. Revised copyright © 1972 by Downe Publishing, Inc. Reprinted by permission of M. Evans and Company, Inc., 216 East 49th Street, New York, N.Y. 10017. "Curried New Potatoes,"

"Right Away Rice Pudding," from *The Quick and Easy Vegetarian Cookbook* by Ruth Ann Manners and William Manners. Copyright © 1978 by Ruth Ann Manners and William Manners. Reprinted by permission of M. Evans and Company, Inc., and International Creative Management. **Fairchild Publications** "Indonesian Beef" ("Beef and Indonesian Rice"), from *Greenwich Village Cookbook* by Vivian Kramer. Reprinted by permission of Fairchild Publications. **Fannie Farmer Cookbook Corp.** "Orange Cream Sauce," from *The Fannie Farmer Cookbook,* revised by Wilma Lord Perkins. Copyright © 1979 by the Fannie Farmer Cookbook Corp. Reprinted by permission of the Fannie Farmer Cookbook Corp. **Farm Journal Inc.** "Corn Bread Topping," from *Complete Pie Cookbook,* edited by Nell B. Nichols. Reprinted by permission of Farm Journal Inc. "Beef and Noodles with Two Cheeses" ("Beef-Cheese Casserole"), from *The Busy Woman's Cookbook.* Reprinted by permission of Farm Journal Inc. **Harper & Row, Publishers, Inc.** "Buttermilk Gazpacho," "Corn Chowder" ("Cherokee Chowder"), "Creamed Diced Carrots with Green Pepper," "Plantation Peanut Soup," from *Half a Can of Tomato Paste and Other Culinary Dilemmas* by Jean Anderson and Ruth Buchan. Copyright © 1980 by Jean Anderson and Ruth Buchan. Reprinted by permission of Harper & Row, Publishers, Inc. "Spicy Oriental Beef" ("Chungking Beef Shreds—Hot"), from *Joyce Chen Cookbook,* J.B. Lippincott. Copyright © 1962 by Joyce Chen. "Beef with Curry Sauce" ("Beefsteak in Curry Sauce"), from *Jim Lee's Chinese Cookbook.* Copyright © 1968 by Jim Lee. Reprinted by permission of Harper & Row, Publishers, Inc. "Sweet-and-Sour Broccoli," from *Fast and Fresh* by Julie Dannenbaum. Copyright © 1981 by Julie Dannenbaum. Reprinted by permission of Harper & Row, Publishers, Inc., and Edward J. Acton, Inc. **Hastings House, Publishers Inc.** "Baked Sea Trout" ("Baked Fish with Savory Green Pepper Stuffing"), "Broiled Fish with Peppery Almond Butter" ("Broiled Fillets with Almond Sauce"), "Broiled Deviled Fish Fillets" ("Oven Deviled Fillets"), from *The Blue Sea Cookbook* by Sarah D. Alberson. Copyright © 1968 by Sarah D. Alberson. Reprinted by permission of Hastings House, Publishers. **The Haywood County Council of Extension Homemaker Clubs** "Asparagus with Pimiento and Cheese" ("Asparagus Casserole"), from *Favorite Recipes.* "Ham and Cheese Strata" ("Cheese and Ham Strata"), from *Home Made Kitchen Magic.* Reprinted by permission of the Haywood County Council of Extension Homemaker Clubs. **Holt, Rinehart & Winston** "Curried Tomatoes," "Sausage Fried Rice," from *Quick and Easy Meals for 2* by Louella G. Shouer. Copyright © 1952 by Louella G. Shouer. Reprinted by permission of Holt, Rinehart & Winston, Publishers. **Homestead Welfare Club** "Carrots Amana Style" ("Gelbe Rüben"), from *Amana Colony Recipes.* Reprinted by permission of Homestead Welfare Club. **Houghton Mifflin Company** "Chinese Baked Fish with Green Onions and Ginger" ("Chinese Baked Fish"), "Curried Rice," "Lamb with Green Onions" ("Lamb with Scallions"), from *Make It Easy in the Kitchen* with Laurie Burrows Grad. Copyright © 1982 by Laurie Burrows Grad. Reprinted by permission of J.P. Tarcher, Inc., and Houghton Mifflin Company. **The Junior Charity League of Monroe** "Crustless Swiss and Onion Quiche" ("Swiss Onion Quiche"), from *The Cotton Country Collection.* Reprinted by permission of the Junior Charity League of Monroe. **The Junior League of Corpus Christi, Inc.** "Pork Chops with Orange Sauce" ("Pork Chops à L'Orange"), from *Fiesta-Favorite Recipes of South Texas.* Reprinted by permission of the Junior League of Corpus Christi, Inc. **The Junior League of Greenville Inc.** "Sweet and Sour Pork," from *300 Years of Carolina Cooking.* Reprinted by permission of the Junior League of Greenville Inc. **The Junior League of San Antonio Inc.** "Copenhagen Cabbage Casserole," "Curried Beef Casserole," "Beef and Tomato Stew" ("Green Tomato Stew"), "Italian Cutlets with Tomato Sauce" ("Italian Cutlets"), from *Flavors.* Reprinted by permission of the Junior League of San Antonio Inc. **The Junior League of Shreveport Inc.** "Mushroom and Barley Casserole" ("Barley Casserole"), "Ham and Egg Casserole," "Hot Chicken Salad," from *A Cook's Tour of Shreveport.* Reprinted by permission of the Junior League of Shreveport Inc. **Junior Service League of McAllen Inc.** "Sunday Eggs and Bacon" ("Egg and Bacon Casserole"), from *La Pinata.* Reprinted by permission of the Junior Service League of McAllen Inc. **Louise Tate King** "A Garden Casserole," "Oyster and Mushroom Pie" ("Oyster Pie"), from *The Martha's Vineyard Cook Book* by Louise Tate King and Jean Stewart Wexler. Copyright © 1971. Reprinted by permission of Louise Tate King. **Alfred A. Knopf, Inc.** "Sautéed Chicken Scallops with Marsala" ("Sautéed Veal Scaloppine with Marsala"), from *The Classic Italian Cook Book* by Marcella Hazan. Copyright © 1973 by Marcella Polini Hazan. Reprinted by permission of Alfred A. Knopf, Inc. "Miniature Meat Loaves" ("Meat Loaf"), "Paprika Beef" ("Sauté de Boeuf Minute Hongroise"), "Salisbury Steak with Onion Sauce" ("Salisbury Steak"), "Bread and Butter Pudding," from *The Classic French Cuisine* by Joseph Donon. Copyright © 1959 by Joseph Donon. Reprinted by permission of Alfred A. Knopf, Inc., and Macmillan Publishing Co. **Ladies' Home Journal** "Caesar Salad," "Green Beans Italian Style" ("Wax Beans Italian Style"), "Baby Lima Beans with Herbs" ("Lima Beans Termière"), "Sweet and Sour Spinach" ("Spinach with Sweet-Sour Sauce"), "Bean Sprout and Bacon Sal-

INDEX

A

Acadian cod and potato pancake, 158
All-purpose barbecue sauce, 164
Almond(s)
  butter, peppery, broiled fish with, 153
  company chicken with orange and, 94
  frosting, 236
Ambrosia, peach, 215
Appetizers, 20–25
  artichoke spread, 20
  black olive pâté, 20
  caviar pie, 22
  cheese puffs, 24
  cheese wafers, 24
  chicken liver pâté, 22
  cocktail cheese spread, 21
  crispy chicken tidbits, 25
  egg chutney Madras, 23
  herbed cream cheese, 21
  Middle Eastern chick pea spread, 21
  pastrami canapés, 25
  pimiento cheese canapés, 24
  sardine pâté, 23
  sausage and cheese balls, 25
Apple(s), 10
  and beet salad with yogurt dressing, 44
  in brown sugar sauce, 214
  chicken with onions and, 87
  –cream cheese sandwiches, 225
  -nut muffins, 231
  -oatmeal crunch, 241
  and onions, 71
  pork curry with cream and, 133
  red cabbage with, 65
  rings, glazed, ham steak with, 135
  salad with sour cream dressing, 57
  sausages and, 141
Apples as substitute
  in carrot cake, 234
  in curried chicken salad with green grapes, 40
  in pear, celery, and pecan salad, 57
Apricot breakfast shake, 219
Armenian pilaf, 144
Artichoke spread, 20
Asparagus
  Chinese style, 58
  with pimiento and cheese, 165
  skillet, 58
Avocado dressing, 52

B

Baby lima beans with herbs, 61
Bacon, 10, 12
  and bean sprout salad, 45
  bulgur with, 206
  and eggs, Sunday, 181
  lettuce and tomato sandwich with peanut butter, 226
  macaroni with tomato, sweet pepper, and, 213
  -spinach salad with warm dressing, 48
  as substitute in cranberry–cream cheese sandwiches, 225
  yellow squash with, 169
  ziti with tomatoes, hot pepper, and, 200
Baked bananas, 215
Baked bluefish with olives and tomatoes, 155
Baked cheeseburger casserole, 174
Baked cornmeal and cheese, 207
Baked deviled tuna, 158
Baked eggs with onions and cheese, 185
Baked fish with tomatoes and tarragon, 212
Baked ham steak, 136
Baked sliced potatoes, 73
Baked stuffed sea trout, 154
Baked stuffed tomatoes, 81
Baked whitings with cucumbers, dill, and cream, 154
Baked winter squash, 80
Baked zucchini with tomatoes, 79
Baking powder drop biscuits, 227
Banana(s)
  baked, 215
  banananog breakfast shake, 219
  Foster, 237
  frosting, 236
  and peanut butter spreads, 226
  pudding, 238
Barbecued hamburgers, 114
Barbecue sauce, all-purpose, 164
Barley and mushroom casserole, 168
Basic broiled chicken, 83
Basic potato salad with variations, 47
Beans, dried, 10
Bean sprout and bacon salad, 45
Béarnaise sauce, 161
Beef, 104–124
  and cabbage soup, 34
  casserole, curried, 173
  creamed dried, on toast, 124
  croquettes, 106
  with curry sauce, 111

Beef *(continued)*
  French-style, and onions, 105
  and green beans, Chinese, 210
  hash, 106
  kebabs, Greek, 113
  and noodles with two cheeses, 173
  paprika, 112
  roast, 104
  salad, spicy, 39
  with scrambled eggs, 104
  slices, deviled, 105
  spicy oriental, 111
  Stroganoff, 110
  sukiyaki, 112
Beef, cooked (leftover)
  and cabbage soup, 34
  croquettes, 106
  hash, 106
  and onions, French-style, 105
  salad, spicy, 39
  with scrambled eggs, 104
  slices, deviled, 105
Beef, cooked (leftover), as substitute
  in Armenian pilaf, 144
  in grilled ham salad sandwiches, 221
  in shepherd's stew, 144
  in spicy curried chicken with tomatoes, 87
  in spicy pork tacos, 126
Beef, ground, 113–124
  Brazilian beef bake, 171
  chili frittata, 187
  Copenhagen cabbage casserole, 172
  curried beef casserole, 173
  easy taco supper, 124
  and ham balls, oriental, 139
  Indian spiced chick peas and, 123
  Indonesian beef, 173
  Italian cutlets with tomato sauce, 115
  and noodles with two cheeses, 173
  quick chili con carne, 122
  and rice porcupines, 118
  Salisbury steak with onion sauce, 116
  skillet macaroni and, 122
  stew, spicy Texas, 121
  sweet and sour cabbage and, 117
  and sweet potato stew, 120
  Tex-Mex tortilla bake, 123
  and tomato stew, 120
  tomato and noodle supper with, 210
  and vegetable chowder, 35
  See also **Hamburger(s); Meatballs(s); Meat loaves.**

Beef, ground, as substitute
  in pork balls with mushrooms, 134
Beef liver
  in basil tomato sauce, 149
  in mustard tarragon cream, 149
Beef liver as substitute
  in chicken livers in sherry, 150
  in chicken livers with mushrooms and tomato, 211
  in chicken livers with sage, 150
Beet(s)
  and apple salad with yogurt dressing, 44
  grated, Russian style, 61
Biscuits, baking powder drop, 227
Black bean soup, Spanish, 26
Black olive pâté, 20
Blender chocolate mousse, 242
Blender mayonnaise, 161
Blintz pancakes, 217
BLT sandwich with peanut butter, 226
Blueberry swirl, 219
Blue cheese
  dressing, creamy, 51
  romaine salad with walnuts and, 53
Bluefish
  baked, with olives and tomatoes, 155
  baked fish with tomatoes and tarragon, 212
  Greek fish and potato bake, 178
Blue ribbon chicken curry, 88
Braised Chinese chicken, 97
Braised pork chops with pears and onions, 132
Brazilian beef bake, 171
Bread(s), 19, 227–231
  baking powder drop biscuits, 227
  and butter pudding, 239
  corn, buttermilk, 229
  crumb coffee cake, 231
  hush puppies, 228
  johnnycakes, 228
  magic mix, 227
  Maritime oatcakes, 229
  pancakes, 227
  See also **Muffins.**
Breaded pork chops with herbs, 130
Breakfast, 214–219
  See also **Bread(s); Egg(s).**
Broccoli, 62–63
  and chicken bake, 169
  chowder, 27
  dry-sautéed, 62
  sweet and sour, 62
  with sweet red peppers, 63